American Exceptionalism in the Age of Globalization

American Exceptionalism in the Age of Globalization

The Specter of Vietnam

William V. Spanos

State University of New York Press

Published by
State University of New York Press, Albany

For information, contact State University of New York Press,
www.sunypress.edu

Production by Kelli Williams
Marketing by Fran Keneston

Library of Congress Cataloguing-in-Publication Data

Spanos, William V.
    American exceptionalism in the age of globalization : the specter of Vietnam /
William V. Spanos.
        p. cm.
    Includes bibliographical references and index.
    ISBN 978-0-7914-7289-7 (alk. paper) — ISBN 978-0-7914-7290-3 (pbk. : alk. paper)
1. American literature—History and criticism.   2. English literature—History and
criticism.   3. National characteristics, American, in literature.   4. Vietnam War,
1961–1975—Literature and the war.   5. America—In literature.   6. Literature and
history—United States.   I. Title.

PS169.N35S63   2008
810.9'358—dc22

2007001681

10 9 8 7 6 5 4 3 2 1

For Susan and Adam,
from the "rag and bone shop of my heart"

The individual is interpellated [called] as a (free) subject in order that he shall submit freely to the commandments of the Subject, i.e. in order that he shall (freely) accept his subjection; i.e. in order that he shall make the gestures and actions of his subjection "all by himself."

—Louis Althusser, "Ideology and Ideological
State Apparatuses"

In this very attitude did I sit when I called him, rapidly stating what it was I wanted him to do—namely, to examine a small paper with me. Imagine my surprise, nay, my consternation, when without moving from his privacy, Bartleby in a singularly mild, firm voice, replied, "I prefer not to."

—Herman Melville, "Bartleby, the Scrivener"

Liberation as an intellectual mission, born in the resistance and opposition to the confinements and ravages of imperialism, has shifted from the settled, established, and domesticated dynamics of culture to its unhoused decentered and exilic energies. . . .

—Edward Said, *Culture and Imperialism*

CONTENTS

PREFACE

In this book I contend that the consequence of America's intervention and conduct of the war in Vietnam was the self-destruction of the ontological, cultural, and political foundations on which America had perennially justified its "benign" self-image and global practice from the time of the Puritan "errand in the wilderness." In the aftermath of the defeat of the American Goliath by a small insurgent army, the "specter" of Vietnam—by which I mean, among other things, the violence, bordering on genocide, America perpetrated against an "Other" that refused to accommodate itself to its mission in the wilderness of Vietnam—came to haunt America as a contradiction that menaced the legitimacy of its perennial self-representation as the exceptionalist and "redeemer nation." In the aftermath of the Vietnam War, the dominant culture in America (including the government, the media, Hollywood, and even educational institutions) mounted a massive campaign to "forget Vietnam." This relentless recuperative momentum to lay the ghost of that particular war culminated in the metamorphosis of an earlier general will to "heal the wound" inflicted on the American national psyche, into the "Vietnam syndrome"; that is, it transformed a healthy debate over the idea of America into a national neurosis.

This monumentalist initiative was aided by a series of historical events between 1989 and 1991 that deflected the American people's attention away from the divisive memory of the Vietnam War and were represented by the dominant culture as manifestations of the global triumph of "America": Tiananmen Square, the implosion of the Soviet Union, and the first Gulf War. This "forgetting" of the actual history of the Vietnam War, represented in this book by Graham Greene's *The Quiet American*, Philip Caputo's *A Rumor of War*, and Tim O'Brien's *Going After Cacciato* (and many other novels, memoirs, and films to which I refer parenthetically), contributed to the rise of neoconservatism and the religious right to power in the United States. And it provided the context for the renewal of America's exceptionalist errand in the global wilderness, now understood, as the conservative think tank the Project for the New American

ix

Century put it long before the invasion of Afghanistan and Iraq, as the preserving and perpetuation of the *Pax Americana.*

Whatever vestigial memory of the Vietnam War remained after this turn seemed to be decisively interred with Al Qaeda's attacks on the World Trade Center and the Pentagon on September 11, 2001. Completely immune to dissent, the confident American government, under President George W. Bush and his neoconservative intellectual deputies— and with the virtually total support of the America media—resumed its errand in the global wilderness that had been interrupted by the specter of Vietnam. Armed with a resurgence of self-righteous indignation and exceptionalist pride, the American government, indifferent to the reservations of the "Old World," unilaterally invaded Afghanistan and, then, after falsifying intelligence reports about Saddam Hussein's nuclear capability, Iraq, with the intention, so reminiscent of its (failed) attempts in Vietnam, of imposing American-style democracy on these alien cultures. The early representation by the media of the immediately successful "shock and awe" acts of arrogant violence in the name of "civilization" was euphoric. They were, it was said, compelling evidence not only of the recuperation of American consensus, but also of the rejuvenation of America's national identity.

But as immediate "victory" turned into an occupation of a world unwilling to be occupied, and the American peace into an insurgency that now verges on becoming a civil war, the specter of Vietnam, like the Hydra in the story of Hercules, began to reassert itself: the unidentifiability or invisibility of the enemy, their refusal to be answerable to the American narrative, quagmire, military victories that accomplished nothing, search and destroy missions, body counts, the alienation of allies, moral irresolution, and so on.

It is the memory of *this* "Vietnam"—*this* specter that refuses to be accommodated to the imperial exceptionalist discourse of post-Vietnam America—that my book is intended to bring back to presence. By retrieving a number of representative works that bore acute witness, even against themselves, to the *singularity* of a war America waged against a people seeking liberation from colonial rule and by reconstellating them into the post-9/11 occasion, such a project can contribute a new dimension not only to that shameful decade of American history, but also, and more important, to our understanding of the deeply backgrounded origins of America's "war on terror" in the aftermath of the Al Qaeda attacks. Indeed, it is my ultimate purpose in this book to provide directives for resisting an American momentum that threatens to destabilize the entire planet, if not to annihilate the human species itself, and also for rethinking the very idea of America.

I

The seven chapters that make up this book are "essays" in the original sense of the word: variations on the theme of spectrality as it pertains to the present volatile post-9/11 occasion. The first two chapters, which constitute Part I of the book, are theoretical.

The first, "History and Its Specter," attempts to establish the philosophical and political contexts that have precipitated the crisis of thinking in "posthistory." It consists of a critical reading of Francis Fukuyama's announcement of the end of history and the advent of the New World Order under the aegis of American capitalist democracy in *The End of History and the Last Man* (1992). It underscores his obliteration of the history of the Vietnam War, a history that would contradict his triumphalist Hegelian thesis. In the process of this critique, the chapter points to the various theoretical and praxis-oriented postmodern discourses that, more or less independently of each other, have borne witness against Fukuyama (and similar intellectual deputies of the dominant American culture) to the emergence of the spectral negative *of* the triumphalist rationality of Enlightenment modernity, especially in its American instrumentalist mode. This chapter further suggests that this "negative"—the ontological nothing (*das Nichts*) that Heidegger, Derrida, and Foucault made visible by disclosing its belongingness (not its antithetical relationship) to the discourse of "Truth"—is indissolubly related to the invisible Vietnamese insurgents—the "nonbeings" who defeated the American war machine in Vietnam—and to the unhomed, the migrants, the refugees, the displaced persons, and the nomads, who, precipitated as a political reality on a global scale by the fulfillment of the logic of Western imperialism, threaten the global hegemony of the West and particularly America at the present historical conjuncture.

The second chapter, "Althusser's 'Problematic'," undertakes a close theoretical study of the anti-ocularcentrism that has been fundamental to the posthumanist critique of Enlightenment modernity. By way of the example of Althusser, it traces the genealogy of the coercive and banalizing global triumph of the gaze of reason, as exemplified by Fukuyama, Richard Haass, Samuel Huntington, Niall Ferguson, Michael Mandelbaum, and other influential deputies of the dominant American culture, back to the privileging of vision in inquiry by the Enlightenment. It shows that this ocularcentrism of modernity *territorializes* the temporal be-*ing* of being—reduces its differential material force to a fixed space to be conquered or mastered. In so doing, this chapter also makes visible this spectral force that is invisible to but has always haunted the imperialist vision informing Western thinking. Harking back to the theme of the West's spectral Other in the previous chapter, the argument of this one concludes by demonstrating the remarkable relevance of Althusser's poststructuralist critique of Western ocularcentrism for understanding America's "errand in the wilderness" of Vietnam. The chapter thus introduces a crucial theoretical motif to American studies to which the New Americanists, because of their vestigial exceptionalist perspective, have remained more or less blind.

The next three chapters, which make up Part II of the book, constitute close ("symptomatic") readings of texts about the Vietnam War written by an exilic outsider (Graham Greene), and two articulate American veterans whose experience in Vietnam had turned them against the war (Philip Caputo and Tim O'Brien).

Chapter 3 shows how remarkably proleptic Greene's novel *The Quiet American* (1955) was of the essence of America's representation and conduct of its mission in Indochina, not least, of the American literature that was to emerge in the wake of the defeat of the United States in the Vietnam War. In foregrounding the Cold War/Orientalism of the policy expert York Harding, it anticipates the poststructuralist and postcolonial overdetermination and critique of representation (what Edward Said calls "the textual attitude") of the Orientalists, who represented the Orient according to the imperatives of the imperial Western gaze. In portraying Alden Pyle as the caricatured epitome of the Anglo-Protestant American pioneer (a modern Leatherstocking figure) and his "mission" in Vietnam according to the imperatives of the "errand in the wilderness," Greene, anticipating the New Americanists, also discloses the centrality of the American exceptionalist ethos in the psyche of the American soldiers who fought in Vietnam.

Chapters 4 and 5, on Philip Caputo's *A Rumor of War* and Tim O'Brien's *Going After Cacciato*, show the degree to which this exceptionalist ethos was inscribed not only in these representative young Americans who fought the war, but in the military command, the Pentagon planners, and ultimately the American public that initially supported it. Despite their refusal in the end to acknowledge the realities this *singular* war had disclosed, both are what I call *threshold texts* in the sense that what is actually said about the war is in excess of the American exceptionalist ideology that would contain and domesticate "it." They both thus symptomatically disclose a reality that haunts the closure they would impose on their narratives.

The chapter on Caputo's *A Rumor of War*, which amplifies my discussion of Althusser's problematic, constitutes a reading of this highly acclaimed memoir about the Vietnam War, which the author, the media, and academic critics have, in its troubled aftermath, represented as paradigmatic of that large body of autobiographical writing by veterans that lent itself to "healing the wound" suffered by the American body politic. Taking its point of departure from the televising of former Senator Bob Kerrey's "confession" on CBS's *60 Minutes II* on April 29, 2001, this chapter shows, on the one hand, that Caputo's will to bring the history of the Vietnam War to closure takes the form of individualizing his collective status (as American) and universalizing *the singularity*—the *thisness*—of the war to war-in-general. It thus shows that this impulse is a typically American ideological move ultimately intended to obscure the complicity of the American national identity with a terrorist "war of attrition," one that perpetrated a form of indiscriminate killing of innocent Vietnamese civilians (the body count, search and destroy missions, defoliation, B-52 bombings) that was tantamount to mass murder. On the other hand, the chapter shows that Caputo's very candid account of his experience betrays his inscribed retrospective will to narrativize the war, that is, to lay its ghost to rest. It discloses, symptomatically, precisely that which he does not want to, or is incapable of, facing: that his Ahab-like crime (against innocent Vietnamese civilians) is a synecdoche of the crime committed against the Vietnamese people, not simply by the U.S. war machine or even the U.S. government, but by "America" itself. In thus focalizing this irresolvable crime, the chapter shows that Caputo's representative memoir points proleptically to the specter that continues to haunt the American national identity in the aftermath of 9/11 and the second (stalled) invasion of Iraq.

The chapter on Tim O'Brien's novel *Going After Cacciato*, which underscores the remarkable similarity between its author's and Caputo's autobiographical representations of the war, analyzes its tripartite structure—the protagonist's past, present, and (imagined) future. It shows that the narrative he is obsessively imagining in the present (in the observation post) as an escape from the abyssal conditions of his past experience in combat is intended to relieve him of the anxiety ("the purple biles," which has "*no thing*" as its object), that has been precipitated by *this* war: a war, that, unlike the one his father fought in, is utterly indecisive, the consequence of a spectral enemy that refuses to fight according to the imperatives of the American narrative. Like the chapter on Caputo's memoir, this one shows that Paul Berlin is a representative young American whose identity undergoes a traumatic self-destruction in the face of a war that he cannot accommodate to his American exceptionalist perspective; thus, he is compelled into an irresolvable dilemma: either to go on fighting in a war for which he cannot attribute a just cause or to leave the war and thus exile himself from his homeland. In the end, he chooses the former. But the case he makes for this decision in the highly ritualized scene he imagines as the end of his narrative—it is in fact a deus ex machina—is incommensurate with the realities of the war that Berlin has borne witness to in the sections of the novel that refer to his experience in combat. Like Caputo's memoir, in other words, O'Brien's novel is a threshold text the "excess" of which belies its author's effort to accommodate the singularity of the Vietnam War to the American exceptionalist ethos. In the strained effort to reduce *this* war to war-in-general or to personalize the terrible collective contradictions of the Vietnam War, the novel betrays the latent violence inhering in the "benign" logic of American exceptionalism. Like the chapter on Caputo's *A Rumor of War*, this one on O'Brien's *Going After Cacciato* shows that American violence was not restricted to the site of the political, as too much criticism of the Vietnam War has maintained (implying the *betrayal* of the ideals of American democracy). As the underscored presence in these texts of the polyvalent myth of American exceptionalism emphatically suggests, it was perpetrated across a continuum from the sites of being as such (the ontological) and the subject, through the ecos (the land), to the cultural and social (gender, race), and the imperial.

Having, in what precedes, retrieved the *singularity* of the Vietnam War from the oblivion to which it had been relegated by the custodians of the American cultural memory, having, that is, disclosed the "Ahabian" violence inhering in the accommodational logic of American exceptionalism that had justified America's "errand in the [Vietnamese] wilderness," the last two chapters reconstellate *this* war into the post-9/11 occasion to disclose the genealogy of the George W. Bush administration's "benign" mission to bring American democracy to the benighted Islamic world in the Middle East and, by way of this retrieved shameful history of the Vietnam War, to suggest its likely horrific "end."

In chapter 6, this project takes the form, not of a direct confrontation of the Bush administration's practice in Afghanistan and Iraq, but of a deconstructive reading of the theoretical justifications of America's policy of preemptive wars, particularly that extremist and therefore telling version articulated by the highly influential policy expert Samuel P. Huntington in his most recent book, revealingly entitled *Who Are We?: Challenges to America's National Identity*. What is especially illuminating about this book written in the aftermath of 9/11 is not simply its frank invocation of the Puritan origins of the American national identity (the divinely ordained errand in the New World wilderness and its rejuvenating frontier allotrope). Equally illuminating is its utilization of the discourse of the exceptionalist American jeremiad (brilliantly analyzed and criticized by Sacvan Bercovitch) in Huntington's argument for recuperating what he calls "the Anglo-Protestant core culture"—threatened since the 1960s by the "deconstruction of America" and the rise of "subnational cultures"—in behalf of the "civilizational" war against "militant

Islam." In short, this chapter shows that at least one powerful strain of America's post-9/11 global policy is repeating *the very deep structure* of the American national identity that America's arrogant intervention and brutal conduct of the war in Vietnam delegitimated.

In chapter 7, the project of reconstellating the singularity of the Vietnam War into the post-9/11 occasion takes the form of a recapitulation of the disclosures about American exceptionalism articulated in the previous chapters for the purpose of unconcealing the imperial will to power that informed the Bush administration's representation of the attacks on the World Trade Center and the Pentagon and the essence of its form of retaliation. As in the Vietnam War under the aegis of the American presidents from Dwight Eisenhower to Richard Nixon, both the theoretical justification of the Bush administration's "war on terror" and its ensuing "shock and awe" practice involved a gross ontological, cultural, *and* sociopolitical reduction of the differential complexities of the Middle East to a single personification—first, Osama bin Laden and then Saddam Hussein. This collective American reduction, especially exemplified in Caputo's symbolic execution of the Vietnamese civilians and Paul Berlin's will to "Kill Vietnam," was, not incidentally, absolutely analogous to Captain Ahab's monomaniacal reduction of "all that maddens and torments; all that stirs up the lee of things; all truth with malice in it" to "Moby Dick" to make "him" "practically assailable." But this concluding chapter also reminds the reader that, like Captain Ahab's promethean project in the face of the nothingness of being (the whiteness of the whale), the American Ahabian project in Vietnam "ended" in the defeat of the "invincible American war machine" by an infinitely less powerful Other that, like Moby Dick (and on a different register, Bartleby), refused to be answerable to its powerful opponent's ontological, cultural, military, and political rules. As such, the book concludes, Vietnam—this singular war—has much to teach Americans and those who, in Noam Chomsky's apt phrase, would "deter America" about the theory and practice of the United States in the aftermath of 9/11.

II

The American national identity was radically destabilized, if not shattered, during the decade of the Vietnam War under the intense pressures of the protest movement, the civil rights movement, and the feminist movement. During the same time—and probably as an indirect consequence of this decentering—the world bore witness to the remarkable rise of transnational capitalist corporations and the free market and the spectacular

advances of electronic information production and dissemination.[1] This
combination induced many oppositional intellectuals to believe that the nation-state system (and the idea of national culture and the imperialism endemic to it) inaugurated by the Treaty of Westphalia in 1648 was coming
to it end and being replaced by the networking dynamics of a globalization
process determined by a decentered or "postmodern" or "posthistorical"
logic of commodity (late) capitalism. Generally indifferent to the visible
and sustained effort of the dominant culture in the United States to recuperate its pre-Vietnam War image as redeemer nation, which, following the
implosion of the Soviet Union, the event of Tiananmen Square, and the first
Gulf War, culminated in the announcement of the "end of history" and the
"advent of the New World Order" under the aegis of the United States,
these oppositional intellectuals—most notably, Fredric Jameson (*Postmodernism; or, The Logic of Late Capitalism*, 1990); Bill Readings (*The University in Ruins*, 1996); Masao Myoshi (*Globalization, Culture and the
University*, 1998), Antonio Negri and Michael Hardt (*Empire*, 2000, and
The Multitude, 2002)—not only underscored the obsolescence of the nation-state; they also claimed that the oppositional criticism identified with
poststructuralism—the antimetaphysical or anti-identitarian criticism that
had sought to liberate difference from the bondage of (Western or national)
culture—was unwittingly complicitous with the new sovereignty of transnational capital. As Negri and Hardt argue:

> The structures and logics of power in the contemporary world
> are entirely immune to the "liberatory" weapons of the post-
> modern politics of difference. In fact, Empire too is bent on
> doing away with those modern forms of sovereignty and on set-
> ting differences to play across boundaries. Despite the best inten-
> tions, then, the postmodern politics of difference not only is
> ineffective against but can even coincide with and support the
> functions and practices of imperial rule. The danger is that post-
> modern theories focus their attention so resolutely on the old
> forms of power they are running from, with their heads turned
> backwards, they tumble unwittingly into the welcoming arms of
> the new power.[2]

But this interpretation of the post-Vietnam world was rendered problematic when, in the wake of the attacks by Al Qaeda on the World Trade
Center and the Pentagon, the United States, supported by a massive explosion of justificatory intellectual and mediatic information, reasserted itself
with a vengeance not simply as a nation-state but also as an avowedly

imperial nation-state committed to imposing a *Pax Americana* on a global scale. This is not to say that this version of globalization is misguided; there is much to commend its argument, not least its attempt to think a global polity that is neither tethered to the nation-state nor subject to the decentered biopolitics of transnational consumer capitalism. It is to say, rather, that in concluding that the nation-state and the nation-centered imperialism that held sway in modernity are now, in the "postmodern" period, anachronistic, that the sovereignty of transnational capital is a fait accompli (not to say that the triumph of "the multitude" is thus imminent), this global theory is clearly—and disablingly—premature insofar as it deflects attention away from the American elite's recuperation of the United States as redeemer nation in the wake of the end of the Cold War and the attacks on American soil by Al Qaeda. Equally important, though in a related way, for my purposes, it is also to say that this contradiction, which highlights the contemporary occasion as an *interregnum* rather than the triumph of one kind of global polity over another, points acutely to the imperative of retrieving the singular history of the Vietnam War in behalf of underscoring the deeply embedded nationalism that is concealed by America's "contractual" origins and thus misread by Negri and Hardt and others as susceptible to decentering and constitutive of the dynamics of transnational imperial networking. This history has been all too hastily obliterated not only by the custodians of the American national identity, but also, ironically, by those "postmodern" global theorists who would deflect critical attention from the nation-state in their respective efforts to validate their visions of the contemporary global occasion. Retrieving its singularity will enable one to see that the contemporary human occasion is indeed an interregnum and that the way of resisting and overcoming both the nation-state momentum, which would precipitate the imperial *Pax Americana*, and that which would precipitate the global sovereignty of transnational capitalism resides not in acknowledging the demise of the nation-state as accomplished fact and in encouraging transnationalism to produce its antithesis, the uncentered sovereignty of "the multitude," as Negri and Hardt seem to advise. Retrieving the singularity of the Vietnam War, rather, would enable us to perceive that the way of resisting and overcoming both the nation-state and "empire" resides in challenging the United States' effort, based on its mythological status as redeemer nation, to achieve global sovereignty in behalf of a decentered global polity, or, in Edward Said's resonant phrase, "'the whole consort dancing together' contrapuntally." There is, as I will show in this book, no more powerful weapon ready at hand for this task of resistance and overcoming than the singularity of the Vietnam War, which delegitimated America's perennial claim to be God's or History's chosen nation.

It is not the main intention of this book to argue against the global theory that posits the demise of the nation-state and the rise of transnational capital to global sovereignty. Its purpose, rather, is to retrieve and underscore the perennial mobilizing force of the myth of American exceptionalism and the American nation-state it defines in the context of a traditional and postmodern representation of the United States that accepts the myth of exceptionalism as a reality. I mean a representation that, in acknowledging the radical difference between its nontraditional multicultural (and contractual) essence and the traditional monocultural essence of the European nation states, has, on the one hand, enabled its defenders to distinguish America as essentially democratic and anti-imperialist from the nations of Europe, and, therefore, on the other, as a nation susceptible to the kind of decentering endemic to transnational capital in a way that the European nations are not. To put my primary purpose in this way in the wake of the coming to prominence of the globalization theory that posits the demise of the nation-state, is, however, to indicate that what follows in the book does constitute a tacit challenge to it.

ACKNOWLEDGMENTS

This book is a sequel to *America's Shadow: An Anatomy of Empire*, published before September 11, 2001, but in my mind uncannily proleptic of America's response to Al Qaeda's attacks on the World Trade Center and the Pentagon. Like the latter in relation to the invasion of Iraq in the post-Cold War period, its purpose is to reiterate the enormous importance of the Vietnam War not simply for understanding this latest and most dangerous American exceptionalist global initiative, but also for providing directives of resistance that, unlike earlier modes, are adequate to the conditions that pertain to power relations at this postmodern conjuncture of world history.

In the six-year process of putting this book together, I incurred too many intellectual debts to be able to acknowledge them individually. Still, since I believe, more than ever now, as the American juggernaut advances and oppositional critics compete with each other, that truly productive oppositional criticism is collaborative, I feel the obligation to express, however inadequately, my gratitude to a number of former and recent graduate students who contributed significantly, through these years, in conversation, by e-mail, or telephone, both directly and indirectly, to my understanding of various topics in this book: Aliki Bakopoulou-Halls, R. Radhakrishnan, Giovanna Covi, Jan McVicker, Michael Clark, Patrick McHugh, Madeline Sorapure, David Randall, Bob Marzec, Assimina Karavanta, Mei Ling Wu, Liana Vrajitoru, Firat Oruc, Michael Logan, Racheal Forlow, Taras Sak, Deborah Poe, Catherine Dent, and Christine Battista. I also wish to thank my English and Comparative Literature Department colleagues, David Bartine, Susan Strehle, Joseph Keith, and Donette Francis, whose global perspectives helped me maintain mine, and the three anonymous readers of the original manuscript, both for their positive response and their wise recommendations for making the book stronger. Of the many scholars who have been influential in providing me with directives for understanding the American mind, I wish to single out Sacvan Bercovitch, Paul Bové, and Donald Pease. I have not always agreed with some of their positions on the matters that are central to this book, but I cannot imagine having written it without the presence of their inaugural and challenging work.

I also wish to extend my gratitude to Ruth Stanek, assistant to the chair of the Binghamton University English Department, and Anita Pisani, secretary to the chair, for their gracious assistance in helping me prepare the original manuscript for submission; to the editorial staff of SUNY Press, particularly Larin McLaughlin, my editor, and Kelli W. LeRoux, the former for her enthusiastic support of my work, the latter for her efficiency in seeing this book through the production process; and to Susan Strehle for the photograph of the Vietnam Veteran War Memorial that became the cover of this book, to Geoffrey Gould, who re-shot it to emphasize the "bar sinister" running through it, and to Ken Schrider for the final design.

Finally, I dedicate this book to Susan Strehle and our son Adam Spanos for being there.

Earlier versions of chapters 1, 2, 3, 4, and 6 were previously published as essays: chapter 1 as "The Specter of History: Rethinking Thinking in the Post-Cold War Age," *Mosaic,* 34, 4 (December 2001), 21–46; chapter 2 as "Althusser's Problematic in the Context of the Vietnam War: Towards a Spectral Politics," *Rethinking Marxism,* 10 (Fall 1998), 1–21; chapter 3 as "Who Killed Alden Pyle? The Oversight of Oversight in Graham Greene's *Quiet American,*" *Critical Zone 2: A Forum of Chinese and Western Knowledge* (University of Hong Kong Press, 2006), 11–45; chapter 4 as "A Rumor of War: 9/11 and the Forgetting of the Vietnam War," *boundary* 2, 30, no.3 (Fall 2003), 29–66; chapter 6 as "American Exceptionalism, the Jeremiad, and the Frontier: From the Puritans to the Neo-Con-Men," *boundary* 2, 34, no. 1 (Spring 2007). All have been substantially extended and revised for this book. I wish to thank the editors of *Mosaic* (Dawn McCance), *Rethinking Marxism* (David Ruccio), *boundary* 2 (Paul Bové), and *Critical zone 2* (Q. S. Tong, Wang Shouren, and Douglas Kerr) for granting me permission to reprint.

Chapter 1

HISTORY AND ITS SPECTER
Rethinking Thinking in the
Post-Cold War Age

On the basis of the Greeks' initial contributions towards an
Interpretation of Being, a dogma has been developed which
not only declares the question about the meaning of Being to
be superfluous, but sanctions its complete neglect. It is said
that "Being" is the most universal and the emptiest of concepts. As such it resists every attempt at definition. Nor does
this most universal and hence indefinable concept require any
definition, for everyone uses it constantly and already understands what he means by it. In this way, that which the ancient philosophers found continually disturbing as something
obscure and hidden has taken on a clarity and self-evidence
such that if anyone continues to ask about it he is charged
with an error of method.

—Martin Heidegger, *Being and Time*

In 1927, in the midst of the disintegration of modern Europe precipitated by
the fulfillment of its fundamentally "imperial" logic, Martin Heidegger, following Nietzsche, called for the retrieval of *die Seinsfrage*, the question of
being that Occidental philosophy had forgotten since it was first asked by
the pre-Socratic Greeks. In so doing, he instigated an alienation effect that
amounted to a Copernican revolution in the advanced thinking of the twentieth century. To put it essentially, in retrieving the question of being from
the oblivion to which it was relegated by the increasing technologization
and institutionalization of thinking, Heidegger enabled or, perhaps more accurately, catalyzed four integrally related epochal disclosures that radically
called the "objective" problematic of the Occidental philosophical tradition
into question: (1) the disclosure that this tradition was "onto-theo-logical,"

1

which is to say, a three-phased history (the Greco-Roman, Medieval/Reformation, and Enlightenment eras) that, despite its historical variations, has continuously privileged metaphysics—a mode of inquiry informed by a *Logos* or principle of presence, outside of or prior to time and history, as the essential ground of thinking; (2) the disclosure that this tradition had reduced the (temporal) be-*ing* of being understood as an indissoluble, if uneven, historical continuum extending from the subject and the ecos through gender and race to culture, economics, and sociopolitics, to a reified entity, a *Summum Ens*; (3) the disclosure that the perception/representation of being in this tradition was enacted not in-the-midst (*interesse*), but from after or above or beyond (*meta*) the emergent things themselves (*physis*); and, most tellingly, (4) the disclosure that this metaphysical representation of being *as* Being was informed by the totalizing will to power over the relay of differences that being *as temporality* always already disseminates.

The years following Heidegger's announcement have borne witness to the emergence of a number of postmodern or post-ontotheological discourses—deconstruction, genealogy, neo-Marxism, feminism, gay criticism, new historicism, cultural criticism, postcolonialism, global criticism, New Americanist studies, and so on—that, despite crucial resistances, have assimilated Heidegger's fundamental transformative disclosures in some degree or other into their particular perspectives. These "new" discourses, in turn, have been (unevenly) assimilated into most of the traditional disciplines of knowledge production. But have the implications for both critique and emancipation of this potentially polyvalent revolution in thinking been fully realized? My answer is an emphatic negative. And the reason for this failure is that the project of thinking or rethinking the *Seinsfrage* has come to a premature closure. This is not simply because of the widespread and ideologically driven identification of Heidegger's thought with Nazism in the wake of Victor Farias's *Heidegger et le nazisme* (1987). It is also because of the growing sense on the part of the current Left, especially in the context of the reemergence of praxis to privileged status over "theory," that ontology or rather ontological representation is so rarefied a category of thought that it is virtually empty of, if not hostile to, politics. In other words, the rethinking of thinking Heidegger's interrogation of the ontotheological tradition enabled has come to its end because the emancipatory "postmodern" discourses that his thought catalyzed have, in putting ontological inquiry ("theory") in a disabling binary opposition with cultural and "worldly" political praxis, again forgotten the question of being. In so doing, they have forfeited the advance in thinking enabled by the *Seinsfrage* to those metaphysical traditionalists it was intended to disarm.

It will be one of the purposes of this introductory chapter, therefore, to retrieve the question of being as an especially urgent imperative of thinking and emancipatory practice at the present—*post-Cold War*—historical conjuncture, which, after Setermber 11, 2001, has entered its most dangerous phase. More specifically, I will attempt, in a prolegomenal way, to think more fully the unevenly thought "Heideggerian" ontological disclosures enumerated above in the context of the resurgence of metaphysical interpretations of the post-Cold War occasion: the "triumphalist" representations of the epochal implosion of the Soviet Union by the liberal democratic/capitalist "victors" as the "end of history" and the advent of "the New World Order"—and the annulment of any lingering vestige of the "Vietnam syndrome," which is to say any remaining doubt as to the ontological rightness of America's perennial exceptionalist errand in the global wilderness. (In later chapters, I will address the modifications of this triumphalist representation of the post-Cold War occasion compelled by the resurgence of Iraq after the first Gulf War and later by the attacks on the World Trade Center and the Pentagon by Al Qaeda. Here, it will suffice to say, by way of anticipation, that these later modifications by the "intellectual deputies"—Gramsci's phrase—of the dominant culture did not entail a radical rejection of the initial end-of-history thesis; rather, they *accommodated* the events that seemed to contradict it.)

On the basis of the recent (mis)identification of Heidegger's thought with Nazi practice, both the liberal and radical left will surely question the legitimacy of such an appeal to a Heideggerian model in behalf of an emancipatory discourse adequate to the post-Cold War occasion. To justify such a project, it will therefore be necessary to undertake a brief "detour" into recent history. By "recent history" I mean, of course, the dominant culture's massive "triumphalist" representation of the uprising in China (Tiananmen Square) and the "revolutions" in Eastern and Central Europe and the Soviet Union in the late 1980s and early 1990s as the end of history and coming of the New World Order and, of course, the ensuing advent of the free world market. But I also mean—and this should always be kept in mind—the historically specific history—*the specter*—that this global History would obliterate in order to legitimize its claim to universality: not least, the Vietnam War.

I

This History, both what it affirms and what it has repressed, is, because of the euphoric excess of its representation, conveniently epitomized by Francis Fukuyama's *The End of History and the Last Man* (1992).[1] This book by an intellectual deputy of the triumphant capitalist culture was immediately canonized on its publication not only by the emergent neoconservative movement in the United States, but also by many liberals, that has saturated the cultural discourse of America, both high and low, since its origins. It informs, as we shall see in Chapter 6, the "American jeremiad," which, from John Winthrop, Cotton Mather, and Jonathan Edwards, through Timothy Dwight and John Adams, Andrew Jackson, Daniel Webster, to Theodore Roosevelt, John F. Kennedy, Ronald Reagan, and, most extremely, George W. Bush, has always functioned to secure—and rejuvenate—the American national consensus in behalf of its providentially ordained mission to domesticate (and dominate) what is beyond the frontier.[5] It informs the historiography of official national historians of the United States like Francis Parkman, George Bancroft, and Frederick Jackson Turner.[6] It informs the narratives of canonical American writers like John Filson, Joel Barlow, Robert Montgomery Bird, James Fenimore Cooper, and William Gilmore Simms.[7] And it informs the Hollywood westerns, which have functioned to naturalize what one New Americanist historian has called the American "victory culture."[8] Indeed, as I will show at length in chapter 6, it is this deeply backgrounded myth in all its historical specificity that Samuel P. Huntington, one of the most influential historians or, more accurately, neoconservative policy experts, of the American future, has invoked in the wake of September 11, 2001, *now overtly*, in his aptly titled book *Who Are We?: Challenges to America's National Identity* for the purpose of mobilizing America against the "internal threat" posed by the "deconstruction of America" and the rise of "subnational cultures" in behalf of "the clash of civilizations" heralded by the Al Qaeda attacks on the World Trade Center and the Pentagon.[9]

Reconstellated into the context of Haass's revisionism, Fukuyama's overdetermination of History in his announcement of the end of history undergoes a suggestive estrangement. What in its naive exaggerations seems on the surface easily dismissable, comes to be seen as demanding rigorous analysis. That is, such a reconstellation reveals Fukuyama's text to be a symptomatic fulfillment of a deeply inscribed American assumption about Being (in the form of its historical allotrope) whose origin is simultaneous with the founding of America. As the inflation of Fukuyama's book into a media event itself suggested, it is an assumption that the actual history of (post)modernity has turned into a national, (meta)narrative need. I cannot undertake such an extended analysis here. It will suffice for my purposes to invoke briefly that dimension of Fukuyama's argument that epitomizes the triumphant post-Cold War discourse's representation of contemporary history in the context of the "Heideggerian" destruction of the ontotheological tradition or, more specifically, of its late, post-Enlightenment or "anthropological" phase. I am referring to Fukuyama's overt appropriation of a Kojèvian version of Hegel's dialectical history to interpret the contemporary historical events as the final and permanent "triumph" of liberal capitalist democracy over communism and the precipitation of (a modified version of) the idea of the "universal and homogeneous state" (*EH*, xxi and chapter 19).

What this "Heideggerian" context demands focusing on in Fukuyama's representation is the radical incommensurability between the *actual* history of recent global politics and the universalist conclusion he draws from this history:

> But the fact that there will be [after the decisive triumph of liberal/capitalist democracy in the Cold War] setbacks and disappointments in the process of democratization, or that not every market economy will prosper, should not distract us from the larger pattern that is emerging in world history. . . . What is emerging victorious, in other words, is not so much liberal practice, as the liberal *idea*. That is to say, for a very large part of the world, there is now no ideology with pretensions to universality that is in a position to challenge liberal democracy, and no universal principle of legitimacy other than the sovereignty of the people. (*EH*, 45)

This representation of the relationship between the historically specific history of the modern age and the History subsuming it constitutes the underlying structural principle of Fukuyama's history—the problematic, in Althusser's term, that determines actual history's visibilities and invisibilities. Its specific multidimensional lineaments can, therefore, serve as a revelatory synecdoche of the fixed, undeviating, and deeply backgrounded whole of Fukuyama's book.

To begin with, we could say in a general way that Fukuyama's historiography—his representation of *this* particular history—takes the essential and foundational form of Western literary narrative, by which I mean a *mimesis* in the "Aristotelian"/"Horatian" mode: a story with a beginning, middle, and end, in which the end—understood as the goal, the truth, and thus the principle of legitimacy—is present from the beginning through the middle to the termination of the action. It partakes, that is, of a (timeless) movement that always already determines the "directionality"—an important word in Fukuyama's Hegelian discourse—of the temporal process. To put this general movement in the more specific ideological rhetoric he employs, Fukuyama's story is, as his representation of the "triumph" of liberal capitalist democracy in the mode of the annunciation of "good news" suggests (*EH*, xiii), informed by the "promise/fulfillment" structure of eschatological (and, as in the case of Virgil's *Aeneid* or Cotton Mather's *Magnalia Christi Americana*, imperial) narrative.

But this, though not inaccurate, is to put the teleology of Fukuyama's narrative too abstractly and simply. As its rhetoric of conflict/triumph suggest, the narrative informing Fukuyama's representation of modern history is complicated by a post-theological dialectical economy. It is a logical economy that, while appearing to allow temporality to do its corrosive work, in fact precipitates an always promised Absolute out of temporal ideological momentums. It is not adequate simply to say that this representation *subordinates* time/history to "a larger pattern." More significant, this maneuver, as the mythology of this "white writing" suggests, transforms time, which is intrinsically unpresentable, unnamable, and incomprehensible, into a presentable, nameable, and graspable spatial or territorial image. That is, Fukuyama's projection of modern history as a conflictual (dialectical) narrative movement that in the end has precipitated "the liberal *idea*" as the truth of History is informed, in Derrida's terms, by a philosophy of Presence, which posits existential time as *merely* apparent and, as such, potentially *"distractive"* from the essential object of the historian's gaze. To foreground the presiding metaphorics of this synecdochical passage, Fukuyama's representation of modern history is a re-presentation (German, *Vorstellung*): a *placing* of time—that which cannot in essence be *placed*—*before* the panoptic and commanding eye. Put alternatively, Fukuyama's "secular" narrative of the history of the Cold War is informed by a *metaphysical ontology*: the perception of being—the always emergent "things-as-they-are" (*physis*)—from *after* or *above*, as, in other words, a totalized structure.

In the above synecdochical passage Fukuyama's rhetoric strategically maneuvers the reader's attention toward the "larger pattern"—the promised structure—that the dialectics of History will bring forth in the "fullness of time." (I am pointing provisionally to the affiliative relationship between the metaphorics of the centered circle, of the gaze/picture, and of the patriarchal/theological seed "planted" in the womb of time, all tropes intrinsic to the Occidental—and especially American—imperial project.) Understood in terms of the de-sedimented context precipitated by this interrogation of Fukuyama's spatial rhetoric, we are enabled to resist this enticement and to refocus our attention on "the setbacks and disappointments in the process of democratization" that Fukuyama foresees, but which he represents as seductive "distractions" from "the larger pattern" to which we should not succumb. That which distracts means an inessential or accidental or irrelevant or, more resonantly, marginal force—a differential Other— that draws our attention—our gaze—away from the "essential" direction and that "stirs up or confuses us [as subjects] with conflicting emotions or motives."[10] In Fukuyama's discourse, this distraction refers to the historically specific events of modernity that have collectively generated a pervasive pessimism, especially among advanced (poststructuralist?) intellectuals, a pessimism that, accordingly, has made it difficult to "recognize good news when it comes" (*EH*, xii). This is the history he abstractly and neutrally characterizes as "the truly terrible political events of the first half of the twentieth century—two destructive world wars, the rise of totalitarian ideologies, and the turning of science against man in the form of nuclear weapons and environmental damage" (*EH*, xiii). That is, what the "distraction" that "distracts" refers to is the actual—catastrophic—history, both past and future, that would disrupt the promissory dialectical economy of History. Derrida thematizes the eschatological provenance of Fukuyama's annunciation of the end of history as "good news" (I would add its "*providential*" origins to foreground the visual metaphorics of this prophetics):

> Why a gospel? Why would the formula here be neo-testamentary? This book claims to bring a "positive response" to a question whose formation and formulation are never interrogated in themselves. It is the question of whether a "coherent and directional History of mankind" will eventually lead "the greater part of humanity" . . . toward "liberal democracy" (p. xii). Of course, while answering "yes" to this question in this form, Fukuyama admits . . . to an awareness of everything that allows one to have one's doubts: the two world wars, the horrors of totalitarianism—Nazi, fascist, Stalinist—the massacres of Pol Pot, and so forth. . . . But according to a schema that organizes the argumentation of this strange plea from one end to the other, all these cataclysms (terror, oppression, repression, extermination, genocide, and so on), these "events" or these "facts" would belong to *empiricity*. . . . Their accumulation would in no way refute the *ideal* orientation of the greater part of humanity toward liberal democracy. . . . Even if one admitted the simplicity of this summary distinction between empirical reality and ideal finality, one would still not know how this . . . anhistoric *telos* of history gives rise, very precisely *in our day* . . . to an event which Fukuyama speaks of as "good news" and that he dates very explicitly from "The most remarkable evolution of the last quarter of the twentieth century." (p. xiii) . . . This "move toward political freedom around the globe". . . would have been everywhere accompanied . . . by "a liberal revolution in economic thought." The alliance of liberal democracy and of the "free market," there's the "good news" of this last quarter century. This evangelistic figure is remarkably insistent.[11]

Derrida's analysis constitutes a powerful and, however belated, much welcomed thematization not simply of the reductive ontological priority of the transhistorical *Logos* over actual history in Fukuyama's historiography, but of the theological provenance of its will to power over the *singular event*: of what I will provisionally call the imperialism of Fukuyama's metaphysical ontology. But the actual history to which Derrida refers does not adequately differentiate itself from the examples that Fukuyama calculatively enumerates in accounting for the "blinding" pessimism of advanced thinking in the late twentieth century. This is because Fukuyama can dissociate the limitations of liberal democracy from the violent events Derrida invokes as witness against the end of history. Indeed, it is the fundamental assumption of Fukuyama's post-Enlightenment discourse that the violence perpetrated by liberal democracy is radically distinguishable from the kind of violence perpetrated by the "political" ideologies that have fallen by the historical wayside in the wake of the dialectical "triumph" of liberal capitalist democracy. Unlike the latter, he would argue, the violence of the former is not—of course—inherent in its logic. As in the binarist rhetoric of the perennial Occidental colonialist project, it is, rather, the consequence of liberal capitalist democracy's unwanted but necessary historical responsibility to "defend" itself from evil aggressors:

> The wars unleashed by these totalitarian ideologies were also of a new sort [sic], involving the mass destruction of civilian populations and economic resources—hence the term, "total war." To defend themselves from this threat, liberal democracies were led to adopt military strategies like the bombing of Dresden or Hiroshima that in the earliest ages would have been called genocidal. (*EH*, 6)

More usually, these apparent violences are rationalized as the consequence of the *betrayal* of liberal capitalist democracy's fundamental principles or of a partial or imperfect view of its logic's benign practical imperatives. As such they can be understood, as in the case of the culture industry's latest representation of America's defeat in Vietnam, as "mistakes" that are correctable or problems that are ultimately solvable.[12] (It is, as I will show later, by way of invoking Michel Foucault's analysis of the "repressive hypothesis," an assumption that has been fundamental to the truth discourse of liberal democratic societies since the Enlightenment.) As Fukuyama puts this perennially articulated American duplicity:

> Assuming that liberal democracy is, for the moment, safe from external enemies, could we assume that successful democratic

societies could remain that way indefinitely? . . . There is no doubt that contemporary democracies face any number of serious problems, from drugs, homelessness, and crime to environmental damage and the frivolity of consumerism. But these problems are not obviously insoluble on the basis of liberal principles, nor so serious that they would necessarily lead to the collapse of society as a whole, as communism collapsed in the 1980s. (*EH*, xxi)

In saying that Derrida's examples can be accommodated to the logic of liberal capitalist democracy, I do not want to suggest that he is blind to the contradictory violence inhering in it. Returning to his thematization of Fukuyama's end-of-history discourse as "teleo-eschatological good news," Derrida in fact identifies the "legitimate" violence perpetrated by liberal democracies with the illegitimate violence to which Fukuyama refers. But characteristically his representation of these contradictions takes the indirect and distancing form of an ahistorical philosophical insight. The gap between the actualities of liberal democratic practice and the *idea* that Fukuyama declares "could not be improved on" (*EH*, xi) is, "by definition, a priori, characteristic of all democracies" (*SM*, 64).

What is surprising about Derrida's otherwise decisive indictment of Fukuyama's privileging of History over the jagged and dislocating singularities of actual history is his failure or refusal to invoke as witness against Fukuyama's representation a decisively *other* history than that which is amenable to accommodation by Fukuyama's imperial teleological dialectic. I mean the very actual violent histories enacted, not as a defense or a betrayal of or a blindness to the logical imperatives of the liberal democracy problematic, but by way of the *fulfillment* of its restricted logical economy. I mean the terrible events of modern history that, ironically, more than any philosophical textual momentum, instigated the postmodern or poststructuralist or posthumanist interrogation of the ontological principles informing the liberal democracies—and their humanist cultures—of Enlightenment modernity. I mean, in short, the very actual histories that have, in their facticity, brought history to a quite different kind of end from that euphorically announced by Fukuyama and celebrated by the American culture industry. This difference to which I am referring is the end—the *telos*—which, in historically fulfilling the theoretical and practical possibilities of the founding ontological principles of liberal capitalist democracy, also discloses its limits: "that" which it cannot finally accommodate and contain within its imperial orbit. Which is to say, the contradictory imperial violence against its Other inhering in its "benign" (teleo)logical economy.

II

These violent modern histor*ies* that would destroy the "History" that both precipitated them and relegated their delegitimizing memory to oblivion are, in fact, everywhere ready at hand, if only symptomatically: the brutalization of the native populations of North Africa, India, and Southeast Asia by Western imperialist nations—Great Britain, The Netherlands, Portugal, France, and Germany—in the name of the *mission civilisatrice*; the histories of the enslavement of black Africans and the rapacious exploitation of their "dark" or "empty" lands in the name of the "white man's burden"; and, more immediately, the histories of the removal and subsequent annihilation of the native Americans and their culture in the name of America's exceptionalist "errand in the wilderness" and its inexorably directional Manifest Destiny.[13] But because these histories tend to subordinate the idea of liberal democracy to the more inclusive category of the "civilized" West, they could (illegitimately) be interpreted as histories perpetrated by and in the name of the generalized West or by an unfinished version of the idea of liberal democracy. For this reason, the history that I will invoke here, and in the chapters that follow, as decisive witness to the illegitimacy of the History that announces the end of history is the coruscating history of the Indochinese War. I mean the inordinately violent imperial history of Southeast Asia that culminated in the United States' invasion of Vietnam or, to be more faithful to the hegemonic rhetoric that "justified" America's intervention, in the American "errand in the wilderness" of Southeast Asia.

It will be the purpose of the second half of this book to fully show in what sense this twentieth-century "event" was an epochal event in modern, post-Enlightenment history, in what sense, that is, this history disclosed the radical contradiction—the unaccommodatable violence—that inheres in the benign discourse and practice of liberal capitalist democracy.[14] Here it will suffice to recall the provenance of postmodernist, or poststructuralist, or posthumanist theory against the reductive tendency of its current practitioners (and its postcolonial and humanist opponents[15]) to forget its historical origins—a tendency incumbent on its institutionalization and exacerbated by the end of the Cold War and the mediatization of one version or other of the "end-of-history" discourse. The advent of "theory," it should be remembered, understood as the interrogation of the Western metaphysical tradition (logocentrism) and the pretensions of its imperial truth-claims to global authority, was precipitated by the implosion of the logical economy of imperialism in the aftermath of World War II. But its immediate origins lay in the thirty-year period of the Indochinese War (1945–1975), especially in its exorbitantly violent late planetary phase, after the United States assumed its "exceptionalist" burden to "save" Vietnam for "democracy" from the decadent Old World colonialism of France and the communism of the Soviet Union. More specifically, the effort of postmodern "theory" to think from and within the margins the polyvalent critical/projective imperatives of a decentered Occidental *Logos* was, however indirectly and unevenly, instigated by the spectacle of the *self*-destruction of the *idea*—the *Logos/Eidos*—of the modern Occident in its post-Enlightenment (anthropological), which is to say, its liberal democratic/capitalist historical allotrope.

The war in Vietnam, it should not be forgotten, was inaugurated and escalated to its most intense and destructive violence by both liberal Democratic and conservative Republican presidential administrations (Dwight Eisenhower, John F. Kennedy, Lyndon Johnson, and Richard Nixon) and was debated globally, not in terms of the fate of democracy in America, but of the very idea of liberal capitalist democracy. This spectacle of the self-destruction of the "benign" logic of liberal democracy—this inadvertent rendering visible of the genocidal violence latent in its otherwise invisible because banalized imperial "center elsewhere"—was the essential witness of the Vietnam War at large. It was, if the grotesquely comic banality (to which the highly serious American speaker is utterly blind) is understood as a carnivalesque trope of the inexpressible horror of the event he, like the Pentagon planners of the war, routinizes,[16] perfectly imaged in synecdochical form by the major who, in the aftermath of a large-scale search and destroy operation, told a reporter, "in a successful attempt at attaining history, 'We had to destroy Ben Tre in order to save it.'"[17] Ben Tre, it should be remarked, was not simply a geographical/political space nor one occupied by the "enemy"; it is an earth, as we shall see later in this book, inhabited by a community of people whose culture sacralized this earth's very (spatial and temporal) being.

We must, that is, not be seduced by the emergent "larger pattern" of History into forgetting that America's intervention in Southeast Asia was undertaken in the name of "winning the hearts and minds" of the Vietnamese people to the fundamental and historically realized ontological principles of "the free world" and that it eventually took the visibly contradictory form of an all-out—undiscriminating—linguistic, ecological, cultural, economic, and military violence. We must also not forget that this polyvalent violence was read by a significant portion of the people of the United States, of Europe, and of the Third World, including responsible representative Western intellectuals such as Jean-Paul Sartre, Bertram Russell, Noam Chomsky, and Martin Luther King, as genocidal in its intent and in its proportions. Nor must we forget that, however symptomatically enacted, the protestation of the war in the United

States—its "refusal of spontaneous consent" to the truth discourse of liberal capitalist democracy, to invoke Antonio Gramsci[18]—brought the American government to a crisis that only the disruption of the Civil War has surpassed in critical intensity. The examples (among many others) of President Lyndon Johnson's decision not to run for reelection and the ensuing violence unleashed by Mayor Richard Daley at the Democratic national convention in Chicago and a little later by Governor James Rhodes at Kent State University attest to this crisis of hegemony.

What, in other words, happened in that time, which must not be forgotten—but which, since then, an entire culture industry has made it its priority to erase from the American national memory—was, to appropriate Michel Foucault's language, something akin to an epistemic break. The unspeakable violence perpetrated in the name of the principles of freedom by the United States during the Vietnam War symptomatically disclosed at multiple sites on the continuum of being the contradictions inhering in the truth discourse of liberal capitalist democracy. To put it concretely and positively, America's inordinately violent conduct of the war made visible the polyvalent global imperial will to power that, under normal conditions, strategically remains invisible in the (onto)logic of the "free world."

It is this decisive shaking of the epistemic foundation of liberal capitalist democracy that explains the continuing unappeasable anxiety of the American people about a war that officially "ended" in 1975: its spectral refusal to be deposited in the main—monumental—stream of American history. It is also this rupturing of the sutured American discourse of hegemony that explains the continuing paranoidal and massively mobilized representational effort of the culture industry—the news media, television, the film industry, mainstream publishing houses, and even educational institutions—to "heal the wound" opened up in the collective American psyche by the United States' brutal and contradictory conduct of the war, the wound, it should be marked, that, since the end of the Cold War and the first Gulf War, has tellingly been rerepresented negatively as "the Vietnam syndrome": that is, a national neurosis.[19] In short, the decentering of the liberal democratic *episteme* also explains the obsessive, but unrealizable, will to forget the haunting specter of Vietnam by remembering it recollectively: by reifying and accommodating its disruptive differential force to the American (democratic/capitalist) cultural memory.

What is remarkable, to emphasize the disclosive paradox, about Fukuyama's representative announcement of the end of history (and the variations on this theme by later deputies of the dominant culture such as Richard Haass, Samuel P. Huntington, Niall Ferguson, Michael Mandelbaum,[20] and many other neoconservatives) is its virtual silence about or blindness to the cacophonously visible history of the Vietnam War. His book purports to be a true history of the world, focusing on its last stage of "development": the dialectical struggle of political systems during the Cold War that terminates (eschatologically) in the demise of a self-contradictory communism and the absolutization of liberal capitalist democracy. But in the process, it literally effaces or, to use a metaphor invariably applied (and restricted) by the Cold War discourse to Stalinist narratives of modernity, it "airbrushes" this singular history. I am referring to the violent history that includes not only the thirty years of actual conflict, but also the twenty years following the defeat of the American military command (1975, the year that bore witness to the humiliating spectacle of the fall of Saigon) to the present post-Cold War, indeed, post-9/11, conjuncture. What should be immediately visible and legible to anyone who, against the grain of the amnesiac American discourse of hegemony, remains attuned to the global scope and epochal significance—the "postmodernity"—of the radically differential history of the Vietnam War is not simply Fukuyama's (and his revisionary neoconservative colleagues') studied indifference to this singular history. It is also, and more important, his arrogant indifference to the difference this history might make in his "report" on the global operations of History, more specifically, in Derrida's apt terms, in his eschatological tidings of "good news."

As his reassuring representation of the likely future "setbacks and disappointments in the process of democratization" as mere *distractions* "from the larger pattern that is emerging in world history" inexorably ordains, Fukuyama's "Hegelian" metaphysical problematic *compels* the trivialization of the history of the Vietnam War, if not the complete obliteration of its epochal significance. In his only more or less direct reference to that globally disruptive occasion, he violently reduces the resonant double difference that was/is the Vietnam War to the reified status of one in a series of vaguely affiliated historical "accidents" (a "fluke") that deflects our attention from the planetary *eventness* of *this* war. From his Hegelian perspective—and reminiscent of the nineteenth-century American discourse of Manifest Destiny—Fukuyama transforms the Vietnam War into a minor, passing, and mere (i.e., fundamentally irrelevant) digression in the grand, inexorable, and necessary progress of the dialectical (meta)narrative of History toward its self-devouring end. In short, just as his mentor effaces the historical presence of Africa from his dialectical history of the world—"At this point we leave Africa, not to mention it again. For it is no historical part of the World; it has no movement or development to exhibit"—so Fukuyama pacifies the disruptive force of the (non)event of Vietnam:

of the brutality of the imperialism of the Turks, the Spanish, the Portuguese, or the Belgians (as in Defoe's *Robinson Crusoe*, Conrad's *Heart of Darkness*, and H. Ryder Haggard's *King Solomon's Mine*—and later, as I will show at length in chapter 6, of American colonialism—its systematic invocation of the French and especially the Spanish, as in James Fenimore Cooper's Leatherstocking novels, William Gilmore Simm's *The Yemassee,* Francis Parkman's *The Conspiracy of Pontiac*, and George Bancroft's *History of the United States*) to define what their colonialism is not. As Conrad's spokesman, Marlowe, puts this perennial post-Enlightenment justificatory logic in *Heart of Darkness*:

> Mind none of us [Marlowe and his British countrymen] would feel exactly like this. What saves us is efficiency—the devotion to efficiency. But these chaps [the Romans in the past and the Belgians in the present] were not much account really. They were no colonists, their administration was merely a squeeze, and nothing more, I suspect. They were conquerors, and for that you wanted brute force. . . . It was just robbery with violence, aggravated murder on a great scale, and men going at it blind—as is very proper for those who tackle a darkness. The conquest of the earth, which mostly means the taking it away from those who have a different complexion or slightly flatter noses than ourselves, is not a pretty thing when you look into it too much. *What redeems it is the idea only.* An idea at the back of it, not a sentimental pretense but an idea; and an unselfish belief in the idea—something you can set up, and bow down before, and offer a sacrifice."[22]

And it is precisely this duplicitous logic of the repressive hypothesis, pushed to its nuanced extreme, that, as in the case of Fukuyama's argument, contemporary liberal democratic societies, especially the United States, employ to justify their colonialist interventions in Third World countries. The fundamental representation of U.S. involvement in Vietnam bears witness to this. Even before the demise of French control in Indochina with the fall of Dien Bien Phu (May 7, 1954), America—the presidency, the Congress, the Pentagon, the culture industry—predictably justified its intervention by insistently distinguishing its motives as radically different from those informing the decadent colonialism of Old World France. As I will show as length in chapter 3, the fraudulence of this benign American exceptionalist justification was proleptically exposed—if not acknowledged by the American public—long ago by Graham Greene's portrayal of the young, idealist American Alden Pyle in his novel *The Quiet American* (1955). Pyle, it will be recalled, comes to Vietnam inscribed by the writing of York Harding, an American "Asian expert"—an "Orientalist" as Edward Said would put it—whose discourse about the Orient is informed not only by the "domino theory" and the strategy of the "Third Force," but also by the profound disdain for Old World colonialism that has characterized American culture since its origins in the Puritan's genocidal exceptionalist "errand in the wilderness." And, in the name of his culture's assumed moral and racial superiority—and its certainty of "winning the hearts and minds" of these backward Asiatics—this Cold War American Adam, armed with Harding's *The Advance of Red China*, the implacable Word or, as Said calls this dangerously quixotic vision, the "textual attitude,"[23] leaves a trail of innocent blood in his inexorably undeviating wake.

IV

What should be remarkable to anyone attuned to the dissonance of the actual history of this century is not only the failure of oppositional discourses—for example, deconstruction, Marxism, the new historicism, feminism, cultural critique, and even postcolonialist criticism—to perceive the rigorously logical counterrelationship between the Vietnam War and the triumphalist representation of the post-Cold War as the end of history and the advent of the New World Order or its later accommodational variants. These oppositional discourses, which include New Americanist studies, had their provenance in and continue to identify themselves with the post-Enlightenment countermemory. It should also be remarkable, therefore, that they have been blinded by their vestigially disciplinary problematics to the rigorously logical complicity of the American cultural memory's massive and obsessively sustained effort in the thirty-year aftermath to obliterate the radically differential actual history of the Vietnam War (and to discredit the posthumanist discourses it precipitated)[24] with the triumphalist post-Cold War discourse's more subtle obliteration of this radically disruptive event by *accommodating* it to the logical economy of the (Hegelian) dialectics of "the larger pattern" of History.

Given the glaring visibility of Fukuyama's invisibilizing of the Vietnam War—a process further abetted by Richard Haass's, and, as I will show later, Samuel P. Huntington's and the numerous Straussian neoconservatives' "realisitic" representation of the post-9/11 world—it is surprising, in other words, that these oppositional discourses should have been blind to his arrogant (or incredibly naive) re-visionary/recuperative strategy, to the fact that this end-of-history discourse of what, since then, has come to be called "the American Century" relies on a now anachronistic ontological justification. I mean a rationale that reverts to the very *episteme*—the ground of legitimacy—that the singular event of the Vietnam War and the "theory" it precipitated had decisively delegitimized by revealing the truth discourse of liberal capitalist democracy to be a social construction—that of the "Anglo-Protestant core culture," as Huntington will put it after 9/11—infused by a totalizing will to power that is characterized by its suppression or accommodation, the colonization, as it were, of the entire relay of Others composing the continuum of being to its polyvalent Identity.

To put that which these oppositional discourses overlook succinctly, Fukuyama's representation of the end of the Cold War or, to emphasize that it is the hegemonization of this end-of-history discourse with which I am concerned, the mediatization of his representation, is informed by a metaphysical ontology that willfully subdues actual history, its differential dynamics, to its secularized transcendental *Logos*. In short, the calculative/instrumentalist thinking it privileges as the agency of truth is *essentially* imperial. It is not so much liberal capitalism's practical colonization of the planet as such that this end-of-history discourse is celebrating. After all, Fukuyama, Haass, and the culture they and their neoconservative colleagues represent acknowledge the possibility of future setbacks and disappointments in this geopolitical "American" project. It is, rather, its planetary colonization of thinking in its technological/instrumentalist mode, though the two are not mutually exclusive, indeed, are indissolubly related. The fundamental ideological purpose of this discourse is to delegitimize *every other* form of thinking than that dialectical/instrumental reasoning that, according to the Kojèvian/Hegelian perspective informing it, History's *Aufhebung* has precipitated as the planetary absolute—the *Pax Metaphysica*, as it were.

This total "victory" of a historically "perfected" calculative metaphysics means, of course, the decisive preclusion as a viable option of the kind of ontological/political thinking precipitated as an imperative by the recognition of the Vietnam War as a radical contradiction in the discursive practices of liberal capitalist democracy, the kind of differential thinking, that is, that haunts the legitimacy of the latter's "benign" global narrative. The massive post-Cold War representation of every manifestation of such thinking first as "politically correct," a "new McCarthyism of the Left," by the "victors" has contributed significantly to the demise of the little authority it originally achieved, indeed, as I will show, to their demonization after 9/11 as complicitous with, if not acts of, terrorism as such. It thus bears emphatic witness to the success of the dominant culture's recuperative project of delegitimizing—which is to say, of colonizing—a thinking that would think the spectral difference that cannot finally be contained by the imperial (onto)logic of liberal democracy.

More tellingly, the success of this imperial project is also witnessed by the seeming indifference of most alternative discourses—those that have emerged in the wake of the demise of "theory" to oppose the New World Order—to Fukuyama's and the contemporary policy elite's representation of the post-Cold War occasion and by their seeming blindness to this representation's synecdochical cultural status.[25] That is, these "emancipatory" discourses, as Fukuyama predicts, seem to have no recourse to any other way of thought than that imperial logic informing and prescribed by the triumphant liberal democracy.This disabling condition of oppositional thought, I want to underscore, is one significant reason why the retrieval of the actual history—the *singularity*—of the Vietnam War is an urgent imperative, especially in the wake of 9/11 and the American government's unleashing of its "war on terrorism."

V

We must ask what remains unthought in the call [by Hegel and Husserl] "to the matter itself." Questioning in this way, we can become aware that something that is no longer the matter of philosophy to think conceals itself precisely where philosophy has brought its matter to absolute and to ultimate evidence.

—Martin Heidegger, "The End of Philosophy and the Task of Thinking"

We are thus compelled by the impasse in which the existing oppositional discourses find themselves to return, despite the invidious associations, to what I take to be Martin Heidegger's fundamental contribution to the philosophical history of this benighted century and of the present post-Cold War occasion. I am referring to his enabling reminder in *Being and Time* that the modern West has forgotten the question of being, or, to put this estranging inaugural assertion in its later form, to his proleptic announcement of the "end of philosophy." This, to be more specific, was his warning to the modern age of the impending global triumph of technology, the total enframing [*Ge-stell*] and reduction of the differential being of being to standing or disposable reserve (*Bestand*) *and* the coming of thinking to its banalized end in the modern "age of the world picture":[26] precisely, that is, the imperial planetary condition that the post-Cold War, end-of-history discourse (and practices) of the dominant American culture celebrates. The retrieval of Heidegger's diagnosis of the culminating moment of modernity as the age of the world picture is thus important because it constitutes a profoundly different and less sanguine understanding of the end of history from that of Fukuyama and the dominant ideological culture he represents.

In other words, the recent philosophical and cultural obliteration of the contradictory history of the Vietnam War, coupled with the impasse of oppositional thinking in the face of the ensuing announcement of the end of history and the New World Order, compels us to understand the end of the Cold War in terms of its *polyvalent* global manifestations. The imperative precipitated by these conditions is to understand this end not only as an epochal *political/economic* event as such—the imperial triumph of the liberal democratic/capitalist United States and its global free market system over the communist Soviet Union and any other polity—but also, and more fundamentally, as an epochal *ontological* event. This end does not simply mean, as Fukuyama's emphasis implies, the imperial triumph of the *interpretation of being* informing the liberal capitalist democracy of the United States (and the European Community that has aped its cultural and political identity) over the interpretation of being underlying the totalitarianism of Nazi Germany and the communism of the Soviet Union. This end means as well, as the United States' willful effort to impose American-style democracies in Afghanistan and Iraq clearly bear witness, the imperial triumph of this metaphysical ontology over *all other unthought* interpretations of being that might inform and enable future cultural formations and polities. The triumphant culture's airbrushing of the actual history of the Vietnam War, that is, demands, against the disciplinary tendency to separate theory and practice (a tendency exacerbated by the new historicism and the initiative "against theory"), that we perceive the American (neo)imperialist project of the post-Cold War era to be a *polyvalent* one, in which ontological representation—the *Pax Metaphysica*—is a praxis that is *indissolubly related* to imperial political praxis—the *Pax Americana*. Such a perception of this increasingly hegemonized representation of the contemporary occasion, in turn, would convey to oppositional intellectuals the urgency of breaking this insidiously polyvalent "peace." It would disclose the urgency of retrieving the unfinished poststructuralist ontological project *to rethink thinking* itself. By this I mean the need to dis-close, to open up, to thought *that which* the triumphant metaphysical/calculative-technological/disciplinary logic of the imperial West has closed off and accommodated or repressed. To rethink thinking means, in short, to *liberate* precisely that relay of differential forces that the structuralizing and disciplinary imperatives of the ontotheological tradition has *colonized* in its final "anthropological" phase.

VI

The urgency of the need to break the peace of the *Pax Metaphysica*—and the general direction that such a project is compelled to take by the contemporary, post-Cold War occasion—is not only the symptomatic testimony of the present impasse of traditional and vestigially traditional forms of emancipatory thought in the face of the planetary triumph of technological reason and the new ("ameliorative") imperialism of the New World Order. It is also suggested by the growing, *if still unthought*, awareness of a small but increasing number of advanced, but otherwise heterogeneous intellectuals on the "Left"—Jacques Derrida, Jean-François Lyotard, Gilles Deleuze and Félix Guattari, Fredric Jameson, Paul Virilio, Rosi Braidotti, Giorgio Agamben, Bill Readings, Homi Bhabha, Gayatri Spivak, Enrique Dussel, Ranajit Guha, Edward Said, and Michael Hardt and Antonio Negri, to name only a few of the most suggestive—that the impasse of emancipatory political practice in the post-Cold War period is in some significance degree *an impasse of thinking itself*. Against the increasing pressure to "forget theory," emanating from spokespersons of the ostensibly practice-oriented new historicism, cultural studies, neo-Marxism, feminism, postcolonialism, and so on, these radical thinkers, like a "certain spirit" of Heidegger before them (whatever their interpretation of the political implications of his thought), recognize this impasse as a failure on the part of currently privileged oppositional discourses to perceive the spread of (visual) technological thinking in the modern age as its global triumph. To put this recognition in Heidegger's resonantly inaugural terms, they symptomatically understand this impasse as a failure to acknowledge the present occasion as "a destitute time"—a time that has totally circumscribed and banalized thinking and thus, paradoxically, a time of renewed possibility insofar as its destitution activates this *awareness* of the total colonization and banalization of thinking *and* its practical corollary. This is their symptomatic recognition of the need to rethink thinking from the perspective of its marginality, now understood as the delegitimizing *contradiction* precipitated by the imperial "triumph" of technological/calculative thinking. In other words, these thinkers of the ontological difference that traditional thought has obliterated in the name of the "objective" truth of empirical science are now beginning, however tentatively, to understand the present historical conjuncture, the *limit occasion* that has enabled the deputies of the dominant mode of thought to name the moment of its triumph "the end of history," as an "interregnum,"[27] a time between the end—the closure—of the reign of philosophy and the beginning of thinking, and the oppositional intellectual as the alienated exile. In Heidegger's resonant term, this unhomed or migrant thinker is the *Abgeschiedene*, the one a-part, who, aware of the global colonization of originative thinking by the total technologization and banalization of "enlightening" thought, has parted from, but is always already a part of, this solar "at-homeland." He is the "ghostly" stranger,[28] the specter, who wanders nomadically "at the fringe of the technically-economically oriented world of modern mass existence" (*LP*, 196). In this "realm of Between," this "No-more of the gods that have fled and the Not-yet of the god that is coming,"[29] as Heidegger alternatively calls this state of a-partness (*Abgeschiedenheit*), the imperative for this oppositional intellectual is precisely to think the excess that the globalization (the end) of technological thinking cannot finally contain and to which it is blind. To underscore the presiding "white metaphor" that inhabits this truth discourse, it is to think the shadow that technological thinking's high noon sun cannot finally enlighten. In the interregnum, the task of the thinker is to think the spectral "reality" that he or she, as *Abgeschiedene*—as the "errant" one, who is "always under way" (*LP*, 163)—"is" as such.

This, for example, is the symptomatic testimony of Jacques Derrida in *Specters of Marx*. Motivated in part by the inflation of Fukuyama's book into a global media event and undertaken, all too belatedly, in the name of reconciling deconstructive theory with "a certain spirit of Marx," Derrida in this enormously suggestive, if finally limited, late book attempts to think the historical and transdisciplinary emancipatory imperatives of Heidegger's decentering ontological project (the latter's effort to think positively "the nothing" *of*—that belongs to—the triumphant instrumentalist thought of modernity) in the context of the globalization of the (onto)logic informing liberal capitalist democracy. With the annunciation of the end of history and the advent of the New World Order—and against a politically conservative theory and practice that represents itself as liberalism—Derrida prioritizes the task of thinking the recalcitrant "spirit" of the difference that the triumphant "Spirit" of the "new Holy Alliance"—the liberal capitalist/providential Christian coalition that Fukuyama and other American neoconservative intellectuals celebrate—would but finally cannot bury once and for all. I am referring to the "specter"—Derrida's more current, and resonant, allotrope of his earlier *differance*—that returns, precisely at the moment of the triumph of the "Spirit," as "spirit" or "*revenant*" to "haunt" or, to thematize the visual metaphorics that are fundamental to this global initiative, to "visit" (to return the gaze of) the imperial "visitor" (from the Latin, *videre*, to see).[30]

But this symptomatic witness—this recent initiative of the *Abgeschiedene* to think the political implications of the Other *of* metaphysics in its completed technological phase—is not, it is important to reiterate, limited to the theorists of the ontological difference (e.g., Martin Heidegger, Emmanuel Levinas, Jacques Lacan, Jacques Derrida, Jean-François

Lyotard, Gilles Deleuze and Félix Guattari, Louis Althusser, Giorgio Agamben) or to those postcolonialists who overdetermine the thought of the ontological difference in their critique of colonialism (e.g., Gayatri Spivak, Homi Bhabha, R. Radhakrishnan, Ranajit Guha, Dipesh Chakrabarty, Partha Chatterjee, Arjun Appadurai, Ernesto Laclau and Chantal Mouffe, Enrique Dussel). It is also the symptomatic testimony of certain politically exiled and/or "postcolonial" thinkers, who have been interpreted, sometimes rightly so, as antitheorists in some degree or other (Frantz Fanon, C. L. R. James, Paul Gilroy, Theodor Adorno, Michel Foucault, Antonio Negri, and, especially, Edward Said). Confronted by the impotence of emancipatory thought in the "postcolonial" interregnum, Said, for example, adapts Adorno's and Deleuze and Guattari's theoretical version of the *Abgeschiedene*—the migrant and the "nomad," respectively—to the global demographics of dislocation (diaspora) that constitutes the terrible legacy of the fulfillment of the Western imperial project proper. He thus calls for "a new critical consciousness" that, unlike all the available oppositional discourses, will refuse, in its strategically contradictory "ec-centricity," its "unaccountability," and its "measurelessness," to be answerable to the thinking/saying of the "triumphant" imperial culture, will not, to invoke Althusser, be interpellated by the dominant liberal democratic discourse:

> It is no exaggeration to say that liberation as an intellectual mission, born in resistance and opposition to the confinements and ravages of imperialism, has now shifted from the settled, established, and domesticated dynamics of culture to its unhoused, decentered, and exilic energies whose incarnation today is the migrant, and whose consciousness is that of the intellectual and artist in exile, the political figure between domains, between forms, between homes, and between languages. . . .
>
> "The past life of emigrés is, as we know, annulled, says Adorno in *Minima Moralia*. . . . Why? Because anything that is not reified, cannot be counted and measured, ceases to exist," and, as he says later, is consigned to "background." Although the disabling aspects of this fate are manifest, its virtues or possibilities are worth exploring. . . . Adorno's general pattern is what in another place he calls the "administered society" or, insofar as the irresistible dominants in culture are concerned, "the consciousness industry." There is then not just the negative advantage of refuge in the emigré's eccentricity; *there is also the positive benefits of challenging the system, describing it in a language unavailable to those it has already subdued.*[31]

VII

I will return later in this book to Said's provocative retrieval of empire's spectral Others—his bringing of this marginalized figure out of the shadows of imperialism's periphery to center stage, as it were. It will suffice here to suggest that by thus assuming the exilic perspective of the *Abgeschiedene* in addressing the question of global colonialism, it should now be clear that my intervention has not been intended to mimic the by now commonplace critical imperative of a certain "postcolonial" discourse, usually identified with Salmon Rushdie and Malek Alloula, in which "the Empire writes back" to the imperial "center."[32] This critical initiative, perhaps needless to say, has contributed significantly, especially by way of identifying the colonial project with cultural, specifically literary, production, to the inauguration of an anticolonial discourse that would be commensurate to the complex and multisituated operations of American (neo)colonialism in the "postimperial" age of globalization, above all, in that phase that has been represented by its intellectual deputies as the "end of history" and is now bearing witness to America's unilateral imposition of capitalist democracy on "rogue states" that threaten the "American Peace." But, as I have suggested, it remains inadequate to this most difficult of tasks, not impossible. This inadequacy is not simply the result of this criticism's vestigial adherence to the kind of imperial thinking it would interrogate (i.e., its not being *postcolonial*—exilic or, rather, "a-part"—enough).[33] It is also, and primarily, the result of a paradoxically limited historical sense. Despite its insistent appeal to history against theory, this praxis-oriented "postcolonial" criticism, like the genealogical criticism of Foucault and even Said, from which it ultimately derives, *is not historical enough*. In keeping with its indifference to, if not its antitheoretical bias against theory, it has, in fact, reduced the critical potential of this resonant motif of resistance by restricting the genealogy of imperialism by and large to the modern era—from the age of exploration in the fifteenth century to the age of imperialism in the late eighteenth and nineteenth centuries. In overlooking its own origins *in* the exilic "theory" that emerged in response to the decisive self-destruction of the imperial (onto)logic of the discourse of the Occident in the middle of the twentieth century, this postcolonial discourse, in other words, has also lost sight of an earlier, deeper, and polyvalent structural origin of the colonial project. I mean the very epochal moment of the founding of the idea of the Occidental polis in late Greek and especially (imperial) Roman antiquity. This was the moment that bore witness to the West's self-conscious inscription of metaphysics—of thinking the transitory and singular (contingent or always incomplete) event from the exclusionary or accommodational prov*ide*ntial/panoptic vantage point of its (preconceived) "completion"—as the

truth of being and history at large.[34] As a consequence of this forgetting
of the provenance of imperialism in the Roman transformation of the
"errant" thinking of the Greeks into a "correct" (and, in Fukuyama's term,
"directional") thinking, the discourse of postcolonialism has delimited its
genealogy of Western imperialism to the Enlightenment and after and thus
the ideological parameters of imperialism to the *practice* of empire, that
is, to the site of cultural geopolitics. Despite its suggestive spontaneous
probings beyond it (mostly in the form of its inadequately thought reitera-
tion of the relay of "white" metaphors—center/periphery; light/darkness;
plantation/wilderness; settler/nomad, development (improvement)/under-
development—that systematically informs the "truth" discourse of metaphysics), they therefore remain vestigially and disablingly disciplinary.

In other words, this privileged version of postcolonialist discourse
is determined by a problematic that restricts itself to an idea of the imperial that remains indifferent to or, more accurately, *over*looks the inaugural ontological ground on which the developing structure of the
West *as* the West rests—a ground that, as I have shown, visibly reasserts
itself in the neo-Hegelianism of the post-Cold War end-of-history discourse. As such, it is a critical discourse that addresses an imperialism
that has been rendered anachronistic, if not exactly obsolete, by the triumphant culture's representation of the end of the Cold War as the end
of history and the annunciation of this "good news" as the advent of the
New World Order. I mean, to retrieve and reconstellate into the present
historical occasion the forgotten and decisively important ideological
function of the ruse of the *Pax Romana*, the peace of what I have been
calling the *Pax Americana*.

On the other hand, I do not want to suggest that the theoretical perspective of Heidegger's *Abgeschiedene* as such (or, for that matter, its
poststructuralist allotropes) is entirely adequate to this task of resistance
either, since the consequences of his (and, in a different way, of those he
influenced) failure to adequately think the political imperatives of his interrogation of Western ontology are now painfully clear. We must,
rather, think the *Abgeschiedene*—the "ghostly" ontological exile evolving a way of "errant" thinking that would be able to resist the global imperialism of Occidental/technological logic—*with*, say, Said's political
Deleuzian nomad: the displaced political emigré evolving, by way of his
or her refusal to be answerable to the "Truth" of the Occident, a politics
capable of resisting the polyvalent global neo-imperialism of Occidental
political power. The *Abgeschiedene*, the displaced thinker, and the migrant, the displaced political person, *are not incommensurable entities;
they are two indissolubly related, however uneven, manifestations of the
same world-historical event.*

The "political Left" of the 1980s, which inaugurated the momentum "against theory," was entirely justified in accusing the "theoretical" discourse of the 1970s of an ontological and/or textual focus that, in its obsessive systematics, rendered it, in Said's word, "unworldly"—indifferent to the "imperial" politics of historically specific Western history. But it can be seen now, in the wake of the representation of the global "triumph" of liberal democratic capitalism in the 1990s as the end of history, or, at any rate, of America's arrogant will to impose capitalist-style democracy on different, "destabilizing" cultures, that this Left's focus on historically specific politics betrays a disabling indifference to the polyvalent imperial politics of ontological representation. It thus repeats in reverse the essential failure of the theoretically oriented discourse it has displaced. This alleged praxis-oriented discourse, that is, tends—even as it unconsciously employs in its critique the *ontologically produced* "white" metaphorics and rhetoric informing the practices it opposes—to separate praxis from and to privilege it over theory, the political over the ontological. Which is to say, it continues, in tendency, to understand being in the arbitrary—and disabling—disciplinary terms endemic to and demanded by the very panoptic classificatory logic of modern technological thinking, the advanced metaphysical logic that perfected, if it did not exactly enable, the colonial project proper.[35] In so doing, this praxis-oriented discourse fails to perceive that being, however it is represented, constitutes a continuum, which, though unevenly developed at any historically specific moment, nevertheless traverses its indissolubly related "sites" from being as such and the epistemological subject through the ecos, culture (including family, class, gender, and race), to sociopolitics (including the nation and the international or global sphere). As a necessary result, it fails to perceive the emancipatory political potential inhering in the relay of "differences" released (decolonized) by an interrogation of the dominant Western culture's disciplinary representation of being. By this relay of positively potential differences I do not simply mean "the nothing" (*das Nichts*) or "the ontological difference" (Heidegger), "existence" (Sartre), "the absolutely other" (Levinas), "the *differance*" or "trace" (Derrida), "the differend" (Lyotard), the "invisible" or "absent cause" (Althusser) that belong contradictorily to and haunt "white"/totalitarian metaphysical thinking.[36] I also mean "the pariah" (Arendt), "the nomad" (Deleuze and Guattari), "the hybrid" or "the minus in the origin" (Bhabha), "the nonbeings" (Dussel), the subaltern (Guha), "the emigré" (Said), "the denizen" (Hammar), "the refugee" (Agamben), "the queer" (Sedgwick, Butler, Warner), "the multitude" (Negri and Hardt),[37] and, to point to the otherwise unlikely affiliation of these international post"colonial" thinkers with a certain strain of post"modern" black American literature, "the darkness" (Morrison) that belong contradictorily to and haunt "white"/imperial culture politics:

The images of impenetrable whiteness need contextualizing to explain their extraordinary power, pattern, and consistency. Because they appear almost always in conjunction with representations of black or Africanist people who are dead, impotent, or under complete control, these images of blinding whiteness seem to function as both antidote for meditation on the shadow that is the companion to this whiteness—a dark and abiding presence that moves the hearts and texts of American literature with fear and longing. This haunting, a darkness from which our early literature seemed unable to extricate itself, suggests the complex and contradictory situation in which American writers found themselves during the formative years of the nation's literature.[38]

In this chapter, I have overdetermined the ontological perspective of the *Abgeschiedene*, the errant thinker in the interregnum who would think the spectral "nothing" that a triumphant empirical science "wishes to know nothing" about,[39] not simply, however, for the sake of rethinking the question of being as such, but also to instigate a rethinking of the uneven relay of *practical* historical imperatives precipitated by the post-Cold War occasion. My purpose, in other words, has been to make visible and operational the substantial and increasingly complex *practical* role that ontological representation has played and continues to play in the West's perennial global imperial project, a historical role rendered disablingly invisible as a consequence of the oversight inherent in the vestigially disciplinary problematics of the privileged oppositional praxis-oriented discourses, including that of all too many New Americanists. In accordance with this need to reintegrate theory and practice—the ontological and the sociopolitical, thinking and doing—and to accommodate the present uneven balance of this relationship to the actual conditions established by the total colonization of thinking in the age of the world picture, I would suggest, in a prologemenal way, the inordinate urgency of resuming the virtually abandoned destructive genealogy of the truth discourse of the post-Enlightenment Occident, now, however, *reconstellated* into the post-Cold War conjuncture. I mean specifically, the conjuncture that, according to Fukuyama (and the strategically less explicit Straussian neoconservatives that have risen to power in America after 9/11), has borne apocalyptic witness to the global triumph of liberal capitalist democracy *and* the end of history. Such a reconstellated genealogy, as I have suggested, will show that this "triumphant" post-Cold War American polity constitutes the fulfillment (end) of the last (anthropological) phase of a continuous, historically produced, three part ontological/cultural/sociopolitical Western history: what Heidegger, to demarcate its historical itinerary (Greco-Roman, Medieval/Protestant Christian, and Enlightenment liberal humanist), has called the "ontotheological tradition." It will also show that this long and various history, which the neoconservatives would obliterate, has been from its origins imperial *in essence*. I am referring to the repeatedly reconstructed history inaugurated by the late or post-Socratic Greeks or, far more decisively, by the Romans, when they reduced the pre-Socratic truth as *a-letheia* (unconcealment) to *veritas* (the adequation of mind and thing), when, that is, they reified (essentialized) the tentative disclosures of a still originative Platonic and Aristotelian thinking and harnessed them as finalized, derivative conceptional categories to the ideological project of legitimizing, extending, and efficiently administering the Roman Empire in the name of the *Pax Romana*.

To be more specific, this reconstellated destructive genealogy will show that the reality of the "triumphant" American democratic/capitalist polity rests on a fabricated ontological base that privileges the hierarchically structured binarist principle of principles—that *identity is the condition for the possibility of difference and not the other way around*—and that, therefore, this polity is imperial *in essence* as well as in its multisituated political practices. It will show, in other words, that, in representing being *meta ta physica* (from after or above being's temporal disseminations), this ontological base generates a "truth" discourse that, far from being transparently "objective," open to the "empirical" event, is actually re-*presentational*, pan-*optic*, and retro-*spective* and, as such, utterly metaphorical—and ideological. To retrieve the now virtually forgotten, but extraordinarily resonant phrase Derrida coined to identify this truth discourse with European origins and interests, it will show that the alleged disinterested truth discourse of the West is, in fact, a binarist "white mythology."[40] It will show that its "truth" *structuralizes* or, more telling in the proximity of its sublimated metaphorics of temporal closure to the operations of colonization, *spatializes* or territorializes the differential dynamics of temporality *around* a polyvalent (Eurocentric) *Logos*. I mean by this *Logos* a Transcendental Signified or Principle of Presence invariably represented in Western history since the Romans' codification of the domiciled *colonus* ("farmer"/"settler") as the binary opposite of the nomadic *sylvestris* ("savage," literally, "of the woods") in the form of a combination of indissolubly related, hierarchically structured binary tropes of resolution or accommodation—most notably and enablingly, *the centered circle, the panoptic eye (and its light), and, not least, the maturation process* (the clearing of the wilderness and the planting and cultivation of the original seed). It is, for example, this relay of imperial tropes emanating from and circulating around the presiding *Logos* that informs Hegel's imperial *Philosophy of History*, epitomized by the incantatory repetition of "World History") in the following famous passage on "Enlightenment":

The History of the World travels from East to West, for Europe is absolutely the end of History, Asia the beginning. The History of the World has an East *kat' exochen* (the term East in itself is entirely relative), for although the Earth forms a sphere, History performs no circle round it, but has on the contrary a determinate East, viz., Asia. Here rises the outward physical Sun, and in the West it sinks down: here consentaneously rises the Sun of self-consciousness, which diffuses a nobler brilliance. The History of the World is the discipline of the uncontrolled natural will, bringing it into obedience to a Universal principle and conferring subjective freedom.[41]

And, I will show in chapter 6, it is this relay of imperial tropes, subsumed to the Hegelian paradigm by Fukuyama, that has pervaded the unexceptionalist discourse of American exceptionalism from the Puritan jeremiad in behalf of the "errand in the wilderness," through the discourse of the frontier in behalf of the fulfillment of America's Manifest Destiny, to that of the post-9/11 effort to recuperate the American national identity in the wake of the Vietnam War.

More immediately, the reconstellation of destructive genealogy into the post-Cold War occasion will show that the relay of binarist "white" metaphors informing the truth discourse of the "triumphant" post-Enlightenment democratic/capitalist society constitutes a naturalized "diagram of a mechanism of power reduced to its ideal form."[42] Contrary to the representation of the reigning disciplinary interpretation of being, this hegemonic diagram of power is operative simultaneously, however unevenly at any particular historical specific occasion, throughout the continuum of being, from the representation of being and the subject as such, through gender and race, to culture, economics, and the national and international polity. It is, in short, polyvalent in its imperial applications.

VIII

As the foregoing remarks suggests, my argument for the urgency of reconstellating the earlier, ontologically oriented destructive genealogy of the truth discourse of the Occident into the present historical conjuncture under the aegis of America has emphasized the negative or critical phase of its disclosive function. It has thematized the imperial essence of the metaphysical ontology of liberal capitalist democracy as it is synecdochically represented by the kind of Enlightenment thinking that culminates with Fukuyama's unexceptionalist de Tocquevilian and Hegelian representation of the post-Cold War occasion. But it should be remembered, against a tendency of deconstruction[43] (and of a certain postcolonialist critique of deconstruction in general[44]) to forget that the de-structive project, as its etymology makes clear, is not historicist in the traditional sense, but genealogical[45] and, therefore, not only negational but also, indeed primarily, positive or "projective" in its purpose. It destroys or, more clearly, de-structures a historically constructed operative structure in order *to release*—to liberate—for the historically futural present that which structure would close off, subdue, and pacify: that is, *colonize*. "On its negative side," Heidegger says inaugurally, "this destruction does not relate itself towards the past; its criticism is aimed at 'today' and at the prevalent way of treating the history of ontology, whether it is headed towards doxography, towards intellectual history, or towards a history of problems. But to bury the past in nullity [*Nichtigkeit*] is not the purpose of this destruction; its aim is *positive*."[46]

The task of oppositional criticism in the American "age of the world picture," in other words, is to articulate a way of thinking that would be adequate not simply to the "postcolonial" occasion understood as the promising aftermath of the demise of imperialism proper, but also and primarily to the condition of "silence" imposed by the global "triumph" of the truth discourse of liberal capitalist democracy, the "end" that has given the "post" of the word "postcolonial" another, less sanguine, resonance. I am referring to the occasion that has precipitated a new form of dedifferentiating, pacifying, and exploitative imperialism, a global neocolonialism that, in its appeal to the benignity of "objective" Truth and its practical imperatives for legitimation, is far more invisible, that is, more subtle and insidious and difficult to resist, than the vulgar imperialism that characterized European conquest and exploitation of other worlds from the sixteenth through the nineteenth centuries: the more or less overt and visible imperialism that most postcolonial critics, whether those who are indigenous to the West or those who are indigenous to the worlds colonized by the West or those who are a hybrid amalgamation of both, continue to envision in their critical discourses. By this new imperialism I do not mean that decentered or "postmodern" imperialism that Fredric Jameson, Masao Miyoshi, Arjun Appadurai, Bill Readings, Michael Hardt, and Antonio Negri and others[47] have identified with the rise of transnational capitalism and the waning of the nation-state. These diagnoses and critiques of the globalizing momentum that link the postmodern global occasion with the logic of late capitalism have much to teach us about contemporary power relations. As the response of the United States and its "people"—and the intellectual deputies who would justify its concentered ferocity—to the attacks on the World Trade Center and the Pentagon testifies, however, they are premature in affirming the waning of the nation-state—and thus the obsolescence of the center/periphery model of empire—as a fait accompli and alleging the complicity of the poststructuralist thinking with transnational capital:

> When we begin to consider the ideologies of corporate capital and the world market, it certainly appears that the postmodernist and postcolonialist theorists who advocate a politics of difference, fluidity, and hybridity in order to challenge the binaries and essentialism of modern sovereignty have been outflanked by the strategies of power. Power has evacuated the bastion they are attacking and has circled around to their rear to join them in the assault in the name of difference. These theorists thus find themselves pushing against an open door. . . . This new enemy [TNCs] not only is resistant to the old weapons but actually thrives on them, and thus joins its would be antagonists in applying them to the fullest. Long live difference! Down with essentialist binaries![48]

However complicated by the processes of globalization, however attenuated the lines of communication that hold the terms together, the center/periphery, nation-state/empire, model, as the various pre- and post-9/11 representations of world history of Fukuyama, Haass, Huntington, Ferguson, or Mandelbaum forcefully testify, remains intact. It, therefore, highlights the urgent need of oppositional criticism to think decentered difference in the context of the center and periphery, and "the multitude," or, as Edward Said put it, the spectral migrants, who now constitute the majority of the planet's population, in the context of the global imperialism that produced their recalcitrantly eccentric subjectivities at the moment of the fulfillment of its (onto)logical economy.

The project of rethinking thinking in this interregnum is an urgent one because we cannot know the ghostly *Abgeschiedene* (his or her uncanny "state of mind") without knowing how this informing ontology of the modern "age of the world picture" has precipitated him or her as an instability and a potential threat to its totalized biopolitical world order in the very process of attempting to preclude that possibility. Nor can we think the different thought that would transform the instability and potential threat the *Abgeschiedene* represents into a positively productive, collective anti-imperial practice without knowing how the inexorable logic that has precipitated the New World Order affiliates this spectral thinker—this intellectual "nobody" precipitated by the fulfillment of the logical economy of Western thought—and the multiply situated political emigré—the political non*being* precipitated by the fulfillment of the logical economy of imperialism—in the very process of attempting to preclude that possibility.

We must first learn, that is, how the "end of [Occidental] history" renders these unlikely identityless identities "between domains, between forms, between homes, between languages"[49]—the alienated, unhomed, spectral thinker and his or her silence and the alienated, the unhomed, spectral political refugee and his or her silence—comrades in the projective task of transforming the dedifferentiated, at-homed, and utterly banalized age of the world picture into a dynamically differential global world order in which, as Edward Said, invoking T. S. Eliot with a resonant twist, says, "'the complete concert danc[es] together,' contrapuntally."[50]

This is why, it seems to me, retrieving the Vietnam War from the oblivion to which the dominant culture in American has, in the thirty-year aftermath of that disclosive disaster, obsessively (but finally unsuccessfully) attempted to relegate it is a crucial inaugural moment in this urgent project. But before undertaking the effort to induce its silent specter to speak, it will be necessary to focus in greater detail on two indissolubly related but inadequately thought aspects of the exceptionalist American mindset that planned and conducted the war in Vietnam and that the singularity of the war, to which the respective literary texts I will examine bear witness, exposed to anxiety-provoking view: the specific nature of the *blindness of its vision* and the spatialization or territorialization of temporality and history that is endemic to this metaphysical or super-visory way of seeing.

Chapter 2

ALTHUSSER'S "PROBLEMATIC"
Vision and the Vietnam War

We called the enemy ghosts. "Bad night," we'd say, "the ghosts
are out." To get spooked, in the lingo, meant not only to get
scared but to get killed. "Don't get spooked," we'd say. "Stay
cool, stay alive." Or we'd say: "Careful, man, don't give up the
ghost." The countryside itself seemed spooky—shadows and
tunnels and incense burning in the dark. The land was haunted.
We were fighting forces that did not obey the laws of twentieth-
century science.

> —Tim O'Brien, *The Things They Carried*

The perspective [of traditional thinking and language] has to
be reversed, once again: ghost or *revenant*, sensuous-non-sensuous, visible-invisible, the specter first of all sees *us*. From the
other side of the eye, *visor effect*, it looks at us even before we
see *it* or even before we see period. We feel ourselves observed, sometimes under surveillance by it even before any apparition. Especially—and this is the event, for the specter is *of*
the event—it sees us during a *visit*.

> —Jacques Derrida, *Specters of Marx*

Although Louis Althusser's central and enabling concept of the "problematic" has been assimilated into the discourse of contemporary Marxism—
indeed, of Left-oriented criticism at large—it has not, I submit, been
adequately thought in the Anglophone world, especially in the wake of the
Vietnam War. It has, in fact, become a counterterm whose meaning is
assumed to be self-evident. Often, as in the case of much cultural and even
postcolonial criticism that has appropriated this Marxist word, it is

understood to mean something like a thorny question or difficulty in the "field" of investigation or a problem within the epistemological apparatus of knowledge production. In virtually all cases, whether "neo-Marxist" or "cultural" criticism (including New Americanist studies), Althusser's resonant term has been divested of the ontological basis that is essential to its meaning. More specifically, this habitual usage is now virtually blind to the metaphysical ground—and the *visual metaphorics* this ground enables and relies on—of the re-presentational discourse, whether post-Enlightenment humanist, capitalist, or Marxist, that it is Althusser's project to call into question.[1]

This failure to adequately think the concept of the problematic has not only resulted in a disabling distortion of Althusser's Marxist thought as such. It has also rendered his thought anachronistically irrelevant as an agency of resisting the conditions of the late postmodern conjuncture. For my purposes in this book, it has prevented the Americanists, old and new, from perceiving the extraordinary relevance of Althusser's concept of the problematic as an agency of resisting the conditions of the post-Cold War occasion, in which, as I observed in chapter 1, the intellectual deputies, both theorists and crisis managers, of the "triumphant" neo-conservative culture, have announced the end of history and the advent of the New World Order—or, after 9/11, posited more nuanced versions of this euphoric annunciation such as those of Richard Haass, Niall Ferguson, and Samuel P. Huntington, among others. I mean specifically their annunciation of the dialectical triumph of the essential(ist) democratic/capitalist principles on which the polity of the United States is founded: a deeply backgrounded teleology indissolubly related to its democratic politics, the *Pax Metaphysica* and the *Pax Americana*, as it were. In this chapter, my purpose is to proffer a more adequate reading of Althusser's concept of the problematic, not for its own sake, but to demonstrate its urgent relevance to the post-Cold War occasion, indeed, its fundamental value as an agency not only of disclosing the limits of the various versions of the end-of-history discourse, but of thinking the positive possibilities of these limits. But, to do this, it will be necessary, against the oppositional New Americanists' vestigial tendency to remain exceptionalist, to reconstellate the discursive context (the representation of Marx's thought) into which Althusser (and those "Althusserians" after him) applies the problematic. In Althusser's Marxian language, it will be necessary to undertake by violence a witting shift of the "terrain" of knowledge production, to read the problematic, more specifically, in the context of the fate of the *singular event* of the Vietnam War at the hands (of the eye) of the problematic informing the end-of-history discourse and the idea of the *Pax Americana*.

I

It is now a commonplace that the Vietnam War precipitated a deep and abiding anxiety in the American cultural memory. But this national anxiety has not been adequately thought by those Left-oriented intellectuals, including the New Americanists, who would invoke the Vietnam War as testimony to the illegitimacy of the United States' intervention in Vietnam and its conduct of that war. This is because this critical inquiry has been conducted according to the logical imperatives of the frame of reference of the American symbolic order. In Althusser's language, this failure of the American Left is the consequence in large part of continuing to think this national anxiety from *within* the exceptionalist "problematic" of the dominant constituency of American society that deplores its corrosive effects on the American national identity and consensus so crucial to the American mission in the "global wilderness." To *think* the significance of this anxiety from the perspective of estrangement—from the point of view of the "outsider in the [representational] machine" or of "the intellectual and artist in exile . . . between forms, between homes, and between languages," to appropriate Gayatri Spivak's and Edward Said's allotropes of Althusser's trope[2]—is to precipitate a remarkable sea change in the meaning attributed to this national anxiety by the dominant culture. To be specific, thinking this national anxiety that refuses to be accommodated to a name—this *Angst*, which, according to Heidegger, has no *thing* as its object—in the context of the history of the *representation* of the Vietnam War discloses this representational history to be a sustained, virtually systematic, effort by the American government, its intellectual deputies, and the culture industry (the dominant symbolic order) to renarrativize the war according to the accommodational logical economy of the American exceptionalist problematic. It comes to be seen, that is, as a remembering of the war that, in fact, is willfully intended to forget its corrosive history. It is precisely the exposure to visibility of this will to forget the Vietnam War that, as we shall see, solicits a meaning from the phrase "national anxiety" that is radically different from that which has been attributed to it by the representational discourse of the dominant culture in America. And it is to render explicit this different and differential meaning that my rethinking of Althusser's concept of the "problematic" is intended.

This recuperative representational process—reflected in the public policy of *both* Republican and Democratic administrations, the film industry, television, the news media, the churches, and even educational institutions (i.e., the ideological state apparatuses)—began with the dedication of the Vietnam Veterans War Memorial in Washington, D.C., in 1982 in terms of an insistent rhetoric calling for "healing the wound" inflicted on the body politic by a war that the United States did not win: a benign rhetoric, that is, urging a vaguely articulated and (apparently) ideologically neutral restoration of a national consensus disintegrated by the rancors precipitated by the war. And it culminated in a radical transformation of this trope of healing that exposed the ideological agenda hidden beneath its apparently ameliorative connotations. I am referring to the transformation represented by President George Bush's euphoric announcement that "By God, we've finally kicked the Vietnam syndrome once and for all!,"[3] following the United State's "decisive" victory in the first Gulf War. This symbolic locution represented the protest movement against the war and the healthy national self-examination it precipitated as a national neurosis that had prevented the United States from winning the war in Vietnam, of fulfilling its "exceptionalist" global mission. It is no accident that this metaphor and its ideological/mythic agenda became the supreme theme of the American culture industry's representation of global events in the aftermath of the Gulf War.

With the simultaneous closure of the Cold War—the collapse of Stalinist communism in Eastern and Central Europe and the Soviet Union—the policy makers of the "triumphant" culture were thus enabled to represent this "end" euphorically as the end of history—which is to say, as the end of a universal dialectical historical process—and the advent of a New World Order under the aegis of American democracy. In this pervasive representational discourse, the memory of Vietnam— the violence perpetrated against the Vietnamese people and their land by the American military machine—was obliterated from being, implying, of course, that this memory, and the anxiety informing it, was also obliterated from the collective consciousness of the American public. The amnesia to which I am referring is, as we have seen in chapter 1, borne witness to by the astonishing omission of reference to the Vietnam War by Francis Fukuyama in *The End of History and the Last Man* (1992), his neo-Hegelian account of world history written from the perspective of the end of the Cold War. This highly mediatized book, it will be recalled, begins and ends with the announcement that the dialectical process of universal history has precipitated the *idea* of liberal capitalist democracy—the very ontological principle of freedom in the name of which the United States intervened and conducted the war in Vietnam— as the fulfillment of the spiritual potential inhering in actual history. As for differential events, whether past (like Vietnam) or future, that apparently contradict this interpretation, they are simply reduced to negations within the teleologic of the dialectic and thus seductive "distractions" from "the larger pattern that is emerging in world history," distractions that deflect our sight away from the central thrust of the developmental (circular) historical process to the superfluous and irrelevant margins. With the victorious emergence of "the liberal *idea*" of capitalist democracy, Fukuyama tells us, "there is now no ideology [for the large part of the world] with pretensions to universality that is in a position to challenge liberal democracy, and no universal principle of legitimacy other than the sovereignty of the people. . . . *Even non-democrats will have to speak the language of democracy in order to justify their deviation from the single universal standard.*"[4]

I will provide a more specific critical genealogy of the representational history that culminates in the metamorphosis of a productive national self-doubt into a pernicious national mental sickness later in this book.[5] It will suffice for my present purpose to enumerate those aspects of the history of the representation of the Vietnam War that are crucial to the rethinking of Althusser's problematic.

1. The obliteration of the historical reality of the Vietnam War means the obliteration of a war bordering on genocide initiated by the United States in the name of the myth of American exceptionalism, which is to say, in the name of the ontological principles that allegedly distinguishes this New World from the Old World.

2. This "forgetting" of the war has been enabled by a metaphysical thinking (in its post-Enlightenment, i.e., technological or instrumental allotrope), a mode of inquiry that, as the etymology of "metaphysics" suggests (*meta ta physika*, "from after or above the be-*ing* of being"), privileges visual perception over all the other, immediate, earthbound, senses in the pursuit of truth. Metaphysical thinking, in other words, reduces the "matter" of its interest—the differential dynamics of being—to a totalized spatial object (picture, map, theatrical stage). Thus, knowledge production becomes inquiry into a "field," "area," "province," "domain," "realm," "region," "territory" to be dominated ("region," e.g., derives from the Latin, *regere*, "to rule" or "regulate"; "domain, from *dominus*, "master").

3. As the various appropriations of the Hegelian dialectical view of history make clear, the announcement in the post-Cold War period of the universal "triumph" of the "idea" of liberal democracy is synchronous with the global "triumph" of metaphysics, that is, with the world hegemony of representational thinking.

4. Insofar as it means the annulment of an understanding of being that acknowledges its radically differential temporality, the advent of the "end of history" also means, therefore, the advent of a *totally* spatialized world, the "age of the world picture" (*Die Zeit des Weltbildes*) as Heidegger calls the advent of modernity.[6]

5. If one attends to the spatial metaphorics that saturates, indeed, *informs* the structure of thinking in the age of the world picture, it can be said, without putting quotation marks around the words, that the

globalization of visual perception is tantamount to the *colonization* of thinking itself. It means, in other words, the establishment of the *Pax Metaphysica*, the peace that has subdued and accommodated the "errant" and "warring" forces of originative and differential thinking.

6. This *Pax Metaphysica*, in turn, has justified, if it has not entirely enabled, the *Pax Americana*. I use these Latin terms harking back to the ruse of the *Pax Romana* not only to suggest that the representational/panoptic thinking of the age of the world picture is imperial *in essence*, but to suggest as well that the globalization of this spatializing thinking—what Martin Heidegger proleptically called "the planetary triumph of technology" of the world system[7]—constitutes the historical fulfillment of its dialectical logical economy. Under the gaze of its luminous imperial eye, any *other* that cannot be contained within or accommodated to its circumferential horizon is a "shadow," and any truly *other* kind of thinking is now necessarily inconceivable, impossible, that is, "nonexistent," "no(-)thing." We might say, with Heidegger, a thinking "other" than metaphysical in its culminating technological mode is "*phantasmic*" and thus an "outrage" against truth.[8]

7. But our *knowing* now—at this limit situation—that science wishes to know nothing of the nothing is also an *awareness* of the limits of this privileged way of thinking that claims to know no limits. At this "end," in other words, the "nothing" transforms itself into a "phantasm" that provokes anxiety in the scientific observer. To appropriate Derrida's *Specters of Marx* to my purposes, the nothing becomes a *revenant* that returns to haunt the discourse and practices of this "triumphant" science that has relegated "it" to the status of nonbeing. To thematize the empowering visual metaphorics informing this truth discourse, "it" returns to "visit" the visitor."[9]

The "closure" of the history of the representation of the Vietnam War constitutes such a limit situation. In announcing in the same breath the end of history and the healing of the *trauma* precipitated by the Vietnam War—the "Vietnam syndrome"—the closure of this history *recalls* (calls back) what has been represented as decisively forgotten. Since the implosion of the Soviet Union and the first Gulf War, the inaugural triumphalist end-of-history discourse has undergone significant modifications, especially in the wake of the Al Qaeda attacks on American soil on 9/11 and the American government's announcement of its "war on terrorism." But, as I argued in chapter 1, these events, as well as the ensuing modifications of the end-of-history thesis in the discourse of policy experts such as Richard Haass and Samuel P. Huntington, have not dissolved the force of the specter of the Vietnam. Indeed, they have exacerbated it.

The closure of the representational history of the Vietnam War has precipitated the phantasm of Vietnam—in all its corporeality—precisely at the moment of its triumphant proclamation that it has laid it to rest. In what follows I want to think this phantasm that reveals itself—becomes invisibly visible *as a revenant* at the limits, that is, at the very moment of the fulfillment of the visual logical economy of the representational thinking that claims to have achieved global scope, that is: to have become hegemonic—the Truth of being in *all* its allotropes. And I want to do this by way of invoking Althusser's concept of the problematic. My purpose in this undertaking is not simply to address the question concerning what precisely "it" is that the amnesiac history of the representation of the Vietnam War would forget, or, put alternatively, what "it" is that the end-of-history discourse and its more recent allotropes would render unsayable (silent). My purpose is also to suggest what it is about Althusser's effort to think the problematic *ontologically* that renders it especially relevant to this urgent political question.

II

My interrogation of the representational discourse that has produced a re-vision of the "political" event we call "the Vietnam War" or simply "Vietnam" (the Vietnamese refer to it as "the American War") in terms that overdetermine the metaphorics of imperial vision derives ultimately from Heidegger's de-struction of the metaphysical discourse of the ontotheological tradition—its perennial visualization of being from after or above (*meta*) its temporal disseminations (*physika*). But my immediate source is, significantly, the neo-Marxist Louis Althusser's interrogation of the ideology informing the political economy of humanist capitalism, in particular, its *ontological* ground. Althusser's critique of ideology, not least in "Ideology and Ideological State Apparatuses" (an essay, not incidentally, written in the aftermath of the events of May 1968 and thus indissolubly related to the Vietnam conflict) is indebted first and foremost to Antonio Gramsci's cultural/political analysis of hegemony.[10] But, it is important to add, it is also indebted to Heidegger's disclosure of the ontological ground of the way "things are publically interpreted,"[11] that is, of the discourse of "everyday life" in the modern "age of the world picture." I am referring to what Althusser calls "the problematic" informing the truth discourse of "classical political economy," his anti-Hegelian analysis of which constitutes one of the most significant contributions of neo-Marxism to the postmetaphysical (or, more specifically, posthumanist) interrogation of the discourse of the bourgeois/capitalist cultural memory. For this analysis thematizes the *indissoluble relationship* between ontological representation (in this case the *vision* that informs re-presentation) and the economic, cultural, and political sites of inquiry that are privileged at the expense of the ontological in most Marxist (and neo-Marxist) theory and practice.

"[Science], Althusser says, "can only pose problems on the terrain and within the horizon of a definite theoretical structure, its problematic, which constitutes its absolute and definite condition of possibility, and hence the absolute determination of *the forms* in which all problems must be posed, at any given moment in the science."[12] Most commentators' accounts of the problematic restrict reference to that aspect of Althusser's definition that invokes "the problem" or "question." Indifferent, if not blind, to the centrality of the visual/spatial metaphorics that inform his rhetoric, they usually gloss the problematic as the ideological frame of reference of a liberal humanist capitalist inquiry that represents itself as objective or disinterested (nonideological) science. In other words, it constitutes a transparent "framework" that establishes the "parameters" of inquiry into the truth, which is to say, determines in advance the questions that can be asked of an "object" or "field" of inquiry, not only within its cultural jurisdiction but everywhere, and, therefore, the answers it can get. According to this view, the problematic functions primarily to assure the confirmation of the ideological assumptions that inform it by representing these answers as having universal validity. What is at stake in this usual definition is the content of the definition: the issue of the questions the problematic can ask and the answers it can arrive at:

> PROBLEMATIC (*problematique*). A word or concept cannot be considered in isolation; it only exists in the theoretical or ideological framework in which it is used: its problematic. A related concept can clearly be seen at work in Foucault's *Madness and Civilization.* . . . It should be stressed that the problematic is not a world-view. It isn't the essence of the thought of an individual or epoch which can be deduced from a body of texts by an empirical, generalizing reading; it is centered on the absence of problems and concepts within the problematic as much as their presence; it can therefore only be reached by a symptomatic reading (*lecture symptomale* . . .) on the model of the Freudian analyst's reading of his patient's utterances.[13]

But this way of putting the problematic, though not wrong, is inadequate to Althusser's ontological insight and, even more important, to situating it within the larger context of contemporary theory. I mean, for example, in relation to the structure of *Ge-stell* (enframing) that, according to Heidegger, determines the discourse and practice of modernity, of what he appropriately calls the the age of the world picture, and to the related "panopticism" that, according to Michel Foucault and Edward Said, determines the discourse and practice of the "disciplinary society" and the Western Orientalist project, respectively. As I will suggest, this definition is also inadequate to the critical possibilities of Althusser's concept of the problematic in a world in which being in its totality has been colonized by the spatializing/reifying imperatives of technological/calculative thinking. As in the case of the above example, which fails to read *"absence"* in the visual terms that Althusser consciously stresses, this is because it is impervious (blind) or indifferent to, even as it inadvertently employs and makes visible, the spatial tropes ("framework") that inform Althusser's definition of the problematic: the tropes, that, as Althusser goes on to point out—and other posthumanist thinkers such as Heidegger, Derrida, Lyotard, and Foucault have shown—decisively inform and determine the polyvalent re-presentational discourse and imperial practice of liberal humanist capitalism.

Althusser in fact initiates his meditation on the problematic in the introduction to *Reading Capital* by affirming what he takes to be a revolutionary imperative of history concerning representation laboriously disclosed by Marx's reading of the "classical political economy": the necessity of breaking the epistemic hold that *mimesis* has had on Western thought through Hegel, Smith, and Ricardo, even on a certain Marx, and, not least, the Marxist followers of this certain Marx. "We must," he writes, "completely reorganize the idea we have of knowledge. We must abandon the *mirror* myths of *immediate* vision and reading, and conceive knowledge as a *production*" (CMP, 25). What Althusser is saying here is not simply that the West, especially in that phase of its history that has borne witness to the rise of classical (liberal capitalist) political economy, has privileged visual perception in the pursuit of knowledge. He is also saying that the (mind's) eye the West has privileged in the name of objectivity is no more immune to prejudice than the other senses that have been relegated to subordinate status, that it does not reflect, but *produces reality* or, rather, that reflection *is* in fact production. Knowledge, that is, is not inherent in phenomena. The end of *mimesis*, copying, reflection, representation, is, as the visual metaphorics informing these transparent counters of the tradition make clear, an ideological construction. To suggest the continuity of Althusser's ontological insight into the contradiction between mimesis and the "immediacy" it claims with such theorists of representation as Heidegger, Derrida, and Foucault, the mimetic orientation toward knowledge reifies or spatializes or structures time and the differences it disseminates: *transforms being into a territory to be conquered.* It is thus a productive *oversight* whose sightings are essentially characterized by *oversight.*

Althusser thinks the contradictory operations of *mimesis*—the "oversight" of its over-sight—in terms of the metaphorics of vision (and non-vision) informing the mirror image of knowledge production. This, above all, constitutes Althusser's major contribution to the critique of the (empirical) problematic of classical political economy and to a still to be thought mode of thinking *not* dependent on its spatializing—imperial—imperatives. Althusser summarizes this profound insight in the following paradoxical way:

> What classical political economy does not see, is not what it does not see, it is *what it sees*; it is not what it lacks, on the contrary, it is *what it does not lack*; it is not what it misses, on the contrary, it is *what it does not miss.* The oversight, then, is not to see what one sees, the oversight no longer concerns the object, but *the sight* itself. The oversight is an oversight that concerns *vision:* non-vision is therefore inside vision, it is a form of vision and hence has a necessary relationship with vision. (CMP, 21; Althusser's emphasis; see also 24)

Althusser here distinguishes between the understanding of oversight—which is also the privileged (distanced) perspective of classical political economy—as not seeing (yet) what it sees (what eludes its imperfect, but perfectible vision) from an understanding of this oversight precisely as what it *does* see, what, as he puts it later, "it produce[s] itself in its operation of knowledge and [what] did not pre-exist it" (CMP, 24). In so doing, he distinguishing between two Marxes. One is the classical Marx (the Marx of the "Marxists") who remains trapped within the metaphysical ontology and the truth understood as *adaequatio intellectus et rei* (the correspondence of mind and thing). This is the metaphysical epistemology that informs the very classical political economy he and the "Marxists" would oppose. More precisely, it is the Marx who remains inscribed by a limited understanding of the imperial operations of the *adaequatio:* one which, in authorizing a spatial understanding of the *inside* and the *outside* of the concept of truth as the correspondence of mind and thing, does not question the ontological priority of vision in the pursuit of knowledge, but simply calls for the *correction* of a faulty vision. It is the Marx, in other words, who ironically allows for the relegitimation of vision's imperial authority and, in so doing, precludes the possibility of thinking the problem of time and difference differently—and differentially.

The other Marx is a radically revolutionary—poststructuralist—Marx, a Marx who recognizes that the "objectivity" of classical political economy is informed by a metaphysically grounded epistemology in which vision and nonvision are not, as it claims (and as it is assumed in "Marxism") external to each other—a matter of the finer tuning of the visual apparatus and its prosthetic extensions and the correction of its former mistakes. It is a Marx, to put it positively, who recognizes that the "objectivity" of classical political economy is grounded in a metaphysical epistemology, in which nonvision *belongs* essentially to, "is inside" of, "vision"—haunts its sightings, as it were—and thus whose subversive "activity" should not be overlooked. Or, to put it in terms of a resonant allotrope of this formulation, this other, revolutionary, Marx is one who not only interrogates the practice of capitalism, but also the very "*saying*" of the *adaequatio* that subsumes this practice. He is thus a Marx who inaugurates the thinking of the (spectral) "*silence*" that inheres in this privileged mode of saying:

> Thus Marx [in his "symptomatic reading" (*lecteur symptomale*) of Adam Smith] makes us *see* blanks in the text of classical economics' answer; but that is merely to make us see what the classical text itself says while not saying it, does not say while saying it. Hence it is not Marx who says what the classical text does not say, it is not Marx who intervenes to impose from without on the classical text a discourse which reveals its silence—*it is the classical text itself which tells us that it is silent: its silence is it own words.* (CMP, 22)

This second Marx, that is, is a Marx who not only manifests a profound awareness of the effaced ontological depth of the "imperial" ideology of liberal capitalism. In thematizing, if not actively thinking the positive possibilities of, this "nonvision/silence" that *belongs* ontologically to and that *haunts* the "vision/saying" of the truth discourse of classical political economy, he is also a Marx who prefigures the overdetermination of the "nothing," the "trace" (or "*differance*"), the "differend," the "catachrestic remainder," the "minus in the origin, "the "nomadic rhizome" in the antimetaphysical discourses of Heidegger, Derrida, Lyotard, Spivak, Bhabha, and Deleuze and Guattari, respectively, as well as the preoccupation with "silence" in the neo-Marxist discourse of Althusser. By way of his related attunement to the affiliation of the metaphorics of vision/saying and blindness/silence and that of the (speaking) center and (silent) periphery, this Marx points proleptically to a certain inaugural, though still to be adequately thought postcolonial discourse that, unlike the privileged contemporary oppositional discourses (e.g., the new historicism, cultural criticism, postcolonial criticism, and even Jamesonian neo-Marxism), is not subject to the disabling "imaginative geography"[14] of the *adaequatio* of the imperial metaphysics of post-Enlightenment modernity. I am referring to those various initiatives of postcolonial and global theory—identified with Deleuze and Guattari, Said, Guha, Spivak, Bhabha, and, most recently, Antonio Negri and Michael Hardt—that shift the emphasis of the critique of imperialism from the colonizer to the colonized, specifically, to the "exile," the "migrant," the "emigré," the "hybrid," the "nomad," the "subaltern," the "multitude": to those hitherto invisible constituencies of the global humanity unhomed or displaced by the depredations of Western imperialism that, as the present global demographics massively testifies, have returned, like the nothing, to haunt the imperial metropolis and its order—that is, to "visit" the "visitor." This other Marx, in other words, is a Marx who inaugurates a way of inquiry that would think the polyvalent emancipatory possibilities inhering in the nonvision/silence of (that belongs to) the vision/saying informing the liberal capitalist problematic.

Understood in terms of the above, Althusser's "Marxist" symptomatic reading of bourgeois humanist representation lends itself to a remarkably productive interrogation of the history of the dominant American culture's representations of "Vietnam" from the beginning of the United States' intervention in the early 1950s to its announcement of the end of history and the advent of the New World Order (i.e., to the effacement of the singular event of the Vietnam War) and, then, after the Al Qaeda attack on American soil, the unleashing of its global "war on terrorism." This is because Althusser's emphasis on the ontological "ground" of the problematic (and the metaphorics this "ground" enables), and his thematization of the invisibility/silence that belongs to and haunts the sighting/saying of the problematic, enables a critical instrument that is more adequate to this crucial task than the available oppositional discourses—the new historicism, cultural criticism, certain neo-Marxisms (most notably that of Terry Eagleton, Aijaz Ahmad, Christopher Norris, Timothy Bewes, and Perry Anderson),[15] postcolonial criticism, and even the secular humanism recuperated by Edward Said in his last, posthumously published book, *Humanism and Democratic Criticism*[16]—that have displaced destruction, deconstruction, and even critical genealogy as the privileged discourses of resistance. I mean those discourses that, in their binarist view of the relationship between theory and *praxis*, remain blind not only to the powerful, if not enabling, ideological role that, as I will show in what follows, ontology has played in the representational history of the Vietnam War, but also, and more important, to the epistemic rupture that has both delegitimized that representational discourse and instigated the need to think differently.[17]

To be more specific, Althusser's analysis of the problematic lends itself to a deeper understanding than heretofore of the imperial hegemonic discourse *and* practices that compelled the United States to intervene in the "wilderness" of Vietnam, to conduct the war in the violent way it did, and to represent "Vietnam" in the long aftermath of the war in order to "obliterate" "it" from the American cultural memory. Further, Althusser's analysis of the problematic, especially his interpretation of the "nonvision/silence" inhering in its vision, is eminently appropriatable for the purpose of thinking the resistant discourse and practice of the notorious, if still to be understood, guerrilla strategy—the silent, nomadic "invisibility"—of the National Liberation Front (Viet Cong), what, on the analogy of the discourse of representation itself, I am calling the "spectrality" of the Vietnamese Other. Finally, in thematizing this invisible/silent Other of the discourse and practice of the political economy of liberal capitalism, Althusser's analysis of the problematic also points to, if it does not itself enact, the unthought emancipatory potentialities inherent in the "postcolonial" occasion described by Edward Said in *Culture and Imperialism*. I am referring to the global condition bearing witness to the precipitation of the Other as the other *of* Western colonialism, the displacement and transformation, that is, of a large mass of the world's population into migrants or nomads, or, most tellingly, the "homeless"—if one understands this resonant word in Said's vocabulary in terms of the condition of not being answerable to, of being *actively* "silent" in the face of, the imperatives of the dominant discursive "realities" of the contemporary historical occasion.[18]

The overdetermination of the visual in Althusser's analysis of the problematic has not been adequately thought. As one of the consequence of this failure, it is likely to be objected that Althusser would not concur with my conflation of his "Marxist" thought with that of Heidegger and (perhaps) Derrida and with my appropriation of the problematic to a reading of "Vietnam." In order to facilitate a preliminary understanding of these relationships (they will be addressed more fully and concretely later in this book), it will therefore be necessary to amplify on the visual metaphorics of the problematic. I mean Althusser's analysis of the two "phases" (that are indissolubly one) of the problematic: the operation of vision and of the nonvision that belongs to—is *inside*—it. About "the determination of the *visible* as visible," Althusser writes, "any object or problem situated on the terrain and within the horizon, i.e., in the definite structured field of the theoretical problematic of a given theoretical discipline, is visible. We must take these words literally. The sighting is thus no longer the act of an individual subject, endowed with the faculty of 'vision' which he exercises either attentively or distractedly; the sighting is the act of its structural conditions" (CMP, 25).

This metaphysical epistemology of the liberal capitalist dispensation reifies or, more precisely, "*structures*" being (its be-*ing*) in its entirety, transforms its temporal dynamics into a totalized and inclusive (strategic) "terrain" or "field," or "region," in which *every thing/time* has its proper place under the metaphysical eye's gaze. To emphasize what is essential about Althusser's analysis, it projects a space in which there is no outside that the gaze has not yet but might see at some future time. This is a crucial, though overlooked, moment in Althusser's analysis of the problematic. For, as I have suggested, it points to the inadequacy of a critique of the privileged empiricist idea of truth as the correspondence of mind and thing that continues to see it in the binarist terms of an inside and an outside in which the will to power manifests itself as simple exclusion. And, in thus disclosing the complicity of such a critique with what it opposes, it provides a more satisfactory way of understanding the spatial metaphorics of the liberal capitalist problematic and thus of exposing to view and countering the invisible polyvalent imperial project that this problematic enables and empowers. Althusser does not think this global extension of the social focus of his analysis (its limitation to the "subject" understood as the interpellated individual—the "subjected subject"—in a society). But, as it will be increasingly seen, it is important for my purposes in this book to point out that this extension inheres in his rhetoric (not least in his pointedly deconstructive utilization of geographic-geopolitical metaphors, which are fundamental to the metaphysical languages of the Occident, to specify the broader visual metaphorics):

> In the development of a theory [the word must be understood in terms of its etymology: Greek, *theoria*: sight], the invisible of a visible field is not generally *anything whatever* outside and foreign to the visible defined by that field. The invisible is defined by the visible as *its* invisible, *its* forbidden vision: the invisible is not therefore simply what is outside the visible . . . . the outer darkness of exclusion—but the *inner darkness of exclusion*, inside the visible itself because defined by its structure. In other words, the seductive metaphors of the terrain, the horizon and hence the limits of a visible field defined by a given problematic threaten to induce a false idea of the nature of this field, if we think this field literally according to the spatial metaphor as a space limited by *another space outside it*. . . . [A]ll its limits [of the problematic's vision] are *internal*, it carried its outside inside it. (CMP, 26–27)

Because of this totalizing (imperial) structuralizing/territorializing operation, in which vision "carries its outside in it," it is not, as the dominant liberal capitalist culture essentially and forcefully claims, "the subject" that determines what is seen. The truth is not dependent on the attentiveness of the subject's vision so that, if attentive, it will see everything, if not, it will miss "things" that are *there*. The subject's vision (and its truth) in this dispensation are determined by the vision of the problematic. What is seen is "the act of its structural conditions." This "sighting" is "the relation of immanent reflection between the field of the problematic and *its* objects and *its* problems" (CMP, 25), the "objects" and "problems," that is, that are intrinsic to its proper structural space. The subject, in other words, is assigned its sight by the totalizing problematic. In the more familiar language of Gramsci's analysis of the discourse of hegemony or of Foucault's analysis of the archival rules of discursive formation, both of which Althusser is clearly appropriating, the problematic *speaks* for, which is to say, *thinks for,* the subject. "It is literally no longer the eye (the mind's eye) of a subject which *sees* what exists in the field defined by a theoretical problematic: it is this field itself which *sees itself* in the objects or problems it defines—sighting being merely the necessary reflection of the field on its subject" (CMP, 25). For the subject within the dispensation of the problematic, every other "object," is not an object; every other "problem" is not a problem. That is, every thing/time that does not properly belong to the problematic has *no existence*—is not, therefore, an object "visible"—to the subject. This condition, in which the very *thought process* of the subject is determined— we might say, in accord with the interpretive imperatives of symptomatic reading, is "colonized"—by the liberal capitalist (empirical) problematic, is what Althusser means by the famous but still to be adequately understood, phrase "the interpellated subject."[19]

But, we are compelled to ask, what about the *existence* of these "nonexisting objects" and "nonexisting problems"? Althusser does not provide an adequate answer to this compelling question. Nevertheless, the "second" phase of his analysis of the problematic prepares the ground for that provocatively unfulfilled possibility. We have, in fact, already encountered it in his analysis of the first phase, the visible, in the form of his identification of the "what" of the oversight of vision as "the invisible *of* the visible," "the forbidden vision" of vision, the "inner darkness *of* exclusion," the "denegation" *of* the affirmed visible. This potential becomes especially clear if Althusser's insights into the invisibility that *belongs* to the vision of the problematic—or, more resonantly, the "*shadowy* obverse" *of* the visible (my emphasis)—are understood in the context of the

two epigraphs that inaugurate this chapter: Derrida's recent, more radical equation of deconstruction with a "certain spirit of Marx" and his
representation of the *differance* in terms of the *revenant*, the specter that
returns to visit the visitor; and, not least (because experiential), Tim
O'Brien's representation of the American soldier who identifies the Vietnamese guerrillas with spectral "forces that did not obey the laws of
twentieth-century science":

> The same connexion that defines the visible also defines the in-
> visible as its shadowy obverse. It is the field of the problematic
> that defines and structures the defined excluded, *excluded* from
> the field of visibility and *defined* as excluded by the existence and
> peculiar structure of the field of the problematic; as what forbids
> and represses the reflection of the field on the object, i.e., the nec-
> essary and immanent inter-relationship of the problematic and
> one of its objects. . . . These new objects and problems are neces-
> sarily *invisible* in the field of the existing theory, because they are
> not objects of this theory, because they are *forbidden* by it—they
> are objects and problems necessarily without any necessary rela-
> tions with the field of the visible as defined by the problematic.
> They are invisible because they are rejected in principle, re-
> pressed from the field of the visible; and that is why their *fleeting
> presence* [my emphasis] in the field when it does occur (in very
> peculiar and symptomatic circumstances) *goes unperceived*, and
> becomes literally an undivulgeable absence—since the whole
> function of the field is not to see them, to forbid any sighting of
> them. Here again, the invisible is no more a function of *a sub-
> ject's sighting* than is the visible: the invisible is the theoretical
> problematic's non-vision of its non-objects, the invisible is the
> darkness, the blinded eye of the theoretical problematic's self-
> reflection when it scans its non-objects, its non-problems without
> seeing them, *in order not to look at them.* (CMP, 25–26)

The fundamental objection to Althusser's account of the problematic—
not only by his liberal humanist antagonists, but by his neo-Marxist followers and others, such as Edward Said, on the Left he has influenced—is that,
in announcing "the death of the subject," he ends up disallowing agency to
oppositional discourses and practices. This objection is symptomatic of a
fundamentally disabling weakness of the "advanced criticism" that has
emerged in "the wake of theory,"[20] not least in the oppositional cultural
and political criticism that would resist the announcement of the end of history in the post-Cold War period and the imperial practice of imposing lib-

eral capitalist democracies (the *Pax Americana*) on "rogue states" like Afghanistan and Iraq. In its studied indifference to the ontological depth to which Althusser takes his inquiry into the capitalist/empirical problematic, this criticism fails to "see" that the kind of agency this "advanced" criticism assumes and calls for is one whose meaning is determined by the thinking demanded by the problematic informing the (repressive) practices it would contest. "Even non-democrats will have to speak the language of democracy," Fukuyama has told us, "in order to justify their deviation from the single universal standard." It is a disabling blindness that, admittedly, Althusser encourages by not calling specific attention to it. Nevertheless, his analysis of the "two" phases of the operations of the problematic has as its revolutionary imperative a radically different kind of agency, or rather an agency or *praxis* informed by a different kind of thinking. It is a mode of thinking that, like the epistemological projects of Heidegger, Derrida, Lacan, Lyotard, Levinas, Spivak, Deleuze, and other postmetaphysical philosophers, has its point of departure (not its end, as it is in some degree the case with some of these others) in the interrogation of liberal capitalist modernity's (implicit) representation of being and its understanding of understanding.

Althusser does not articulate what this far-reaching different understanding of agency involves, because, like the others, he does not think *positively* the "what"—the "dark inside"—of the problematic's oversight that he discloses. But a symptomatic reading of his enabling analysis suggests that such a positive understanding of this "what" has to do with the nonvision that *belongs* to vision, just as Heidegger's has to do with the "nothing" that modern science "knows [will know] nothing of"; as Lacan's has to do with "the lack" that disrupts the identity of the subject;[21] as Levinas's has to do with the "radical Other" of the "imperial ontology" of European modernity;[22] as Derrida's has to do with the "specter"—the *revenant*—that returns to "visit" the Spirit of the "new [post-Cold War] Holy Alliance";[23] as Lyotard's has to do with the "*differend*" that refutes "the prejudice that there is 'man,' that there is 'language'";[24] as Deleuze and Guattari's has to do with the "rhizome" that resists the capitalist state's "apparatus of capture."[25] If, that is, we attend carefully to the unthought metaphors in Althusser's text that I have underscored—"the shadowy," "the denegational," "the invisible," "the lacunae," "the blanks," and so on—it will be seen that the nonvision that is inside vision is a potentially *active* force—a material or corporeal immateriality—insofar as it *haunts* the structural totality that the vision of the problematic produces.

In short, attending to this unthought metaphorics in Althusser's remarkably suggestive text demands thinking *productively* that which all the thinkers, including Althusser himself, who have thematized the invisible *of*—that belongs to—the visible have more or less been satisfied merely to make visible. An agency that would escape the subjectivized agency ("the subjected subjectitivity") prescribed by the dominant discourse must begin from the recognition that the "shadowy obverse" *of* vision—its "nonobjects" and its "nonproblems," is *material*, that it *is* the contradictory "reality" that, resisting colonization, rises up precisely at the moment of its death not only to ward off but also to haunt the Truth. I mean the "totalized " reality produced by the (visualist) thought that informs what we can now call, without resorting to quotation marks, the imperial problematic of classical political economy.

"To see this invisible, to see these 'oversights', to identify the lacunae in the fullness of this discourse, the blanks in the crowded text," Althusser tells us, "we need an *informed gaze*, a new gaze, itself produced by a reflection of the 'change of terrain' on the exercise of vision, in which Marx pictures the transformation of the problematic" (CMP, 27). But he does not address, at least not clearly, the question of the historical origins of this "new gaze." Because he overdetermines the critique of the "subject" of the problematic (and its understanding of agency), Althusser simply assumes the transformation as a historical fact, though in passing he refers to "the mechanism that unleashed it and completed it" as "a process" involving "the dialectical crisis of the mutation of a theoretical structure in which the 'subject' plays, not the part it believes it is playing, but the part which is assigned to it by the mechanism of the process" (CMP, 27). Whatever Althusser means here by "the dialectical crisis," the logic of his *lecteur symptomale* of Marx's reading of "Smith-Ricardo's" classical political economy would suggest that the crisis that triggered the estrangement that transformed Marx's gaze into an *"informed gaze"* had to do, however broadly, with a historical moment very much like that to which Heidegger is referring in claiming that "philosophy comes to its end" (*both* fulfillment *and* demise) with the planetary triumph of technological thinking (*Ge-stell*: "enframing") in the modern age (i.e., *"die Zeit des Weltbildes"*); to which Derrida is referring in speaking about the "event" of the "rupture" in "the history of the concept of structure" (which "is as old . . . as Western science and Western philosophy),"[26] precipitated by the fulfillment of the structuring imperatives of Western metaphysics; to which Foucault and Deleuze are referring in implicitly pointing to the "epistemic break" incumbent on the completion of the logical economy of the Enlightenment in the "panoptic" or "disciplinary society"; to which Said is referring in pointing to the prevalence of the migrant in the radically transformed global demographics precipitated by the logic of imperialism; and to which Negri and Hardt are referring in announcing the coming to be of the multitude as the necessary consequence of the very mechanisms of capital.

Despite his rarefied representation of the dark, negational side of the modern Western problematic, the witness that Althusser bears to this "changed terrain," like Marx before him, and like his contemporaries, Heidegger, Derrida, Foucault, and Deleuze and Guattari, is finally a historical or, in Said's word, "secular" witness. He becomes aware of this "shadowy obverse" of vision—this spectral reality, as it were, that haunts the "Truth" of Western representation—by way of bearing witness to an epochal historical "event" precipitated by "the West" that brings the West to its self-destructive "end." I mean an event in which the very fulfillment of the logical economy of Western thought—the completion and global triumph of the process of knowledge production that transforms and reduces the be-*ing* of being to a strategic "terrain"—precipitates its delegitimation and demise. For Marx that "event" may have been the historical conjuncture that witnessed the violent repression of virtually the entire European working-class movement in the name of the Holy Alliance he refers to in *The Communist Manifesto*. For Heidegger, it may have been the global devastations of World War I precipitated by the concatenation of European imperialism and the mass slaughter enabled by a planetary triumphant technology. For Derrida and Lyotard, it may have been the event called "Auschwitz," in which, according to one of Derrida's ablest disciples, *"ce n'est ni plus ni moins que l'Occident, en son essence, qui s'est révéler—at qui ne cesse, depuis, de se révéler"* (it is nothing more nor less than the Occident, in its essence, which was revealed—and which since then does not cease to reveal itself).[27] For Said, it may have been the implosion of Western imperialism at the beginning of the twentieth century. For Foucault, Deleuze, and Althusser it may have been the general, but no less disclosive historical conditions in France and its colonies—Algeria and Indochina—that precipitated the socalled events of May 1968.

III

All these historical events and others, I suggest, constitute the single larger event of epistemic "fulfillment" to which I am referring. But the self-destruction of the idea of the West to which they bear witness is not immediately self-evident for different reasons: the euphorically positive image of the achievements of bourgeois capitalism in the middle of the nineteenth century (Marx); the ambiguities of the global carnage of World War I precipitated by a conflict internal to the West, in which each side claimed the status of defending the idea of Western civilization against the other (Heidegger); the unmitigating evil of Nazism that obscured what Hannah Arendt persuasively called its "banality" (Derrida, Lyotard, Adorno); the nostalgia for a "lost" humanism (Said); the localism of historical reference to, if not of, the events of 1968 themselves (Althusser, Foucault, and Deleuze). Because of the ambiguous status of the relationship between the adversary and the protagonist, each of these events could, therefore, be and have been all too easily represented as *betrayals* of the fundamental principles and values of the "West" and thus as their vindication rather than their delegitimation.

As the national anxiety that, above all, is evident in the obsessively sustained effort of the American cultural memory to forget it suggests, the shameful history of the Vietnam War (and the enormously body of discourse it has spawned), on the other hand, bears a more self-evident witness to the radical contradiction—the dark side—of the vision of the West. I am referring not only to the radically contradictory spectacle of America's destruction—bordering on genocide—of a Third World nation and its culture in order to "save" it for, and in the name of the principles of, the "free world," which, according to the moral imperatives of its "exceptionalist" mission, the United States had assumed as its burden in the wake of their betrayal by a decadent Europe. I am also referring to the ineffaceable testimony of an ostensibly weak Other that defeated the formidable American military machine, not by force of arms as such, but by intuiting the ontological Achilles' heel of the power of the most powerful nation-state in the history of the world, by, that is, turning the visually oriented "problematic" of the First World aggressor against itself. This, as we shall see more fully in the following chapters, was the "guerrilla" strategy that transformed the intrinsic oversight (and the "terrain" it oversees) that reduced this "Third World" people to nonexistence—to the "nonobject," the "nonproblem," the "shadowy obverse," the "nonvision," the "denegation," *of* the inclusive (imperial) vision of the First World invader—into a highly effective (unorthodox) praxis. To invoke the metaphorics that, as I will show in greater depth and more specifically, came to saturate American discourse from the lowliest American "grunt" through the military commands in Saigon and the Pentagon, to the culture industry that represented the war to the American people and the world, it was the strategy of "low intensity warfare" that appropriated the blindness *of* American vision—the oversight *of* its over-sight—to a nomadic *spectral* practice that baffled its panoptic eye and disintegrated the military directionality its reifications made possible. It is as if the Vietnamese insurgents had proleptically put into practice Enrique Dussel's remarkably Althusserian announcement of a philosophy of liberation that would enable weak Third World (i.e., "barbarian") countries to resist the otherwise irresistible power of First World imperialism:

> Against the classic ontology of the center . . . a philosophy of liberation is rising from the periphery, from the oppressed, *from the shadow that the light of Being has not been able to illume.* Our thoughts [Dussel's and the Other he represents] set out from non-Being, nothingness, otherness, exteriority, the mystery of no-sense. It is, then, "a barbarian" philosophy.[28] (my emphasis)

Let me put it alternatively—and more specifically—this time in terms of the trope of the "terrain" of knowledge that is the intrinsic complement of the light of Western vision. In refusing to show themselves to the gaze of the American problematic, in, as it were, thinking the possibilities of resistance inherent in their status *as* the "*shadow* that the light of Being has not been able to illumine," the Vietnamese insurgents developed a military practice remarkably similar to the nomadic strategy against the capitalist state theorized by Deleuze and Guattari in *A Thousand Plateaus.* I mean, more specifically, the decentering and molecularizing strategy incumbent on the deterritorialization of the Western, especially American, "panoptic" representation of space—and of *the narrative structure of action* such a representation enables—into a "rhizome"—"an acentered, nonhierarchical, nonsignifying system" in Deleuze and Guattari's resonant language, "without a General and without an organizing memory or central automaton, defined solely by a circulation of states" or, even more tellingly, a rhizomatic landscape "a region of unceasing intensities, vibrating upon themselves, which develop by avoiding every orientation towards a culminating point or towards an exterior end."[29] In thus destructuring the American command's metaphysically grounded (imperial) assumptions about space, the Vietnamese insurgents disarticulated the charted (territorialized and disciplined) terrain projected by the distant eye of the American command and neutralized the otherwise invincible power of the war machine that is that terrain's effect. In other words, they made it impossible for the inordinately more powerful U.S. army to engage in the *decisive battle* that is endemic to *Western* warfare: to the kind of military tactics that is intrinsic to the vision of the problematic.[30]

   If, in short, we are attuned with Althusser (and the other poststructuralist thinkers who have focused on metaphysics in their interrogation of Western perception and practice) to the metaphorics of vision that the amnesiac representation of the history of the Vietnam War has overdetermined, if, to be specific, we heed the invisible (and the silence) that *belongs* to the visible (and saying) of the representational discourse of the modern

Western problematic, we will *see* (and hear) something different from that which this discourse compels us to see (and hear). In this "changed terrain," we will see (and hear) that the degree to which this representational history would annul the memory of Vietnam in order, first, to proclaim the end of history (the *Pax Metaphysica* and the *Pax Americana*) and then, in the wake of 9/11, the preemptive wars intended to secure humanity against itself is the degree to which this representational history itself precipitates Vietnam—its singularity—into spectral visibility. We will see, in other words, the degree to which the (non)*event* of Vietnam, like the invisible/silent (non)*being* of the Vietnamese insurgents vis-à-vis the American army in the Vietnam "wilderness" in the 1960s, haunts the American cultural memory as, now, after the Al Qaeda attacks, the triumphalist American government wages its implacable "war on terror" in behalf of establishing what its neoconservative intellectual deputies call the "New American Century."[31] Instigated by the retrieval of this spectral Vietnam, such an "informed gaze," to use Althusser's language, will enable us, as New Americanists, to realize the urgency in this interregnum of thinking the positive ontological, social, and political possibilities that are latent in the spectrality that has been disclosed by the fulfillment of the logical economy of representational thinking.

We must not be satisfied with Heidegger, Derrida, Lyotard, and even Althusser simply to force the invisibility of the visible into visibility. The "change of terrain" precipitated by the coming to its end of Western modernity in America's unending war on terror in the name of the *Pax Americana* also compels us to *think* this "shadowy obverse" of metaphysical *vision*—the specter—positively. This task of thinking is no marginal matter, one that can therefore be considered separate from or subordinate to the more "practical" sites of economics and politics. It must be *polyvalent*. As I hope to show in what follows by way of examining the symptomatic struggle of American veterans to come to terms with the specter of the Vietnam War, it is this polyvalency that is the imperative of thinking in an age that has become the "Age of the World Picture." Thinking the spectral Other of modern metaphysics positively is a task that *belongs with*, if it is not indeed the source of, a future emancipatory politics that would resist the *Pax Americana* and its dehumanizing logic in the name of a global humanity, a "new humanism" in Frantz Fanon's proleptic phrase.[32]

Chapter 3

WHO KILLED ALDEN PYLE?

The Oversight of Oversight in Graham Greene's The Quiet American

All of Orientalism stands forth and away from the Orient: that Orientalism makes sense at all depends more on the West than on the Orient, and this sense is directly indebted to various Western techniques of representation that make the Orient visible, clear, and "there" in a discourse. And these representations rely upon institutions, traditions, conventions, agreed-upon codes of understanding for their effects, not upon a distant and amorphous Orient.

—Edward W. Said, *Orientalism*

The sun that rose over Hue on the morning of February 25, 1968, illuminates a dead city. . . . Wise, like Solomon, we converted Hue into rubble in order to save it.

—Gustav Hasford, *Short-Timers*

Graham Greene's *The Quiet American,* first published in 1955, is a novel whose mis-en-scène is the Indochina of the period between 1946—when, in the aftermath of the withdrawal of the Japanese at the end of World War II, the French colonial army was fighting the Viet Minh to regain France's authority over its former colony—and 1954, immediately before the decisive defeat of the French by the Viet Minh at Dien Bien Phu (May 7, 1954). This was the period when the United States was locked into the Cold War scenario (specifically, the domino theory), which, from its typically panoptic perspective, saw the Vietnamese people's struggle for their independence from a long and degrading history of foreign colonial rule as a geopolitical initiative masterminded by the Soviet Union. It was also the period when the United States, impatient with the failure of the

French to reestablish control over what it then called Indochina, began to intervene clandestinely in that part of Southeast Asia with the ultimate intention of securing it for the West, the "free world." This novel about American exceptionalism begins in medias res and is written from a first-person preterite point of view, that of Thomas Fowler, a cynical, politically detached opium-smoking British reporter, who, having borne witness to the violence endemic to the French *mission civilisatrice* in Indochina, has become disillusioned with the West and alienated from its ideals. His alienation has taken the form of a refusal to become politically involved or, in the language of the existentialism of that time, "*engagé.*" From this estranged and neutral present perspective, this expatriate retells the story of his relationship to a young idealist American, Alden Pyle, who has been mysteriously assassinated. Ostensibly a member of a fact-finding U.S. "economic mission" in Indochina, Pyle, Fowler informs us in his retrieval of the events leading up to the assassination, was, in fact, a counterinsurgent, profoundly influenced in his views of Southeast Asia by the books on American foreign policy of a certain American area expert, York Harding. Pyle was working clandestinely to establish a "Third Force" that disavowed both French colonialism and Stalinist and Maoist communism in favor of a "national democracy" aligned with the Cold War policy of the United Sates. The story Fowler retells also involves a young Vietnamese woman, Phuong, clearly a personification of Indochina, with whom he is in love, but whose affection had been alienated by the quiet American. (When, for example, Phuong leaves him for Pyle, Fowler remarks: "It was as though she were being taken away from me by a nation rather than a man."[1])

As this brief summary suggests by way of stressing the various perspectives on the struggle over Indochina, Greene's novel is fundamentally about representation or, rather, the relationship between representation and power. More specifically—and this is what I wish to contribute, in the wake of 9/11 and the United States' global "war against terror," to the prolific retrospective commentary on Greene's novel and the Vietnam War—it is both a detective story and an allegory or, more precisely, an antidetective story and an anti-allegory. It is, in other words, a narrative that begins with an assassination that provokes the question, "Who killed the quiet American, Alden Pyle?," and "ends" with an "answer" that subverts the expectation it conjures. Told from a perspective *outside* those of the French colonial, Soviet communist, and especially American democratic problematics, it also deconstructs and thus estranges the rigid and reductive allegorical, indeed, Manichaean, discourse of America: its representation of the Cold War between democracy and communism as a struggle between good and evil. And it does this in a way that is remarkably proleptic not only of the historical future of America's inexorably determined—we might say missionary— intervention in Vietnam, its mindlessly brutal conduct of the war, and its humiliating defeat, but also of the poststructuralist and/or postcolonialist, and New Americanist, critical analyses of this shameful epochal moment of Western, particularly American history. Further, dislocating Greene's novel from the discursive matrix in which it has been embedded and reconstellating it into the present post-9/11 historical conjuncture will go far to disclose the secret history that the George W. Bush administration and the media— the consciousness industry, as Adorno called it—have obfuscated by way of representing its "preemptive" invasions of Afghanistan and Iraq and its missionary effort to impose American-style democracies in the Middle East as its unilateral global responsibility.

What Greene is suggesting by way of overdetermining representation (knowledge production) and its relationship to power, to put it provisionally, is that this "quiet American's" "objective" or "universal" truth is a construction—a "truth discourse," to appropriate the poststructuralist language he anticipates—that is grounded in an imperial metaphysical interpretation of being (the perception of the be-*ing* of being from after or above its temporal disseminations) that coerces alterity, whether ontological or cultural or political, into a preconceived self-identical *whole*, or what is the same thing, a *structured totality*. It is what Antonio Gramsci calls a "hegemonic" discourse,[2] a discourse that is understood by those who speak, write, and live it to be natural, the articulation of the way things really are, but which, in fact, is a gradually evolved fabrication of the dominant culture, whose end is the disabling of subaltern resistance and the maintenance and aggrandizement of its authority. It is also, therefore, a discourse that represents itself as a progression from and opposition to the discourse and practice of the overt and direct use of power. Though it always exudes the aura of benignity, it is, in fact, a discourse of domination. A hegemonic discourse, in other words, represents itself in a binary opposition to indoctrination, the calculated, deliberate, and arbitrary imposition of its truth by a dominant culture on a differential community. Thus, unlike those in a totalitarian society, who are consciously aware of the agents of their oppression and therefore always constitute a potential force of resistance, in a society in which a hegemonic discourse obtains, those who are exploited by the dominant culture—those, to underscore the effaced metaphorics of the term, who are *marginalized*—are silently compelled to represent the disabling lack in their lives not as the fault of the system, but as their own fault, and thus to think that they can achieve the full benefits of its truths if they abide by the prevailing (normative) "truth." The majority of those who live within a society that is determined by a hegemonic discourse *see* only the questions that are within, endemic to the inclusive hegemonic discourse. Any question that is outside the parameters—the *circle*—of the hegemonic discourse are thus not questions at all. They may become questions for those who are outside the circumference of the hegemonic discourse, its Other, like Graham Greene's exilic and nomadic Fowler, for example, but they cannot be questions for those, like Pyle, who live entirely within it—give their spontaneous consent to its truth. This, to anticipate, explains why Fowler says that "there was a quality of the implacable in Pyle" (*QA*, 59) and why Pyle is constantly bewildered by the dislocating ironies of Fowler's discourse and practice.

Let me supplement this Gramscian cultural insight by putting his definition of hegemony in terms of the metaphor of sight I analyzed in chapter 2, a metaphor that, in deepening Gramsci's analysis of the cultural, economic, and political imperialism of Western democracy to include the (onto)logical site, is more adequate than the general definition in determining the nature of Graham Greene's portrayal of the "quiet American" and of his contribution to our understanding of the essence of America's intervention in Vietnam. In a hegemonic society, one can only *see* what the discourse of hegemony allows one to see. Anything *other*, anything that contradicts the hegemonic discourse, is not visible to those who live within it. (This is one reason, not incidentally, why contemporary "theory," specifically poststructuralist thought, has been such a powerful agency of interrogating the discourse of the West and especially of America, and why traditionalists and the deputies of the dominant culture have mounted a massive campaign to delegitimize its fundamental counter- or "il-logic"). Having its point of departure outside the parameters of the American hegemonic discourse, it is able to see that which is invisible to the eyes of those who think inside this discourse, just as Fowler sees what Pyle is blind to: not least, the blood of the victims of his "innocent" and "benign" American perspective, the symbol, that is, of the dark side of the myth of American exceptionalism.

My extension of Gramsci's analysis of hegemony in terms of the invisible "white" metaphorics of vision[3] derives ultimately from Heidegger's ontological interrogation of the metaphysics (the perception of being from after or above its disseminations) that has determined the various philosophies of the Western tradition, but its immediate source is, as I have observed in the previous chapter, the neo-Marxist Louis Althusser, a *political* thinker whose critique of Western (bourgeois) ideology, not least in "Ideology and Ideological State Apparatuses" (an essay written in the aftermath of the events of May 1968 and thus indissolubly related to the Indochinese conflict) is deeply indebted to Gramsci's cultural/political analysis of hegemony.[4] I am referring specifically to what Althusser calls "the problematic," his analysis of which, in its anti-Hegelian focus on the more nuanced modernist allotrope of the metaphysical thinking that has dominated in the West and his thematization of the indissoluble relation between ontological and cultural, economic, and political representation, constitutes one of his most significant contributions to the poststructuralist interrogation of the hegemonic discourse of the liberal capitalist democracy. As such, it sheds remarkable new light on *The Quiet American*, especially on (1) Thomas Fowler's relation to Alden Pyle (the exilic outsider to the American insider) and, more broadly, as I have suggested in chapter 2, on (2) the hegemonic discourse and global practice of "America," and on (3) the discourse and practice of America's Vietnamese Other during the Vietnam War.

Like Heidegger's ontological account of *Ge-stell* (enframing), Althusser's analysis of the problematic in "From *Capital* to Marx's Philosophy" constitutes, as I have shown, a radical critique of the kind of vision (seeing) that determines *representation* in the post-Enlightenment modernity. In their critique, both thematize and deconstruct the (white) metaphorics of sight that the West has privileged over the other senses in opting for a metaphysical interpretation of being, which—in perceiving being from the distance of the *meta* (after or above), spatializes time (and "nothingness")—transforms its temporality into an inclusive *structure*. What distinguishes Althusser's critique from Heidegger's is that, whereas the latter's critique of Western metaphysical representation is generalized and by and large restricted to the site of ontology, the former focuses on the historical moment of the rise of liberal capitalist democracy and encompasses the ontological and the economic and sociopolitical sites of the continuum of being. Althusser's account of the problematic in this important but neglected text demonstrates perhaps more clearly than any poststructuralist discourse the indissoluble relationship between ontological representation, on the one hand, and cultural, ecological, economic, and sociopolitical representation, on the other, in liberal capitalist modernity. More specifically, if only implicitly, it demonstrates this relationship in the history of America (which, contrary to the myth of American exceptionalism, is the self-appointed heir of Europe), not least, in the history of America's intervention in Vietnam. In what immediately follows, therefore, I will re-cite the crucial passage on liberal capitalist representation from the introduction of *Reading Capital*, "From *Capital* to Marx's Philosophy," in which Althusser, via Marx's "symptomatic reading"—a reading that refuses to adhere to the visual imperatives of a metaphysical understanding of knowledge production—explains the operations of the problematic in terms of "sight" and "oversight" (which means "not seeing," "seeing from above," and "supervising").

Althusser, it will be recalled, begins his analysis of the problematic by asserting that "we must abandon mirror myths of *immediate* vision and reading, and conceive knowledge as a *production*"[5] (my emphasis). What he is insisting on is that the mind's eye privileged by classical political economy is no more immune to prejudice than the other senses, that, in fact, it produces "reality," that knowledge is constructed rather than somehow inherent in phenomena and therefore available to be mimetically disclosed or copied or mirrored or reflected. From the traditional mimetic perspective vis-à-vis inquiry into the truth, what it cannot see is a matter of not having seen what is there *yet*. This kind of mimetic reading, in other words, is grounded in the principle of *correctness* and its binary opposite, falseness. The false is a misinterpretation or misrepresentation of what is there. It is thus subject to correction by way of a visual instrumentality that is not available to the inquirer at the particular moment of inquiry. This is, of course, what Heidegger identifies as the traditional metaphysical concept of truth: *adaequatio intellectus et rei* ("the correspondence of mind and thing")—which, as I have shown in chapter 1, has its origins in the Roman translation of the Greek concept of truth, *a-letheia* (unconcealment) to *veritas*, an originary into a derivative or calculative—and imperial—mode of inquiry, that reifies time into a visible and graspable object or structure.

From Althusser's secular (antimetaphysical) perspective, on the contrary, what the classical mimetic perspective does not see in its seeing is "the *object it produced itself* in its operation of knowledge and which did not pre-exist it": precisely "the production itself, which is identical with the object"(CMP, 24). In its production of "an answer without a question," it produces "a new question, but *unwittingly*" (Althusser's emphasis). This unwitting question or "new problem," which "is impenetrable for its author"—to which, in other words, his super-visory metaphysical perspective is blind—becomes the point of departure for Althusser's discussion of the problematic proper:

> This introduces us to a fact peculiar to the very existence of science [by which he means the pursuit of knowledge in general]: it can only pose problems on the terrain and within the horizon of a definite theoretical structure [the frame of reference inscribed in the mind's eye], its problematic, which constitutes its absolute and definite condition of possibility, and hence the absolute determination of *the forms in which all problems must be posed*, at any given moment in the science. (CMP, 25; my emphasis)

The problematic, in other words, determines that which constitutes problems. As in Gramsci's understanding of the discourse of hegemony, anything outside the purview of the problematic is not a problem; it is invisible to the inquiring mind's eye and its prosthetic instruments. This recognition of the structural essence of the problematic "opens the way to an understanding of the determination of the *visible* as the visible, and conjointly of the invisible as invisible, *and the organic link binding the invisible and the visible*" (my emphasis): that which is within and that which is outside the problematic, now understood as a construction, the effects of which are taken to be the truth. That is, the "sighting is no longer *the act of an individual subject,* endowed with the faculty of 'vision' which he exercises either attentively or distractedly"—if attentively, the subject will see everything, if not, he or she will overlook that which is not there. Rather, "the sighting is *the act of its structural conditions,* it is the relation of immanent reflection between the field of the problematic and *its* objects and its *problems."*

What Althusser is saying here is crucial, not only to an understanding of his particular poststructuralist Marxism, but, to anticipate, to Graham Greene's understanding of Alden Pyle's American "problematic" (and, beyond that, to the perspective on Vietnam of the American military command, of the planners in the Pentagon, and ultimately of the American public: his inscribed exceptionalist ethos in its contemporary Cold War avatar, which is represented, above all, by Pyle's avid commitment to the truth of the books on American foreign policy in the East written by the American area expert York Harding). In the world of the bourgeois capitalist dispensation it is not, as it is insistently claimed against totalitarian societies (their collectivism), the free individual—the subject—who is the agent of the truth. The individual, without knowing it, is spoken for, is ventriloquized, by the discourse of the dominant culture: his or her vision and its truth are determined by the problematic, what Gramsci calls the discourse of hegemony, Foucault, the "rules of discursive formation," and Said, "the textual attitude"[6]: "The sighting is the act of its structural conditions." What counts as the truth are those objects and problems (or questions) that the problematic appropriates, incorporates, or accommodates, makes its own; everything outside *its* proper structural space does not properly belong to the problematic, are not problems, that is, *have no being,* are, so to speak, *nothing.* From this analytical perspective, "it is literally no longer the eye (the mind's eye) of a subject which *sees* what exists in the field defined by a theoretical problematic: it is this field itself which *sees itself* in the objects or problems it defines—sighting being merely the necessary reflection of the field on its objects" (CMP, 25).

At this point, in an ontologically revolutionary move that has yet to be noticed—one recalling Heidegger's invocation of the "nothing that science [metaphysics in its modern, anthropological, phase] will have nothing to do with"[7]—Althusser invokes the *necessary* binary opposite of the privileged visible: the invisible.

It is the field of the problematic that defines and structures the invisible as the defined excluded, *excluded* from the field of visibility and *defined* as excluded by the existence and peculiar structure of the field of the problematic; as what forbids and represses the reflection of the field on its objects. . . . They are invisible because they are rejected in principle, repressed from the field of the visible: and that is why their fleeting presence in the field when it does occur (in very peculiar and symptomatic circumstances) *goes unperceived.* (CMP, 26)

By means of this symptomatic reading of the liberal capitalist problematic, the invisible other *of*—that *belongs* to—vision becomes "visible," not only at the site of ontology, but all along the continuum of being: from the "nothing" of metaphysical perception through the reified earth to the various classes of beings (not only the laborers that Althusser overdetermines, but also women, racial and ethnic minorities, gays, and the peoples of the Third World), who have been violently reduced, both ideologically and corporeally, to nonbeing by the "benign" polyvalent binary visualist logic of the liberal capitalist problematic. Indeed, this visibility of the polyvalent invisible becomes the spectral "shadow" that haunts the light of the imperial truth and practice of liberal capitalist modernity. If we recall his overdetermination of culture in his critique and revision of the orthodox Marxist base/superstructure model in "Ideology and Ideological State Apparatuses," we might say that Althusser's symptomatic reading of the problematic constitutes the definitive critique, not simply of the classical *capitalist* economics of Adam Smith and David Ricardo, but also of the cultural and sociopolitical discourse of those modern classical humanists, British and American, whose "disinterested" visualist inquiry was epitomized by the latent violence inhering in Matthew Arnold's privileging of "culture" over "anarchy."[8]

In short, the "symptomatic reading" Althusser practices and calls for is one that not only discloses the "oversight" (the blindness) of the oversight of the interpellated subject (the subject that has been inscribed and ventriloquized by the hegemonic truth discourse).[9] It also and simultaneously makes visible *for positive thought* the hitherto "undivulgeable absence," the "objects" and "problems" that it is the "whole function of the field" to "forbid any sighting of." A *lecture symptomale*, then, entails—and this is broadly fundamental to the interpretive practice of poststructuralsit or posthegemonic or postmodern theory—a reading that attends to the *margins* as well as to the center of the text, or, what is the same thing on a more practical register, the *provinces* as well as the metropolis. To put this in Walter Benjamin's terms, it reads texts "against the grain" or in Edward Said's, "contrapuntally." More specifically, it calls for a reading that attends not only to what is there in a text, but also what is not there, what is left unsaid, what the text is blind to. To read symptomatically is to read what is not there in the text by way of reading what is there, to read what is there in order to discover what is not there, since what is *not* there is the necessary consequence of what *is* there, since what is invisible is precisely the consequence of what is visible. Put in a way that evokes the indissoluble relationship between *poesis* (representation) and politics, to read symptomatically is to enable that which the text marginalizes and can be seen, if at all, only at the periphery of the spectatorial eye—as "a fleeting presence"—to return to center stage. This, I suggest, is what Greene is attempting not only in the content of *The Quiet American* by way of his evocation of the terrible consequences of Alden Pyle's American exceptionalist "problematic," but also in the novelistic form he has chosen to articulate this content. I am referring to the detective story, the genre that brings the teleologic informing the "realist" narratological aesthetic of post-Enlightenment modernity to its fulfillment, in which the murdered eventually turn out in the end to be in some significant sense the murderer.

I

The historical context of *The Quiet American*, as I have said, involves the Vietnamese peoples' insurgency, under the leadership of the Viet Minh, the "Marxist" political/military arm of this nationalist initiative, against French colonial rule in the aftermath of World War II. But it also, and more fundamentally, involves the initial intervention of the United States in the affairs of this Third World space. At the outset of this fateful inaugural intervention in what was then called Indochina, the United States, first under the Truman and then under the Eisenhower administration, supported France's effort to maintain its colony both ideologically and materially by way of virtually financing its military effort to quell the insurgency. The American support of the French, which took the form of massive economic and military aid and, not least, the sending of Americans to "South Vietnam" as advisors, was motivated primarily by the American hysteria over the emergence of the Soviet Union as a global power after the war, and over the victory of Mao Tse Tong's communist revolution in China, that is, because of the communist "threat" to (American) capitalist hegemony in the world. More specifically, its support of the French colonial project was determined by the highly allegorical "domino theory," the Manichaean geopolitical prediction that if one of those Southeast Asian countries were allowed by the "West" (capitalist democracy) to fall to the "East" (communism), all of them would inevitably follow suit. (I will return later in this chapter to this allegorical narrative, that, like a paranoia, inexorably determined the official American representation of global relations and its practice throughout the Cold War period, from the time of the United States' intervention in Southeast Asia to the collapse of the Soviet Union.)

But America's support of France in the Indochina War was, significantly, far from wholehearted. It was, in fact, fractured by a deeply backgrounded, ambiguous attitude of great consequence toward its European ally, one that Greene overdetermines and thus is crucial to an understanding of *The Quiet American*. As old as the founding of America, this was the American government's (and the American public's) historically inscribed mistrust of, if not disdain for, the Old World, here represented primarily by France. I am, to be more specific, referring to the myth of American exceptionalism, which had its origins in the American Puritans' divinely ordained "errand in the wilderness" to build "a City on a Hill," as John Winthrop put it in his sermon on board *The Arabella* in 1620;[10] its secularized adolescence in the period of westward expansion under the aegis of Manifest Destiny; and its apogee in the post–World War II period, when the United States assumed the status of a global power.[11] Taking its lead from the exemplary self-reliant pioneering or westering spirit of the archetypal backwoodsman or frontiersman—for example, the legendary Daniel Boone or the fictional Leatherstocking figure of James Fenimore Cooper's novels of the American frontier—who, like their Puritan ancestors' rejection of the Old World, always shuns the town (i.e., the corruptness of the civilized settlements), this is the myth that (1) represents Europe as the Old World, understood as a sedentary civilization that, having betrayed its providential responsibility, had become senile and degenerate in its pursuit and refinement of the things of this world, three of the most important manifestations of which were its dependence on tradition, its tyrannical forms of government, and its rapacious colonialism. Conversely, it is the myth that (2) represents America as the antithesis of Europe: a New World, understood as a civilization that, true to the Word of God or History, is *always* youthful, dynamic, creative, forward-looking, whose supreme manifestations are its privileging of self-reliance, its idealization of the perpetual frontier (a violent forwarding that always already renews the spirit of the settlement),[12] its democratic polity, and its "benign" mission to create a garden—a New Jerusalem—out of the anxiety-provoking but promising wilderness (thus the pervasive reference to "clearing," "improvement," or "betterment" in the discourse of colonial America")[13] and to save the Old World from its suicidal decadent tendencies.

This, as I will show at length in chapter 6, is the inaugural American myth, first theorized paradoxically by a European, Alexis de Tocqueville,[14] that, in the process of American history, especially after the Civil War, became naturalized, that is, accepted as the essence or truth of the American national identity until it was rendered problematic during the Vietnam War (only to be recuperated in the aftermath of the terrorist attacks on the World Trade Center and the Pentagon on September 11, 2001). It is no accident that it was President John F. Kennedy who, reacting to the national debate instigated by the publication of William Lederer and Eugene Burdick's American jeremiad, *The Ugly American*, in 1958— two years after Greene's *Quiet American*[15]—identified his administration as "the New Frontier," a name that was intended both to shock the American public into awareness of its precarious drift into decadence and to instigate a rejuvenation of the original "idealism" of its authentic national identity in behalf of the global struggle against the evils of Soviet communism. Nor was it an accident that, in the name of the New Frontier, he sent American soldiers to Vietnam, first as advisors to train the army of the "democratic" government of South Vietnam newly established by the United States, but increasingly and in larger numbers to participate, in violation of the protocols of the Geneva Accords that brought the Indochina War to its end, in covert combat missions against the National Liberation Front (Viet Cong). Nor is it an accident that one of Kennedy's first projects as president was the creation of the "Special Forces," the most visible of which was the Green Berets, the counterinsurgency military unit that, consonant with the idea of the New Frontier, was intended to recall the national cultural heroes of the colonial period, the legendary descendants of the Puritan elect. I am referring to mythicized historical figures like Daniel Boone, Kit Carson, Davy Crocket, and James Bowie, and mythicized fictional figures like Natty Bumppo, who, having learned the ways of the native Americans—their knowledge of and intimate relation to the land, their endurance of pain, their perseverance in the face of hardship, their tactics of indirection, their self-reliance—were, as James Fenimore Cooper put the American errand in the wilderness in 1823, "the foremost in that band of Pioneers, who are opening the way for the march of the nation across the continent."[16]

Though Greene does not invoke the myth of American exceptionalism overtly, it is, nevertheless, precisely this naturalized historical construction— its indissolubly related ontological, cultural, and political manifestations— that he is alluding to and deconstructing in *The Quiet American* by way of the allegorical *psychomachia* between Thomas Fowler and Alden Pyle. Despite the seeming realism of the novel, Greene does not represent Fowler and Pyle as unique individuals. They are, rather, symbols, indeed, virtually allegorical figures, who represent the Old World and the New World, respectively. Fowler, a middle-aged expatriate British reporter who has been in Indochina for a long time, is consciously European in his decadent lifestyle, his cynicism, his tacit acknowledgment, if not affirmation, of the value of experience, of tradition, and of historical depth, his appreciation of the complexity of the human condition—the "tragic" sense of life endemic to the cultural perspective of the Old World—and his general identification with French civility, if not with France's colonialist cause. Pyle, on the other hand, is *American*—young, innocent, enthusiastic, idealistic, vital, practical, and indifferent to history and tradition: the adventurous modern avatar of the American national identity—the secularized Puritan elect/westering pioneer driven by his History-ordained "errand" in the "wilderness" of Indochina to build "a Citty on a Hill."[17] To put it in the satirical term Michael Herr coined to characterize the type of straightforward, adventurer/idealist imperialist patriot (Father Finian, Gilbert MacWhite, Edwin Hillandale, Tex Wolchek, Homer Atkins), Burdick and Lederer's jeremiad posited in opposition to the careless and self-indulgent career diplomats the U.S. State Department was sending to Southeast Asia—and to whom Greene is referring—in the earliest phase of the United States' involvement, Pyle is an American "spook":

> It was spookwar then [in 1963], adventure; not exactly soldiers, not even advisors yet, but Irregulars, working in remote places under little direct authority, acting out their fantasies with more freedom than most men ever know. Years later, leftovers from that time would describe it, they'd bring in names like Gordon, Burton and Lawrence, elevated crazies of older adventures who'd burst from their tents and bungalows to rub up hard against natives, hot on the sex-and-death trail, "lost to headquarters." There had been Ivy League spooks who'd gone bumbling and mucking around in jeeps and beat-up Citroens. . . . There'd been ethnologue spooks who loved with their brains and force that passion on locals, whom they'd imitate, squatting in black pajamas, jabbering in Vietnamese. . . . There were spook deities, like Lou Conein . . . and Edward Landsdale [sic] himself, still there in '67, his villa a Saigon landmark where he poured tea and whisky for second generation spooks who adored him, even now that his batteries were dead.[18]

In fact, as it has often been observed, Greene modeled Alden Pyle on the legendary American Colonel Edward Lansdale, who, in violation of the Geneva Accords, was commissioned in 1954 by John Foster Dulles, the brinksman secretary of state in the Eisenhower administration, to inaugurate clandestine psywar (the euphemism for terrorism) in Vietnam on the basis of the "successful" work he had done in countering the communist insurgency (HUK) in the Philippines after the Japanese were driven out during World War II and in facilitating the emergence of the anti-communist, pro-American Ramon Magsaysay, who eventually became president of the Philippines. As Lansdale makes clear everywhere in his megalomaniacal autobiography, *In the Midst of Wars*, appropriately subtitled *An American's Mission in Southeast Asia* (1972), he saw himself as a kind of missionary/pioneer of the Cold War era (without being aware of the irony that he was, in Marx's terms, repeating history, but now as farce). Like the Leatherstocking figure, but now armed with the creed of the American Revolution, he represented himself as a loner, who, impatient with the conventional strategies of American civilian and military officialdom, chose to learn the ways of the natives in the forests and their methods of survival the better to contribute to the advance of "civilization" in a benighted Southeast Asia:

When a man leaves home, he sometimes travels more than mere physical distance. This happened to me in the middle years of the century when the U.S. government sent me to help our Asian friends in the Philippines and Vietnam cope with wars of rebellion and insurgency. I went far beyond the usual bounds given a military man after I discovered just what the people on these battlegrounds needed to guard against and what to keep strong. The needs are so universal in today's world that I decided to share the story of those days with others. . . .

You should know one thing at the beginning: I took my American beliefs with me into the Asian struggles, as Tom Paine would have done. Benjamin Franklin once said, "Where liberty dwells, there is my country." Tom Paine had replied, "Where liberty dwells not, there is my country." Paine's words form a cherished part of my credo. . . . Along with other Americans, I feel a kinship with Thomas Jefferson when he declared, "I have sworn upon the altar of God eternal hostility against every form of tyranny over the mind of man."[19]

And in between Fowler and Pyle, these representatives of the Old and the New Worlds, is, of course, the prize of this psychomachia: the Vietnamese girl Phuong (meaning, ironically, phoenix, the fiery bird that is reborn out of its ashes), who, in this allegorical context, is clearly a personification of Indochina itself: helpless in the face of her deracination by

the imperial West and always spoken for—represented—by its two manifestations. As Fowler recalls, "One always spoke of her [Phuong] like
that in the third person as though she were not there. Sometimes she
seemed invisible like peace" (*QA*, 44). Though Fowler's acute observation is a self-indictment of his vestigial colonialist perspective, the novel
makes it quite clear that Greene is far more sympathetic with this alienated European despite his opium habit, his ennui, his cynicism, his infi-
delity to his wife in England, and his refusal to commit himself to any
cause, than he is with the undeviatingly innocent and honorable, but
"morally" committed (Fowler's term, we recall, is "implacable," *QA*,
58), "quiet American," Alden Pyle.

II

The American exceptionalism—Pyle's New World disdain for the Old
World—Greene deconstructs is not ideological as such, a self-conscious
privileging of the American democratic creed over French colonialism; it
is, rather, a deeply felt belief, a "structure of feeling," in Raymond
Williams's[20] phrase, a "structure of attitude and reference," in Edward
Said's,[21] that Pyle understands to be commensurate with the truth of being
and, therefore, benign: a disinterested, universal truth that transcends the
limitations of the older, anachronistic, and interested imperial ideology of
the Old World and thus a far more viable means of winning "the hearts
and minds" of the Vietnamese people in the struggle against communism.
Like his historical and mythical originals, he undeviatingly believes that a
primitive Indochina would embrace his disinterested truths and the practical benefits they would bestow on its benighted people: freedom, prosperity, moral decency, civilization—the "good life" of the (Anglo-Protestant)
American dream or, to put it alternatively, of American democracy, what
the American government and the media relentlessly and misleadingly
called "the free world." Pyle's unshakably innocent and crude exceptionalist New World perspective is epitomized in *The Quiet American* when
Fowler recalls the conversation he had with Pyle in Phat Bien, a battle zone
to which the American had come ostensibly to confess his love for Phuong.
In this conversation, during which Pyle tells Fowler that Phuong needs his
protection from the decadence of French colonial Saigon, the European
exile replies prophetically that it is Phuong who needs to be protected from
the Bostonian (Puritan) morality of Pyle's care:

> He said, "You know, I think it was seeing all those girls in that
> house [a brothel to which Fowler has earlier taken Pyle]. They

were so pretty. Why, she might have been one of them. I wanted to protect her."

"I don't think she's in need of protection. . . ."

"You've seen so much more of the world than I have. You know, in some ways Boston is a bit—cramping. Even if you aren't a Lowell or a Cabot. I wish you'd advise me, Thomas."

"What about?"

"Phuong."

"If it's only her interests you care about, for God's sake leave Phuong alone. Like any other woman she'd rather have a good. . . ." The crash of a mortar saved Boston ears from the Anglo-Saxon word.

But there was a quality of the implacable in Pyle. . . .

"Why don't you just go away, Pyle, without causing trouble?"

"It wouldn't be fair to her, Thomas," he said quite seriously. I never knew a man who had better motives for all the trouble he caused. He added, "I don't think you quite understand Phuong." (QA, 58–60)

Despite Fowler's cynical evaluation of Phuong's (and women's) preferences—its crudity is motivated more by exasperation than considered belief—it is this recognition not only of the blindness of the American's oversight by an outsider, but also of the inevitable consequence of this blindness—his acute awareness that the Indochinese people need protection from their would-be New World protector—that the novel as a whole will enact.

As the above passage makes clear, Pyle is not a conspirator—a *political* manipulator—in the duplicitous sense of the word. His representation of Phuong—and the Indochina she personifies—is not the consequence of deliberation and calculation. Though he is clandestinely instigating a plot intended to create an indigenous "Third Force" favorable to the policies of the United States that would transcend the violence of French imperialism and the Soviet-style communism of the Viet Minh, Pyle believes that what he thinks and feels about Phuong and the Indochinese is the objective truth and that his actions are manifestations of it. He thus also believes his motives are morally honorable. From Fowler's external point of view, however, Pyle's benign truth and his honorable "honesty" is precisely what renders him Phuong's and Indochina's worst enemy.

Alden Pyle's American exceptionalism is not simply a matter of his inscribed and deeply backgrounded disdain for French imperialism and his missionary zeal to facilitate the imposition of an American-style democracy on a radically different culture, which he represents not simply as politically and morally primitive but also as being impeded in its desire for democracy by a decadent French colonialism and a totalitarian Soviet and Chinese communism. It is also a matter of his affective (mindless) adherence to the missionary Cold War scenario, which constitutes the contemporary instrumentalist avatar of this American missionary exceptionalism. This "scenario"—I use this ubiquitous visual metaphor not only to highlight the reduction of complex *historical* global phenomena to an inclusive spatial image, a microcosm that can be seen all at once, but also to make explicit the willful *simplification*, the dedifferentiation, such a reduction entails—is epitomized by the policy books of York Harding, the American East Asian area studies expert on whom Pyle relies to give credibility to his American exceptionalist ethos and practice in Indochina. This Cold War scenario, indissolubly related to the American exceptionalist mission in the Southeast Asian wilderness, as Fowler's repeated ironic references to York Harding's books suggest, is remarkably analogous to the functioning of the problematic Althusser analyzes. It inexorably determines not only Pyle's representation of the struggle in Indochina, but also its relationship to the complex global context, what in Pyle's eyes is visible and invisible, what he sees and what he is utterly and absolutely incapable of seeing in Indochina, even if it is there in all its stark singularity staring him in the face. York Harding, whose name floats insistently in and out of Fowler's narrative, is crucial not only to the content but also, as I will show, to the form of Greene's *Quiet American*. And since the role of this absent present figure in the novel has, despite his omnipresence, been overlooked or minimized, it behooves us to attend to it.

The first of the numerous references to York Harding in Fowler's narrative occurs immediately after his interrogation about the mysterious murder of Pyle by the detective Vigot (a reader, not incidentally, of Pascal) of the French *Sûreté*, which prefaces his account of the origins of his relationship with Pyle. In an unspoken flashback during this interrogation, Fowler, recalling his first meeting with Pyle, had imagined this "serious" and "very quiet American" as one who "Perhaps only ten days ago . . . had been walking back across the Common in Boston, his arms full of the books he had been reading *in advance* on the Far East and the problems of China" and had characterized his mission as a "determ[ination] to do good, not to any individual but to a country, a continent, a world" (my emphasis). And, alluding to his death (and resurrection) as well as the American errand in the wilderness, he had added, "Well, he was in his element now with the whole universe to improve" (*QA*, 18). Here, Fowler remembers Pyle asking,

"Have you read York Harding?

"No. No, I don't thinks so. What did he write?"

He gazed at a milk-bar across the street and said dreamily, "that looks like a soda-fountain. . . .He looked reluctantly away from the milk-bar and said, "York wrote a book called *The Advance of Red China*. It's a profound book.

"I haven't read him. Do you know him?"

He nodded solemnly and lapsed into silence. But he broke it again a moment later to modify the impression he had given. "I don't know him well," he said. "I guess I only met him twice." . . . I was to learn later that he had an enormous respect for what he called serious writers. That term excluded novelists, poets and dramatists unless they had what he called a contemporary theme, and even then it was better to read the straight stuff as you got it from York.

I said, "You know, if you live in a place for long you cease to read about it."

"Of course I always like to know what the man on the spot has to say," he replied guardedly.

"And then check it with York?"

"Yes." (*QA*, 23–24)

Following this resonant exchange, Fowler goes on to tell Pyle what he knows about the situation in Indochina, stressing its complexity—the inconsequentiality of guerrilla war in the north, in which the enemy of the French is never visible, the precariousness of French control of the south, the private armies (Caodaists, Hoa-Hoa, and the Binh Xuyen, "who sold their services for money or revenge" and "now . . . there's General Thé. He was Caodaist chief of Staff, but he's taken to the hills to fights both sides, the French, the Communist"). At this point, as if the complexity of Fowler's history of the Indochina War was inconsequential, Pyle interrupts him: "York," Pyle said, "wrote that what the East needed was a Third Force" (*QA*, 24–25).

Later in the novel, Fowler informs us that it was precisely to clandestinely organize such a "Third Force" between a degenerate French colonialism and a brutal Viet Minh communism by way of enlisting the services of General Thé[22] that lay behind Pyle's ostensible attachment to the American economic mission. I will return to the nature and consequence of this collaboration, in which York Harding's books are complicitous. Here, I want both to elaborate Greene's ideological intention in introducing this American journalist "scholar," who, like the facile area expert the U.S. government, as Said insistently reminded us, has come increasingly to rely on for its foreign policy decisions, is, in fact, physically remote from the turbulent locus and action of the story Fowler is telling, and to suggest in what sense this intention is proleptic of the poststructuralist critique of representation as well as the New Americanist critique of American imperialism.

York Harding is an American journalist, specifically a "diplomatic correspondent," who specializes in the "Far East," one who, Fowler tells Vigot at the end of the novel, "had been here [in Indochina] for a week on his way from Bangkok to Tokyo" (*QA*, 168). Greene, in fact, insistently emphasizes Harding's geographical remoteness from Indochina to suggest the inordinate degree to which his several books about the West's relationship to the Far East—*The Advance of Red China, The Challenge to Democracy, The Role of the West*" (*QA*, 28)—derive, not from immediate knowledge, but from the visualist logic of the Cold War *scenario* as it pertained to Maoist China, if not from other books about the Far East written from a Western, particularly American, perspective, and therefore of the blindness of his oversight to the corrosive realities of that inordinately complex and fractured world. Greene's portrayal of York Harding, in other words, not only anticipates Althusser's analysis of the metaphysics/international politics of the liberal capitalist problematic. It is also proleptic of Edward Said's similar analysis of the onto-imperial logic of Orientalism—of the authors of the *Description de l'Égypte*, who had accompanied Napoleon's imperial legions to Egypt, the "disinterested" European scientific scholars of the Orient such as Sir William Jones, Edward Lane, Sir Hamilton Gibb, Silvestre de Sacy, and Ernest Renan, and, not least, the area studies "experts," such as Walt Rostow, Henry Kissinger, Paul Wolfowitz among many others, who came to replace these earlier Orientalist models in the wake of America's ascendancy to global dominance after World War II—in precisely the sense Said gives the term in identifying this Occidental representational discourse about the Orient with the dangerously quixotic "textual attitude":

> It may appear strange to speak about something or someone as holding a *textual attitude*, but a student of literature will understand the phrase more easily if he will recall the kind of view attacked by Voltaire in *Candide*, or the attitude to reality satirized by Cervantes in *Don Quixote*. What seems unexceptionable good sense to these writers is that it is a fallacy to assume that the swarming, unpredictable, and problematic mess in which human beings live can be understood on the basis of what books—texts—say; to apply what one learns out of a book literally to reality is to risk folly or ruin. . . .

There is a rather complex dialectic of reinforcement by which the experiences of readers in reality are determined by what they have read, and this in turn influences writers to take up subjects defined in advance by readers' experience. . . . A text purporting to contain knowledge about something actual, and arising out of circumstances similar to the ones I have jut described [the public "success" of its representation] is not easily dismissed. Expertise is attributed to it. The authority of academics, institutions, and governments can accrue to it, surrounding it with still greater prestige than its practical successes warrant. Most important, such texts can *create* not only knowledge but also the very reality they appear to describe. In time such knowledge and reality produce a tradition, or what Michel Foucault calls a discourse, whose material presence or weight, not the originality of a given author, is really responsible for the texts produced out if it.[23]

More specifically, York Harding's Cold War Orientalism is everywhere informed by the "domino theory"—or, more precisely, a domino theory that was indissolubly related to the Protestant American exceptionalist disdain of the Old World colonialism of France—that pervaded the discourse and practice of America in the aftermath of World War II, especially in the immediate wake of the Chinese revolution, as the enormous influence of such Cold War/Orientalist books as Tom Dooley's *Deliver Us from Evil* (1956) and Burdick and Lederer's *The Ugly American* (1958) had on the policies of the American government in the early stages of its involvement in Vietnam testifies. This was the fallacious but unshakable assumption that the Viet Minh insurgency against French colonial rule was not simply communist dominated, but was masterminded by the Soviet Union and/or Maoist China and that if Indochina (Vietnam) were allowed to fall to the communists, this soft and unmanly policy would encourage further communist aggression that would eventually end in the "loss" of all of Southeast Asia (and eventually the entire Third World) to the free world and its absorption into the expanding orbit of the communist East. This assumption rigidly determined the foreign (and domestic) policy not only of the Truman and Eisenhower administrations, which were contemporary with the historical occasion of *The Quiet American*, but also of the Kennedy, Johnson, and Nixon administrations, which, as Greene anticipates, escalated the clandestine "spook" war in the immediate aftermath of the Geneva Accords into an all-out— virtually genocidal—military war.

This exceptionalist Cold War Orientalism pervades *The Quiet American*, but it is epitomized in the conversation Fowler recalls between himself and Pyle when, after their car has broken down on the way back from the Caodaist festival at Tanyin to Saigon (where Pyle had secretly met with General Thé), they are trapped in a watchtower manned by two frightened Vietnamese soldiers who had been conscripted by the French:

> "No French officer," I said, "would care to spend the night alone with two scared guards in one of these towers. . . . You and your like are trying to make a war with the help of people who just aren't interested."
>
> "They don't want Communism."
>
> "They want enough rice," I said, "They don't want to be shot at. . . . They don't want our white skins around telling them what they want. "
>
> "If Indo-China goes. . . ."
>
> "I know the record. Siam goes. Malaya goes. Indonesia goes. What does 'go' mean? If I believed in your ["Unitarian"] God and another life, I'd bet my future harp against your golden crown that in five hundred years there may be no New York or London, but they'll be growing paddy in these fields, they'll be carrying their produce to market on long poles wearing pointed hats. . . ."
>
> "They'll be forced to believe what they are told, they won't be allowed to think for themselves."
>
> "Thought's a luxury. Do you think the peasant sits and thinks of God and Democracy when he gets inside his mud hut at night?"
>
> "You talk as if the whole country were peasant. What about the educated? Are they going to be happy?"
>
> "Oh, no," I said, "we've brought them up in *our* ideas. We've taught them dangerous games, and that's why we are waiting here, hoping we don't get our throats cut. We deserve to have them cut. I wish your friend York was here too. I wonder how he'd relish it."
>
> "York Harding's a very courageous man. Why, in Korea. . . ."
>
> "He wasn't an enlisted man, was he? He had a return ticket. With a return ticket courage becomes an intellectual exercise, like a monk's flagellation. How much can I stick? Those poor devils can't catch a plane home. Hi," I called to them, "what are your names?" . . . They think we are French," I said.
>
> "That's just it," Pyle said. "You shouldn't be against York, you should be against the French. Their colonialism."
>
> "Isms and ocracies. Give me facts." (*QA*, 94–95)

Though Fowler's perspective is problematic (for it, too, is Orientalist, though vestigially and far less devastating in its effects), what Greene is suggesting here, in underscoring York Harding's spatial remoteness from the recalcitrant singularities of the Indochinese occasion, is the revelatory irony of a discourse that, by miniaturizing these global singularities—by reducing their elusive force to a microcosmic-territorizlized/geopolitical, picture— this enables him to see *all*—from a distance, that is, to render what counts—the corrosive realities—invisible and unsayable. In other words, in focusing York Harding's adherence to the domino theory—the aspect of his Cold War Orientalism pertaining to Southeast Asia—that determined his view of the complex realities of the struggle between the French and the Viet Minh in Indochina, Greene shows that American democracy and the individualism it privileges over the collective, espoused in Harding's books against the totalitarianism of China and the Soviet Union, on the one hand, and the colonialism of France, on the other—Said would call their purpose "crisis management"—are both informed by a Quixotic or Panglossian totalizing teleological perspective. No less than the colonialism of the French and the communism of China and the Soviet Union, this democratic teleopanopticism coerces (colonizes) the recalcitrantly differential historicity of the Vietnamese history it is representing into conforming with its preestablished American exceptionalist end (*telos*), renders it, that is, an integral part of the larger *design*. But in thus *mediating* (or territorializing) the *immediate* (temporality), it also exposes—makes visible to an outsider—the differential reality—not least, the existential humanity of the Vietnamese people, if not their anticolonialist struggle for independence from colonial rule—which Harding's problematic makes invisible.

To put it alternatively, this Hardyan anticommunist and anticolonial democratic discourse is no less totalitarian than the totalitarianism it always measures itself against, insofar as it is inscribed by a concealed teleo-panoptic perspective. Like the French colonialism and Maoist or Stalinist communism that Pyle vilifies, it is informed by a will to power over alterity that has as its end the totalization of the differential phenomena of being. The difference is that this transcendental perspective is rendered invisible by a discourse of imminence, "a natural supernaturalism," to use the term Said borrows from M. H. Abrams to indict the "objective science" of the Orientalist Ernest Renan,[24] that privileges the "free" individual. This distinction, as Foucault, Said, and other poststructuralist theorists have decisively shown, has been fundamental to the justification of liberal capitalist democracy since the period of the Enlightenment, which bore witness to the rise of the bourgeoisie and the "disinterested" or "objective" discourse of liberal humanism. I am referring to what Foucault has called the "repressive hypothesis," which, in assuming the truth (as it has been interpreted in Western democratic societies) to be external to power—its antithesis or natural adversary (as in the phrase "the truth will set you free"), obscures the fact that this "truth" is disciplinary and thus complicitous with power, that the discourse of the free individual, unlike the collectivist totalitarian societies where power is overt, hides the machinery of its power:

> The individual is no doubt the fictitious atom of an *"ideological"* representation of society; but he is also a reality fabricated by this specific technology of power that I have called "discipline." We must cease once and for all to describe the effects of power in negative terms: it "excludes," it "represses," it "censors," it "abstracts," it "masks," it "conceals." In fact, power . . . produces reality.[25]

Seen from the outside, this "'changed terrain'"[26] that Fowler's alienated Europeanism enables, Alden Pyle's assimilation of York Harding's books to his American exceptionalist ethos has, despite his commitment to democracy and the free will it apotheosizes against totalitarianism, annulled his agency and rendered him a puppet ventriloquized by Harding's Cold War Orientalism. To put it in terms of Althusser's analysis of the liberal capitalist problematic, Pyle's "sighting," is seen to be "no longer the act of an individual subject, endowed with the faculty of 'vision' which he exercises either attentively or distractedly; the sighting is that of its structural conditions. . . . It is literally no longer the eye (the mind's eye) of a subject which *sees* what exists in the field defined by a theoretical problematic; it is this field itself which *sees itself* in the objects or problems it defines—sighting being merely the necessary reflection of the field on its objects." Fowler invokes precisely this metaphorics of sight and its *other*—oversight—early in the novel, in anticipation of the "denouement" of the narrative of Pyle's assassination that is to follow, when, irritated by the bathos of the cable the American economic attaché sends to Pyle's parents ("Grieved to report your son died a soldier's death in the cause of Democracy"), and the duplicity of his reference to Pyle's work for the economic aid mission, he recalls:

> Vigot's phrase came back to me. . . . He was a very quiet American.
> "Have you any hunch, he asked, "why they killed him and who?" Suddenly I was angry. I was tired of the whole pack of them with their private stores of Coca Cola and their portable hospitals and their too wide cars and their not quite latest guns. I said, "Yes. They killed him because he was too innocent to live. He was young and ignorant and silly and he got involved. He

had no more of a notion than any of you what the whole affair's about, and you gave him money and York Harding's books on the East and said, "Go ahead. Win the East for democracy." He never *saw anything* he hadn't heard in a lecture hall. And his writers and his lecturers made a fool of him. When he *saw* a dead body he couldn't even *see* wounds. A red menace. A soldier of democracy. (*QA*, 31–32)

It is the terrible paradoxical consequences of this single-minded American exceptionalist Cold War problematic—this "very, very *serious*" (*QA*, 23)[27] and innocent blindness to difference—that Greene's Voltairean novel will enact.

III

Fowler's retrospective narrative following Pyle's murder takes the form of what Edward Said would call a "contrapuntal" structural movement in which the personal theme—the struggle between Fowler and Pyle over the affections of Phuong—is counterpointed by the political—Fowler's struggle to remain disengaged in the context of his increasing awareness of the destructive potential of Pyle's Hardyan Cold War Orientalist perspective on Indochina. Fowler tells the reader at the outset that he was suspected by the Pascalian French detective Vigot of having committed the murder in the name of revenge against Pyle's alienation of Phuong's affection. This information is counterposed by his informing us that he had, through his Indian assistant, Dominguez, discovered that the "quiet American's" real mission in Indochina was to establish a Third Force (just as the United States, in violation of the Geneva Accords of 1954, had installed Ngo Dinh Diem as the "president" of South Vietnam) that, he, following York Harding' scenario, believed would save Indochina from the ravages of European (French) imperialism and Maoist communism:

"How much do you know of your friend Pyle?" [Dominguez asks.]

"Not very much. Our tracks cross, that's all. I haven't seen him since Tanyin." [This was the area "where General Thé, the dissident Chief of Staff who has recently declared his intention to fight both the French and the Viet Minh", held out. *QA*, 84.]

"What job does he do?"

"Economic Mission, but that covers a multitude of sins. I think he's interested in home-industries—I suppose with an

American business tie-up. I don't like the way they keep the French fighting and cut out their business at the same time.

"I heard him talking the other day at a party the Legation was giving to visiting Congressmen. They had put him on to brief them."

"God help Congress," I said, "he hasn't been in the country six months."

"He was talking about the old colonial powers—England and France, and how you two couldn't expect to win the confidence of the Asiatics. That was where America came in now with clean hands."

"Hawaii, Puerto Rico," I said, "New Mexico."

"Then someone asked him some stock question about the chances of the Government here ever beating the Vietminh and he said a Third Force could do it. There was always a Third Force to be found free from Communism and the taint of colonialism—national democracy he called it; you only had to find a leader and keep him safe from the old colonial powers."

"It's all in York Harding," I said. "He had read it before he came out here. He talked about it his first week and he's learned nothing."

"He may have found his leader," Dominguez said. (*QA*, 124)

Following this lead, Fowler learned from Dominguez's contact, a communist or a member of the Vietminh named Heng, that the plastics Pyle had been importing from the United States were intended to make bombs and that they were being sent to General Thé. Later, in the context of an altercation over Phuong, during which Pyle's reassertion that he "want[s] to protect her" makes explicit once more the allegorical character of the novel, Fowler reacts to the blindness of Pyle's benignly innocent motives—they are, it is important to point out, simultaneously ontological, epistemological, and political—by alluding to the plastics and warns him: "'I hope to God you know what you are doing there. Oh, I know your motives are good, they always are.' He looked puzzled and suspicious. 'I wish sometimes you had a few bad motives, you might understand a little more about human beings. And that applies to your country too, Pyle'" (*QA*, 133).

At the end of this exchange, which brings Part 2 of the novel to its close, Fowler recounts his exasperation with Pyle's unshakable American innocence, telling him to "Go to your Third Force and York Harding and the Rôle of Democracy. Go away and play with plastics." Nothing he might tell this quiet, serious, and optimistic American about the human condition and the political situation in Indochina could have penetrated his implacable

Hardyan perspective. He was, in Althusser's terms, irretrievably the instrument of the American exceptionalist/Cold War/Orientalist problematic. Having finally realized that Pyle's contempt for Old World colonialism, his certainty of the benignity of America's exceptionalist mission in the wilderness of Indochina, and his assumption that his interlocutor's warning is tainted by his European decadence are absolute, he adds, "Later I had to admit that he had carried out my instructions to the letter" (*QA*, 132–134). Pyle's "accomplishment" of these "instructions," which, in fact, was the utterly destined—and self-destructive—end of his exceptionalist Hardyan problematic, brings Fowler's story to its horrifically paradoxical end. In a moment of self-criticism, Fowler again, this time sympathetically, in a way that invokes the blindness of his own decaying Old World self as a means of penetrating the New World certainty of Pyle's textural attitude, pleads with Pyle not to "trust too much in York Harding":

> "We are the old colonial peoples, Pyle, but we've learned a bit of reality, we've learned not to play with matches. This Third Force—it comes out of a book, that's all. General Thé's only a bandit with a few thousand men: he's not a national democracy. . . . But, Pyle, you can't trust men like Thé. They aren't going to save the East from Communism. We know their kind."
> "We?"
> "The old colonialists."
> "I thought you took no sides."
> "I don't, Pyle, but if someone has got to make a mess of things in your outfit, leave it to Joe [the American attaché]. Go home with Phuong. Forget the Third Force." (*QA*, 157)

But Fowler's plea, which, it should be noted, calls on Pyle to abandon his panoptic perspective of mediation for the existential situation of immediacy, goes unheard. In the inexorable name of establishing this Third Force in Indochina, Pyle conspires with General Thé to undertake a series of terrorist bombings in the heart of Saigon that were calculated to be attributed to the communists. The second of these, Fowler recalls, occurs while he is in a cafe across the way from a milk-bar where Phuong habitually went at that precise time of day, wondering what the two American girls sitting nearby meant when one of them had said that they had been warned to leave before eleven twenty-five. Following the explosions, Fowler, anxious about Phuong's safety, rushes out into the smoking carnage of the square and encounters Pyle, who, in response to Fowler's anxiety over Phuong's safety, informs him that he had warned her beforehand to stay away from the milk-bar. With this information, "the pieces," Fowler says, "fell together in my mind" (*QA*, 161). I quote this climactic moment of Fowler's story at some length not only to suggest the disclosive power that Greene achieves in juxtaposing Pyle's mindless and indiscriminate enactment of the "truth" of the American exceptionalist ethos, as that deeply backgrounded myth was incorporated into the Cold War problematic, with its murderous consequences for innocent human life, but also to suggest how proleptic of the bloody history of America's benign global "vision" it has been ever since this pre-Vietnam War moment about which Greene is writing, including the United States' post-9/11 "war on terror"

"There mustn't be any American causalities, must there?" [Fowler tells Pyle] An ambulance forced its way up the rue Catinat into the square and the policeman who had stopped me moved to one side to let it through. . . . I pushed Pyle forward and ahead of me into the square before we could be stopped.

We were among a congregation of mourners. The police could prevent others entering the square; they were powerless to clear the square of the survivors and the first-comers. The doctors were too busy to attend to the dead, and so the dead were left to their owners, for one can own the dead as one owns a chair. A woman sat on the ground with what was left of her baby in her lap; with a kind of modesty, she had covered it with her straw peasant hat. She was still silent, and what struck me most in the square was the silence. . . . The legless torso, at the edge of the garden still twitched, like a chicken which has lost its head. From the man's shirt, he had probably been a trishaw driver.

Pyle said, "It's awful." He looked at the wet on his shoes and said in a sick voice, "What's that?"

"Blood," I said, "Haven't you ever seen it before?"

He said, "I must get them cleaned before I see the Minister." I don't think he knew what he was saying. He was seeing a real war for the first time: he had punted down into Phat Diem in a kind of schoolboy dream, and anyway in his eyes soldiers didn't count.

I forced him, with my hand on his shoulder, to look around. I said, "This is the hour when the place is always full of women and children—it's the shopping hour. Why choose that of all hours?"

He said weakly, "There was to have been a parade."

"And you hoped to catch a few colonels. But the parade was cancelled yesterday, Pyle."

"I didn't know."

"Didn't know!" I pushed him into a patch of blood where a stretcher had lain. "You ought to be better informed."

"I was out of town," he said, looking down at his shoes. "They should have called it off."

"And miss the fun?" I asked him. "Do you expect General Thé to lose his demonstration? This is better than a parade. Women and children are news, and soldiers aren't, in a war. This will hit the world's Press. You've put General Thé on the map all right, Pyle. You've got the Third Force and National Democracy all over your right shoe. Go home to Phuong and tell her about your heroic dead—there are a few dozen less of her people to worry about." (QA, 161–162)

It is precisely this violent "end" of the logic of Pyle's—and America's—mediated exceptionalist perspective—this blindness of his benign, all-encompassing Hardyan oversight, the visualist (onto)logic of which necessarily terminates in the dreadful banality of his (and America's) indifference to the indiscriminate killing of his (its) "invisible" Other (now, in the wake of the Vietnam War, grotesquely called "collateral damage")[28]—that Greene's novel about sighting discloses:

Unlike them [the people who were already flocking into the nearby cathedral] I had reason for thankfulness, for wasn't Phuong alive? Hadn't Phuong been "warned"? But what I remembered was the torso in the square, the baby on its mother's lap. They had not been warned: they had not been sufficiently important. . . . A two-hundred-pound bomb does not discriminate. How many dead colonels justify a child's or a trishaw driver's death when you are building a national democratic front? (QA, 163)

By way of Pyle's Panglossian inability to *see* the blood he sees on his shoe, Fowler realizes definitively that this exceptionalist American puppet, ventriloquized by York Harding's Cold War problematic, cannot be deflected from his preordained, single-minded "errand in the wilderness" of Indochina—his mission to build a national democracy ("the City on a Hill") in a culturally foreign land—no matter how powerfully historical and cultural reality impinges on his deeply inscribed consciousness: "He was impregnably armoured by his good intentions."[29] Fowler thus silently concludes: "What's the good? He'll always be innocent, you can't blame the innocent, they are always guiltless. All you can do is control them or eliminate them. Innocence is a kind of insanity." He goes to the Quai Mytho, where his communist contact, Heng, lives. Against his will to remain disengaged, Fowler finally becomes *engagé*: he arranges with Heng for the assassination of Pyle.

IV

The beginning of the last part of *The Quiet American* returns overtly to the detective-story motif that, as I indicated earlier, constitutes the fundamental structural principle of Greene's novel. I am referring to the occasion immediately after Pyle's body has been found in the muddy water under the bridge to Dakow, when Fowler is again being interrogated by Vigot, the French detective, in his apartment, an interrogation, not incidentally, over which the absent yet ubiquitous presence of York Harding presides in the form of his book *The Role of the West*, which Fowler had taken from Pyle's apartment "as a keepsake" after his death (*QA*, 29). In this final interrogation, which precedes Fowler's retrospective account of his meeting with Heng and his last conversation with Pyle before his death, Greene's deconstruction of the structural (onto)logic of the traditional detective story (and, by extension, of the narrative of American Cold War/Orientalist exceptionalism) comes to its bitterly paradoxical end: the ostensible victim of the crime comes to be seen as its perpetrator

> I held the whiskey out to him [Vigot] so that he could see how calm my nerves were. "Vigot, I wish you'd tell me why you think I was concerned in Pyle's death. Is it a question of motive? That I wanted Phuong back? Or do you imagine it was revenge for losing her?"
>
> "No, I'm not stupid. One doesn't take one's enemy's book as a souvenir. There it is on your self. *The Rôle of the West.* Who is this York Harding?"
>
> "He is the man you are looking for, Vigot. *He killed Pyle—at long range.*"
>
> "I don't understand."
>
> "He's a superior sort of journalist—they call them diplomatic correspondents. *He gets hold of an idea and then alters every situation to fit the idea.* Pyle came out here full of York Harding's idea. Harding had been here once for a week on his way from Bangkok to Tokyo. Pyle made the mistake of putting his idea into practice. Harding wrote about a Third Force. Pyle formed one—a shoddy little bandit with two thousand men and a couple of tame tigers. He got mixed up." (*QA*, 167–168; my emphasis)

From the panoptic perspective of the detective story—the form that brings the spatializing metaphysical or beginning-middle-end logic of Western narrative to its positivist fulfillment in its privileging of Identity over difference, the One over the many, Space over time, the Eye over the other senses, the Visible over the invisible[30]—one is, of course, compelled to conclude that it is Fowler who killed Pyle insofar as he informed the communists about Pyle's clandestine mission and told them that "he's got to be stopped." (*QA*, 173). But from the imminent or situated perspective—the "changed terrain"—of *The Quiet American*, which rejects the metaphysics of traditional detective fiction, the "retrospective" or panoptic gaze, and the reductive binary logic endemic to these, this factual evidence is absolutely irrelevant insofar as its appropriation for a preconceived design (plot) is the consequence of the blindness of oversight. The murderer of Pyle, Greene's antinovel implies, is Pyle himself or, more precisely, the Pyle who, ventriloquized by York Harding's exceptionalilst/Cold War/Orientalist problematic, becomes its agent, or, to put it alternatively, the Pyle who cannot *see* what he sees when he looks at the blood of the innocent victims of his murderous American innocence.

Not the least irony of Greene's "detective story" (*QA*, 170) is that its literal detective, Vigot, the Old World reader of Pascal's *Pensées*, who has inferred Fowler's complicity by way of his meticulous empirical logic, refuses to act on this "knowledge." In the classical detective story (and the literature of the Western tradition in general), the detective, armed with an acute empirical mind, solves the mystery in the end and recuperates the order and peace that have been shattered by the crime. In Greene's novel, the detective, Vigot, "solves" the crime, but does not act on it. This is because he, like Fowler, comes to perceive the crime on an entirely different moral register than that of the laws of cause and effect that structure detective fiction, that is, from outside the American, New World, exceptionalist problematic. In the end, he reconstellates Fowler's "crime" against Pyle into the larger ontological, moral, and sociopolitical context that has been precipitated by the latter's terrorist fulfillment of his Hardyan problematic—not simply his slaughter of innocents, but also his establishment of a Third Force destined to exacerbate rather than ameliorate the volatile conditions in Indochina—and his callous inability to see the blood of his innocent victims on his shoe: what Hannah Arendt, a few years later and in another, but not dissimilar context, would come to call "the banality of evil."[31] What is at stake for Vigot—and Greene—is not Fowler's empirical mind, but his soul, that is, his comportment toward being at large. This is not only suggested by his Pascalian perspective (the imperative to choose in the context of the *deus absconditas*) (*QA*, 16, 138–139), but also by Fowler's acute sense of Vigot's priestly calling and by his Dostoievskian account of their last interview in the language of the confessional:

> "You would have made a good priest, Vigot. What is it about you that would make it so easy to confess—if there were anything to confess?

"I have never wanted confessions."

"But you've received then?

"From time to time."

"Is it because like a priest it's your job not to be shocked, but to be sympathetic. . . .

"You have a whimsical imagination. Aren't you drinking, Fowler?"

"Surely it's unwise for a criminal to drink with a police officer?"

"I have never said you were a criminal."

"But suppose the drink unlocked even in me the desire to confess? There are no secrets of the confessional in your profession."

"Secrecy is seldom important to a man who confesses: even when it's to a priest. He has other motives."

"To cleanse himself?"

"Not always. . . . You are not a criminal, Fowler, but I would like to know why you lied to me. You saw Pyle the night he died." (QA, 168)

Unlike the classical detective story, the crime in *The Quiet American*, in short, remains unsolved and the reader, seeking closure, is denied the sense of an ending, is dislocated into a "changed terrain," where the invisible of the American problematic becomes visible and hauntingly *thought-provoking.*[32]

All this is not to say that Fowler is simply Greene's spokesperson. On the contrary, Greene is implicitly critical of him. After all, Fowler is a cynical and decadent European, who admits his kinship with "the old colonial peoples" (QA, 157); he is a fallen Catholic alienated from his wife in England; he smokes opium to obliterate his consciousness of the morass of his personal and public life; he is plagued by jealously over Phuong; he *speaks for* the subalterns: two Vietnamese soldiers in the tower, and, not least, Phuong (and the Indochinese people) whom he treats as if she were an object at his command, though, unlike Pyle, he is aware of this: "She's no child," he tells Pyle,

> "She's tougher than you'll ever be. Do you know the kind of polish that doesn't scratch? That's Phuong. She can survive a dozen of us. . . . she won't scratch, she'll only decay." But even while I made my speech and watched her turn the page (a family group with Princess Anne), I knew I was inventing a character just as much as Pyle was. One never knows another human being; for all I could tell, she was as scared as the rest of us; she didn't have the gift of expression, that's all. And I remembered that first tor-

menting year when I had tried so passionately to understand her, when I had begged her to tell me what she thought and had scared her with my unreasoning anger at her silences. Even my desire had been a weapon, as though when one plunged one's sword towards the victim's womb, she would lose control and speak. (*QA*, 133)

It is quite clear, furthermore, that Fowler feels a peculiar, if ambiguous, kind of attraction to Pyle that derives, no doubt, from a recognition of his own fundamental (European) corruption, one manifestation of which is his awareness of his moral paralysis (what he calls non-involvement)—his inability to make any positive contribution to the solution of the moral and sociopolitical morass that is Indochina. It is, no doubt, this complex feeling of inadequacy instigated by European fallenness that in some sense initially drew him to his opposite: the American idealist for whom the world is new and filled with potential; or, to put it in the terms Americans have perennially used to refer to their optimistic national identity, the American Adam.[33] And in the end, we find that he was also, and all along, filled with a kind of remorse for his act. As he gazes at York Harding's book, *The Rôle of the West*, which "stood out like a cabinet portrait—of a young man with a crew-cut and a black dog at his heels," Fowler reiterates that he "could harm no one any more." And yet, despite his awareness that "everything had gone right with [him] since he had died," he "wished there existed someone to whom [he] could say that [he] was sorry." (*QA*, 188–189)

Nevertheless, it is precisely Fowler's fallenness, his identification with the decadent Old World that enables him, as it were, to *see* the blood on Pyle's shoe to which Pyle is blind. This Europe is not imperial Europe in its prime; it is a postcolonial Europe, a Europe whose imperial logic and practice has come to its end in the double sense of its fulfillment and demise, a Europe, in other words, that, in fulfilling the potential of empire has paradoxically self-destructed: disclosed or, better, precipitated its hitherto invisible *Other*: that which has haunted the logic and practice of European imperialism from the beginning, but which, now, at its end, when its logic has been fulfilled, can no longer be contained within its circumference. Understood in this sense, Fowler's identification with the decadence of "the old colonial peoples" also entails his awareness of his alienation from it, an awareness that is epitomized by his revulsion for the decadent French rubber planter whose apartment, with its pornographic art, he wanted to purchase: "I was glad Pyle had not seen him; the man might have lent his features to Pyle's imaginary 'old colonialist,' who was repulsive enough without him" (*QA*, 158). He, too, as his exile from his homeland makes quite clear, is a displaced person, an emigré, a nomad in Edward Said's terms, who, precisely because of his decentered condition is enabled to *see* what Pyle's exceptionalist/Cold War/Orientalist problematic renders invisible to him: the blood of his innocent victims on his shoe that is the inevitable consequence of his act of terror—for that is what Pyle's act really is.[34] That is to say, Fowler's being outside/in (apart, from/of) the imperial problematic enables him to see Pyle's American exceptionalism as a myth that obfuscates the continuity between America's "benign" "errand in the wilderness" of Indochina and the Old World's imperial history and his covert effort to create a Third Force, as the beginning of a process that will repeat the European imperial experience: the colonization of a Third World country that will inevitably devastate that which it would "save" for democracy, but in the end will self-destruct, that is, produce the very differential forces that will defeat it. This, I suggest, is why, immediately after its publication in 1955, *The Quiet American* was condemned by American reviewers as a reactionary affirmation of the anachronistic Old World ethos—"'an exercise in national projection' by a member of the British Empire history had passed by,"[35] and was willfully misrepresented—recast to reverse Greene's condemnation of Pyle's (and America's) blundering Panglossian New World intervention in the wilderness of Vietnam—in the film of the same name by Joseph Mankiewitcz (1958), which made Pyle (Audie Murphy) its sympathetic protagonist.[36]

Coda
The Quiet American and 9/11

As I have suggested, Greene's fictional representation of America's initial intervention in Indochina anticipates the volatile future history of the Vietnam War: (1) the United States' implacable but finally futile effort to create a Third Force—a "National Democracy"[37]—that would transcend the corrupt exploitative practices of Old World colonialism and the oppressiveness of communism in a land whose inhabitants constituted an entirely foreign culture; (2) its relentless and indiscriminate (i.e., terrorist) devastation of Vietnam—its land, its people, and its culture—in the name of its undeviating exceptionalist mission to save Vietnam for "the free world";[38] and (3) the self-destruction of this exceptionalist logic at the very moment of its fulfillment in practice.

Equally, if not more important, *The Quiet American*, in its revelatory focus on the overdetermined role that York Harding's Cold War/Orientalist books play in Pyle's deadly benign mission in the Vietnam "wilderness," is proleptic of the New Americanist critique of the undeviating reliance of the United States on what Antonio Gramsci calls "the discourse of hegemony"; Louis Althusser, "the problematic"; Michel Foucault, "discourse"; and, most lucidly, Edward Said, "the textual attitude," in its determination of the "truth" of Vietnam and of its cultural, political, and military practices. I mean that mediated perspective on history that, in privileging the eye and the distance from and miniaturization of the world it enables, not only blinds it to the differential reality on which it gazes, but also eventually atrophies the perceiver's affective sense.

Read in the context of this "changed terrain," *The Quiet American*, long before the New Americanists, spoke the truth to the appalling reductiveness—and the devastating banality—of the representations of Vietnam proliferated endlessly by the Pentagon planners, the military strategists in Saigon, the media, Hollywood, and, as we shall see in the next two chapters, all too many of the American soldiers who fought the war (during and after it), all of whom in some degree or other were blinded by the oversight of their textual attitude, that is, were rendered, like York Harding and his enthusiastic ephebe, incapable of *seeing*—of bearing witness to—the carnage they wrought and saw in Vietnam.[39]

But my intention in retrieving Graham Greene's *The Quiet American* from its past has not simply been to demonstrate its significance as a proleptic counterhistory of the period of the Vietnam War and its immediate aftermath. I have also wanted to suggest its uncanny relevance to the contemporary American occasion: 9/11 and America's global "war on terror." As I have shown elsewhere[40]—and will reiterate in the chapters that follow—the aftermath of the Vietnam War bore witness to the systematic forgetting of its historical actualities by way of the combined efforts of the American government, the media, and Hollywood (what Adorno called the culture industry) to recuperate the consensus, that is, the American national identity, that was shattered when the inordinately violent sociopolitical and military practices of the United States in a small Third World country delegitimized its theoretical justification of the war. I am not simply referring to the American cultural memory's airbrushing of the United States' clandestine subversion of the Geneva Accords that had brought the long struggle between the French colonial army and the Viet Minh to it end; its killing and maiming of untold numbers of Vietnamese civilians in its unrelenting and undiscriminating war of attrition in the face of a strategically invisible enemy (its search and destroy missions, scorched earth operations, and massive B-52 bombings); its devastation of the Vietnamese land (the defoliation of its forests and the use of chemical herbicides like Agent Orange); and, not least, its mindlessly indifferent reduction of a traditional rice culture to a deracinated society of refugees—all in the unrelenting name of saving Vietnam for the "free world." I am also referring to the cultural recuperation of the myth of American exceptionalism and the benign rhetoric, popular and intellectual, circulating around the "divinely" or "historically" ordained mission (errand) in the world's wilderness. This willful national amnesia and reaffirmation of the American national identity—this "textual attitude"—(re)produced by the narcotics of the culture industry and relegitimized by the intellectual deputies of the dominant culture—enabled the first Bush administration to undertake the Gulf War of 1991 and that president's declaration in its immediate aftermath that Americans had "kicked the Vietnam syndrome at last." Greatly aided by the Al Qaeda attacks on the World Trade Center and the Pentagon on 9/11/01, this amnesia also mobilized this negative into a highly energized positive—a virtually hysterical patriotic—and religioracist—fervor that prompted the second Bush administration to undertake the enactment of the global scenario its neoconservative intellectual deputies (PNAC), like York Harding in *The Quiet American*, had conceived long before 9/11: its announcement, more or less unilaterally, to the world—and in defiance of international law—of a global "war on terrorism"; its unleashing of preemptive wars first against the Taliban regime in Afghanistan and then against Saddam Hussein's Iraq; and its installation of puppet regimes intended to impose American-style capitalist democracies on these Islamic cultures (and any other that it deemed a threat to the *Pax Americana*), in the name of its rejuvenated exceptionalist global errand, now represented by its policy experts as saving the world for "civilization."

In the process of achieving a "benign" end in the Middle East, America, like the fictional America of *The Quiet American*—represented by the Pyle ventriloquized by the exceptionalist Cold War/Orientalist problematic of York Harding—has been compelled to see in the Middle Eastern world only that which its renewed global vision allows it to see, a telling example of which is the Bush administration's undeviating assertion before and after the invasion of Iraq, against massive evidence to the contrary, that Saddam Hussein had and was intent on using weapons of mass destruction. America, in other words, has been compelled by its exceptionalist problematic to reduce the differential dynamics of the complex and recalcitrant past and present history of the Middle East, the legacy, ironically, in large part of the depredations of European and American imperialism, to a simple Manichaean struggle between good and evil (Western, particularly American) civilization and (Islamic) barbarism. As in Greene's novel, this violent theoretical reduction and simplification of the differential historicity of Middle Eastern history to fit the American problematic has not only resulted in an implacably resolute military practice that has killed and maimed thousands of innocent Iraqi civilians; it has also precipitated an unfore*seen* opposition, not only by the Iraqi people, who were represented by the American army spokesmen (and the media) immediately after the defeat of Saddam Hussein's army as jubilant over the prospect of democracy, but also by a substantial and growing body of militant Iraqis who have inaugurated a guerrilla war whose *hit-and-run,* that is, *invisible,* tactics, like those of the Viet Cong in the Vietnam War, has molecularized and rendered ineffective the formidable American occupation army and, therefore, is compelling it to resort to indiscriminate killing, a practice that, in turn, promises to increase and diversify the opposition to America and its capitalist version of democracy.

The remarkable relevance of Greene's depiction of Alden Pyle's typically American exceptionalist/Cold War/Orientalist textual attitude in *The Quiet American* to the contemporary global occasion that is bearing witness to the repetition of America's intervention in Vietnam will be fully developed in chapter 6 ("American Exceptionalism, the Jeremiad, and the Frontier"). Here, for the sake of orientation, it will suffice to briefly reconstellate what I have taken to be the essential insight of Greene's novel—his brilliantly proleptic invention of the absent presence of the area-studies expert York Harding in Indochina—into the representational discourse that is increasingly coming to be seen as determining the post-9/11 global policies and practices of the United States. For this purpose I could invoke any number of policy books and papers written by the neo-conservatives who now constitute the official and unofficial intellectual deputies of the second Bush administration. For the sake of economy, however, I will briefly cite only the last two best-selling books of the prestigious Harvard University professor and founder of the influential journal *Foreign Affairs,* Samuel P. Huntington—*The Clash of Civilizations and the Remaking of the World Order* published before 9/11, and *Who Are We?: The Challenges to America's National Identity,* published after 9/11.[41] For these, as their very titles suggest, like York Harding's American-centered Cold War representation of the Orient, reflect most precisely and systematically *both* the overt *and* hidden, conscious and unconscious, ideology that informs the Bush administration's global war on terror: the general spatializing/binarist logic of it global vision and its specific manifestation in the deeply backgrounded myth of American exceptionalism, whose origin is simultaneous with the founding of America.

In *The Clash of Civilizations,* for example, Huntington, responding to the rise of anti-American sentiment on a global scale in the wake of the fall and disintegration of the Soviet Union and America's assertion of global hegemony, modifies Francis Fukuyama's "end-of-history" thesis. Taking the latter to be premature, he substitutes a geopolitical paradigm

that represents contemporary, post-Cold War history in terms of the conflict between a Western civilization led by the United States and other
hostile civilizations, above all, Islamic and Confucian (Chinese) for the
paradigm of the Cold War. Nevertheless, this American-centered global
paradigm, precisely like that of the Cold War, reduces history to an inclusive strategic *spatial* "scenario" that can be *seen* all at once, thus mirroring the York Harding problematic that undeviatingly determines the
quiet American's innocently brutal practice in Southeast Asia. "The West
[led by the United States]," Huntington writes summarily,

> is and will remain for years to come the most powerful civiliza-
> tion. Yet its power relative to that of other civilizations is declin-
> ing. [This way of putting America's power is not to be taken
> factually, but, as I will show in chapter 6, as an American jere-
> miadic strategy intended to provoke the anxiety that is the nec-
> essary condition for the mobilization of national consensus.] As
> the West attempts to assert its values and to protect its interests,
> non-Western societies confront a choice. . . . A central axis of
> post-Cold War world politics is thus the interaction of Western
> power and culture with the power and culture of non-Western
> civilizations. (CC, 29)

Then, in a move reminiscent of York Harding's problematic (his spatialization of time), Huntington goes on, undeviatingly, to reassert the practical cultural and political value of this reductive metaphysical and
cartographic mode of inquiry that, in implicitly privileging (over)sight
and thus transforming time into *manageable* (i.e., conquerable) space—
a map, a *tableaux vivante*, or "world picture"[42]—enables the inquirer,
now understood, not as scholar, but crisis-manager, to *shape/predict* the
future. This integrally related metaphorics of vision and picturing, seeing
and territorializing, unconsciously pervades his discourse:

> *Maps and Paradigms.* This picture of post-Cold War world pol-
> itics shaped by cultural factors and involving interactions among
> states and groups from different civilizations is highly simplified.
> It omits many things, distorts some things, and obscures others.
> Yet if we are to think seriously about the world, and act effec-
> tively in it, some sort of simplified map of reality, some theory,
> concept, model, paradigm, is necessary. . . ."Finding one's way
> through unfamiliar terrain," John Lewis Gaddis also wisely ob-
> served, "generally requires a map of some sort. Cartography, *like
> cognition itself*, is a necessary simplification that allows us to see
> where we are, and where we may be going." (CC, 30)[43]

Despite his token acknowledgment that this spatial paradigm "omits many things, distorts some things, and obscures others," Huntington's "indispensable guide to international politics" (no less than Fukuyama's) clearly, if implicitly, recalls York Harding's (and Pyle's) panoptic Cold War problematic: above all, its tacit indifference to the radical difference that time always already disseminates, more specifically, the cultural and sociopolitical difference that deconstructed the American problematic, its geography of Vietnam, and its formidable forwarding war machine in the Vietnam War. These differences, which are not only ontological but human—as the fourth of the five advantages of the paradigm asserts, it enables us to "distinguish what is important from what is unimportant" (CC, 30)—are, like the blood on Pyle's shoe, irrelevant: "collateral damage."

Published in the aftermath of 9/11, Huntington's next book, *Who Are We?* is a sequel to *The Clash of Civilization,* one that, as the title suggests, "historicizes" the American national identity. In it, Huntington modifies his post-Cold War scenario to incorporate a diagnosis of post-9/11 American civilization and his nationalist recommendations as to what "we" must do to maintain "our" global hegemony in the face of the emergent challenges of Islamic and other civilizations. As its subtitle—*The Challenges to America's National Identity* suggests in echoing the title of one of York Harding's books, *The Challenge to Democracy*—Huntington, very much like Graham Greene, if far more explicitly and from an entirely antithetical perspective, traces the post-Cold War problematic determining the United States' representation and practice in the world back to the founding of the American national identity. Just as Greene's genealogy of Alden Pyle's representative Cold War/Orientalist problematic locates its origins in his deeply inscribed exceptionalist Puritan/pioneer individualism, so Huntington locates the origins of the American post-Cold War problematic that would be adequate to the task of winning in the "clash of civilizations" in the "chosen" Puritan founders of American civilization. It was not, he asserts tellingly, the founding fathers' "American Creed" (liberal democracy) as such that was the source of the American national identity—and of the future "greatness" of American civilization. It was, rather, as Greene's portrayal of Pyle/Harding also implies, the Puritans' divinely ordained "errand in the wilderness," more specifically, their evangelical Protestant Christianity (on which the American Creed was founded) (*WAW*, 64).

Furthermore, just as Pyle's American Protestant identity compels him to see himself (America) in no other way than as "saving" Phuong (Vietnam) from the self-destroying errancy of her backward culture and the oppression of French colonialism and Maoist communism by marrying (i.e., Americanizing) her (this is a recurrent motif in the novel), so also

Huntington sees and affirms this founding American Protestantism as the "core culture" (*WAW*, 145, 171, 176) or center that, in its ability to assimilate ethnic and racial minorities, has rendered America a unified civilization and enabled its global hegemony. Anticipated by the reductive rhetoric Pyle uses to represent his Americanism—a rhetoric, as I have shown, blind to the violence that is its inevitable consequence—Huntington writes: ["the assimilation of different groups into American society"] enabled America to expand its population, occupy a continent, and develop its economy with millions of dedicated, energetic, ambitious, and talented people, who became overwhelmingly committed to America's Anglo-Protestant culture and the values of the American Creed, and who helped to make America a major force in global affairs" (*WAW*, 183).

This assimilated national identity, then, the key elements of which are "the English language; Christianity; religious commitment; English concepts of the rule of law; the responsibility of rulers, and the rights of individuals; and dissenting Protestant values of individualism, the work ethic, and the belief that humans have the ability and the duty to try to create a heaven on earth, a 'city on the hill'" (*WAW*, xvi), according to Huntington's twenty-first century American jeremiad, has been jeopardized by "the deconstruction of America" in the 1960s and the consequent "rise of subnational identifies" ("multiculturalism") in its aftermath. Analogous to Pyle's (and Harding's) exceptionalist Cold War problematic, Huntington's vision of America's future is blinded by its oversight to the significant historical role the West has played in producing such a divide, to the complexity of the realities of history, and to the oceans of human blood that the fulfillment of its practical imperatives has spilled and would spill. Nevertheless, it is, according to Huntington, this Anglo-Protestant national identity, adapted to the Manichaean world picture that sees the contemporary occasion as a simply a clash of civilizations, that the United States must recuperate at all costs from the "deconstructionist movement" if America is to maintain the unified civilization that will be necessary to compete and triumph over Islam and the other civilizations that now "threaten" American hegemony in the world.

Finally, and not least, as chapter 6 will bear witness, *The Quiet American* is proleptic of the essential characteristic of the exceptionalist American national identity that lies at the heart of *Who Are We?*: its need for a frontier or, as Huntington everywhere puts it, a "fault line," that always already serves to regenerate its flagging and disintegrating collective energies,[44] which is to say, to preclude its repeating of the imperial Old World's decline into decadence. This motif is exemplified in the novel, not simply by Pyle's (and the American reporters') reiterated American exceptionalist disdain for the decadent French colonialists and his clandestine efforts to establish a ventriloquized Third Force, but also by the means he uses to do so, which is at the paradoxical heart of the novel. I am specifically referring to his (and the American mission's) blind reliance on General Thé to undertake terrorist bombings in Saigon which, reported in the media as communist acts of terrorism, would produce an enemy who, in becoming visible to the "free world" and to the American public at home, would justify America's more direct involvement in Vietnam.

Huntington, too, like virtually all of the neoconservative deputies of the Bush administration, posits the dependence of a unified civilization (a mobilized national identity) on an "Other," a rival civilization it can define itself against. In keeping with the binarist logic of this assumption, he and his fellow conservatives not only celebrated the "triumph" of American democracy over the Soviet Union in the Cold War. Invoking the tradition of the American jeremiad (to which I will return in chapter 6, these nationalists also began to lament its end in that it meant the loss of an enemy that could "reinvigorate their core culture" (*WAW*, 20). As Huntington puts this primary agenda at the beginning of his book, "The dissolution of the Soviet Union eliminated one major and obvious threat to American security and *hence* reduced the salience of national identity compared to subnational, transnational, binational, and other-national identities. Historical experience and sociological analysis show that the absence of an external 'other' is likely to undermine unity and breed divisions within a society" (*WAW*, 17; 277). The attacks by Al Qaeda on the twin towers of the World Trade Center and the Pentagon on 9/11, according to Huntington (and the Bush administration), did not simply fill this disturbing void; these "militant Islamic" terrorist acts also catalyzed the disintegrating essential American national identity, that is, its Protestant "core culture": "When Osama bin Laden attacked America and killed several thousand people, he also did two other things. He filled the vacuum created by Gorbachev with an unmistakably dangerous new enemy, and he pinpointed America's identity as a Christian nation" (*WAW*, 357–358; see also 263).

To reiterate, I have invoked Samuel Huntington's latest books in my attempt to demonstrate the quite remarkable relevance of Greene's *The Quiet American* to the post-9/11 global occasion, not for their uniqueness, but because they are, like York Harding's books in the context of the Cold War, representative of the discourse of the policy makers of the Bush administration about America's global war against terror. The difference—and it is a crucial one, as we shall see when I return to him in chapter 6—is that Huntington makes quite explicit the deeply backgrounded religiocultural or "civilizational" foundation of this extremely dangerous—but finally self-defeating—national initiative that most of his other neoconservative colleagues conceal behind the geopolitical "realism" of their global vision. I mean specifically the American exceptionalist problematic of the frontier (the Puritan "errand in the wilderness"), epitomized by the American jeremiad, that determined the theory and practice of those who inaugurated and executed the American war in Vietnam—and, in the fulfillment of its oversight, inadvertently turned that which was invisible to it into a spectral force that defeated the most powerful army in the world.

As I have been suggesting by way of pointing to the indissoluble relationship between York Harding's policy books and Alden Pyle's American Protestant "textual attitude" and its disastrous practical consequences, Greene's novel about America's initial intervention in Vietnam is proleptic of the post 9/11 occasion. In perceiving the United States' original intervention in Vietnam in terms of the perennial American exceptionalist/Cold War/Orientalist problematic, it enables us a half-century later to retrieve the singular actualities of the Vietnam War from the oblivion to which they were relegated by the American culture industry in its aftermath. By overdetermining the role of York Harding's books in the clandestine terrorist practice of Alden Pyle, Greene anticipates not simply that this American exceptionalist problematic, in privileging oversight, in spatializing time/history, manifested itself in the following decade as an oversight that ultimately resulted in the devastation of an inordinate number of innocent Vietnamese people (it is estimated that about half of the two million that were killed were civilians) and of their land in the name of saving them for the free world. Insofar as this problematic was necessarily blind to the blood of its subaltern victims, it also rendered that invisible blood visible—made it a specter that haunted the American exceptionalist problematic, a specter whose visible invisibility molecularized and eventually defeated the most powerful army in the history of warfare.[45]

By thus anticipating these paradoxical consequences of the American exceptionalist problematic in the Vietnam War, Greene's novel also anticipates the disastrous consequences of the exceptionalist "civilizational" problematic of the intellectual deputies of the Bush administration that is now *determining* America's global "war on terror": not simply the carnage its relentlessly single-minded (Ahabian) perspective ("staying the course," as the president has insistently put it) is wreaking in the Islamic Middle East in the name of saving it for the "civilized world," but also, as the sporadic and dispersed but increasingly frequent acts of a "terrorism" suggest, the emergence of a spectral force—one that promises to become global—the visible invisibility of which, as in the Vietnam War, is molecularizing the American juggernaut and thus threatens to eventually produce an impasse that is likely to terminate in the peculiar kind of defeat that America suffered in the Vietnam War—or the annihilation of the planet.

Unlike the imperial and totalitarian societies it measures itself against, killing its Other—and all too many of its own—"at long range" seems to be the American way: this kind of killing—and the specter it activates—is, to put it succinctly, what renders Graham Greene's *Quiet American*, especially in its focus on the remote immediacy of York Harding, a prophecy not only of what was to happen in Vietnam in the years following the United States' violation of the Geneva Accords, but also of what is happening in the Middle East in the aftermath of 9/11. Much of the literature written by American veterans of the Vietnam War will bear witness to these unpleasant realities that Greene foresaw at the origins of America's intervention in Vietnam. As I will show in the following two chapters, Philip Caputo's memoir, *A Rumor of War*, and Tim O'Brien's *Going After Cacciato*, are, in their very resistance to its disclosures, remarkably exemplary of this witness.

Chapter 4

RETRIEVING THE *THISNESS* OF THE VIETNAM WAR

A *Symptomatic Reading of Philip Caputo's* A Rumor of War

Serve me? Ye cannot swerve me, else ye swerve yourselves! Man has ye there, Swerve me? The path to my fixed purpose is laid with iron rails, whereon my soul is grooved to run. Over unsounded gorges, through the rifled hearts of mountains, under torrents' beds, unerringly I rush! Naught's an obstacle, naught's an angle to the iron way!

—Herman Melville, *Moby-Dick*

"Kill Nam," said Lieutenant Calley. He pointed his weapon at the earth, burned twenty quick rounds. "Kill it," he said. He reloaded and shot the grass and the palm tree and then the earth again. "Grease the place," he said. "Kill it."

—Tim O'Brien, *In the Lake of the Woods*

Vietnam Vietnam Vietnam, we've all been there.

—Michael Herr, *Dispatches*

Since the end of the Vietnam War in 1975, there have been numerous disclosures of atrocities committed by American soldiers during that war, a fact that clearly suggests that these acts were common and that the specter of Vietnam continues to haunt America long after the deputies of the dominant American culture had thought the war had come to its closure. What is of primary significance for the purpose of this chapter is that in each case the representation of these disturbing disclosures of American atrocities in Vietnam has taken the form of individualizing what was fundamentally a state project sanctioned by a national cultural code and, closely related, reducing *this* historically specific war to war-in-general. Such a dislocating disclosure occurred as late as May 2001 when it was revealed that the former senator from Nebraska and later president of the New School for Social Research, Bob Kerrey, on a raid as the commander of a U.S. Navy SEALS unit on Thanh Phong, a Vietnamese hamlet in the Mekong Delta, on February 25, 1969, had ordered and participated in the execution of at least thirteen defenseless Vietnamese civilians—women and children.[1] Both his own representation of that event and that of the media followed this by-now predictable pattern. Kerrey's account focused on the deeply felt guilt he has borne all these years after the war for the acts he committed on that unfortunate occasion. In the nationally televised interview with Kerrey conducted by Dan Rather for CBS's *60 Minutes II*, Rather undeviatingly fed Kerrey questions that allowed him in his responses—even when the questions pertained to the testimony of Gerhard Klann, one of Kerrey's men, which contradicted his undeviating assertion that the villagers had fired on them first—to remain within the framework of his individualized representation of an event that was essentially national in scope and meaning. And the coverage by the media at large followed suit.[2] In the end, in fact, this act of gratuitous mass murder, which was the inevitable consequence of the American military policy of attrition that identified any Vietnamese in a "free fire zone" as an enemy, was transformed into a story that tacitly made Kerrey the hero of a tragedy—a hero who has nobly suffered the excruciating guilt of the crime he committed in Vietnam thirty years before—that culminated in a *catharsis* that obliterated the audience's historical consciousness. What haunted Kerrey's representation of this terrible event and the media's representation of his representation was not simply the specter of the Vietnamese women and children who were brutally murdered that night, but also the question of *the role played by the military command in Saigon, by the Pentagon, by the American state, and finally, but not least, by the American national identity in this gratuitous act of terror.* By the last, I mean the image the American cultural memory has constructed of itself and naturalized ever since the Puritans identified the "clearing," "settlement," and "improvement" of the New World as their "errand in the wilderness," ordained by God's providential design. It was as if the interview with Bob Kerrey was staged for the American public precisely to deflect attention (once again) from this irrepressible public question by way of restricting the parameters of this representation to the individual himself, who is then universalized according to the humanist imperatives of the Western tragic tradition. There is nothing new about this duplicitous American strategy of remembering

Vietnam in order to forget the actualities of the history of the United States' intervention in that Third World country and its conduct of the war. It has been repeated in one form or another over and over again throughout the thirty-year aftermath of the war, even by those who, like Bob Kerrey, sometime along the way turned against the war.

In this chapter, I want to invoke an early instance of these unwanted but insistently recurrent irruptive disclosures not simply because it is especially paradigmatic of this particular strategy of forgetting, but also because the event is represented in such a sincerely candid way that it comes, despite itself, to the threshold of disclosing precisely that which this kind of remembering would attempt to repress. It can thus help us not only to analyze the complex mechanism of forgetting that is involved in this amnesiac re-presentation, but also to thematize the spectrality of that which finally refuses to be forgotten in this representational history of the Vietnam War. That text is Philip Caputo's *A Rumor of War*, a memoir, published in 1977 and written from the perspective of a Marine lieutenant who had turned against the war, about his tour of duty between March 1965 and July 1966 in Vietnam, during which he, like Bob Kerrey, had ordered the execution of innocent Vietnamese civilians.

I

To render visible the ideological significance that lies behind yet haunts Philip Caputo's retrospective representation of the events culminating in the murder of two innocent Vietnamese civilians and the court-martial trial that ensued, it must be reconstellated into that huge body of autobiographical writing—the collections of the letters home by the soldiers fighting in Vietnam, of the reminiscences of veterans long after their return to the unwelcoming if not entirely hostile "world," of the memoirs of officers who had served in Vietnam—that suddenly, after the dedication of the Vietnam Veterans Memorial in Washington in 1982, emerged as a visible alternative to the then current, largely negative, representation of the veteran and the war that had been influenced by the protest movement and had been given its definitive form by the humiliating image of the chaotic flight of the last Americans in Vietnam.[3]

This inordinately large body of auto- and biographical writing was epitomized by Al Santoli's best-selling and highly acclaimed *Everything We Had: An Oral History of the Vietnam War by Thirty-Three American Soldiers Who Fought It* (1981), a text that was intended to contribute to the emergent campaign to rehabilitate the Vietnam veteran, more specifically, to counter the received understanding of the war—an ideological construction damaging not only to the veteran but to the American national identity—that had been imposed on the American public by those who had not fought it, had not *been there* (above all, those in the United States who protested the war). As Santoli puts this complaint in his much quoted preface, this "oral history" would allow those who had fought the war, those who had *been there*—"*the soldiers themselves*," whose voices "the American people have never heard in depth"—to tell their more authentic stories: "It is often said that it is impossible for the uninitiated to understand war. But in our book we hope you will see what we saw, do what we did, feel what we felt. Until the broader public fully comprehends the nameless soldier, once an image on your television screen, the nation's resolution of the experience called Vietnam will be less than adequate."[4]

What Santoli's appeal to the eyewitness accounts, to the witness of being there, against "mere" "re-presentations" written from an ideological distance (like that of the reporter Beckford in John Wayne's *Green Berets*) occludes is that his book, whatever the degree of its sincerity, is no less ideologically motivated. More specifically, in rereremembering the Vietnam War in this particular way in 1981, the book's ultimate intention was not simply to rehabilitate the ostracized veteran, but, more important, to forget—to deflect attention from—the actual history of the United States' intervention in Vietnam and its brutal conduct of the war in behalf of recuperating the national consensus that had been shattered by the protest movement. Indeed, as his own witness suggests—"It wasn't the NVA [North Vietnamese Army] that beat us, it was our own politicians" (*EWH*, 151)—his book enables the possibility, exploited later in the period of the conservative Reagan administration, by films such as the *Rambo* trilogy and the *Missing in Action* series, of a revisionist history of the Vietnam War that transformed the ideologically "neutral" initiative, inaugurated with the dedication of the Vietnam Veterans Memorial, to "heal the wound" suffered by the national psyche into the "Vietnam syndrome": a national neurosis precipitated by the protest movement that prevented America from using its full military power to "win" the war. Despite its appeal to the eyewitness, the testimony of *Everything We Had* is no less informed by "the textual attitude" as that of the fictitious Alden Pyle.

I cannot in this context undertake a full analysis of this end of Santoli's recuperative project. It will suffice for my purpose to invoke briefly the three epigraphs that are intended to epitomize the informing spirit of the multiple voices of the text that, according to Santoli, "bear witness" to the "truth" of the "story" about the Vietnam War they collectively are telling. The first is from Thucydides' *The Peloponnesian War*, which generalizes from the responses of both Athenian and Spartan young men about the natural enthusiasm of (male) youth to the call of war: "At the beginning of an undertaking the enthusiasm is always greatest. And at that time both in the Peloponnesus and in Athens there were great numbers of young men who had never been in a war and were consequently far from unwilling to join in." The second epigraph is from the nationally televised speech delivered to the American public by President Lyndon Johnson on July 28, 1965, announcing his decision to escalate the war by sending American soldiers into overt combat in Vietnam: "I have asked Commanding General William Westmoreland what more he needs to meet this mounting aggression and he has told me. And we will meet his needs. . . . We do not want an expanding struggle with consequences that no one can foresee, nor will we bluster or bully or flaunt our power. But we will not surrender and we will not retreat." The last epigraph takes the form of a haiku by an Asian poet, Chosu: "Though it be broken— / Broken again—still it's there, / The moon on the water." A specific reference to the inaugural moment of the United States' overt use of combat forces—the "idealist" youth of America—in Vietnam (which represents its intervention in Southeast Asia as a heroic defensive war against aggression) sandwiched between two texts from the distant past that are also representative of the point of view of different races, in fact, the two that are locked in deadly conflict in Vietnam. Coming as the prelude or *pretext* of the thirty-three reminiscences by the American veterans that will follow—the collective body of which will offer the American public an "alternative" history to that assumed to be holding sway at the time of publication—the ultimate intent of these epigraphs is clear. They not only constitute an effort to transform the American soldiers who participated in the devastation of Vietnam into soldiers-in-general and the Vietnam War—*this particular war*—into war-in-general. They also constitute in synecdochical form a story—*the* humanistic narrative—that begins with the idealist innocence of youth ("we were idealistic young people confronted by the awesomeness of fighting other human beings" (*EWH*, xv) then tells of its disintegration under the corrosive assaults of the experience of warfare, and ends, through the heroic will to survive, in the recuperation of a higher and more noble (*Western*) manhood. Like the glorious moon in Chosu's poem—the irony that this epigraph was written by an Asian should not be overlooked—that is shattered again and again, but always recovers its glorious wholeness, so these American soldiers, who experienced the fracturing horrors of the war in Vietnam, now understood collectively as the triumphant human spirit, recover their luminous humanity—a humanity, not incidentally, that the highly racialized discourse and practice of America did not grant to the Vietnamese subalterns (the "gooks," "slopes," "slants") they were killing wholesale.

Despite this generalizing process—and the editor's careful selection of his contributors (most of them are, like Pyle, ventriloquized by the discourse of America, and only one is black)—it is clear that the actual testimony of a number of the veterans who compose this book often contradicts its intention. For this reason, Santoli is compelled to impose a narrative structure on the thirty-three voices of the veterans by means of organizing them chronologically in such a way as to give them the appearance of closure—a beginning, middle, and end: "Our book . . . will take the reader more or less chronologically from December 1962, when John F. Kennedy was still alive, to the fall of Saigon in April 1975, when Gerald Ford was president. Our personal accounts span almost the entire period of the nation's overt involvement in that distant place" (*EWH*, xv), and, as in a traditional novel, it is separated into five continuous chapters, the titles of which clearly imply the same narrative structure implied by the three epigraphs: "I: Gathering Clouds," "II: Sand Castles," "III: Peaks and Valleys," "IV: Barren Harvest," and "V: Operation New Wind."

In other words, despite the appearance of realistic spontaneity and the unpremeditated nature of the story that these oral reminiscences unfold, the fact is that the end, in both senses of the word, is there at work from the beginning, determining their narrative shape. That end, that is, constructs a history of the Vietnam War that reduces its historical scope and concrete density to the individual perspectives of some of those who fought in it, then universalizes their narratives to deflect the attention of the American public, to which the book is consciously addressed, away not simply from the contradictions that pervade the individual texts of Santoli's metatext, but to obliterate the larger historically specific sociopolitical context of the war, specifically, the relation between the soldiers, on the one hand, and the nation-state and the cultural mythos that has given the American people, including the soldiers, their sense of national identity, on the other. Despite the appeal to America's "exceptionalist" character that is intended to differentiate itself from the decadent imperialism of the Old World (in this case, as in Greene's *The Quiet American*, the repressive colonialism of France in Vietnam), the structure of *Everything We Had* is the structure of all official Western narratives of particular imperialist wars whose domestic subtext has always been to shift the focus from their *thisness*—from the dominant culture that sacrifices the young in wars it wages for dubious ideological purposes—by way of invoking the perennial universal humanist paradigm of the young soldier who endures the horrors of war and survives it in a noble, "manly" way. It is the all-too-familiar Western story of the "triumph of the human spirit" that always obscures the degree to which the nation-state has reduced the flesh and blood of the young who fight them to collective cannon fodder. Like so many others of its genre, Al Santoli's "oral" history of the Vietnam War, for all its underscored claim to authenticity, is, in short, an amnesiac history, a remembering that is finally intended to forget the singularity of the Vietnam War. Or rather, it is a history that lends itself to the official culture's obsessive will to inter, once and for all, the specter that haunts its national discourse in the name of recuperating its former imperial authority.

Philip Caputo's *A Rumor of War* is a sustained personal account of the war that essentially replicates the retrospective narrative structure that informs Santoli's *Everything We Had.* It is no accident that the epigraph from Vegetius, a "Roman military writer, fourth century A.D.," which Caputo chooses to introduce his memoir proper, repeats precisely the generalized point of view informing the quotation from Thucydides' *The Peloponnesian War* that Santoli uses to introduce his text: "No great dependence is to be placed on the eagerness of young soldiers for action, for the prospect of fighting is agreeable to those who are strangers to it."[5] This same point of view is reflected in the biblical passage from Matthew 24:6–13 from which Caputo derives his title. Indeed, all the epigraphs for each of the eighteen chapters are drawn from Western texts about war, ranging from the New Testament through Shakespeare to Ernest Hemingway, Wilfred Owen, and Siegfried Sassoon, thus disclosing Caputo's inscribed effort to generalize the individual soldier to the universal soldier and the Vietnam War to war-in-general. Nor is it accidental that, like *Everything We Had* and so many others of this autobiographical genre, Caputo's narrative "ends" with the humanistic archetype of survival: "The plane banked and headed out over the China Sea, toward Okinawa, toward freedom from death's embrace. None of us was a hero. We would not return to cheering crowds, parades and the pealing of great cathedral bells. We had done nothing more than endure. We had survived, and that was our only victory" (*ARW*, 320).[6] These structural coordinates will determine the shape of Caputo's ("eyewitness") representation of his fracturing tour of duty in Vietnam. Like Santoli's text, his will be a story whose beginning will depict a young idealistic American, certain about his country's call to sacrificial duty and hungry for the glory of accomplishing a decisive act of courage; whose middle will plunge him into "the heart of darkness," the dislocating and bewildering dynamics of which will compel him to commit an act of violence that, far from heroic, is, in fact, akin to an act of murder; and its end will transform him—his shattered individual/American self—into a timeless tragic figure, that is, will represent him as a type of the universal soldier who, by enduring the corrosive fires of the "crucible of war," transcends his occasion—and effaces the ignoble history of *this* war.[7]

But there is a crucial difference between Caputo's and Santoli's representation of the Vietnam War that manifests itself not only in Caputo's less sanguine attitude toward his endurance and survival, but also and primarily in his far more forceful and revealing articulation of the betrayal of the young American soldiers by those institutions—the army, the nation, the state—that thrust them into the situation that rendered Vietnam a hell with no exit. The unmitigated honesty of Caputo's indictment of his actions, and of the overall American military strategy it was his duty to carry out, manifests itself in a rhetorical "excess" that, far more than Santoli's patriotic text, calls his own personal narrative into question. His integrity, that is, forces the language of his narrative to the threshold of a disclosure that belies the closure induced by the denouement of surviving war-in-general and points menacingly—and *synecdochically*—to the larger and deeper history this latter is intended to obscure. And it is this marginal excess haunting Caputo's representational discourse that I want eventually to think in this chapter. It will clarify what I mean by referring to *A Rumor of War* as a "threshold text" that, however inadvertently, verges on disclosing the larger sociopolitical history its narrative (and, above all, the media industry's reception of the book that unanimously took its point of departure from it) would occlude: the complicity not simply of the nation-state but also of the national culture of which he is a representative in the climactic murder of the two Vietnamese civilians. It will also, by way of thinking the spectrality of this excess, problematize the official determination of the beginning and, especially, the end of the Vietnam War.

II

Despite its seeming personal realism, Caputo's *A Rumor of War*, like so many of the novels, autobiographical works, films, documentaries, and histories of the Vietnam War, is deeply backgrounded in American cultural history, specifically, as I have insistently underscored, that history that has its origins in the Puritan "errand in the wilderness" of the "New World" and that was secularized in the inexorable westward expansionist momentum from frontier to frontier led by the manly "pioneer" or "frontiersman" or "borderer": the symbolic male (and phallic) figure inscribed in the American cultural memory by James Fenimore Cooper as the trail-blazing "Leatherstocking," "the foremost in the band of Pioneers, who are opening the way for the march of the nation across the continent,"[8] and the historiography of Francis Parkman, George Bancroft, William Prescott, and Frederick Jackson Turner. It is no accident that Caputo begins his story by declaring that he enlisted in the Marine Corps partly because he "got swept up in the patriotic tide of the Kennedy era" (*ARW*, 4)—the era, he later recalls, the new president aptly called the "New Frontier," in which "the War Corps" would "do the man's work of battling Communist guerrillas, the new barbarians who menaced the far-flung interests of the new Rome" (*ARW*, 16). Though he attributes his primary motive to the deadly boredom and aimlessness of his life in a modern suburban prairie town near Chicago, it is this resonant sense of the American frontier, once fundamental to that midwestern space but now utterly domesticated, commercialized, and emptied of certain purpose, that dominates his rhetoric:

> The only thing I liked about my boyhood surroundings were the Cook and DuPage County forest preserve, a belt of virgin woodland through which flowed a muddy stream called Salt Creek. It was not polluted then, and its sluggish waters yielded bullhead, catfish, carp, and a rare bass. There was small game in the woods, sometimes a deer or two, but most of all a hint of the wild past, when moccasined feet trod the forest paths and fur trappers cruised the rivers in bark canoes. Once in a while, I found flint arrowheads in the muddy creek bank. Looking at them, I would dream of that savage, heroic time and wish I had lived then, before America became a land of salesmen and shopping centers. (*ARW*, 5)

This is not simply the expression of a bored young man's need for excitement, or even a nostalgia for an earlier America as such. It is, above all, as the echoes of the American jeremiad suggests, a deeply inscribed repetition of the essential ethos of the American national character that, since the Puritans, both separates and relates the idea of America and the idea of Europe. This, specifically, is the coded exceptionalist ethos that not only distinguishes the *manly* inhabitant of the New World from the *feminized* citizen of the Old World—the sense of difference, of newness, of vitality, of potential, of creative purpose, of virile action endemic to the very idea of the frontier wilderness from the sameness, the decadence, the enervation, the sterility, the conformity, the effeminate passivity that is the consequence of overcivilization—but also recognizes and relies on their problematic relational dependency. I am referring to the anxiety that is always incumbent on the knowledge that penetrating the wilderness necessarily involves clearing, settling, and improving it,[9] and thus the urgent need of a perpetual frontier between them, which is to say, the need always to re-new the civilization, which is the result of settling and improving the wilderness, by violence.[10] However subdued in his rhetoric, it is this perennial, culturally inscribed polyvalent American ethos, so prominent in the representational history of the Vietnam War, that Caputo will bring with him to the wilderness of Vietnam and will resonate subliminally throughout his narrative—and, as I will show at length in chapter 6, will speak significantly to the official representations of the post-9/11 occasion.

Caputo finds this productive purpose that will break the unmanning pattern of the routine of modern American suburban life in the mythicized figure of the U.S. Marine, the (ironic) contemporary allotrope of the colonial frontiersman whose border violence rejuvenates the civilized city. In the paragraph following his expression of nostalgia for an earlier American Midwest, he ironically recalls the poster displayed by a recruiting team in the student union of Loyola University that convinced him to enlist in the Marine Corps: "[A] trim lieutenant who had one of those athletic, slightly cruel faces considered handsome in the military. . . . *Clear and resolute*, his blue eyes seemed to stare at me in challenge. JOIN THE MARINES, read the slogan that appeared above his white cap. BE A LEADER OF MEN" (*ARW*, 8; my emphasis). Caputo's attraction to this phallic image may be read from a feminist perspective, especially since this passage is followed by insistently repeated expressions, reminiscent of Stephen Crane's *The Red Badge of Courage*, of his anxiety about his manliness: "I needed to prove something—my courage, my toughness, my manhood, call it what you like" (*ARW*, 6). Nevertheless, it would be inadequate to restrict the ideological register of Caputo's narrative to the site of gender. As I have suggested by pointing to the relatedness of the American mythos of the pioneer and the legendary figure of the U.S. Marine in his rhetoric, what is at stake in Caputo's ironic account of this inaugural moment of his story is not simply the question of American gender relations, but the indissoluble relay of characteristics that make up the American national identity: his ontology, his subjectivity, his cultural ethos, his understanding of gender and race, his politics, his comportment toward the land, and his view of warfare. Specifically, what Caputo, as a representative of American exceptionalism, is symptomatically suggesting—no doubt largely against his intention—is that his decision to enlist in the Marine Corps was, in fact, informed by a *European* way of thinking being that reads its temporal disseminations from the end (*meta ta physika*), that is, as a *narrative* (with a beginning, middle, and end); a subjectivity, therefore, that is grounded in certainty and directionality, an optimistic one, reminiscent of Alden Pyle's, that operates according to a binary logic that privileges identity over difference, (instrumental) reason over *poiesis*; and a racial, patriarchal, and imperial politics that justifies the representation of its Others as inferior and thus subject to its command; and, most prominently, a form of warfare that, like the structure of narrative itself, is essentially Western in the sense that it assumes a directional and con-fronting movement toward a preconceived end (the decisive battle).

This—and because they constitute the thematics Caputo will over-determine in his story—is why I have italicized the words "clear and resolute" in the quotation referring to the Marine in the poster. Clarity, the essential value of Western epistemology (as it is reflected, e.g., in the privileged concept of the Enlightenment) implies a *charted field* of (super-) vision that is not impeded by diversionary obstacles or, rather, as my epigraph from Melville's *Moby-Dick* has it, that sees contradictions *as* obstacles to the decisive achievement of the end and thus to be obliterated. Resoluteness implies not simply the certainty of purpose but also of the end to be accomplished. Together, they assume a disciplinary epistemology that spatializes temporal events before they occur—reduces their errant, obscure, and menacing livingness to a strategic map in which no detail is superfluous or unaccounted for to the calculative mind—and, crucial to Caputo's text, they enable *getting something done.*

In identifying with the Marine in the poster, in other words, the older, ironic Caputo *intends* to imply, the young Caputo is also identifying himself with a caricatured version of the empirical pragmatic American character, the self-reliant "leader of men," who has his origins in the image of the path-breaking and civilization-rejuvenating frontiersman and his "maturity" in the problem-solving of a Benjamin Franklin, but who comes down to Caputo (as it did to virtually all the young Americans who fought in Vietnam) mediated by the melodramatic Hollywood western and its World War II allotrope and symbolized by the ubiquitous image of the actor John Wayne. This image or, rather, this simulacrum, he identifies with, that is, constitutes the fulfillment of the logical economy of the original, but in such a caricatured way that it discloses its absurdity and its contradictory essence. What the retrospective Caputo *symptomatically* implies is that the younger Caputo *is also identifying himself with a relay of analogous, more concrete, but no less grotesque, national identities*: the military command in Saigon, which would arrogantly carry out the jungle war in Vietnam in terms of the incommensurate European model of warfare (the related ideas of the front and decisive battle); the planners of the war in the Pentagon, who, under the aegis of Robert McNamara's management skills and in the name of the instrumentalist metaphorics of cost efficiency, would reduce the combatants to statistics in a comprehensive table; and the intellectual representatives of the nation-state—the "best and the brightest," who, as David Halberstam characterized these "can-do" thinkers,[11] intervened in Southeast Asia in the name of the truth of the free world and pursued its instrumentalist logic to the edge of genocide, where it self-destructed.[12] In the process of retelling his story, Caputo will pursue this symptomatic intuition about his identity to the threshold of an epochal disclosure.

In his account of the young Caputo's period of stateside training, from the summer of 1961 when he goes to Officer's Training School through the spring of 1964 when he enrolls in Officer's Basic School to the moment he (and his platoon) lands in Danang in March 1965, it is, however unevenly, this ideological relay emanating from the symbolic clarity and resoluteness of the figure of the Marine of the poster that Caputo overdetermines. For the sake of convenience, I will identify this relay as one in which metaphysical perception (in its instrumentalist and performative mode—i.e., seeing time in spatial or reified terms and in the form of narrative structure; a self-identical subjectivity, which is simultaneously optimistic, certain, manly, disciplined, calculative, and directional (in control); a forwarding practice, which is inexorably committed to accomplishment; and a self-righteous morality that understands value in quantitative terms (all of which are understood in binary opposition to a thinking, practice, and morality that this ideological relay would call errant, unmanly, unproductive or wasteful, and so on) are indissolubly related.[13]

Thus, for example, when Caputo tells us that during his training period it was above all the fear of being identified as "one of the marginals, as they ["who were borderline cases"] were known in the lexicon of that strange world" (*ARW*, 10–11), this typical young American is not simply invoking the will to be strong and manly against an effeminate weakness that he associates with his earlier interest in literature. That manliness that he is willing himself to achieve is inseparable from a disciplinary epistemological process that is transforming his sense of the living earth—its beauty and (to press his insight beyond where he takes it) its anxiety-provoking mystery—into a quantified space—a territory—to be classified, mastered, and occupied:

> We had become self-confident and proud, some to the point of arrogance. We acquired the military virtues of courage, loyalty, and esprit de corps, though at the price of a diminished capacity for compassion. There were other alterations. In my case, it was the way I looked at the world around me. A year earlier, I would have seen the rolling Virginia countryside through the eyes of an English-major who enjoyed reading Romantic poets. Now I had

the clearer, more pragmatic vision of an infantry officer. Landscape was no longer scenery to me, it was terrain, and I judged it
for tactical rather than aesthetic value. (ARW, 21)

Caputo understands the metamorphosis he is describing in terms of the
reduction of nature as an aesthetic phenomenon; but just below the surface of his insight another, more telling meaning is struggling to be born.
It was not simply the "beauty" of nature that this inscribed manly, technological, American consciousness effaced; it was also its ineffable mystery, the finally irreducible being that, as Foucault and other critics of the
"truth" of the post-Enlightenment, such as Deleuze and Guattari have
shown, modern Western epistemology and its technology of knowledge
production, has (futilely) reified—reduced to "a field," a "domain," "a
province," "a region," "a terrain" to be conquered.[14] As I will suggest,
this irreducible "nature"—this baffling uncanniness that finally resists
spatializing, territorializing, mapping—will come increasingly to haunt
Caputo—and, as the symptomatic testimony of virtually all the veterans
included in such autobiographical texts as Santoli's *Everything We Had*,
of the American soldiers who came to fight in the jungles of Vietnam.

In turn, this "manly" process that reduces the vital landscape Caputo
encounters to fixed "terrain" is also inseparable from the military tactics
he learns on simulated or, to thematize their narrative structure, "staged"
battlefields, all of which could be subsumed under the rubric of the "offensive," which means not only the act of attacking, but also a progressive forwarding, which, like narrative movement itself, is oriented toward
an end that is blocked by an enemy.

The offensive was the only tactic worthy of the name. . . . The
Army retreated, the Marines did not. . . . The essence of the offensive was the frontal assault: "Hey diddle diddle, straight up
the middle"; this was the supreme moment of infantry combat;
no tricky flanking or encircling movements, just a line of determined men firing short bursts from the hip as they advanced on
the enemy at a stately walk. (*ARW*, 14)

Thanks to this disciplining of his inscribed desire to be self-reliant (i.e., an
essential—male—American), by the time Caputo arrives in Vietnam he
has become precisely the Marine in the poster: a "leader" or "individual"
who has been interpellated and ventriloquized by the collective, historically constructed Voice of America. It was this indissoluble relay of "clear
and resolute" expectations embodied in and aroused by this idealized (yet

self-parodic) figure of the Marine that the young Caputo brought to Vietnam: "Could it have been only a year since I was discussing the relative merits of *Tom Jones* and *Joseph Andrews* in a seminar on the English novel? Since my roommate and I were listening to Bach and Vivaldi as we studied for our graduate record exams? What a waste of time that all seemed" (*ARW*, 45). And it was precisely this relay of expectations informing what Tom Englehardt has called American "victory culture" that the "wasteful" reality of Vietnam was to devastate.[15]

III

The inexorable process that deconstructed the narrative image Caputo had of the war—and the positive attitude, the clarity and resoluteness, it enabled—began even before he was assigned to duty in "the boonies," as combat zones in the Vietnamese wilderness were called by the American soldiers. As an officer whose platoon was assigned to participate in defending the perimeter of the Danang airbase, what he realized almost immediately under sniper fire was that the reference point for talking about this war was not light, but darkness: "Around nine or ten, when snipers opened up on our positions, we learned that the Vietnam War was primarily a nocturnal event" (*ARW*, 54). This was both literally and symbolically true. For related to the obscuring nocturnal context was the uncanny facelessness of the enemy. It was simply that Caputo came at once to realize that, unlike the image of warfare he had learned at Quantico (or, for that matter, from the World War II movies like *Guadalcanal Diary, Retreat, Hell!* and *Sands of Iwo Jima*), it was virtually impossible to discriminate between a friendly Vietnamese and an unfriendly one (*ARW*, 52). It was inevitable, therefore, that this moment, which inaugurated the inexorable process entailing the disintegration of the clarity of his gaze, should culminate in the irruption of a metaphor that, for Caputo (and virtually all the Americans who actually fought in Vietnam) would come to represent not simply the invisible enemy but the very mysterious land, indeed, the very *being* of Vietnam: the *phantom*:

> Looking into the gloom beyond the wire, I saw nothing dangerous, only the empty paddies, gray now instead of green. . . . All the same the sniper had to be out there somewhere—with my head in his sights, for all I knew. Before my imagination got the best of me, I climbed out and continue on my rounds, feeling queasy the whole time. Phantoms, I thought, we're fighting phantoms. (*ARW*, 55)

This is a critical moment in Caputo's narrative. And it is not simply because, in underscoring the menacing invisibility of the Vietnamese enemy—the inability of his gaze to identify its object—it shakes the foundations of his certainty. However symptomatically, this moment also inaugurates a reversal of Caputo's deeply backgrounded American phenomenological perspective on the Other, one that will increasingly come to oppress him. Whereas prior to this moment Caputo's American gaze had been oriented in an arrogant one-way relationship toward its object, as if this other's very being (and his own) depended on it—this representational perspective is the deepest structure of the imperial project[16]—now, suddenly, he realizes that it is the gaze of the Other that is seeing and objectifying him. To put this dislocating turn—one that pervades the American veterans' discourse about this war—in a way that incorporates its two indissolubly related epistemological elements, the visual and the spectral, the *visitor* becomes the *visited* or the *visited* becomes the *visitor*.[17]

But even as the young Caputo begins to encounter a world of war bearing little resemblance in its corrosive ambiguities to the straightforward image of war he had brought with him to Vietnam from the United States, he nevertheless remains loyal to it. "Nothing," Caputo writes, "could have been better calculated to give an idea of the kind of war Vietnam was and the kind of things men are capable of in war if they stay in it long enough"(*ARW*, 64) than the anxiety-provoking invisibility of the enemy, the sudden death by sniper fire, the mutilation by booby-trap, the shock of being shown "two brown and bloodstained human ears," "souvenirs" that had been cut off the body of a dead VC (*ARW*, 64). But this early intuition into the difference of the Vietnam War from his inscribed expectations is not yet decisive: "It was a peculiar period in Vietnam, with something of the romantic flavor of Kipling's colonial wars. Even the name of our outfit was romantic. Expeditionary Brigade. We liked that. And because it was the only American brigade in-country at the time, we had a feeling of being special, a feeling of 'we few, we happy few, we band of brothers.' Lieutenant Bradley, the battalion motor transport office, perfectly expressed the atmosphere of those weeks. He called it the 'splendid little war'" (*ARW*, 63). This positive sense of heroic purpose was underscored by Caputo's deeply inscribed belief in America's exceptionalist mission: "I guess we believed in our own publicity—Asian guerrillas did not stand a chance against U.S. Marines—as we believed in all the myths created by that most articulate and elegant myth-maker, John Kennedy. If he was the King of Camelot, then we were his Knights and Vietnam our crusade. There was nothing we could not do because we were Americans, and for the same reason, whatever we did was right" (*ARW*, 66).[18] And this optimistic, indeed, Panglossian, mythology continues to hold even after his unit has been assigned in April to the bush, "a range of heights that formed a natural wall between Danang and the VC-controlled valley to the west" (*ARW*, 64).

It is only when he undertakes his first "search and destroy" mission that his illusions about war (if not this particular war) and the sense of control they enabled begin to crumble decisively. Caputo anticipates this process at the outset of the action, when, airborne on his way into the designated landing zone, he encounters the tremendous difference between that part of Vietnam seen from the panoptic distance enabled by a microcosmic map—and the "hammer and anvil" tactics based on this territorializing vision—and the actualities of entering this nightmarish and menacing jungle landscape:

> We were flying parallel to the mountains; the Cordillera spread out before us, and it was the most forbidding thing I had ever seen. . . . There it was the Annamese Cordillera, hostile and utterly alien. . . . Looking down, I wondered for a moment if the operation was somebody's idea of a joke. Our mission was to find an enemy battalion. A battalion—a few hundred men. The whole North Vietnamese Army could have concealed itself in that jungle-sea, and we were going to look for a battalion. Crush it in a hammer and anvil movement. We were going to find a battalion and destroy it. Search and destroy. I half expected those mountains to shake with contemptuous laughter at our pretense. (*ARW*, 77–78)

This sense of dread activated by the "utterly alien" and menacing "out there" and the consequent intuition into the grotesque impotence of America's arrogant instrumentalist ethos—and its "errand in the wilderness" of Southeast Asia (no doubt precipitated by his study of the English literature he has earlier referred to as "a waste of time")—is, of course, an indirect allusion to that epiphanic moment in Joseph Conrad's *Heart of Darkness* when Marlow, remembering the man-of-war anchored off shore and firing into the heart of Africa, discloses the grotesque folly of the European imperial project: "There wasn't even a shed there, and she was shelling the bush. . . . In the empty immensity of earth, sky, water, there she was, incomprehensible, firing into a continent. Pop, would go one of the six-inch guns; a small flame would dart out and vanish, a little smoke would disappear, a tiny projectile would give a feeble screech—and nothing happened. . . . There was a touch of insanity in the proceeding, a sense of lugubrious drollery in the sight;

and it was not dissipated by somebody on board assuring me earnestly there was a camp of natives—he called them enemies—hidden out of sight somewhere."[19] And though Caputo may not be fully conscious of it, it is another one of those threshold moments in his narrative that, in suggesting the complicity of the American ethos with that of European imperialism, belies the myth of American exceptionalism on which its intervention in Vietnam was based.

Once Caputo's platoon has arrived at the landing zone in the jungle and the helicopter has flown off, this dread and the attendant intuition into the ineffectuality of his American technological fire power in the face of this menacing wilderness becomes a realization that he expresses in the decisive language of crossing a geographical boundary that is also a symbolic boundary: from *terra cognita* to *terra incognita*: "When the helicopters flew off, a feeling of abandonment came over us. Charley Company was now cut off from the outside world. We had crossed a line of departure [a military term] all right, a line of departure between the known and the unknown. The helicopters had made it seem familiar. Being Americans, we were comfortable with machines, but with the aircraft gone we were struck by the utter strangeness of this rank and rotten wilderness. Nothing moved in the paralyzed air, and the only sounds were the gurgling of the river and the rustling of those invisible things in the underbrush. It was not at all a tranquil silence. I thought of that old line from the westerns: 'It's too quiet'" (*ARW*, 79). To appropriate Karl Jaspers' apt vocabulary, we might say that Caputo and his unit have entered a *Grenzsituation*—an "ultimate situation" that, as the etymology suggests, can be equally understood as a "boundary situation" that disintegrates the familiar reference points of the previously charted world (what earlier he has called "terrain"). This "change of terrain," to appropriate Althusser's resonant Marxian phrase, this silent and placeless place, in which one feels dislocated and bereft of language, is what Heidegger calls *die Unheimliche*, the realm of the uncanny or the not-at-home. It is that primordial space, stripped of coordinates and language, that precipitates *Angst*, the existential mood of anxiety that, unlike fear [*Furcht*] has *no thing* as its object, that is, is an invisible presence. Because this enabling Heideggerian distinction has been virtually forgotten by critical discourse in the wake of the triumph of "cultural studies" over poststructuralist theory—and because it is, though unrecognized or repressed by virtually everyone who has written about the Vietnam War, at the abyssal heart of Caputo's and so many American veterans' representation of their experience of the Vietnam War—I will quote Heidegger at some length:

In anxiety, we say, "one feels ill at ease [*es ist einem unheim-lich*]." What is "it" that makes "one" feel ill at ease? We cannot say what it is before which one feels ill at ease. As a whole it is so for one. All things and we our selves sink into indifference. This, however, not in the sense of mere disappearance. Rather, in this very receding things turn towards us. The receding of beings as a whole that closes in on us in anxiety oppresses us. We can get no hold on things. In the slipping away of being only this "no hold on things" comes over us and remains.

Anxiety reveals the nothing.[20]

This nameless "nothing" that is disclosed in and by anxiety, it will be re-called, is the "nothing [*das Nichts*] that, as Heidegger says in his seminal essay, "What Is Metaphysic?," the triumphant "truth" of modern empir-ical science will have nothing to do with: "The nothing—what else can it be for science but an outrage and a phantasm?"[21] The nothing, in other words, is that spectral Other *of*—that belongs to—and haunts the "tri-umphant" global truth of science. This is the way Caputo puts this virtu-ally unrepresentable condition, which, from his perspective, is "a thing malevolent and alive" (*ARW*, 80), when, immediately following his crossing of the boundary, he leads his platoon toward the village he has been assigned to search and destroy:

The patrol that morning had the nightmare quality which charac-terized most small-unit operations in the war. The trail looped and twisted and led nowhere. The company seemed to be marching into a vacuum, haunted by a presence intangible yet real, a sense of being surrounded by something we could not see. It was the in-ability to see that vexed us most. In that lies the jungle's power to cause fear: it blinds. It arouses the same instinct which makes us apprehensive of places like attics and dark alleys. (*ARW*, 80)[22]

The "no thing" that haunts Caputo—this American soldier who par-ticipates in America's errand in the Vietnamese wilderness—is the noth-ingness of being that the truth of Being as it is understood by American instrumentalism will have nothing to do with. But it is more than that. It is also those phantasmic Others—the invisible and menacing Vietnamese insurgents—who, from this instrumentalist perspective (epitomized by the discourse of officials who planned the war from the Pentagon), are subaltern: have no being.[23] And not least it is the spectral difference that contradicts the narrative—the teleological expectation of closure—that Caputo has brought with him to Vietnam.

This inaugural anxiety instigated by the "changed terrain"—the forbidding and foreboding Vietnamese landscape—is greatly exacerbated during this first search and destroy mission. Burdened by his acute awareness that "it was the land that resisted us, the land, the jungle, and the sun" (*ARW*, 82), when his platoon enters the village of Hoi-Vuc to undertake its search, it is not simply his uncertainty about the identities of the enigmatically silent and passive Vietnamese villagers—mostly old people and children—that overwhelms him: "That old woman [whom a Vietnamese Marine lieutenant had identified as "VC; Dai-uy," "explaining that the stakes which she had been hardening in the fire were antihelicopter devices"] shuffled away, a sack of bones covered by a thin layer of shriveled flesh. The Enemy" (*ARW*, 85). It was also, and equally acute, his sense of the dislocating inconclusiveness of the mission. Caputo's platoon is engaged in two hit-and-run firefights initiated by Viet Cong snipers as it leaves the village to "complete" the prearranged hammer and anvil operation. In response to both, the platoon, spurred by Caputo's "Hollywood heroics," which draws fire toward them (*ARW*, 88), fires massively but randomly into the bush at the invisible enemy. In the immediate aftermath of this indecisive engagement, a deeply perplexed Caputo, conscious of the vicious circularity of the structure of this warfare, concludes: "When the skirmish ended, a squad searched the tree line but found only a few spent cartridges. The phantoms had pulled off another vanishing act. Late that afternoon, sunburned, bone-tired, *wondering if we had accomplished anything*, suspecting that we had not, we linked up with D Company and were flown back to base camp" (*ARW*, 89; my emphasis).

In the ensuing months following Caputo's anticlimactic "baptism of fire," during which "in effect, we commuted to and from the war," it is precisely the recurrence of this random anxiety-provoking and frustratingly indecisive action—a happening in which nothing happens, nothing "gets done"—that Caputo, like so many other American soldiers, records: "There was no pattern to these patrols and operations. Without a front, flanks, or rear, we fought a formless war against a formless enemy who evaporated like the morning jungle mists, only to materialize in some unexpected place, it was a haphazard episodic sort of combat. Most of the time nothing happened; but when something did, it happened instantaneously and without warning" (*ARW*, 89). In recounting this chaotic time, Caputo, therefore, cannot give the events a narrative sequence: "Because of the sporadic, confused nature of the fighting, it is impossible to give an orderly account of what we did. With one or two exceptions, I have only disjointed recollections of this period, the spring of 1965. The incidents I do remember, I remember vividly; but I can come up with no connecting thread to tie events neatly together" (*ARW*, 90).

What these recurrent random events Caputo goes on to recount have in common is, above all, the *intensification* of all those earlier intuitions, both individual and collective, that implied that *this war* refused to accommodate itself to the expectations about war that he, as an American, had brought with him to Vietnam: not simply the "clarity" of vision and "resoluteness" of practice whose genealogy extends back from the idealized Marine in the poster in the recruiting booth, through the Hollywood westerns Caputo often invokes, to the self-reliant, trail-blazing frontiersman, but also his American exceptionalist "problematic"—the linear narrative structure of consciousness informing this clear vision and decisive practice, European in origins, whose end, in privileging visual perception, is *in* its beginning. Characteristically, Caputo unconsciously universalizes his response to the increasing corrosiveness of these violent historical events and thus blunts their historical and political significance: "We learned what *war* was about, 'the cares of it, and the forms of it' [the quoted passage repeats the generalizing epigraph from Shakespeare's *Henry V* that introduces this chapter; my emphasis]." But those contradictory intuitions cannot be repressed. They manifest themselves in a contradictory rhetoric, which includes insistent ironic references to the colonial wilderness ("Indian country") (*ARW*, 102, 104, 126), that haunts his generalization of the *thisness* of the Vietnam War and thus demand attending to.

To begin with, this intensification infuses Caputo's repeated representation of the inconsequence of those actions in terms of everyday Americanisms, such as "doing"/"not doing," "happening"/"not happening" as in the above passages, with ideological meanings they normally do not have, thus suggesting that, like the reifying visualist Americanisms that refer to knowledge ("I see what you mean" or "I get your point"), these are "white metaphors" that conceal more than they reveal about the identity of the American user, yet, *as symptoms*, reveal what they conceal. What, in other words, this intensification discloses about these "random" violent events in which "nothing happens" is not simply the inscribed (Franklinian) assumption that *accomplishment*—getting things done—is the American measure of success, a performative measure, as I have suggested (and to which I will return) that determined the scenarios of the instrumentalist ("can do") planners in the Pentagon, the undeviating narrative consciousness informing this measure, and the metaphysical interpretation of the truth of being that produces this narrative consciousness. It also discloses what I have called after Althusser the ocularcentric problematic, the one way—colonizing—directionality, of this relay, which perceives the Vietnamese enemy as the object of the action, not as an agent. When, for example, Caputo recalls, as he all too often does (*ARW*, 100), that the engagements with the enemy were always random and inconsequential, engagements from which he could not come up with a "connecting thread to tie events neatly together," he is not only dimming down the prominence he everywhere gives to the invisibility of the Vietnamese insurgents and their hit-and-run tactics. In so doing, he is also blinding himself to the fact that it is precisely these spectral tactics that are disintegrating his American problematic: his clarity, his resoluteness, his sense of direction and control. These events are random from his inscribed ocularcentric American perspective, which perceives the enemy simply as the object of his narrativizing gaze. But, as Caputo's discourse, especially its insistent references to his unrelieved awareness of always being looked at by an invisible enemy, itself implies, they are not random from the perspective of the Viet Cong. We are thus compelled to ask: what is the raison d'être of the Viet Cong's baffling irregular tactics?

Despite, or perhaps because of, this intensification of the blinding and dislocating anxiety provoked by his having "crossed a line of departure between the known and the unknown" and his intuitions into an other "reality" to which this relay of spectral presences points, Caputo, like virtually all the Americans who fought in Vietnam—and all the "historians," literal and metaphorical, who have chronicled it—does not ask this question that increasingly haunts his narrative. (I will return to this question later in the chapter.) Rather, he responds to these alien and dislocating conditions of guerrilla warfare—the uncanny invisibility of the enemy, the erratic and decentering violence, the senselessness of mounting casualties, the guilt activated by the gratuitous torching of villages, the waning of his sense of direction and control—in a typically American way. He attributes these terrible conditions to the alien Vietnamese land and what he takes to be the animal-like character of Vietnamese villagers who inhabit it, and, above all, to the malevolent Viet Cong insurgents: to their cunningly duplicitous (barbaric) conduct of the war—their refusal to fight in a "manly" or "civilized" manner: "up front," as it were.[24] In a way that exactly mirrors Heidegger's extension of his phenomenological distinction between anxiety and fear, that is, he willfully reduces the anxiety that has no *thing* as its object to fear, this *no* thing that demands recognition to *some thing*, to an object that is nameable and thus comprehensible, that, as the etymology of this word suggests, can be "taken hold of," "managed." To regain the directionality and the control the conditions of warfare in Vietnam have disintegrated, Caputo resorts, in other words, to the pervasive rationalization that "clarifies" the ambiguous status of the Vietnamese subaltern that American soldiers always and necessarily encountered in their search and destroy missions, the very rationalization that had troubled him when he first heard it from his commanding officer prior to this first mission:

> Peterson concluded by reading instructions from brigade concerning rules of engagement. . . . To avoid [killing innocent Vietnamese civilians] brigade again ordered that . . . no fire be directed at unarmed Vietnamese *unless they were running*. A running Vietnamese was a fair target. This left us bewildered and uneasy. No one was eager to shoot civilians. Why should the act of running identify someone as a Communist? What if we shot a Vietnamese who turned out to have a legitimate reason for running? Would that be a justifiable act of war or grounds for court-martial? The skipper finally said, 'Look, I don't know what this is supposed to mean, but I talked to battalion and they said that as far as they're concerned, if he's dead and Vietnamese, he's VC. (*ARW*, 60)

As in my epigraph from Tim O'Brien's *Lake in the Woods*, everything about *this* war that oppresses Caputo—all its irregularities, its ambiguities, it flows, its differential dynamics—is reduced and incorporated into *one* and given an "American" name: "Vietnam." Despite his recurrent and telling recognition that the inhabitants of the ancient villages he and his men—and the American military machine—are ruthlessly burning or bombing or napalming to the ground are human beings and the Viet Cong insurgents they are killing do in fact have human faces, it is this characteristically Western—and especially American—reduction of the differential dynamics of being—*including human being*—to a diabolic identity that increasingly determines Caputo's actions, once he has crossed over (i.e., trangresses) into this *terra incognita*: this labyrinthine, excruciatingly ambiguous, and anxiety-provoking rhizomatic space without geographical, temporal, and moral reference points: "one of the last of the dark regions on earth" or "Indian country" as he repeatedly and tellingly puts it.

But before bearing witness to the inevitable fulfillment in practice of Caputo's inexorable end-oriented and reifying logic, I want now to return to the question instigated by his acute awareness of always being looked at—visited, as it were—by the invisible enemy, the question, as I have said, that haunts his effort to give narrative shape to his experience in the wilderness of Vietnam, but which his "manly" American problematic makes it impossible for him to ask: Why did the Vietnamese insurgents resort to a military strategy that was fundamentally grounded in the principle of invisibility and whose tactics involved the hit-and-run ambush rather than head-on confrontation? The obvious answer to this question is that they had no other recourse in the face of an infinitely more formidable American military machine. This is, of course, true. But if we read texts like Caputo's *A Rumor of War* or Tim O'Brien's *Going After Cacciato* or Ron Kovic's *Born on the Fourth of July* or John Del Vecchio's *The Thirteenth Valley* or W. D. Earhart's *Passing Time*, to name only a few of the memoirs and novels written by Vietnam veterans whose actual witness belies their impulse either to personalize this war or condemn their nation's intervention in Vietnam as a betrayal of the ideals of America, against the grain, which is to say, if we attend to what they visibly marginalize, it will be seen that this negative way of putting the answer in fact obscures the polyvalent positivity of the Vietnamese insurgents' strategy. What I have been suggesting by foregrounding the deeply back-grounded American history that Caputo's bafflement in the face of the spectral invisibility of the enemy and his loss of a sense of control and directionality precipitates is that, despite his effort to personalize and then generalize this war, *he nevertheless reveals that his individual identity is utterly implicated in the American national identity that has its origins in the myth of the exceptionalist errand in the New World wilderness.* This is the collective instrumentalist identity, aptly called *homo faber* by Hannah Arendt (to distinguish it from the *vita activa* of the public realm),[25] that has its origins in Europe (the "West") and is characterized by its (logo-)centeredness, its visualist orientation toward being (which spatializes and reifies its differential dynamics), its hierarchical binarist logic, its linear narrative consciousness, and its practicality, that is, its assumption that *doing* (accomplishment) is the ideal and end—the measure—of man—and, therefore, its representation of that which is radically other as *nonbeing.*

When this American history, which the personalization of his experience cannot quite subdue, is made explicit and reconstellated into Caputo's narrative, especially that crucial aspect of its itinerary that focuses on his anxiety, bafflement, and dislocation, the meaning of the language he insistently uses to refer to the invisibility of the Viet Cong undergoes a sea change. The "phantoms," "chimera" (*ARW*, 95) "mysterious wraiths" (*ARW*, 103, 117), "djinns" (*ARW*, 139), "shadows" (*ARW*, 229) that pervade and haunt Caputo's text become something more than mere metaphors; they become literal, that is, the absolute Other of the instrumentalist ("can do") discourse of America. As such, they suggest that the war these subaltern Vietnamese insurgents fought against the American military machine was not simply determined by a necessarily reactive strategy aided and abetted by a jungle landscape, but by a deliberately active one. It was as if this small and powerless army of Southeast Asian "savages" had discovered the Achilles' heel of the otherwise invincible American war machine in the very Western metropolitan culture—its imperial metaphysics and epistemology—that underlay its concept of war and then refused to obey—to be answerable to—its imperatives of closure. To put it more specifically, it is as if the Viet Cong had discovered that the American war machine was driven by an unexamined commitment to a (Western) narrative structure—the beginning-middle-end or promise/fulfillment model—that, analogous to Western philosophy's and literature's spatialization and linearization of time, has always privileged frontal warfare and the decisive battle and, in response to this knowledge, resisted its imperial project by organizing their tactics around the (non)principles of invisibility, rhizomatic mobility (errancy), and open-endedness: by, that is, positively assuming the spectrality—the nonbeingness—that the West has always attributed to its nomadic subaltern Other. The result of this spectral nomadic strategy is by now familiar, even if its cause is not. In refusing frontal engagement—the "decisive" battle—in adopting instead a tactics of invisible and episodic mobility, the Vietnamese insurgents fractured the inordinately powerful American war machine, immobilized its forwarding movement, and, in the wake of this perpetual stalemate, immobilized its forwarding movement: wearied the United States into defeat. What Caputo—and so many other American veterans—says over and over from the perspective of a small unit about this fracturing, bafflement, and immobilization applies as well to the larger military—and national—context of which his unit is a part:

> My platoon started toward its first objective, a knoll on the far side of the milky-brown stream. It was an objective only in the geographical sense; it had no military significance. In the vacuum of that jungle we could have gone in as many directions as there were points on a compass, and any one direction was as likely to lead us to VC, or away from them, as any other. The guerrillas were everywhere, which is another way of saying they were nowhere. The knoll merely gave us a point of reference. It was a place to go, and getting there provided us with the illusion we were accomplishing something. (*ARW*, 107)[26]

This attribution of strategic deliberateness to the Vietnamese insurgents is, of course, speculation drawn from a poststructuralist "*lecture symptomale*" of Caputo's narrative. But it should be remembered that the revolutionary leadership of the Vietnamese people—this particular constituency of "the yellow hordes," as all too many Americans referred to the subaltern enemy (*ARW*, 179)—had had ample time—a hundred years of brutal French colonial rule, in fact—to experience the *"mission civilisatrice"* of the metropolitan West and to learn under the regime of its ruthless gaze about its deepest operative structures. From early in his career as a revolutionary intent on the liberation of Vietnam from French colonial rule, Ho Chi Minh, for example, fervently believed that "it was necessary to understand the enemy in order to defeat him," and to this end spent half his lifetime in France studying French imperial culture.[27] And it is possible that what Ho learned during that time about the cultural identity of the West is reflected by the words of a member of the NLF (National Liberation Front, i.e., the South Vietnamese insurgents called erroneously by the Americans, including Caputo, the Viet Cong), paraphrased by Herman Rapaport in his brilliant Deleuzian essay to which I referred in chapter 2:

> Truong Son of the N. L. F. reports that the North Vietnamese took very much into account the American expectation that one ought to win "decisive battles" in Vietnam. "Though somewhat disheartened, the Americans, obdurate by nature and possessed of substantial forces, still clung to the hope for a military solution, for decisive victories on the battlefield." Truong Son's comments are based on the perception that an American view of an all-or-nothing victory can easily be converted to a tactic by which the "superior forces," anxious for quick victory, are by way of a certain fracturing, reduced to something less than victory. That is, the North Vietnamese immediately realized that a molecularization of its forces among those of the Southern resisters would force the United States to spread its resources thin. Son's assessment of the American strategy is that "it did not specifically center on anything" and that "the Americans and their puppets had no definite way of utilizing their mobile and occupation forces. . . ." For this reason, even when conflict was "head on," that conflict would be articulated in terms of a certain passivity, since action does not necessarily lead to anything more than action itself. Moreover, the communists saw to it that the "corps" would be disarticulated along various mobile "fronts" all at the same time. In doing so they insured that "action" would be reduced to random or marginalized events which even if successfully won by Americans would not mean victory. As so many soldiers said to themselves over and over again, "what a waste."[28]

IV

It is the memory of this fracturing passive action in this increasingly "haunted dangerous wilderness" (*ARW*, 107)—this decentering of the powerful American war machine inaugurated by the nomadic mobility of the Viet Cong and, despite the carnage, mutilation, and death it left behind (often from "friendly fire"), ending in inconclusiveness—that usurps control of Caputo's retrospective narrative. But instead of attending to the accumulating intimations suggesting that this complex of dislocating and fragmenting conditions are both individual and collective, his and the American military machine's and ultimately America's, he is compelled by the very hegemonic discourse of America—his deeply inscribed belief in its founding "truths' that has rendered him a synecdoche of America—to perceive them in personal terms. Again and again in these engagements with the Viet Cong insurgents in "Indian country," it is *his* frustration at the bloody inconclusiveness—the sense of getting nowhere, of always returning to the same starting point, despite the incremental slaughter of his comrades, that his retrospective discourse overdetermines:

> We fought no great battles. There was not massive hemorrhaging, just a slow trickle of blood in a series of ambushes and firefights. Although there was more action [in the summer of 1965] than in the spring, contacts were still rare. . . . When contacts did occur, they were violent, but nothing ever really changed. . . . Men were killed and wounded, and our patrols kept going out to fight in the same places they had fought the week before and the week before that. *The situation remained the same.* (*ARW*, 182; my emphasis)

Like that of virtually all the young Americans who fought in Vietnam, Caputo's response to this mounting sense of helpless blockage is not to shift his attention to the motives of the Viet Cong, but predictably to yearn for the decisive battle that characterized America's earlier, "civilized," wars. (He repeatedly and appropriately refers to this Eurocentric form of war as the "set-piece battle" *ARW*, xv, 272–273.) As he puts it in his summary "Prologue" (which also underscores what I have said about his related inability to narrativize *this*, first postmodern, war):

> Writing about this kind of warfare is not a simple task. Repeatedly, I have found myself wishing that I had been the veteran of a conventional war, with dramatic campaigns and historic battles for

subject matter instead of a monotonous succession of ambushes and fire-fights. But there were no Normandies or Gettysburgs for us, no epic clashes that decided the fates of armies and nations. The war was mostly a matter of enduring weeks of expectant waiting and, at random intervals, of conducting vicious manhunts through jungles and swamps where snipers harassed us constantly and booby traps cut us down one by one. (*ARW*, xiv–xv)

But Caputo's response to the increasing frustration precipitated by the inconclusive carnage of the guerrilla warfare waged by the Viet Cong is not simply to yearn futilely for the "set-piece battle." Predictably, and more fatefully, it is also, as I have suggested, to blame the victim of American aggression: to transform him or her into the victimizer. More specifically, he identifies the Vietnamese insurgents as the malevolent cause of these conditions and, without considering the stakes for which they were fighting, comes to seek personal vengeance against them. But since they are "everywhere and nowhere," this growing desire for "retribution" (*ARW*, 104) takes the form of objectifying the complex conditions of the war, that is, of reducing them to an inclusive and nameable *image*—"Vietnam"—that would render the otherwise impossible act of revenge possible. This personal state of mind thus manifests itself in a much more tolerant attitude toward the increasingly common practice that flaunted the official "rules of engagement" that were intended to protect the noncombatant peasantry from harm. I mean the indiscriminate killing of Vietnamese people on the basis of the insidious but, given the conditions of *this war*, all too easily rationalizable notion that every dead Vietnamese was a dead Viet Cong.

Though Caputo never condones this brutal practice—whenever he refers to it, it is invariably to other Americans—he nevertheless makes it clear that he can understand why it had become increasingly common. And this is not only because, as one of them, he could identify with their anxiety-driven inability to differentiate between a noncombatant Vietnamese villager and one who was either a Viet Cong guerrilla or a sympathizer. It is also because he was aware that this murderous practice was the necessary consequence of the "war of attrition" that superseded this "splendid little war" when the Pentagon and MACV (Military Assistance Command Vietnam) came to realize that the Vietnamese enemy would not be drawn into decisive battles. This was the bureaucratic euphemism that, in reality, meant the grotesquely inhuman "body count," which, in increasingly measuring success according to the performative "kill ratio"—the proportion of the number of Viet Cong killed to the number of Americans killed—not only reduced the frustratingly ambiguous conditions of this war to quantifiable and manageable data (data that enabled "performance"), but also utterly dehumanized life and death in the name of a "higher" abstract cause, and, in so doing, made the indiscriminate killing of Vietnamese by American combat units inevitable, common, routine, and banal. Caputo comes to know this with a vengeance when, in the summer of 1965, he is reassigned, against his will, to his parent Regimental Headquarters Company as Casualty Reporting Officer, or, as he puts it, "the keeper of Colonel Wheeler's scoreboard":

> The colonel, an easy-going man in most instances, was adamant about maintaining an accurate scoreboard: high-ranking visitors from Danang and Saigon often dropped in unannounced to see how the regiment was performing. And the measures of a unit's performance in Vietnam were not the distances it had advanced or the number of victories it had won, but the number of enemy soldiers it had killed (the body count) and the proportion between that number and the number of its own dead (the kill ratio). The scoreboard thus allowed the colonel to keep track of the battalions and companies under his command and, quickly and crisply, to rattle off impressive figures to visiting dignitaries. My unsung task in that statistical war was to do the arithmetic. If I had been an agent of death as platoon leader, as a staff officer I was death's bookkeeper. (*ARW*, 160)

Eventually, especially after he has been ordered by the colonel to exhume the mutilated and decaying bodies of four dead Viet Cong guerrillas to be put on display for a visiting Marine General from MACV in Saigon, this quantification of the horror of human death comes to appall Caputo. But despite his genuine revulsion in the face of this banalizing arithmetic, it is not the innocent Vietnamese that this war of attrition was indiscriminately killing, nor his uneasiness about America—its intervention in Vietnam and its conduct of the war—to say nothing about its national identity—that he overdetermines in his narrative. It is, rather, the psychological effects of this quantification of death incumbent on the policy of measuring military success on "the body count"—of his becoming "death's bookkeeper." What he emphasizes, in other words, even as these other alternative interpretations haunt his narrative, is his will to repress these visitations, then, his guilt at hearing incrementally of the horrible—and pointless—deaths of his former comrades—Sullivan, Gautier, Reasoner, Parsons, Pappas, Devlin, Lockhart, Bryce—and finally, an ill-defined and ominous sense of uncontrollable rage without outlet that was the consequence of this official indifference to the lives of American soldiers, especially the friends he had come to know intimately as unique individuals, who were dying tragically

> for nothing tangible. Those men might as well have died in automobile accidents. It made me feel guilty about my comparatively safe life on the staff, guiltier still about being the one who had translated their deaths into numbers on a scoreboard. I had acquired a hatred for the scoreboard, for the sight of it. It symbolized everything I despised about the staff, the obsession with statistics, the indifference toward the tragedy of death; and because I was on the staff, I despised myself. It did not matter that I was there by orders, that I had made several attempts to transfer back to a line company. I despised myself every time I went up to the scoreboard and wrote in some new numbers. Maybe it was an extreme form of the cafard. One of its symptoms is a hatred for everything and everyone around you. . . . At other times, I felt urges to kill someone else.(*ARW*, 191)

V

It is this heightened but ill-defined rage, indissolubly related to his mounting frustration over the meaninglessness of his comrades' deaths—their dying "for nothing *tangible*" (my emphasis)—that Caputo brings back to the dark Vietnam wilderness after he is finally reassigned to a line company. The difference between the conditions of combat he experienced prior to becoming "death's bookkeeper" and those he now confronts is a matter of greater intensification. In the wake of the United States' abandonment of the strategy of counterinsurgency for that of attrition, the "splendid little war," of the months before "had become a different war. The casualty rate had increased enough to make death and maiming seem commonplace" (*ARW*, 207). It had become a more cruel, more violent, more savage war. But in essence these conditions remained excruciatingly the same: the invisibility of the enemy, the inability to discriminate between civilian and foe, the randomness and inconsequence of a military engagement when it occurred, the lack of a front-and-rear and progressive movement: all the circumstances of this war that destructured his narrative expectation of closure—of accomplishment—and broke down his sense of control and resoluteness. Caputo underscores the maddening sameness of these recurrent violent passive actions by bringing his accounts of several instances to their identical inconclusive conclusions with the ritual refrain: "All secure. Situation remains the same (*ARW*, 228–231).

Nor, despite certain symptoms, does Caputo's response to these conditions change in any essential way. He has become acutely aware that the "attrition" of this "different" "war of attrition" was an "attrition the enemy inflicted on us and that which we inflicted on ourselves" by way of "friendly fire" and the internal tensions these conditions made inevitable (*ARW*, 207). And as an American inscribed by the economy of the Protestant work ethic, he has come to understand the resonantly dark meaning of the word "wasted": "In that war, soldier's slang for death was 'wasted.' So-and-so was wasted. It was a good word" (*ARW*, 210). This awareness is especially underscored after Caputo learns about the death of Walter Levy, his friend from their time at Quantico, who had been killed in an attempt, while wounded in the legs, to save the life of a corpsman: "a patriot—the best sort, the kind who do not walk around with American flags in their lapels. He had volunteered because it had seemed the right thing to do, and he had done it quietly, easily, and naturally. He had one other attribute rare in this indulgent age: an inflexible fidelity to standards" (*ARW*, 211). But this accumulating recognition that these disabling conditions were as much the consequence of American military policy as they were of the enemy he was fighting does not instigate a different interpretation of them—one that reads them from the perspective of a subaltern people fighting for their independence from foreign intervention and occupation. Despite the emergence in his consciousness of the question of America's moral culpability, Caputo, like Al Santoli and virtually all the other Americans who have tried to come to terms with the Vietnam War in its aftermath, repeatedly wards off this haunting question, which now cannot be interred, by subordinating it to the "benign" ethos of American individualism, the universalist ethos that, in attributing the visibly specific brutal acts of American violence to the "betrayal" of its values, obscures the latent violence, now virtually enacted, in them. This deflection of attention from the historical question of America's moral responsibility for its intervention in Vietnam and its brutal conduct of the war in the name of the "free world," for example, is manifest in Caputo's eulogizing apostrophe, written from the disruptive perspective of the postwar present and invoking Horace's nationalist poem, "Dulce et Decorum est Pro patria Mori," to the memory of Walter Levy, in which he reduces its force to a dependent clause: "Whatever the rights or wrongs of the war, nothing can diminish the rightness of what you tried to do. Yours was the greater love. You died for the man you tried to save, and you died *pro patria*. It was not altogether sweet and fitting, your death, but I'm sure you died believing it was *pro patria*. You were faithful. Your country was not" (*ARW*, 212).[29]

Nor does Caputo's awareness of the waste of lives (it is invariably American lives to which he refers) incumbent on the military policy of attrition deflect his pent-up rage against the elusive Viet Cong that has been precipitated by these disarticulating conditions. Of all the reasons behind his decision to return to a line company in the bush, he tells his reader, the most compelling was retribution:

> Finally, there was hatred, a hatred buried so deep that I could not then admit its existence. I can now, though it is still painful. I burned with a hatred for the Viet Cong. . . . I did not hate the enemy for their politics, but for murdering Simpson, for executing that boy whose body had been found in the river, for blasting the life out of Walt Levy. Revenge was one of reasons I volunteered for a line company. I wanted a chance to kill somebody. (*ARW*, 219)

And it is, above all, this inexorable personal desire for revenge precipitated by the conditions of *this war* that drives him into ordering the fateful act of murderous violence that would bring his tour of duty—and his narrative—to its self-destructive close.

As the ferocity of the guerrilla war intensifies, the frequency of engagements accelerate, and the mutilations and deaths mount, what Caputo focuses on is not the American policy of "attrition" emanating from Saigon and, beyond that, the Pentagon and demanding larger numbers of dead bodies (though he invokes this imperative to justify his will to kill Vietnamese), but, rather, his sense of absolute futility. It was the feeling that this kind of random war, in which one fought against phantoms, actions ended inconclusively, and no ground was gained despite the toll of dead, disintegrated control and resoluteness and precluded arriving at a successful end: the decisiveness and satisfaction of *accomplishment*. Gradually but inexorably this focus coalesces into an implacable need "to *do* something" in this uncanny limit situation, where the phenomena of the world had become epiphenomenal:

> Staring at the jungle and at the ruined temple, hatred welled up in me; a hatred for this green, moldy, alien world in which we fought and died.
>
> My thoughts and feeling over the next few hours are irretrievably jumbled now, but at some point in the early evening [some

time during the month before Caputo's tour of duty terminated],
I was seized by an irresistible compulsion to do something.
"Something's got to be done" was about the clearest thought
that passed through my brain. I was fixed on the company's intolerable predicament. We could now muster only half of our
original strength, and half of our effectives had been wounded at
least once. . . . It was madness for us to go on walking down
those trails and tripping booby traps without any chance to retaliate. *Retaliate.* The word rang in my head. *I will retaliate.* It
was then that my chaotic thoughts began to focus on the two
men whom Le Dung, Crowe's informant, had identified as Viet
Cong. [*ARW*, 292–203] *My mind did more than focus on them*;
it *fixed on them like a heat-seeking missile fixing on the tail-pipe
of a jet.* They became an obsession. I would get them. I would get
them before they got any more of us; before they got me. I'm
going to get those bastards, I said to myself, suddenly feeling
giddy. (*ARW*, 299; the third emphasis is mine)

Thus fixated, Caputo orders three of his men—Allan, Crowe, and
Lonehill—to "*get those goddamned VC*" (*ARW*, 300), but in such a way
that his command would convey the impression that he meant them to
summarily execute the captives, despite the fact that they had been previously identified as civilians (*ARW*, 300). After the patrol leaves for the
village, Caputo begins to doubt his decision, and even entertains the
thought of retracting it. But he "could not bring [himself] to do it. Something had to be done" (*ARW*, 301). And, as he says in the next paragraph. "something was done."

When Caputo's men return from the village, they tell him exultantly
of their clandestine invasion of the hooch where the suspected Viet Cong
lived, the rifle beating of a young Vietnamese girl they found there, the
cold-blooded execution of one of the men, and the capture and later execution of the other on the pretext that he was attempting an escape.
When Caputo goes out to examine the body, which the patrol had
brought back to the perimeter, he finds to his horror that they had "mis-
takenly" killed the "informer," Le Dung:

They walked off. I stayed awhile looking at the corpse. The wide,
glowing, glassy eyes stared at me in accusation. The dead boy's
open mouth screamed silently his innocence and our guilt. In the
darkness and confusion, out of fear, exhaustion, and brutal instincts acquired in the war, the marines had made a mistake. An
awful mistake. They killed the wrong man. The boy's innocent

blood was on my hands as much as it was on theirs. I had sent
them out there. My God, what have we done? I thought. I could
think of nothing else. My God, what have we done? Please God,
forgive us. What have we done?

Clicking off the flashlight, I told Coffel to get a burial party
together. I did nor know what else to do with the body of
Crowe's informant, the boy named Le Dung. (*ARW*, 304)

Caputo's narration of this rapid sequence of events, in which the rhetoric
of "doing" is so disturbingly ironic and prominent, demands careful
attention, not only because it is the climax of his retrospective personal
narrative, but also because it, like the Vietnam War itself, has been insistently read as the denouement of an "American tragedy,"[30] which means,
of course, a story that ends in national *catharsis*, the purgation of the violent political history—the *thisness*—of the Vietnam War from the collective American cultural memory.[31] To begin with, this sequence is
inaugurated by what I will call, after Herman Melville, and for a reason
that will shortly become clear, a telling "concentering" of the dislocating
and disabling conditions of combat in the Vietnam wilderness—its nothingness, as it were—that moves through two phases of objectification intended to make them more intelligible and manageable: take-holdable, as
it were. He first identifies these uncannily undecidable conditions with
Vietnam, "this green, moldy, alien world": America's radical Other.
Then, since his objectification of these always ambiguous conditions of
combat is still too large, amorphous, and unwieldy to understand and
manage, he goes on to further reduce this inclusive image into a minia-
turized version of the same: the image of the two young Vietnamese boys
in the village of Giao-Tri, who are suspected of being Viet Cong. *Everything* that maddens this young American about this war—the elusiveness
of the enemy, the inability to differentiate between friend and foe, the
volatile tropical climate, the randomness of violence, the inconclusiveness
of actions—is now incorporated in this concentered, synecdochical personification. And it is this progressive reduction of an intangible nothing
to something tangible that enables him to "*do* something" about it.

What Caputo is saying symptomatically, what he is trying to repress
by rigorously restricting the point of view to the personal register, is that
the gratuitous violence he committed against innocent Vietnamese civilians was the (self-destructive) culmination of a personal narrative *that
was necessarily re-enacting the (self-destructive) collective American narrative in Vietnam*. Despite the glamorous image of the Green Berets fos-
tered by the Kennedy administration, the military strategy in Vietnam
favored by the military command in Saigon (and the "can do" planners in

the Pentagon) was from the beginning, as Caputo everywhere intimates, oriented by what was known as "the Army Concept," which, as the military historian Andrew Krepinevich observes, was characterized by "a focus on mid-intensity, or conventional, war and a reliance on high volumes of firepower to minimize casualties—in effect, the substitution of material cost at every available opportunity to avoid payment in blood."[32] It was, in other words, a "European" perspective on warfare, by which I mean a metropolitan perspective on war that, like Caputo's, plays itself out in narrative form—according to a beginning, middle, and end structure that is informed by a metaphysical principle of presence and its hierarchical binary logic (identity versus difference), that assumes the space of conflict to be that of the front and the rear and the logical economy of movement, an offensive forwarding that understands military engagement in terms of the decisive battle, and that ends in an unequivocal military victory over the differential enemy that is represented as peace.

When the Vietnamese insurgents refused to accommodate themselves to this metaphysical/Western concept of warfare, the frustrated American military command was forced to revise its strategy. But this revision did not take account of the cultural implications of this systematic refusal on the part of the subaltern Other to abide by its narrative logic. As in the individual case of Caputo, the collective unconsciousness of the American military command was so deeply inscribed by the "truth" of the American narrative that privileged and, in turn, demanded accomplishment—getting something done—that it precluded the possibility of seeing the conditions of this war from the eyes of the subaltern Other. Instead, it sought the same decisive narrative end by other means: the "war of attrition," which rendered the invisible and intangible "enemy"—ultimately Vietnam—visible to the metropolitan gaze, tangible, and thus assailable. This was the strategy of high technological mass destruction that at first (in the period of Caputo's service) took the form of the relentless search and destroy mission preceded and often accompanied by napalm bombings and artillery barrages, but which, when this type of operation accomplished nothing, eventually escalated into the massive B-52 bombings, the systematic defoliation of the Vietnamese wilderness (which also contaminated it with the deadly Agent Orange), and the spraying of herbicides into the Vietnamese rice paddies, all undertaken on the assumption that these tactics of mass technological violence would kill or enable the killing of enough of the enemy to "bring him to his knees." This official strategy of indiscriminate mass destruction—there is no other name for it but "terror"—is precisely that which increasingly preoccupies Caputo's narrative until it comes to culmination shortly before his fatal order:

Having lost about thirty percent of his command the past month, Neal [Caputo's company commander] had become intolerable. I assumed battalion was putting a great deal of pressure on him; since Operation Long Lance ended, the company had killed only three guerrillas and captured two more, while suffering six times as many casualties itself. C Company's kill ratio was below standard. Bodies. Bodies. Bodies. Battalion wanted bodies. Neal wanted Bodies. He lectured his officers on the importance of aggressiveness and made implied threats when he thought we lacked that attribute. . . . So we went along with the captain's policy [of offering extra beer rations for every confirmed VC killed], without reflecting on its moral implications. That is the level to which we had sunk from the lofty idealism of a year before. (*ARW*, 294)

The inscribed will to "perform"—to accomplish, to bring crisis to a productive closure—of the American chain of command extending outward from Caputo's company commander to battalion headquarters and beyond to MACV and the Pentagon was utterly frustrated by the strategic refusal of the Viet Cong to expose themselves to the vastly superior American war machine. And in its arrogant assumption of the rightness of its cause that, I am suggesting, had its ultimate source in the "exceptionalist" origins of America, it tacitly authorized the indiscriminate killing of Vietnamese in the name of the "body count." As author of his narrative, Caputo is unwilling to acknowledge the continuity between his individual actions and those of his military superiors, to say nothing about his country's national identity. Here, for example, he both disassociates his postwar (educated) self from the command's perspective and implies that his and his men's going along with the chain of command's banalizing of human life and death was a betrayal of the "lofty ideals" of America. If, however, we reconstellate this "confession" into the context of Caputo's characterization of his psychological condition prior to his order to "get those goddamned VC," we are compelled, despite, indeed, because of the visibility of his reluctance, to perceive the ineluctable relay between his personal act of violence and the collective act of violence perpetrated against the Vietnamese people and their land by the American military machine, the American government, and ultimately—and most tellingly—by America itself.

In that climactic moment of his memoir, we recall, Caputo tells his postwar reader that he was enabled to "do something"—to break out of the paralyzing psychological and practical impasse into which he had been plunged—by personifying the undecidability of the impossible conditions of warfare in the inclusive image of the two suspected Viet Cong men (later, after they are dead, he will pointedly call them boys) and then, in an astonishingly resonant image, likening this metamorphosis of his hitherto fragmented—benighted and irresolute—mind to a "heat-seeking missile fixing on the tail-pipe of a jet." When one remembers that Caputo virtually repeats this image pertaining to getting something done in his preface (which means that it was written at the end as an essential summing up of the content of his memoir [*ARW*, xix]), we cannot help realizing that Caputo's narrative of this climactic moment of his experience in Vietnam echoes that of another American writer who, much earlier, in the context of a relentlessly genocidal expansionist project undertaken in the name of the American Adamic Word, had made explicit the dark underside of America's national identity as that was inexorably formed by its exceptionalist errand in the world's wilderness. I am referring, of course, to Herman Melville, the nomadic exile from his homeland, who represented Captain Ahab—the American Adam—as the quintessential embodiment of the reifying logical economy of American self-reliance and his "fiery pursuit" of Moby-Dick, which turned the *Pequod* (the ship of state) into a phallic technological instrument of indiscriminate destruction, as an Adamic monomania. I mean by the latter, as a single-minded and unerring, indeed, lunatic, search and destroy mission enabled by a metaphysical representation of being at large (the elusive and ineffable white whale) that reduced ("concentered") its uncontainable (sublime) force to a singular name in order to make its unpresentable temporal disseminations—its spectral nothingness—decidable, presentable, and "practically assailable":

> No turbaned Turk, no hired Venetian or Malay, could have smote him with more *seeming* malice. Small reason was there to doubt, then, that ever since that almost fatal encounter, Ahab had cherished a *wild vindictiveness against the whale*, all the more fell for that in his frantic morbidness he at last came to identify with him, not only *all* his bodily woes, but *all* his intellectual and spiritual exasperations. The White Whale swam before him as the monomaniac incarnation of *all* those malicious agencies which some deep men feel eating in them, till they are left living on with half a heart and half a lung. That *intangible malignity* which had been from the beginning; to whose dominion even the modern Christians ascribe one-half of the worlds; which the ancient Ophites of the east reverenced in their statue devil;—Ahab did not fall down and worship it like them; but deliriously transferring its idea to the abhorred white whale, he pitted himself, all mutilated, against it. He piled upon the whale's

white hump the sum of all the general rage and hate felt by his
whole race from Adam down; and then, as if his chest had been
a mortar, he burst his hot heart's shell upon it.[33]

What I want to suggest, in pointing to the remarkable parallel between
Caputo's and Melville's "furious trope"—his self-portrayal *in this limit situation* and Melville's representation of Ahab and his relentless mission—
is that Caputo's deeply backgrounded narrative belies his sustained retrospective effort to individualize/universalize his experience as a combat officer in the Vietnam War. Its excess discloses instead that the logic that
compelled him to commit a gratuitous act of murderous violence against
innocent Vietnamese is, finally, the (mono)logic, not simply of the military
institution to which he belongs, but also, despite appearances to the contrary, of the culture he represents. It is the reifying "Ahabian" logic that
was founded on the divinely ordained Adamic mission in the New World
wilderness (and always practiced on the frontier) to "build a Citty on a
Hill," whatever the cost to its inhabitants, and which achieved its most efficient (and deadly) form in the secularized instrumental ("can do") logic of
those Cold War policy experts who, like Robert McNamara, McGeorge
Bundy, William Bundy, Walt Rostow, and John McNaughton, planned
and conducted the war in Vietnam.[34] What Caputo *does* in the village of
Giao-Tri, this symptomatic identification with Ahab's monomania suggests, replicates what his country *does* in Vietnam at large.It is the specter
of this *unjustifiable* act of violence against the subaltern Other inhering in
the exceptionalist American national identity but historically obscured by
its representation by the custodians of the American cultural memory as an
unwanted necessity in the "defense" of freedom against tyranny, that the
thisness—the singularity—of the Vietnam War has raised.Despite Caputo's
effort to resist it, this continuity between his private act and the act of
the nation of which he is a member is what emerges spectrally to haunt
his account of the court-martial trial, which brings his narrative to its
troubling "end."

VI

In his representation of the court-martial proceedings, in which he and
his men have been accused of premeditated homicide, Caputo indicates
acute symptomatic awareness that the discourse of the military tribunal
repeats at the site of thought the same (Ahabian) instrumentalism that
informed the United States' conduct of the war in Vietnam, the logic of
the body count, which resulted in the indiscriminate annihilation of any

difference, whether natural or human, that contradicted its truth and prevented it from accomplishing its preconceived (narrative) task. This insight is especially pronounced in his courageously honest climactic attempt, against the self inscribed by the hegemonic discourse of America, to interpret the "conspicuous blank" space on one of the forms containing the charges against him:

> There was a lot of other stuff—statements by witnesses, inquiry reports, and so forth—but one square on form DD457 was conspicuously blank. It was the square labeled EXPLANATORY CIRCUMSTANCES ARE SUBMITTED HEREWITH. Early in the investigation, I wondered why the investigating officer had not submitted any explanatory or extenuating circumstances. Later, after I had time to think things over, I drew my own conclusions: the explanatory circumstance was the war. The killings had occurred in war. They had occurred, moreover, in a war whose sole aim was to kill Viet Cong, a war in which those ordered to do the killing often could not distinguished the Viet Cong from the civilians, a war in which civilians in "free-fire zone" were killed every day by weapons far more horrible than pistols and shotguns. The deaths of Le Dung and Le Du could not be divorced from the nature and conduct of the war. They were an inevitable product of the war. . . . But to raise those points in explanation or extenuation would be to raise a host of ambiguous moral questions. It could even raise the question of the morality of American intervention in Vietnam; or, as one officer told me, "It could open up a real can of worms." Therefore, the five men on the patrol and I were to be tried as common criminals, much as if we had murdered two people in the course of a bank robbery during peacetime. If we were found guilty, the Marine Corps' institutional conscience would be clear. Six criminals, who, of course, did not represent the majority of America's fine fighting sons, had been brought to justice. Case closed. If we were found innocent, the Marine Corps could say, "Justice has taken its course, and in a court-martial conducted according to the facts and the rules of evidence, no crime was found to have been committed." Case closed. Either way, the military institution won. (*ARW*, 305–306)

Caputo tries desperately to *raise* the question of this visible blank space— to give its silence voice, as it were—to his legal council, Jim Rader, who, predictably, had prepared his "case with the hard-minded pragmatism of a battalion commander preparing an attack on an enemy hill" (*ARW*,

312). "In a guerrilla war," Caputo writes in a note to this paradigmatic American, for whom reality is inexorably a matter of facts, "the line between legitimate and illegitimate killing is blurred. The policies of free-fire zones, in which a soldier is permitted to shoot at any human target, armed or unarmed, and body counts further confuse the fighting man's moral senses." In response to Caputo's spectral reminder of a silenced reality about this war that haunts the visible facts, Rader repeats at the level of the logic of the defense not only the violent gesture of the court-martial that would obliterate the differential reality that jeopardizes the authority of the Marine Corps, but also of the self-righteous American nation that would annihilate the ghost that haunts its "benign" intervention in Vietnam and its conduct of the war:

> Radar crumpled up my literary ramblings. . . . "This is all irrelevant, Phil." . . .
> "But *why?*" We didn't kill those guys in Los Angeles, for Christ's sake."
> Radar replied with a lecture on the facts of life. I cannot remember exactly what he said, but it was from him that I got the first indication that the war could not be used to explain the killings, because it would raise too many embarrassing questions. We were indeed going to be charged as if we had killed both men on the streets of Los Angeles. The case was to be tried strictly on the facts. . . . A detective story. The facts, Rader said, are what he wanted. He didn't want philosophy. (*ARW*, 310)

Despite his threshold insight into the willful blindness of American officialdom to its complicity in the synecdochical murder of the two innocent Vietnamese boys—indeed, a blindness that seems to be haunted by an unwanted awareness of the criminality of its conduct of the war—Caputo, *as American*, is finally incapable of facing this other repressed reality—this "real can of worms" as the banal and banalizing language of American officialdom puts the horror of the Vietnam War—the very terrorist reality his narrative cumulatively and symptomatically brings to resonant presence. The closest he comes to articulating it is when, after capitulating to Rader's and American officialdom's factual understanding of the testimony, which eventually exonerates Caputo and his men, he writes: "None of this testimony, none of these 'facts' amounted to the truth. . . . the war in general and the U.S. military policies in particular were ultimately to blame for the deaths of Le Du and Le Dung. That was the truth and it was that truth which the whole proceeding was designed to conceal" (*ARW*, 312). But in the end, after he has signed his separate peace, he backs away from even that minimal accusation—minimal, because its implicit emphasis on the betrayal of the cultural ideals of America allows for its exoneration—by resorting once again to the rationalization adopted by Santoli and so many other veterans—the "eyewitnesses" of the 1980s—who have "remembered" the horrors of the Vietnam War. He withdraws from history into the subjective realm of the personal and, however inadvertently, transforms his historical identity into that of the tragic (universally human) survivor, who suffers the slings and arrows of the outrageous fortunes of war (including the guilt that accrues in the process) but refuses to break under their powerful blows:

> I already regarded myself as a casualty of the war, a moral casualty, and like all serious casualties, I felt detached from everything. . . . I had not broken during the five month ordeal. I would not break. No matter what they did to me, they could not make me break. All my inner reserves had been committed to that battle for emotional and mental survival. I had nothing left for other struggles. The war simply wasn't my show any longer. I had declared a truce between me and the Viet Cong, signed a personal armistice, and all I asked for was a chance to live for myself on my terms. . . . The important thing was to get through this insane predicament with some degree of dignity. I would not break. (*ARW*, 315)

Caputo's effort to inter the *singularity* of the Vietnam War by invoking the dialectics of tragedy compels us to recall Al Santoli's inaugural metonymic invocation of Chosu's haiku—"Though it is broken—/ Broken again—still it's there, / The moon on the water"—to emphasize the pathos of the American veterans who, like Caputo, refused to "break"— endured and survived the ravages of war for the purpose of rehabilitating their tainted image in the minds of the American public—and to deflect attention from its historical realities. More significantly, this dialectics also compels us to remember CBS's *60 Minutes II* staging, twenty years later, of the interview with the winner of the Congressional Medal of Honor, the former senator from Nebraska, Bob Kerrey, the narrative structure of which, like the court-martial proceeding in Caputo's memoir, studiedly precludes raising the question of America's complicity in Kerrey's murderous acts in Thanh Phong in February 1969 by focusing on the personal guilt he has silently—and nobly—endured for so long a time.

In thus universalizing *this war*, the very specific war that in his analysis of the conspicuous blank space he tentatively distinguishes from war in general ("The killings . . . had occurred . . . in a war whose sole aim was to kill Viet Cong, a war in which those ordered to do the killing often could not distinguish the Viet Cong from the civilians"), Caputo, in a now classic gesture of evasion, deflects our attention from the "other reality" that inhabits the blank space in the very process of calling our attention to it. But, as I have tried to suggest, the extraordinary force of the other reality cumulatively disclosed by his "story" overwhelms the feebleness of his conscious effort to exorcize "it": its specter returns in the very "end" of his narrative to visit him and the idea of America he finally cannot call into question. This comes through poignantly—but inexorably—in the multiple ironies of the "Epilogue," in which Caputo, now a reporter, in April 1975, "ten years and one month after [he] had landed at Danang with the 9th Expeditionary Brigade" bears older and "wiser" witness, in the incantatory repetitions of finality, to the "closure" of the American adventure in Vietnam that began when the United States, in the exceptionalist spirit of the New World, took over the burden of the *mission civilisatrice* from the decadent Old World French in the aftermath of Dien Bien Phu: the fall of Saigon and the evacuation of the last Americans in Vietnam:

> The evacuees were processed and sent down to the scorching mess deck for a meal. Most of us were giddy with relief, but one disconsolate diplomat from the American Embassy just sat and muttered to himself, "It's over. It's the end. It's the end of an era. It's a lousy way to have it end, but I guess it had to end some way." Exhausted and sweating, he just shook his head. "The end of an era." I supposed it was, but I was much too tired to reflect on the historical significance of the event in which I had just taken part: America had lost its first war.
>
> The next day, April 30, the ship's captain announced that the Saigon government had surrendered to the North Vietnamese. We took the news quietly. It was over. (*ARW*, 328)

VII

This war. . . . Since the publication of Caputo's *A Rumor of War* in 1977, the representational history of the Vietnam War has been characterized by an obsessive national effort, visible everywhere in what Althusser calls the ideological state apparatuses of America—the media, the culture industry, the schools—to remember Vietnam in order to forget it, to bring its recalcitrant errancy to closure. Or in the rhetoric that pervades yet continues to remain unthought in this dialectical discursive regime, to lay its ghost. Indeed, this amnesiac representational history has been one that has passed through a politically neutral phase inaugurated by the publication in the mid-1970s and early 1980s of personal memoirs like Caputo's—a time for "healing the wound" suffered by the American body politic (i.e., for reconciliation, for recuperating the lost national consensus)—to become in the period of the conservative Reagan administration a retrospective political indictment of the protest movement that, in symptomatically calling the perennial American errand in the world's wilderness into question, precipitated a national neurosis that the ideological apparatuses have called "the Vietnam syndrome." And this amnesiac history was ostensibly brought to its decisive closure with the "surgically executed" defeat of Saddam Hussein in the Gulf War of 1991." But just as the specter of *this war* haunted Caputo's final words in 1975, so it continues to haunt a triumphant post-Cold War America and the New World Order over which it unilaterally presides, even, as I will show in chapter 6, in the wake of the mobilization of the American national identity instigated by the Al Qaeda attacks on the World Trade Center and the Pentagon on September 11, 2001.

Despite the pervasive awareness, both public and private, of the persistent visitations of this significant unsaid—this specter that inhabits the conspicuous blank—in the innumerable histories of the Vietnam War, oppositional criticism in America, however, has done little more than note the phenomenon. It has not undertaken the seemingly obvious, however difficult, task of thinking its meaning, or rather it has understood its spectrality metaphorically rather than literally. As a result, I am suggesting, it has found itself in an impasse in the globalized post-Cold War era, which, in the wake of Al Qaeda's attacks and the resurgence of patriotism and America as a unified *people*, the officials of the second Bush administration overtly began referring to the "New American Century" and America's global errand as the establishment of the *Pax Americana*. We are thus compelled by this impasse of oppositional criticism to ask, "Why?" The answer is not a simple one. But perhaps retrieving those early texts, like Caputo's exemplary *A Rumor of War*, that were written by veterans who came to question America's involvement in Vietnam and its conduct of the war, and reconstellating them into this post-Cold War context might suggest a productive way into and out of this difficulty.

In the corrosive process of guerrilla warfare in the alien wilderness of Vietnam—especially at the limit situation, when Caputo, like the detective of a Borgesian postmodern story, found his American self, the ostensible clear-eyed and resolute agent of deliverance, guilty (as the fictitious Alden Pyle did but did not in *The Quiet American*) of the murder of one of those he came to Vietnam to liberate—the American ideals of this typical, utterly assimilated Italian-American youth underwent a profound dislocating disillusionment. He became, in his own words and actions, an exile from his homeland, a condition that enabled him to see the war America was fighting in Vietnam from a global perspective: with eyes, that is, other than those earlier America-centered eyes whose gaze was relentlessly unidirectional. But when, with these decentered and chastened eyes, he did finally look into the abyss that was the Vietnam War, he was unable, despite his profound honesty, to acknowledge the horror he saw in that "changed terrain" gazing accusingly back at him—"The wide, glowing, glassy, eyes stared at me in accusation. The dead boy's open mouth screamed silently his innocence and our guilt" (*ARW*, 304). Instead, as we have seen, he reduced its dreadful historical void into a personal psychological narrative that erased its self-accusatory national particularity.

Caputo's new consciousness, in other words, was not *exilic* enough. Though his dislocating limit experience enabled him to perceive the gratuitous destructiveness—and even the possible immorality—of the United States' intervention and conduct of the war, his exodus was not determinative. As his summary "Prologue" makes sadly clear, it did not enable him to perceive—or even to entertain the possibility—that the very metaphysically grounded pragmatist values informing the free world that America would unilaterally and with single-minded ferocity "save" Vietnam for were also complicitous with, indeed, foundational of, this massive practical destructiveness: "There has been a good deal of exaggeration about U.S. atrocities in Vietnam, exaggeration not about their extent but about their causes. The two most popularly held explanations for outrages like My Lai have been racist theory, which proposes that the American soldier found it easy to slaughter Asians because he did not regard them as human beings, and the frontier-heritage theory, which claims he was [like Melville's "Indian-hater par excellence] inherently violent and needed only the excuse of war to vent his homicidal instincts. . . . The evil was not inherent in the men—except in the sense that a devil dwells in us all—but in the circumstances under which they had to live and fight" (*ARW*, xviii). In other words, Caputo's decentering was not decisive enough to allow him to perceive that these perennial pragmatist values, whose origins lay in the origins of America itself, and now, at the end of modernity, had metamorphosed into a reifying and deadly banalizing instrumentalist logic, were being invoked monomaniacally—in total indifference to the desires of this subaltern people for independence from Western occupation—to justify a deadly political, military, and cultural practice. I mean a practice that, besides killing Vietnamese people indiscriminately and wholesale, was, as early as the year of Caputo's service, already blindly destroying the very fabric of an ancient earth-oriented rice culture in the name of a global order envisaged by exceptionalist America as preordained by God or

History. It was a self-righteous "Ahabian" destructive process that, by the time Caputo wrote his memoir, had become all too reminiscent of the genocide for which the West had condemned Nazi Germany.[35]

Similarly, I submit, American oppositional criticism—and this includes a great deal of the discourse of the New Americanists[36]—has not been able to extricate itself entirely from the American national problematic—its adherence to the model of culture inhering in the social contract and thus to the concept of power relations in which negotiation is the adjudicator[37]—and as a result has been inadequate to the task of "deterring democracy"[38] in the post-Cold War global age. Though, like Caputo's, it had its origins in the 1960s, which bore witness to America's devastation of Vietnam in the process of "saving" it from communism, the oppositional critical tradition has by and large represented this devastation as a "mistake" or as a "betrayal" of the foundational ideals of America. Its perspective, despite the decline of the nation-state and rise of globalization,[39] has remained too "American"—that is, not global enough in its alienated perspective—to entertain the possibility that the ontologic informing America's brutal conduct of the war was not different from but simply more efficient—and banal—than the totalizing ontologic that informed the imperial and genocidal practices of the Puritans' "errand" in the New World wilderness and of the postrevolutionary Americans' westward expansion under the aegis of Manifest Destiny.[40] Like Caputo's and that of so many other veterans who were disillusioned by America's brutally indiscriminate strategy of attrition in Vietnam, this oppositional criticism, in other words, has failed to perceive that the specter haunting the discourse of America since the fall of Saigon in 1975 (if not before) is not simply a metaphor for defeat or for error or for betrayal, but an *ontological* category. Precipitated into menacing visibility by the limit situation that was *this* Vietnam War, it is *the radical Other of*—that belongs to—the global discourse and imperial practice of America—and for this very reason, its nemesis.

It is this ontological status of the specter of the Vietnam War—and the global scope of its countertruth—that, I suggest, oppositional critics must think along with questions of international politics and economics in this globalized post-Cold War age. But to understand this directive fully, American oppositional critics must also understand the postmodern unhoming precipitated by the limit situation in Vietnam—*the situation that bore witness to the benign global policeman becoming the criminal*—as an ontological as well as a political decentering. Only such a deep—abyssal—sense of exile, announced, it should be recalled, by the poststructuralist theorists—most forcefully and effectively by Edward Said—in the wake of the French and American wars in Vietnam, can preclude its remaining vestigially nationalist. Only such an a-partness, that is, can enable its practitioners to achieve the global/local perspective, the condition of being both outside and in the national problematic, that is the sine qua non of deterring liberal capitalist democracy—the planetary aspirations of what Melville proleptically called this "Leatherstocking Nemesis"—and its homogenizing and banalizing instrumentalism—in the new global age. This is especially true in the aftermath of 9/11, when like, Captain Ahab's monomaniacal reduction of the white whale to "Moby Dick," the second Bush administration, emboldened by a recuperated national unity, has reduced the complexities of the globalized occasion—largely produced by the depredations of Western cultural and political imperialism—and the diversity of humanity to "Osama bin Laden" (or "Saddam Hussein") and made them "practically assailable" in the name of "America."

Chapter 5

"THE LAND IS YOUR ENEMY"
Tim O'Brien's Going After Cacciato

In remembrance of the
exilic life of Edward W. Said

It is common knowledge that nomads fare miserably under
our kinds of regime. We would go to any length in order to
settle them. . . . But the nomad is not necessarily one who
moves; some voyages take place *in situ*, are trips in intensity.
Even historically, nomads are not those who move about like
migrants. On the contrary, they do not move; nomads, they
nevertheless stay in the same place and continually evade the
codes of settled peoples.

—Gilles Deleuze, "Nomadic Thought"

As I have shown in the previous chapters of this book, the history of the
representation of the Vietnam War since 1975, when the last American
was ignominiously airlifted out of Saigon, has been a virtually systematic
forgetting of its corrosive reality. By this forgetting I do not simply mean
the obliteration from the American public memory of the humiliating defeat of the most powerful military machine in the history of warfare by a
small and militarily weak Third World country. Nor do I simply mean
the forgetting of the United States' virtual destruction of Vietnam in the
decade-long process of this defeat. I also mean—and this is primary insofar as it has been a neglected theme in the critical discourse about the
Vietnam War—the forgetting of the revelatory contradiction between the
United States' intervention in Vietnam in the name of a freedom always
identified with the origins of the exceptionalist American national identity in the Puritans' divinely ordained "errand in the wilderness" and its
genocidal conduct of the war, the contradiction that delegitimized the
truth discourse of American liberal capitalist democracy. The polyvalent

145

forgetting I am emphasizing, it will be recalled, was epitomized in the immediate aftermath of the first Gulf War in 1990 when President George Bush, the elder, proclaimed with relief that America had "kicked the Vietnam syndrome at last" and announced the advent of New World Order under the aegis of the United States.

In the aftermath of the fall of Saigon, following a period in which the shame of defeat instigated a collective repression of the memory of the war—a repression that also manifested itself in the vilification of the American soldiers who fought it—the frantic effort of the dominant culture in the United States to recuperate the public consensus that had disintegrated during the decade following the Tet Offensive in 1968 took the form of a pervasive call to "heal the wound" that the war had inflicted on the American national psyche, a metaphor that, however ideologically laden, was represented in neutral terms: neither the American government that inaugurated and conducted the war nor the protest movement that opposed it were to blame for the breakdown of the national consensus. Twenty years later, as a consequence of the systematic rewriting of the history of the war by the governing elite and the American culture industry, the metaphor of the wound had metamorphosed into the "Vietnam syndrome." That is, the healthy national debate over the question of the American national identity precipitated by the protest movement's disintegration of its monolithically benign exceptionalist image had, as in such revisionary films as the *Rambo* trilogy (1982, 1984, 1988), come to be represented and accepted by the American public in the Reagan era as a national neurosis that had prevented the United States' military machine from winning the Vietnam War. This will to forget the horrific actualities of the war and to recuperate the prewar national identity was abetted by the collapse of the Soviet Union, which left the United States as the sole global superpower. And it culminated with Al Qaeda's attacks on the Pentagon and the World Trade Center on September 11, 2001, which came, one could say on the basis of its rhetoric, as a boon to the dominant culture in the United States. The recuperative forgetting not only explained the virtual absence of reference to the Vietnam War in the hegemonic and overtly imperial discourse and practice of the neoconservative/faith-based administration of George W. Bush, when it launched its "war on terror," but also the president's self-righteous—and startlingly crude—announcement to the entire world in the immediate aftermath of the attacks that "You're either with us or against us."

This overtly imperial discourse and practice, which has taken the form of a unilateral perpetual war against "terrorism" in the name of civilization, not only authorized preemptive military invasions of foreign ("rogue") states—Afghanistan and Iraq—the ultimate goal of which is the imposition of an American-style liberal capitalist democracy on the invaded nations, a foreign policy that violates the most basic tenets of international law. In tacitly establishing this post-9/11 occasion as a perpetual state of national emergency, the Bush administration, with the collusion of the Democratic Party leadership, has also authorized itself to police dissent within the United Sates itself. As such this domestic and international practice constitutes, in a fundamental way, the fulfillment and overt manifestation of the global imperatives of the logic that, as I have reiterated, inheres in the myth of American exceptionalism and that has determined America's national and foreign policies ever since the Puritans' divinely ordained "errand in the wilderness" of the "New World." In other words, the second Bush administration's representation of America's planetary role in the post-9/11 era constitutes a recuperation of American exceptionalism (its self-representation as radically different from and morally superior to the peoples of the rest of the world) and, as we have seen, a putting into practice of the ontology informing the global vision of the post-Cold War intellectual deputies of the dominant neoconversative culture in America, for example, Francis Fukuyama's proclamation of the end of history under the aegis of liberal capitalist democracy;[1] or the more nuanced or indirect versions of Richard Haass, which, calling on the nineteenth-century rhetoric of Manifest Destiny, envisions the United States as the "reluctant sheriff" of a "deregulated" post-Cold War world;[2] of the Project for the New American Century, which advocates total military domination of the world by the United States in behalf of "preserving the *Pax Americana*;[3] of Niall Ferguson, who counsels the United States to assume the role of empire, given up by Great Britain, in behalf of the good of postmodern humankind,[4] of Samuel P. Huntington, who calls for the reaffirmation of America's "Anglo-Protestant core culture" in behalf of winning the "clash of civilizations," in the wake of the stalling of the American military/political initiative in Iraq,[5] and of Michael Mandelbaum, who, in the context of a dangerously destabilized world of incompetent nations, argues that the United States is morally obligated to use it Goliath-like stature to govern the planet.[6] This is why, as I have been arguing, the primary imperative of the critical consciousness at this ominous historical conjuncture is to reconstellate the forgotten Vietnam War into the context of the present post-9/11 occasion, that is, to retrieve the history of the Vietnam War that the dominant culture in the United States, including the culture industry, has not only systematically eroded but also transformed into its opposite: the corrosive history, in other words, that had in reality delegitimized the ontological ground of America's perennial exceptionalist ethos and its "errand in the [world's] wilderness."

This chapter will continue the process of retrieving this history from the oblivion to which the custodians of the American cultural memory have relegated it inaugurated in the previous chapters on Graham Greene's *The Quiet American* and Philip Caputo's *A Rumor of War* in the hope that its singularity will undermine the authority of the recuperated "truth" of American exceptionalism. To this urgent end it will invoke the testimony of the novelist Tim O'Brien, one of the very few American veterans who, resisting the power of the discourse that would recuperate the American national identity, has borne symptomatic witness in his fiction to these actualities of the Vietnam War. By "actualities," it is important to emphasize, I do not simply mean the United States' virtually genocidal conduct of the war, but also the ontological, epistemological, and cultural relay that informed and "justified" its inordinately violent political practices. The novel to which I am referring is *Going After Cacciato*, published in 1978, three years after the fall of Saigon and four years before the dedication of the Vietnam Veterans War Memorial in Washington, D.C., at the very time, that is, that the culture industry was inaugurating the massive momentum to forget the shameful history of the war by remembering it. I mean, more specifically, the representational initiative that would eventually transform the pervasive metaphorics of healing a cultural wound to that of curing a cultural neurosis, "the Vietnam syndrome," a "cure" that twenty years later would "resolve" the long "crisis" of the national psyche, recuperate the national consensus and the exceptionalist metanarrative informing it, and enable America to resume its errand in the world's wilderness, now on a global scale, which was interrupted by the defeat of the United States by a small subaltern Third World country in the Vietnam War.

In invoking the "witness" of Tim O'Brien's *Going After Cacciato*, I am referring to an existential form of representation that relies on *being there*, in the midst of a singular event as opposed to a narrative that represents its singularity from a distanced or panoptic perspective, the ideological perspective on the Vietnam War that determined its representation by the governing elite and the culture industry. I am, of course, aware of the fact that this argument for bearing witness was utilized as a ploy by the American media, in fact, in a fundamental way, against those critical accounts of the protestors, who, unlike the soldiers who were fighting the war, *were not there*. This duplicitous ideologically motivated representation is, for example, fundamental to the structure of John Wayne's film *The Green Berets*, in which, at the outset, the state-side reporter of a major newspaper, Beckford, who has been representing the United States' intervention in Vietnam as an immoral act, is compelled by Colonel Kirby's acid reminder that his criticism of the war at long distance is not the truth, but the ventriloquized representation of the "radical" malcontent protest movement, to go to Vietnam with the Marine A-team Kirby commands to "see for himself," a compelled decision that eventuates in Beckford's melodramatic conversion. As I have shown in my reading of Caputo's *A Rumor of War*, this typically American argument for the "objective" truth of the testimony of the eyewitness as opposed to representation from a distance (i.e., from hearsay) is also fundamental, though far more nuanced than it is in *The Green Berets*, to the numerous autobiographical reminiscences of the war by veterans, epitomized by Al Santoli's best-selling *Everything We Had: An Oral History of the Vietnam War by Thirty-Three American Soldiers Who Fought It* that flooded the American market at the time of the dedication of the Vietnam Veterans War Memorial in 1982, when the metaphorics of healing the wound began to become pervasive. But this strategic appeal to the eyewitness account conceals its recuperative ideological agenda. The war Beckford "experiences" after arriving in Vietnam turns out to be a patent, indeed, unwittingly self-parodic, imposition of the Hollywood western on the actual history of the Vietnam War—which, it should not be overlooked, popularized the mythological narrative of the exceptionalist pioneer or backwoodsman or frontiersman experience. Similarly, the narrative of war that Santoli, as editor, constructs, and that virtually all of "the thirty-three soldiers who fought it" represent in their individual reminiscences, reduces the revelatory historically specific singularity of the Vietnam War—its *thisness*, as I have referred to it in the last chapter—to a timeless war-in-general.[7]

Tim O'Brien's *Going After Cacciato* does not entirely escape this complicity with the recuperative ideological agenda of the American culture industry, as we shall see. What redeems his novel, what renders it a text that *bears witness* in the existential or Kierkegaardian sense in which I intend, is, above all, its acute, if only symptomatic, consciousness of precisely the difference between *this* war and all the other modern wars America had fought. There is, as in Caputo's *A Rumor of War*, a deeply felt structural and rhetorical excess about the novel that undermines its inscribed tendency to individualize the protagonist and then incorporate him into a narrative that universalizes his experience, that, in other words, abstracts him from the indissolubly related ontological, cultural, and sociopolitical realities of the Vietnam War. Unlike Santoli's *Everything We Had* and the numerous autobiographical ("eye witness") representations of the Vietnam War that by and large adhere to the structural paradigm inhering in the ideological metaphorics of healing the wound, *Going After Cacciato* is, like Caputo's *A Rumor of War*, what I have called a *threshold text* insofar as the excess that spills across the boundaries of the narrative constitutes a symptomatic refusal to forget the *thisness* of the Vietnam

War, that is, the historically specifically ontological, cultural, and sociopolitical context in which the characters in the novel are embedded. As the insistent and nuanced contrast between the character of the Vietnam War and that of World Wars I and II makes acutely clear (it is a contrastive motif that at a far more unthought level informs a large part of the literature of the Vietnam War written by its veterans), O'Brien, to put it summarily, represents the Vietnam War in *Going After Cacciato* as radically different from its predecessors in this century, indeed, from the essence of modern European warfare. This crucial difference—I will call it tentatively "postmodern"—deconstructs the myth of the benign exceptionalist American national identity (liberal capitalist democracy) and the ontology on which it is grounded that justified the United States' intervention in Vietnam and its relentlessly indiscriminating violent conduct of the war, the very American logocentrism that the postwar discourse of healing the wound was intended to recuperate.

I

Tim O'Brien works out the content of *Going After Cacciato* in terms of a tripartite "structure" that is instigated by the desertion of Private Cacciato, an enigmatic member of a squad of American soldiers operating in the Quang Ngai area in Vietnam, and its effect on Spec Four Paul Berlin, from whose perspective on the war the novel unfolds. One part represents Berlin's *present* (the sections, interspersed throughout the novel, identified as "The Observation Post," which refer to the single night during which Berlin is on guard as the others in the squad of the platoon are sleeping). A second is narrated in the third person from the collective perspective of the platoon and represents the unit's past—the singular events that produce the conditions of *this particular war*—that seem to account for Cacciato's desertion and Berlin's ambivalent, indeed, tortured feelings about the mission to go after him. The third represents the "future" Berlin imagines from his place in the observation post as a way of resolving this agonizing ambivalence that the indeterminacy of the platoon's past up to the time of Cacciato's desertion has precipitated in Berlin.

O'Brien's structuring of the novel in this way is not simply an aesthete decision. What I want to suggest at the very outset is that this tripartite structure not only reflects the psychological effects of the actual combat conditions of this war on Paul Berlin, but, in so doing, also problematizes the very *ontological foundations* of the traditional Western narrative. I mean the representation of human events—in this case the war story—that is grounded in a metaphysical interpretation of being, an ontology that also constitutes the very foundation of the idea of Western civilization and its practice—*including*, as we shall see, *its form of warfare*—and which has arrived at its logical fulfillment (end) in post-Enlightenment modernity, specifically in the construction of the idea of America, the, in fact, unexceptionalist heir of the Old World. I am, of course, referring to the beginning-middle-end structure, formulated decisively by Aristotle in the *Poetics*, which, as his *Metaphysics* testifies, constitutes the literary analogue of the Western metaphysical representation of the be-*ing* of being, the determination, that is, of its differential disseminating dynamics from *after* or *above* the temporal process (*meta ta physika*) or, to put it schematically, the determination that, compelled by the principle of presence, *spatializes* time, turns its primordial randomness into a promise/fulfillment *structure*.[8]

O' Brien, it is important to emphasize, depicts Spec Four Paul Berlin, the young soldier who is perceiving, experiencing, and processing the violent events of the novel in the observation post, not simply as the type of the modern American, but also—and much like Caputo—as I will show, as an American whose thought and practice, indeed, his very being, constitute the fulfillment of the "exceptionalist" logic of the American national identity, which had its origins in the Puritan "errand," its maturation during the period of westward expansion that was driven by the secularization of the Puritan divinely ordained "errand" as the idea of Manifest Destiny, and it's fulfillment in the post-World War II (i.e., Cold War) era when America globalized its frontiers, one of the symbolic manifestations of which was, as I have observed, President John F. Kennedy's identification of Southeast Asia as "the New Frontier."

The novel begins in medias re:

> It was a bad time. Billy Boy Watkins was dead, and so was Frenchie Tucker. Billy Boy had died of fright, scared to death on the field of battle, and Frenchie Tucker had been shot through the nose. Bernie Lynn and Lieutenant Sidney Martin had died in tunnels. Pederson was dead and Rudy Chassler was dead. Buff was dead. Ready Mix was dead. They were all among the dead. The rain fed fungus that grew in the men's boots and socks, and their socks rotted, and their feet turned white and soft so that the skin could be scraped off with a fingernail, and Stink Harris woke up screaming one night with a leech on his tongue. When it was not raining, a low mist moved across the paddies blending the elements into a single gray element, and the war was cold and pasty and rotten. Lieutenant Corson, who came to replace Lieutenant

Sidney Martin, contracted dysentery. The tripflares were useless.
The ammunition corroded and the foxholes filled with mud and
water during the nights, and in the mornings there was always the
next village, and the war was always the same.[9]

A paragraph later, the narrator tells us how the soldiers dealt with these
dreadful conditions of combat in Vietnam:

There was a joke about Oscar. There were many jokes about Billy
Boy Watkins, the way he'd collapsed of fright on the field of battle. Another joke was about the lieutenant's dysentery, and another was about Paul Berlin's purple biles. There were jokes
about the postcard pictures of Christ that Jim Pederson used to
carry, and Stink's ringworm, and the way Buff's helmet filled with
life after death. Some jokes were about Cacciato, Dumb as a bul-
let, Stink said. Dumb as a month-old oyster fart, said Harold
Murphy. (*GAC*, 2)

And then, in a single sentence paragraph: "In October, near the end of
the month, Cacciato left the war" (*GAC*, 2)

In these inaugural pages of *Going After Cacciato*, O'Brien is clearly
not establishing a context out of which a traditional war story will eventually emerge. In this unexpected "beginning," we have, rather, the ingre-
dients of an antistory about an "antiwar": the randomness of death, the
degrading dynamics of violence, the miasmic aura of an uncharted and
seemingly primordial terrain, the lack of directionality and of consequence
("and in the mornings there was always the next village, and the war was
always the same"), the desperately cynical (i.e., disillusioned) representation of death, the evocation of terror rather than bravery or heroics (Paul
Berlin's "purple biles," which, not incidentally, alludes to Sartre's *Nausea*)
and, not least, the impulse to flee from a war that, as these proleptic pages
suggest, seems to make no sense to the common American soldiers who
are fighting it These, we learn in the following chapter, the first of the
"Observation Post" sections, are metonymic of the actual conditions of
combat in Vietnam, the accumulated shards of Paul Berlin's immediate
past, about which he is meditating in the context of the desertion of Cacciato. In the process of this night-long meditation, Berlin will recall his and
the platoon's (now reduced to a squad) past in all its terrible and dread-
provoking specificity to account for his dark state of mind. This young
American soldier will also, and at great length, project his and his squad's
"future" as he tries desperately to imagine it after Cacciato's desertion.

Like Philip Caputo, he will attempt to give the radical contingency—the senselessness—of this war a satisfying *narrative shape*, a shape that will redeem the dislocating actualities–"the bad time"—of the war.

II

Although the sections of the novel in which Berlin's past is incoherently retrieved are primarily devoted to the history of his and his squad's experience in Vietnam, they also, and importantly, refer to his boyhood past in America, a personal but also a symbolic past. Unlike all too many autobiographical accounts of the Vietnam War, in which the writer is more or less unconscious of the degree to which he or she is inscribed by the myth of American exceptionalism, O'Brien, like Caputo, consciously generalizes Berlin's early life in the Midwest to make it clear that he is not only a representative modern young American, but also the inheritor, in a markedly attenuated form, of the exceptionalist legacy of the American frontier—the trail-blazing (forwarding) ethos of the "backwoodsman"— that was inaugurated by the Puritans' "errand" and given its secular avatar in the period of westward expansion or, more accurately, that reductive version of the frontier spirit that was disseminated by the American culture industry, not least, in the Hollywood western.[10]

O'Brien accomplishes this generalization not only by endowing a symbolic resonance on the place in which Berlin was born and grew up, Fort Dodge (*GAC*, 47), the midwestern frontier town that figured prominently in the relentless history of westward expansion and was given legendary status by Hollywood,[11] but in reality was simply another modern mid-American town whose energizing "American sublime"[12] and "pristine" space had long since been domesticated and familiarized, had become what the exceptionalist idea of the frontier existed in large part to preclude by way of the "regenerating violence" it authorized.[13] This mythical resonance is established not simply by O'Brien's insistent references to the pointedly westward direction of Cacciato's flight, but also, and primarily, by the repeated flashbacks to Berlin's childhood memories of his camping excursions along the Des Moines River with his father, a veteran of World War II. All of which are, it should be emphasized, instigated by the young soldier's acute sense of *dis-location* in the Vietnamese bush ("Indian country," as the American soldiers invariably called the jungles in which they fought), a dislocation that, in shattering Berlin's sense of place, did not square with the iconic image of the American frontiersman he had been inscribed by in his childhood, but was never able to emulate adequately.

This was the image, mediated by Berlin's image of his Adamic father, of the self-reliant, resolute, and westward-looking pioneer, who, thanks to the knowledge of the wilderness he had gained by attending to the intimate and subtle relationship between the native Americans and the land, always knew where he was in the threatening forests and thus, to put it in the myth-creating terms of the conclusion of James Fenimore Cooper's *The Pioneers*, enabled the westward forwarding that made the Leatherstocking figure "the foremost in the band of Pioneers, who are opening the way for the march of the nations across the continent."[14]

> And later, as if a mask had been peeled off, the rain ended and the sky cleared and Paul Berlin woke to see stars.
>
> They were in their familiar places. It wasn't so cold. He lay on his back and counted the stars and named those that he knew, named the constellations and the valleys of the moon. He learned the names from his father. Guideposts, his father had once said along the Des Moines River, or maybe in Wisconsin. Anyway—guideposts, he'd said, so that no matter where in the world you are, anywhere, you know the spot, you can trace it, place it by latitude and longitude. (*GAC*, 24)

Indeed, it is, as the repetition of this particular memory of a rite of passage suggests, precisely because Berlin had not been able to emulate him and his multiple avatars in American cultural production (from Robert Montgomery Bird's *Nick of the* Woods and William Gilmore Simms's *The Yemassee*, through Francis Parkman's *The Oregon Trail*, to William Faulkner's, *The Bear* and the movie *Easy Rider* and beyond), in his childhood that this iconic American figure becomes a spectral presence that haunts him in the Vietnamese wilderness:

> His sense of place had never been keen. In Indian Guides, with his father, he'd gone to Wisconsin to camp and be pals forever. Big Bear and Little Bear. He remembered it. Yellow and green headbands, orange feathers. Powwows at campfire. Big Fox telling stories out of the *Guide Story Book*. Big Fox, a gray-haired father from Oshebo, Illinois, owner of a paper mill. He remembered all of it. . . . Then the third day, into the woods, father first and son second, Little Bear tracking Big Bear, who leaves tracks and paw prints. Yes, he remembered it—Little Bear getting lost. Following Big Bear's tracks down to a winding creek, crossing the creek, checking the opposite bank according to the *Guide Survival*

Guide, finding nothing; so deep into the woods—Big Bear!—and deeper, then turning back to the creek but now no creek. Nothing in the *Guide Survival Guide* about panic. Lost, bawling in the big Wisconsin woods. He remembered it clearly. (*GAC*, 40–41)

It is this American archetype, this "textual attitude," as Edward Said calls it,[15] deeply inscribed and utterly determinative, however fragilely, in his very being, that informs Paul Berlin's anxious response to the past—the time he has spent in Vietnam prior to the culminating present moment in the observation post—in the wake of Cacciato's enigmatic desertion—and his orientation toward the future: his ambiguous imagining of the narrative possibilities that this desertion has precipitated.

III The Past and the Present

"It was a bad time. . . . The ammunition corroded and the foxholes filled with mud and water during the nights, and in the morning there was always the next village, and the war always the same." This "beginning," as I have said, is a reflection of the actual conditions of combat in Vietnam as Paul Berlin and his platoon were experiencing them. But as the ironic allusion to Charles Dicken's *A Tale of Two Cities* suggests, this subjective assertion about the particular occasion resonates with a larger significance, one that incorporates a relay of *analogous* sites on a continuum that obviously includes the sites of antagonistic nations and of different kinds of warfare, and, I want to suggest, different cultures and, least visible but no less significant, different ontologies, that is, interpretations of being.More specifically, it is a "bad time" for this young American soldier because *every* aspect of what he has encountered in Vietnam up to this point—above all, the enemy, their tactics, the Vietnamese people, their culture, their land, and even their idea of time—has run counter to—has decentered, as it were—the culturally inscribed expectations he, as an "innocent" American, had brought with him to this "New (American) Frontier" as a "textual attitude." It is the purpose of those parts of the tripartite structure of *Going After Cacciato* devoted to the platoon's immediate past not only to retrieve the particular grotesque events this "beginning" *randomly* enumerates, but also, through this retrieval, to make visible (to "render," in Henry James's word) this indissoluble relay of sites that constitute Berlin's consciousness during the night on watch in the observation post and to suggest the source and the nature of his profound anxiety ("the biles"), of his sympathy with Cacciato's flight from the war, and of "the story" he tries to project.

As the retrieval of the episodes that detail the history of the decimation of the platoon suggests (a retrieval, not incidentally, that is as random as the initial enumeration of their various fates), the war these American soldiers are fighting in Vietnam is not *any war*. *This war*, the Vietnam War, that is, cannot be generalized; as in the case of Caputo's *A Rumor of War*, it is too unique—too singular—to be accommodated to a universal frame. (I will return to this ubiquitous motif of the literature of the Vietnam War later in this chapter.) More immediately, these episodes suggest that *this* war is radically different from the concept of war—its logistics, its tactics, its strategies, the very language through which it is represented—as it has been formulated and practiced by American armies, indeed, by Western armies, not simply in modernity, but, I want to emphasize for a reason that will become clear in the sequel, from the very moment of the founding of Western civilization. Berlin and his comrades (like Philip Caputo) come to Vietnam trained to fight a "conventional" war, a war they have been inscribed to perceive, above all, as a frontal encounter between two massive armies, the movement of which is assumed to be unidirectional (a process of advancing forward and occupying the enemy's territory), involving *decisive* battles, and ending in a climactic victory.[16] It is a kind of war that, however frightening and dislocating to the individual soldier at each immediate moment, can be *foreseen* as coming to a decisive end. One might say that this "European" concept of war is informed by a narrative structure that enables the individual soldier to transcend the terrific immediacy of combat and thus to feel a degree of certainty in the midst of contingency. All the specific events of the past that flesh out the random references in the beginning to the decimation of Berlin's platoon disclose, on the contrary, that *this* war does not conform to the narrative structure of the kind of war they assumed it would be on coming to Vietnam. It is too messy to be rendered intelligible (i.e., comprehended).

This crucial difference is announced laconically in the very first of those chapters of the novel that refers to Berlin's past in Vietnam:

> In the morning the fifty new men were marched to a wooden set of bleachers facing the sea. A small, sad-faced corporal in a black cadre helmet waited until they settled down, looking at the recruits as if searching for a lost friend in a crowd. Then the corporal sat down in the sand. He turned away and gazed out to the sea. He did not speak. Time passed slowly, ten minutes, twenty, but still the sad-faced corporal did not turn or nod or speak. He simply gazed out at the blue sea. Everything was clean. The sea was clean, and the sand and the wind.

They sat in the bleachers for the full hour. Then at last the corporal sighed and stood up. He checked his wristwatch. Again he searched the rows of new faces.

"All right," he said softly. "That completes your first lecture on how to survive this shit. I hope you paid attention." (*GAC*, 37)[17]

As the disciplinary setting suggests, the newcomers to the Vietnam War, seated in an amphitheater facing their teacher, expect the knowledgeable corporal, who has experienced combat in Vietnam and has survived it, to tell them something definitive about the war, something that would render its mystery intelligible, something to "hold on to," as it were, and thus would ease their anxiety. But in a striking short-circuiting of the panoptic paradigm (the centered circle), the authoritative figure—the experienced possessor of the "Word" about the war—turns his gaze away from his pupils without saying a word, and, after a full hour of utter silence, turns to them again and announces decisively that his "lecture" on surviving this war, which he reduces to "this shit," had come to its "end."

"Shit" (or "deep shit" or "a world of shit") was the word that, more than any other one in their vocabulary, the American soldiers used to "name" the abyssal conditions of combat in the Vietnam War. With this word, its ordinary meaning—the waste that is discharged in the process of digesting the food that nourishes the life of the body—undergoes a grotesque reversal. In the discourse of the American soldiers, waste becomes the "essence" of—the Word that unnames—*this* war. Paul Berlin and the new recruits hear in the sad-faced corporal's silence and his summary identification of the Vietnam War with shit, in other words, not simply its murderous randomness, but also its unpresentability. Language or, more specifically, the American language they know, is utterly inadequate to the task of naming, of objectifying, of territorializing, of domesticating, its dread-provoking corrosive realities.

All the episodes recounting Paul Berlin's past experiences in Vietnam, foreshadowed by the random enumeration of the grotesque unheroic deaths of his comrades in the first paragraph of the novel, are intended by O'Brien to disclose this world of "shit." Or, to put the metaphor in terms of its tenor, it is this dislocating and anxiety-provoking contradiction between the unspeakable pointlessness of the war and the straightforward way the American soldiers had been inscribed to read it by a relay of superiors extending from the commanding officer of the platoon back through MACV (Military Assistance Command Vietnam) in Saigon to its sources in the Pentagon, the American government, and, ultimately, but not least, as the insistent and telling, usually ironic, allusions to America's exceptionalist past suggest, the very discourse of the American national identity. No matter how different the details of this past history, everyone of these recounted episodes of Berlin's (and his platoon's) past repeat and at the same time deepen his resistant awareness of the realities of the war that contradict his culturally inscribed textual attitude. Expecting face-to-face encounter with an evil enemy, he finds them invisible; expecting directionality, he finds randomness; expecting an outcome of an engagement, he finds inconsequence; expecting solidarity with his superiors, he finds enmity; expecting closure, he finds openness; expecting determination, he finds indeterminacy; expecting to find location, he finds dislocation. In short, where he expects the movement of warfare to articulate a narrative structure, he finds this movement to be structureless—deterritorialized.

The war, these sections of the novel imply—and this, it is important to reiterate, is the symptomatic witness of virtually all the accounts, both in content and form, of those veterans of the Vietnam War who have written about their experiences—goes nowhere: "and in the mornings there was the next village, the war was always the same." And the consequence for Berlin of these anticlimactic and decentering conditions is "the purple biles" (and his ambiguous attitude toward Cacciato's desertion). In the first of the observation post sections of the novel (chapter 2) that articulate Berlin's present state of mind—the Berlin whose present self is the result of the past I have summarized—he recalls the following disquisition of his "biles" as it is diagnosed by Doc Peret, the platoon's articulate, science-oriented medic:

> "You got an excess of fear biles," Doc had said one afternoon beneath the tower. . . . "And my theory is this: Somehow these biles are *warping your sense of reality*. Follow me? Somehow they're *screwing up your basic perspective*, and the upshot is you sometimes get a little mixed up. That's all."
>
> Doc had gone on to explain that the biles are a kind of glandular substance released during emotional stress. A perfectly normal thing. . . . Doc had listed the physical symptoms: numbness of the extremities in time of extremity; a cloudiness of vision; paralysis of mental processes that separate what is truly happening from what only might have happened; floatingness; removal; a releasing sensation in the belly; a sense of drifting; a lightness of the head. "Normally," Doc had said, "those are healthy things. But in your case, these biles are . . . well, overabundant. . . . This Cacciato business—it's the work of the biles. They're flooding your whole system, going to the head and fucking up reality, frying in all the goofy, weird stuff.
>
> So Doc's advice had been to concentrate. (*GAC*, 28; my emphasis)

Doc's instrumentalist diagnosis of Berlin's centrifugal biles is that of the empirical scientist—one who simply assumes that the condition that is "warping" his patient's "sense of reality," "screwing up" his "basic perspective," "fucking up" the actual—is explicable in quantitative terms and thus curable by *concentration*, that is, by re-concentering what the "oversaturation" of the "glandular substance" has decentered and scattered. To put this otherwise, Doc's cure is dependant on his reification of Paul Berlin's being. But Berlin is too fragilely human to be persuaded that Doc's empirical diagnosis is a valid one:

> True, he was afraid. Doc was right about that. Even now, with the night calm and unmoving, the fear was there like a kind of background sound and was heard only if listened for. But even so, Doc was wrong when he called it dreaming. Bile or no bile, it wasn't dreaming. . . . Blisters on their feet, streams to be forded and swamps to be circled, dead ends to be opened into passages west. No, it wasn't dreaming. It was a way of asking questions. (*GAC*, 29)

Berlin's reaction to Doc's diagnosis seems to be an ambiguous one, since it moves from the question of the meaning of the "biles" to its consequence: the impulse to imagine the narrative possibilities instigated by Cacciato's desertion. But if one attends to his effort to offer an alternative meaning of his biles to Doc's "scientific" definition—"the fear was there like a background sound and was heard only when listened for"—one can understand them as the present consequence of the disorienting (or "unhoming") conditions of combat in Vietnam. From this perspective, the "fear" he feels, like that which Caputo and so many other Americans who fought in the wilderness of Vietnam experienced, metamorphoses into something remarkably similar to Heidegger's Kierkegaardian phenomenological analysis of *Angst* (anxiety or dread), which, unlike *Furcht* (fear) has no *thing* as its object.[18] I am referring to that "mood" (*Stimmung*) of *Dasein* that, according to Heidegger, provides access to an ontological "reality"—the nothingness of being (*das Nichts*)—that the globally hegemonic truth discourse of Western science calls "an outrage and a phantasm" and "wishes to know nothing about it."[19]

It is, I suggest, this ontological anxiety in the face of the nothing that this sensitive young American soldier feels in the face of a war he finds inexorably incomprehensible, which is to say, according to the etymology of this word, not-take-holdable (Latin, *prehendere*, "to take hold of"). He had experienced this anxiety, he insistently, if reluctantly, remembers, on other occasions throughout his earlier life. On his third night after his arrival in Vietnam, he had written to his father to "look up Chu Lai in a world atlas. 'Right now,' he wrote, 'I'm a little lost.'" On his seventh day, he recalls his camping trip with his father as a young boy: "His sense of place had never been keen. . . . Nothing in the *Guide Survival Guide* about panic. Lost, bawling in the big Wisconsin woods. He remembered it clearly" (*GAC*, 40; see also 24, 180). But it is only after he becomes immersed in "the destructive element," to invoke Joseph Conrad's apt phrase from *Lord Jim*—the decentering and estranging war, which the sections of the past powerfully render—that this anxiety which has nothing for its object comes to full presence as a fundamental dimension of his very being, that is, as a condition he must confront.

Following his declaration that "anxiety reveals the nothing," Heidegger adds: "Anxiety robs us [we of the West] of speech. Because beings as a whole slip away, so that just the nothing crowds round, in the face of anxiety all utterance of the 'is' falls silent. That in the malaise of anxiety we often try to shatter the vacant stillness with compulsive talk only proves the presence of the nothing."[20] What Heidegger means by this is that, in the face of the nothingness of being, Western man, the fulfillment of the post-Enlightenment instrumentalist mode of metaphysical thinking, the thinking that enables "the dictatorship of the public realm, which decides *in advance* what is intelligible and what must be rejected as unintelligible"[21]—evades the nothing's imperatives by reifying its unspeakable and unpresentable essence. He is inscribed to find, that is, an object for his anxiety that will transform the nothing into *something* that can be *seen* and "taken hold of," grasped by the mind's eye—comprehended, mastered, occupied—and the uncertainty of his dislocation into the realm of the uncanny into the certainty of a centered, territorialized at-homeness.

This ontological way of putting the effect of the actual conditions of combat in *this war* on Berlin's present being in the observation post foregrounds the structure of the self—its representational perspective—that he, like virtually all his American comrades, brought from "the world' to the "wilderness" of Vietnam as a textual attitude and that the radical corrosive difference of *this* war has destructured. It discloses that his truth discourse is a Western, specifically American, ideological construction that is indissolubly polyvalent, however uneven at any particular historical occasion, in its manifestations: ontological (the representation of being as such), epistemological (the representation of the subject of knowledge), ecological (the representation of the land), sexual (the representation of gender relations), racial (the representation of race relations), cultural (the representation of collective national self), military (the representation of warfare), narratological (the representation of human actions), and sociopolitical (the representation of international relations).

IV

Let me now recapitulate Paul Berlin's traumatic and dislocating past in Vietnam from the vantage point of the ontological anxiety that characterizes his present occasion in the observation post. On the basis of the incommensurability between the kind of war Berlin had been inscribed by his exceptionallist culture to expect and the kind of war he encounters in Vietnam, we might say, with Fredric Jameson, that the Vietnam War was the "first terrible postmodern war."[22] Berlin's anxious meditation on the events of the immediate past, insistently, if only implicitly, informs us that his expectations, like Caputo's and many other young Americans born to the generation that fought World War II, were based on a model of warfare that was assumed by a relay of "commands" extending from his commanding officer, Lt. Sidney Martin the West Point graduate who "believed in mission"—"mission over men" (*GAC*, 162)—through the military command in Saigon to the Pentagon, the American government, the American national identity, and, ultimately, the identity of Western civilization. This deeply backgrounded model of warfare, as I have remarked in chapter 4, assumed a narrative (beginning-middle-end) structure that posited direct confrontation with a *visible* enemy, the decisive battle, the definitive occupation of conquered land, and final victory.[23] This strategy, as O'Brien clearly suggests, had its immediate origins in European warfare beginning with the Franco-Prussian War in 1870 and culminating in World War II, but, I want to add by way of thematizing O'Brien's symptomatic witness, its ultimate and still virtually invisible origins at the very moment of the founding of Western civilization. This was the historical moment that bore witness to the emergence in antiquity, particularly Roman antiquity, of an end-oriented (imperial) metaphysical thinking that, in seeing being (*physis*) from *above*, privileges *vision* (the panoptic gaze) and its *binarist ontologic,* a logic that precipitated not only a relay of hierarchical oppositions between agriculturalist (Latin, *colon*) and the forest dweller (*sylvestris*, which also means "savage"), clearing and wilderness, settler and nomad, civilization and barbarism,[24] but also, and not incidentally, an analogous imperialist mode of warfare that privileged the visualist battle field strategy of con*front*ational massed armies over the mobile "guerrilla " tactics of the peripheral nomadic tribes.[25]

It is this essential and inaugural distinction between the deeply inscribed expectation of the decisive battle and the actual nomadic tactics—the invisible mobility—of the Vietnamese insurgents that has precipitated Berlin's "biles"—his anxiety in the face of the nothing—and his desperate wish, remarkably like Caputo's, that the obscure and erratic war he is fighting was like the clearer and regular war his father had fought earlier in the century.[26]

Such a desperate but futile desire informs every section of the novel that refers to Berlin and his platoon's past, but it receives its definitive and most resonant articulation in one of the last of these sections significantly entitled "The Things They Didn't Know":

> They did not know even the simple things: a sense of victory, or satisfaction, or necessary sacrifice. They did not know the feeling of taking a place and keeping it, securing a village and then raising the flag and calling it victory [a reference no doubt to the Battle of Iwo Jima]. No sense of order or momentum. No front, no rear, no trenches laid out in neat parallels. No Patton rushing for Rhine, no beachheads to storm and win and hold for the duration. They did not have targets. (*GAC*, 270)

But it is more than simply the disintegration of his former certainties about warfare that this now dislocated young American is lamenting. It is also, as what follows immediately after his invocation of the "heroic" warfare of World War II makes resonantly clear, the loss of the relay of ideological, cultural, economic, political, and, not least, ontological, epistemological, and moral certainties that are continuous with the idea of warfare endemic to the American national consciousness:

> They did not have a cause. They did not know if it was a war of ideology or economics or hegemony or spite. On a given day they did not know where they were in Quang Ngai, or how being there might influence larger outcomes. They did not know the names of most villages. They did not know which villages were critical. They did not know strategies. They did not know the terms of the war, its architecture, the rules of fair play. When they took prisoners, which was rare, they did not know the questions to ask, whether to release a suspect or beat on him. They did not know how to feel. Whether, when seeing a dead Vietnamese, to be happy or sad or relieved; whether, in times of quiet, to be apprehensive or content; whether to engage the enemy or elude him. They did not know how to feel when they saw villages burning. Revenge? Loss? Peace of mind or anguish? They did not know.They knew the old myths about Quang Ngai—tales passed down from old-timer to newcomer—but they did not know which stories to believe. Magic, mystery, ghost and incense, whispers in the dark, strange tongues and strange smells, uncertainties never articulated in war stories, emotion squandered on ignorance. They did not know good from evil. (*GAC*, 271)

Following O'Brien's novelistic directives—that we attend to Berlin's point of view—I have, up until this point, described the actual conditions of the Vietnam War as they are perceived and felt by the American soldier Paul Berlin. But, like Caputo's, O'Brien's overdetermination of the metaphorics of vision in his rhetoric, specifically the tension between the heavy reliance on *visibility* intrinsic to the confrontational economy of American warfare, on the one hand, and the uncanny invisibility of the Vietnamese enemy that is at the (absent) core of Berlin's acute awareness of the randomness and sameness of the war, on the other, compels us, whether intentionally or not, to bring the marginalized subaltern Other of the America war machine to center stage. In so doing, it also compels us to ask what O'Brien and his protagonist are reluctant to ask, what they shrink back from: not only why the American soldier's perspective is unidirectional, but also why he refuses the imperatives of this overdetermination of the tension between visibility and invisibility to think the invisibility of America's subaltern Other positively.

In the chapters referring to the inexorably random and absurdly pointless decimation of Berlin's platoon that lead up to the night in the observation post, we witness not simply the gradual destruction of his overcoded American vision of the world and the anxiety-provoking nothing this change of terrain discloses. Besides his nostalgic desire that this war were like World War II, we also bear insistent witness to Berlin's natural(ized) will to annul his anxiety by objectifying the nothing: by bringing "clarity" and "resoluteness" to the dislocating obscurity and erratic mobility of the war or, as the narrator puts it, by imposing "certainty and regularity" on its instability and randomness, which "alone was something to hold to" (*GAC*, 101). Berlin's evasive will to objectify the nothingness of this war, his unwillingness to address its dislocating "anti-imperial" imperatives, is a constant in those sections of the novel that refer to the platoon's corrosive past, but it is epitomized in the chapter entitled "Pick Up Games." This chapter recounts a lengthy "lull" in the platoon's combat operations that is filled in by a series of pickup basketball games—one, not incidentally, of the American national/cultural pastimes—as the members, under the command of the mission-oriented, disciplinary Lieutenant Sidney Martin, "too disciplined for such a lousy war" (*GAC*, 105), move, increasingly anxious, from one village to another in search of an enemy they "could not drive . . .into showing himself."

And the lull continued.
Paul Berlin was the first to feel uneasy. He couldn't quite place it.
A milky film clouding the hot days. Lapping motions at night.
Artificiality, a sense of imposed peace.

> He didn't understand it but he felt it. He wondered how it would end, and the wondering made him nervous.
>
> Still, there was always basketball. Games were won and lost, mostly won, and he found himself looking forward to it. He liked reciting the final scores: 50 to 46; 68 to 40. . . . He liked the clarity of it. (*GAC*, 102)

Later, as the search and destroy mission continues, the tension mounts and the members of the platoon become "sluggish and edgy," "thinking of land mines and trickery and ambush" (*GAC*, 105)—a psychological dislocation Doc generalizes as "a vacuum. Like in emptiness, suction. Can't have order in a vacuum. For order you got to have substance, material. So here we are—nothing to order, no substance. Aimless, that's what it is: a bunch of kids trying to pin the tail on the Asian donkey. But no fuckin tail. No fuckin donkey" (*GAC*, 105). To ward off the anxiety precipitated by the silence—and the specter of the invisible Asian enemy that haunts him—Berlin reverts to basketball, the American sport that analogous to American warfare, epitomizes what Tom Englehardt calls American "victory culture."

> Crouching deeper into a corner of his hole. Paul Berlin bowed his head and closed his eyes and listened hard. But there was nothing. Not the wind or the grass, not even the river now.
>
> A bad place, Buff had said. Bad place, bad time. He tried not to think about it, which started him thinking. In the morning they would cross the river and enter the ville and search it, that was what Sidney Martin said, and . . . still the quiet. The nerveless quiet. It was in his head now. Silence that wasn't silence. And in the morning they would cross the river and enter the ville. . . . He thought about basketball. Winning that was the sweetest part. . . . Winning—you knew the score, you knew exactly. . . . A basket to shoot at, a target, and sometimes you scored and sometimes you didn't, *but you had a true thing to aim at,* you always knew, and you could count on the numbers. And in the morning. . . . (*GAC*, 109; my emphasis)

In this resonant passage, which is haunted by the specter—the "nothingness" or "nonbeing" of Southeast Asia—Berlin is not simply referring to *this* war, the war that has disrupted his American understanding of warfare. His fraught meditative discourse is, consciously or not, referentially polyvalent: it articulates his (futile) will to muffle by reifying his agitated consciousness of a disintegrative momentum that affects an indissolubly relay of sites on the continuum of (American) "truths," ranging back from the immediate American truth of war itself, through American global politics, to—as my emphasis on the penultimate sentence makes quite clear—the increasingly less "practical" but no less important, sites of American culture, American epistemology, and American ontology. I mean that post-Enlightenment empirical perspective (or "problematic") that, as Heidegger, Derrida, Foucault, Althusser, Said and other post-structuralists have observed, determines the truth of being in all its manifestations according to the dictates of *quantifiable beings*, that is, to the inexorable directives of this empirical perspective that Doc exemplifies.[27]

Through Paul Berlin's excessive effort to annul by objectifying his "biles," in other words, *Going After Cacciato* compels us to *think* the *unsaid* of his reiterated—and unthought—characterization of the Vietnamese enemy in the language of spectral invisibility. And, I suggest, such an imperative ends in the hypothesis that the menacing invisibility of this subaltern Other of America was strategic: it put into positive practice the Eurocentric identification of non-Westerners with nonbeing. As we have seen in the case of Caputo's *A Rumor of War*, the insurgent strategy was not simply a deliberate refusal to engage with the American war machine according to the forwarding imperatives of the Western master narrative that informed its theory and practice. It was also a *positive* exploitation of the essential weakness—the Achilles' heel—of this master narrative: the American juggernaut's inability, fatally determined by its identification of its deeply backgrounded ocularcentric vision and it obsession with objects, with truth, with answers, with (victorious) endings, that is, its will to "having nothing to do with the nothing," to accommodate itself to the mobile, lightning-like hit-and-run tactics of "guerilla" or "low intensity" warfare.

Let me put this in the far more precise terms of Deleuze and Guattari. Consonant with inhabiting the land (Xa) (rather than striating and exploiting its smoothness as the West has always done), the Vietnamese insurgents constituted a nomadic war machine whose invisible and rhizomatic flow decentered, molecularized, and dispersed the otherwise concentered, sedentary, and "invincible" power of the American army.[28]

This nomadic strategy of the Vietnamese war machine—this refusal to be answerable to the American metanarrative—not only explains Paul Berlin's reiterated demoralized awareness of the randomness, the inconsequence, the sameness of this war, his sense of being lost in a labyrinth with no exist, his inability to bring the volatile and erratic events leading up to the night in the observation post into a satisfying coherence—an at-homing or territorializing narrative structure. It also goes far to explain his pervasive anxiety, always expressed in contrast with his American unidirectional perspective, over the uncanny invisibility of the enemy and his repeated reference to them as menacing ghosts. We might say, with the Derrida of *Specters of Marx*, keeping in mind the etymology, that the visitor (from the imperial perspective of the American soldier) has become the visited, the see-er, the seen:[29]

> Whenever he thought of the land, he thought first of the paddies. But next, almost in the same thought, he thought of the hedgerows. . . . They were thick, unclipped, untended tangles. Twice the height of a tall man, the hedges served the function that fences serve in richer countries. They held some things in and other things out. But more than that, the hedges were a kind of clothing for the villages. From far off a village was not a village. . . . Guarding, but mostly concealing, the hedgerows in Quang Ngai some times seemed like a kind of smoked glass forever hiding whatever it was that was not meant to be seen. . . . It was only a feeling, A feeling of marching through a great maze; a sense of entrapment mixed with mystery. The hedgerows were like walls in old mansions: secret panels and trapdoors and portraits with moving eyes. (*GAC*, 252)

This passage, as its remarkable similarity to the one quoted in the previous chapter in which Caputo describes his unit as being "haunted by a presence intangible yet real, a sense of being surrounded by something we could not see,"[30] is a synecdoche of virtually all the American soldiers' responses to the uncanny visible invisibility of their Vietnamese "enemy." It symptomatically suggests, perhaps against O'Brien's intention, that the nomadic strategy of the Vietnamese Other—those who have been marginalized by the America metropolitan gaze—not only destructures the theory and practice of the American war machine. It also destructures a relay of cultural structures endemic to the logocentric/panoptic Occidental tradition, especially as this tradition has been appropriated by an unexceptionalist exceptionalist America: above all, its one-way ocular-centric perspective, its instrumentalist/calculative thinking, and, not least, its reduction of the land (the earth) to mapped and conquerable and exploitable territory.

This symptomatic suggestion is, in fact, underscored in the one time in the novel when O'Brien "allows" a Vietnamese soldier to articulate his perspective on America's intervention in Vietnam and its conduct of the war, though his representation is undercut by the fact that he and it are imagined by Paul Berlin in the chapters of the novel in which he attempts to fantasize the outcome of Cacciato's desertion and flight "west" to

Paris. No doubt instigated by the terror-provoking reality of the tunnel complexes his lieutenant demanded his men to crawl into before blowing them up, Berlin imagines that he, his comrades, and the refugee, Sarkin Aung Wan, fall into one of them and find a Viet Cong soldier, aptly named Li Van Hgoc,[31] whom he interrogates in the hope of receiving clear answers that would ease his nameless anxiety instigated by "their" invisibility. The passage deserves quoting at length for its articulation of all the deep-rooted, reason-defying mysteries that baffled the American soldiers fighting in this alien land:

How, he asked Li Van Hgoc, did they hide themselves? How did they maintain such quiet? Where did they sleep, how did they melt into the land? Who were they? What motivated them—ideology, history, tradition, religion, politics, fear, discipline? What were the secrets of Quang Ngai? Why did the earth glow red? Was there meaning in the way the night seemed to move? Illusion or truth? How did they wiggle through wire? Could they fly, could they pass through rock like ghosts? Was it true they didn't value human life? Did their women really carry razor blades in their vaginas, booby traps for dumb GIs? Where did they bury their dead? Which of all the villages were VC, and which were not, and why were all the villes filled with old woman and kids? Where were the men? Did he have information on the battle at Singh In in the mountains? Had he been there? Did he see what happened to Frenchie Tucker? Was he present when Billy Boy Watkins expired of fright on the field of battle? Did he know anything about the time of silence along the Song Tra Bong? Was it really a Psy-Ops operation? What trails were mined and which were safe? Where was the water poisoned? Why was the land so scary—the criss-crossed paddies, the tunnels and burial mounds, thick hedges and poverty and fear?

To these anxious, virtually feverish, questions circulating not simply around the menacing invisibility of the Viet Cong soldiers, but also on the land of which they seem to be organic extensions, Li Van Hgoc replies: "The land."

"The soldier is but the representative of the land. The land is your true enemy." He paused. "There is an ancient ideograph—the word *Xa*. It means—He looked to Sarkin Aung Wan for help."

"Community," she said. "It means community, and soil, and home."

"Yes," nodded Li Van Hgoc. "Yes, but it also has other meanings: earth and sky and even sacredness. *Xa,* has many implications. But at heart it means that a man's spirit is in the land, where his ancestors rest and where the rice grow. The land is your enemy." (*GAC,* 85–86)[32]

Li Van Hgoc's response to the baffled American soldier's questions is not simply focused on the site of warfare: the difference between American and Viet cong military strategy and tactics. Its focus, rather, is on a telling *cultural* difference informing this difference, more specifically, on a continuum of sites—warfare, politics, the subject, the idea of the community—that are grounded in and emanate from an *ontology* of the land. Berlin's questions concerning the baffling invisibility of the enemy presuppose a Western, particularly American, representation of the land. It is a deeply backgrounded representation, one going back at least as far as the revolutionary enclosure movement in England in the seventeenth and eighteenth centuries that, as Rober Marzec has shown following the directives of Heidegger and Deleuze and Guattari, not only reduced the intensely lived common land to fixed sites of capitalist stockpiling (disposable reserved), but also paved the way for the establishment of the British imperial mind-set.[33] And it was informed by an instrumentalist or technological metaphysics that had reified, classified, charted—territorialized—its living being in behalf of mastering its recalcitrant and menacing differential force and exploiting its resources, that is, in behalf of colonizing and administering "it." As Heidegger puts this Western (imperial) comportment to the land, which he claims had its origins in Rome's reification of the originative comportment toward being of the Greeks, in his *Parmenides* lectures:

> For the Romans, the earth, *tellus, terra,* is dry, the land as distinct from the sea; this distinction differentiates that upon which construction, settlement, and installation are possible from those places where they are impossible. *Terra* becomes *territorium,* land of settlement as realm of command. In the Roman *terra* can be heard an imperial accent, completely foreign to the Greek *gea* and *ge.*[34]

So deeply inscribed by this panoptic/cartographic/imperial understanding of the earth (the last in this series is no longer a metaphor), this young midwestern American (like virtually all his fellow soldiers, both fictional and real) and the commands above him, ranging from his immediate superior office to the Pentagon,[35] can only see the living being of the earth—or, more precisely, the indissoluble relation between the Vietnamese people and the land on which they dwell, the land the Americans have invaded—as "territory" or "terrain" to be conquered, occupied, and administered. And this, we can now call it after Edward Said, Orientalism,[36] is why Berlin can make no more of their invisibility than he can of the nothing that his anxiety has revealed.

This—and the typical American response to bafflement in the face of the mystery of the Vietnamese land—manifests itself dramatically in one of the chapters about his past in Vietnam, "Fire in the Hole." It recounts the indiscriminate incineration of the village of Hoi An by American artillery called in by the lieutenant after being dropped in a landing to undertake a search and destroy mission during which Jim Pederson was killed by the friendly fire of the gunners of the helicopter that had brought Berlin's platoon into the rice paddies.

The radio buzzed. There was a whining. The marking round opened high over the southeast corner of Hoi An.

The lieutenant called in an adjustment and asked for white phosphorous.

And again the whine. White phosphorous burned the village.

"Kill it," Paul Berlin said.

The lieutenant watched the village burn. Then he went to the radio and ordered a dozen more Willie Peter, then a dozen HE.

The rounds hit the village in thirty-second intervals. The village went white. The hedges swayed. A vacuum sucked in quiet and a wind was made. Hoi An glowed. Trees powdered. There was crackling, scalding sound. Sitting on their rucksacks, the men watched black smoke open in white smoke. Splinters of straw and wood sprinkled down, and there was light in the village like flash-bulbs exploding in sequence, and then a melting, and then heat. Even high on the hill they felt the heat. Something liquid seemed to run through the center of the village. The fluid burned and ran off into the paddies.

"Kill it," Paul Berlin said without malice.

The lieutenant returned to the radio.

Next came alternating Willie Peter and HE, first white, then black. The men did not cheer or show emotion. They watched the village become smoke. Rounds pounded the smoke. The trees and huts and hedges and fences were gone. White ash fluttered down. Something gleamed in the smoke, as at the center of a furnace, and the rounds kept falling. . . . Then they began firing. They lined-up and fired into the burning village. . . . The tracers could be seen through the smoke, bright red streamers, and Willie Peters and HE kept falling, and the men fired until they were exhausted. The village was a hole.

They spent the night along the Song Tra Bong. They bathed in the river and made camp and ate supper. When it was night they began talking about Jim Pederson. It was always better to talk about it. (*GAC*, 78–79)

Unlike his comrades and his commanding officer, Paul Berlin is deeply aware that there is something radically wrong about the war his country is waging in Vietnam. Nevertheless, his immediate response in this synecdochical episode to the turbulent recalcitrant conditions of combat in Vietnam—his bafflement provoked by the invisibility of an enemy that cannot be distinguished from the land that harbors him—is, as in the case of Philip Caputo, as we have seen, typically American. And, I want to emphasize, it is an Americanness that begins with an ontological (metaphysical) gesture of reduction that manifests itself simultaneously as a violent military and political reduction. The monomaniac Captain Ahab in Melville's *Moby-Dick*, we will recall from my reading of Caputo's *A Rumor of War* in the previous chapter, reduces the nothingness of being (the white whale)—"All that maddens and torments, all that stirs the lees of things, all truth with malice in it; all that cracks the sinews and cakes the brain; all the subtle demonisms of life and thought"—to a malevolent reified One (Moby Dick) to make *it* "practically assailable."[37] In keeping with the inexorably pragmatic American identity and the flattened out world it presupposed, Paul Berlin, in a remarkable gesture reminiscent of Caputo's vengeful Ahabian monomania, similarly reduces the baffling land and the unidentifiable people who are defending "it" and whom "it" is defending to an *it* in order to make it "practically assailable." "'Kill it,' Paul Berlin said." In this sublimely grotesque reduction, he reflects, if only momentarily, the indiscriminate violent imperatives not only of his "mission"-oriented platoon leader, Lieutenant Sidney Martin. More important, though this all-too-evident reality has never been invoked by even the most critical commentators on the war and its multitudinous representations, it also reflects the comportment toward Vietnam of the baffled military command in Saigon, the "can do" policy experts in the Pentagon—and, however invisibly, of the narrative of the exceptionalist American national identity. That this awful locution is not an aesthetic accident, that O'Brien intends in some conscious degree to infuse it with the larger meaning I am suggesting, is made powerfully manifest by his repeating it in his later novel about the Vietnam war, *The Lake in the Woods* (1995), now more pointedly, in the context of the My Lai massacre led by Lieutenant William Calley (March 15, 1969): "'Kill Nam,' said Lieutenant Calley. He pointed his weapon at the earth, burned twenty quick rounds. 'Kill it,' he said. He reloaded and shot the grass and a palm tree and then the earth again. 'Grease the place,' he said, 'Kill it.'"[38]

What my overdetermination of the marginal ontological dimension of Paul Berlin's reaction to the actual conditions of combat into which his country has plunged him discloses—and O'Brien's novel is at the threshold of revealing—is a reality about America's intervention in Vietnam and its conduct of the war that its hegemonic (truth) discourse rendered virtually unthinkable to most Americans in 1968, the time in which the novel is set, or, for that matter, 1978, the time of its publication. I mean that America's (exceptionalist) "mission" in the "wilderness" of this "Third World" Asian country, betrayed the complicity of its truth discourse—ontological, epistemological, cultural, political—with an aggressive, self-certain imperial practice that destroyed the recalcitrant land and the people it ostensibly intended to "save" for the free world (Western civilization). To put it another way, O'Brien's threshold novel, like Philip Caputo's memoir, *A Rumor of War*, is on the verge of disclosing that *this* war bore witness to an epistemic break: that the Vietnam War was not only a matter of the self-destruction of the American military machine, but also of the self-destruction of the hegemonic discourses—the relay of deeply imbedded cultural *narratives*—that "justified" the United States' intervention and military practice in Vietnam. I repeat for the sake of its significance for the post-9/11 occasion: it is this crucial aspect of the novel that is missing in virtually all the commentaries on O'Brien's *Going After Cacciato*.

V The Future

To summarize, the sections of the novel that represent the actual conditions of combat that Paul Berlin and his platoon encountered in Vietnam bear repeated witness to the disintegration of his benign "American" image of reality. All of the deeply inscribed characteristics of the typical practical American embodied in Graham Greene's Alden Pyle—the optimistic innocence of the exceptionalist national ethos, self-reliance, certainty, a sense of location, directionality, clarity, resoluteness, and an end-oriented perspective—are fractured and thrown into turmoil by the spectral enemy's strategic invisibility and the erratic engagements, the indeterminacy and inconsequence of the violent and bloody military actions his unit engages in. As a result, his reality has become "de-realized." He has lost his bearings, his sense of location, of direction, and, not least, of moral purpose. This "breaking of the referential surface" of the world[39]—this erasure of geographical and mental reference points, has thrown Berlin unwillingly into a "changed terrain," the estranged and estranging realm of the uncanny. It has, that is, divested him of all the alibis intrinsic to the exceptionalist "American dream" that would neutralize the anxiety that has nothing for its object ("the purple biles"), including his belief that he is fighting in a just war, and his intolerable condition manifests itself in his ambiguous sympathy with Cacciato, who has "left the war" (*GAC*, 2). Invoking Berlin's own language, we might say that the spectral Asian enemy haunts his American exceptionalist problematic: his will to narrativize—to impose a plot, a beginning-middle-end structure, on what finally cannot be narrativized: the *Xa*.

The Paul Berlin we encounter in the observation post sections (the present), as a consequence, faces a terrible dilemma. In the state of anxiety, he must choose between two equally unsatisfying options: to walk away, like Cacciato, from a war he no longer believes to be a just war, in which case, he must give up his American identity and become, from an American perspective, the most dreaded of all subjectivities—an expatriate, an exilic consciousness—or to remain in the war, in which case he must repress his new historical knowledge and his belief that the war he is fighting as an American is unequivocally an unjust war. The means he chooses to resolve this dilemma is to project the present occasion—the ambiguous mission ordered by his new commanding officer, Lieutenant Corson (who has replaced Lieutenant Martin, whom the platoon has "fragged") to go after Cacciato—into an imagined future, specifically, a narrative: the very Western ontological/cultural apparatus, ironically, that informs the American national identity, its exceptionalist ethos, the American state's representation of historical reality, its imperialist vision, and the violent forwarding strategy of its war machine. This still invisible complicity between narrative (the novel) and imperialism is at the heart of Edward Said's argument in his magisterial *Culture and Colonization*. Referring to Joseph Conrad's *Heart of Darkness*, he writes:

> Conrad encapsulated two quite different but intimately related aspects of imperialism: the idea that is based on the power to take over territory, an idea utterly clear in its force and unmistakable consequences; and the practice that essentially disguises or obscures this by developing a justificatory regime of self-aggrandizing, self-originating authority interposed between the victim of imperialism and its perpetrator. . . . Conrad's argument is inscribed right in the very form of narrative as he inherited it and as he practiced it. Without empire, I would go so far as saying, there is no European novel as we know it, and indeed if we study the

impulses giving rise to it, we shall see the far from accidental con-
vergence between the patterns of narrative authority constitutive
of the novel on the one hand, and on the other, a complex ideological configuration underlying the tendency to imperialism.[40]

Taking its lead from the American innocent, Private Cacciato, and his
determination to walk westward out of Vietnam through Burma, India,
Afghanistan, and Iraq to Europe and finally to Paris, Berlin's imagined
story will reenact, for the purpose of recuperating some semblance of the
American Adamic myth, the westward progress of exceptionalist America
epitomized by the Puritan "errand in the wilderness," by the trailblazing
itinerary of the nation-building Leatherstocking figure of Cooper's novels,
by the doctrine of Manifest Destiny, and, above all, by the American
army's triumphant entry into Paris at the close of World War II, which
brings this historical exceptionalist momentum to its global fulfillment.
Nothing, it seems, will stand in the way of bringing Berlin's story to closure. Indeed, in the beginning, his imagination seems like a dedifferentiating machine, a juggernaut that will not be impeded in its fiery pursuit of
the satisfying end it desires:

Sure, there would be skeptics. But he would explain. Carefully,
point by point, he would show how these were petty details. . . .
A million possibilities. Means could be found. If pressed, he could
make up the solutions—good, convincing solutions. But his imagination worked faster than that. Speed, momentum. Since means
could be found, since answers were possible, his imagination
went racing toward more important matters: Cacciato, the feel of
the journey, what was seen along the way, what was learned, col-
ors and motion and people and finally Paris. It could be done.
Wasn't that the critical point? It could truly be done. (GAC, 125)

In the furious rush of these lines, one cannot help recalling Captain
Ahab's imagined project (quoted as an epigraph to chapter 4): "Swerve me!
Ye cannot swerve me, else ye swerve yourselves! . . . Swerve me? The path
to my fixed purpose is laid with iron rails, whereon my soul is grooved to
run. Over unsounded gorges, through the rifled hearts of mountains, under
torrents' beds, unerringly I rush! Naught's an obstacle, naught's an angle to
the iron way!"[41] Unlike Captain Ahab, however, who is fatally immune in
his monomania to the devastating irony informing the very articulation of
his "fiery pursuit," Paul Berlin, like Ishmael, who has borne witness to the
difference between the unpresentable whiteness of the white whale and the
presentable and practically assailable Moby-Dick, has borne symptomatic

and irreversible witness in Vietnam to the horrendous monomaniacal violence against all the manifestations of the radical Other of America latent in the American exceptionalist identity, but even more important, to the nothingness of being—the "naught" that *is* always already "an obstacle," an "angle to the iron [American Ahabian] way." And so its specter—its otherness—relentlessly haunts—and dissolves—his American imaginative effort to structure a future out of the past and, finally, to "arrive" at a solution—and the cathartic "peace" that arrival brings.

As Katherine Kinney has observed in her persuasive (if partial) reading of *Going After Cacciato*, this dissolution of the benign American exceptionalist narrative Berlin would recuperate takes, above all, the form of his indirect but systematic reference to the crude imperialism of the United States' "realistic" Cold War foreign policy in the Asian and Middle Eastern worlds that Berlin and his squad traverse in their ambiguous "pursuit" of Cacciato, most tellingly after their second arrest in Iran by some officers of SAVAK, the notoriously brutal secret police of the shah of Iran, whose repressive regime had been the intended consequence of the coup initiated in 1953 by the CIA against the democratically elected Muhammad Musaddiq. Noting Berlin's recuperation of "emotional control" in the wake of his reduction of the memory of the death by fright of Billy Boy Watkins as "a fact . . . the first fact, and leading from it were other facts" (*GAC*, 220), Kinney writes:

> But this apparent sense of personal emotional control does not translate into narrative control, for the Vietnam War did not begin with Paul Berlin's first day in country and its meaning cannot be contained by his tour of duty or his personal fears and obsessions. When Berlin resumes his narrative, the squad is again arrested, this time by SAVAK officers considerably less sympathetic than Rhallon [the previous arrester]. Their necks are ominously and ceremoniously shaved each day for eight days until Rhallon brings them the official news that they have been condemned to die for espionage and desertion. Rhallon remains apologetic. . . . His best advice is to "pray for comfort in the certainty of your innocence. In the purity of your motives" (*GAC*, 201). Innocence and good intentions are revealed as ironic fig leafs for a fact more unspeakable than the word "desertion"—the political fact of American imperialism as figured in an Iranian government "where internal security is paramount" (*GAC*, 200).

Historically, this repressive Iranian dedication to internal security reflects the imperatives of the 1953 CIA-led coup which toppled the democratically elected, nationalist government of

Muhammad Musaddiq in favor of the more "stable" authoritarian leadership of the Shah. With this historical legacy literally pressing on their necks, Doc attempts the classic ugly American gesture by invoking the power and prestige of the American embassy, a tactic that before Vietnam was a narrative staple for dealing with intransigent officials in foreign lands, and a gesture that in Iran, in light of the embassy hostages of 1979, takes on ever-deepening levels of historical irony. . . . Rhallon's answer, "your government does not know you. Or chooses not to," preempts Doc's request, suggesting that it is the SAVAK who holds the privileged link of communications with the American government. The SAVAK, which was established with the aid of American intelligence and remained a key CIA ally, functions in *Going After Cacciato* as an instrument of American historical agency. The men have no recourse because they are condemned, literally and figuratively, by American practices and beliefs; their death sentence thus becomes a scene of friendly fire. With the innocence of the American/Iranian relation thus transformed, Rhallon is replaced by his brutal "twin," a SAVAK colonel who breaks noses and scorns explanations, forcing them to confess their so-called *mission* is nothing but a "fiction"—a made up story.[42]

Kinney's reconstellation of the Vietnam War into the larger context of the United State's imperialist Cold War policies constitutes a valuable contribution to the criticism of *Going After Cacciato*. And this insight is enhanced by her further identification of the American imperialist Cold War project with the myth of American exceptionalism. But her discussion of the imagined itinerary of the squad in the Middle East marginalizes what I take to be at the heart of Berlin's witness in Vietnam, however much he wills himself to mute it: the self-destruction of the *truth discourse* of America at the moment of the fulfillment of its (metaphysical) logic and his consequent decentering, his dislocation into the nothing. Her insight, therefore, is partial in the same way that virtually all commentaries not only of O'Brien's novel, but of the literature *and* the histories of the Vietnam War have been partial. And this is because it is primarily this witness to the contradictory violence the American Adamic discourse—so pervasive down to the smallest detail in the novel—more than, *though not in opposition to*, the political witness she overdetermines in her reading of the novel that is the spectral agent of the disruption of the resolving narrative Berlin wants desperately to imagine.

This is why I prefer to focus on the imagined "conclusion" of Berlin's story—the scene of persuasion at the circular "peace table" in the Salle des

Fêtes of the Majestic Hotel in Paris, which, it is crucial to remember, follows directly on Berlin's reluctant "report" of his last imagined encounter with Cacciato to the loquacious Doc Perez, in which Cacciato's silence resonates disturbingly in the turbulent world of Berlin's now haunted American self. In this highly formalized scene at the peace table, the symbolic function and decor of which resonate with the potential of finality— so much so that one is hard put not to read it as an example of the classical deus ex machina (I will return to consider the implications of this question), Paul Berlin pits Sarkin Aung Wan, the Vietnamese refugee,[43] whom he, in his "innocence," has imagined as his love companion in the process of the trek to Paris, against himself. In keeping with the role he has assigned her throughout the imagined narrative of the future, she represents that aspect of Berlin's ambivalence that leans toward withdrawing from this unjust war, signing, like Frederick Henry in Hemingway's *A Farewell to Arms,* a separate peace, though as Katherine Kinney tellingly notes, his representation of this Vietnamese victim of American violence "always verges on the idealized, transnational, and transhistorical Western fantasy of the Asian woman as supreme servant, the 'geisha.' As refugee she should represent what the war has done to the Vietnamese, but this crucial point is ultimately displaced by Paul Berlin's need for her to recognize what the war has done to him, to cleanse and heal his symbolically wounded body."[44]

What should not be overlooked, however, in attending to the speech O'Brien gives Sarkin Aung Wan to speak at the peace table in her effort to persuade Berlin to *realize* his vision—to abandon imaginative "speculation about what might be," to give up "this fruitless pursuit of Cacciato," in favor of a decisive *act*—is that she identifies what she is struggling against not so much in terms of the violence of America's conduct of the war in Vietnam as of the truth discourse of America that saturates Berlin's very being: the myth of American exceptionalism that has become naturalized as the way things really are:

> Even the refugee must do more than flee. He must arrive. He must return at last to a world as it is, however much in conflict with his hopes, and he must then do what he can to edge reality toward what he has dreamed, to change what he can change, to go beyond the wish or the fantasy. "We have fed the heart on fantasies," says the poet [W. B. Yeats], "the heart's grown brutal from the fare." Spec Four Paul Berlin, I urge you to act. . . . Do not be deceived by false obligation. . . . Do not be frightened by ridicule or censure or embarrassment, do not fear name calling, do not fear scorn of others. For what is true obligation? Is it not the obligation to pursue life at peace with itself? (*GAC*, 318)

In the ostensible weakness of its positive content, especially evident in the last question, this speech, like Berlin's self-serving recuperative representation of her victimage by America, is heavily loaded against Sarkin Aung Wan's argument. But when it is read symptomatically—against its grain, as it were—it metamorphoses into a powerful indictment not simply of America's military devastation of Vietnam and its callously violent deracination of a rice culture into a society of refugees like Sarkin, but also of the American "regime of truth"[45] that made the disastrous fate of Vietnam inevitable. At her speech's center is the quotation from William Butler Yeats's poem, "Meditations in Time of Civil War"(VI): "We have fed the heart on fantasies, / The heart's grown brutal from the fare;" which, no doubt, is a metonymic allusion to the very American history, from the genocidal Puritan "errand" in the American wilderness to modern America's genocidal "errand" ("mission" is its modern equivalent) in the "wilderness" of Vietnam. I am referring to the history, that, as invoked by the insistent witness not only of Tim O'Brien, but virtually all the American veterans who have written about the war, was driven by hearts brutalized by the naturalized myth of American exceptionalism, now, however, further reduced and banalized by the routinization of indiscriminate killing inherent in the instrumentalization and technologization of the "truth."[46]

It is no accident, therefore, that the focus of Sarkin's speech at this "final" scene of persuasion is not on America's political and military violence in Vietnam, the political and military justifications of which have, after all, been shattered in Paul Berlin's mind, but, rather, on the one remaining inviolable space of this typical unquieted "quiet American's" being:[47] his *soul*.[48] I mean the personal "obligations" *as an American individual* that the truth discourse of America has taught him to *feel* are in the end prior to political beliefs.[49] Nor is it an accident that it is precisely this inviolable—one is tempted to say, impenetrable—space of his American being to which this ordinary soldier will appeal in his rejection of Sarkin Aung Wan's plea. I am not only referring to the positive aspects of this "structure of *feeling*" that enabled him, as it has enabled virtually the entire 'liberal" culture industry, to interpret the politics of the war as a "tragic mistake" or a "betrayal" of the benign ideals of America:[50]

Friends, I don't pretend to be expert on matters of obligation, either moral or contractual, but I do know when I *feel* obliged. Obligation is more than a claim imposed on us; it is a personal sense of indebtedness. It is a feeling, an acknowledgment. By prior acts of consent we have agreed to perform certain future acts. I have that feeling. I make that acknowledgment. By my prior acts—the acts of consent—I have bound myself to performing subsequent acts. . . .I tied myself to this mission, promising to see it to its end. These were explicit consents. But beyond them were many tacit promises; to my family, my friends, my town, my country, my fellow soldiers. These promises, too, accumulated. I was not misled. I was not gulled. On the contrary, I believe . . . I *feel* . . . that I am being asked to perform a final service that is entirely compatible with what I had promised earlier. A debt, a legitimate debt, is being called in. . . . True, the moral climate was imperfect; there were pressures, constraints, but nonetheless I made binding choices. Again, this is nothing whatever to do with politics or principles or matters of justice. My obligation is to people, not to principle or politics or justice.

I am also, and above all, referring to the negative aspects of this *feeling*, which, to anticipate, have to do with an indissoluble relay of "structures of feeling" that encompass the subject, the family, the culture, and the nation:

But please, I don't want to overemphasize all this. More than a positive sense of obligation, I confess that what dominates is the dread of abandoning all that I hold dear. I am afraid of running away. I am afraid of exile. I fear what might be thought of me by those I love. I fear the loss of respect. I fear the loss of my own reputation. Reputations, as read in the eyes of my father and mother, the people in my home town, my friends. I fear being an outcast. I fear being thought of as a coward. I fear that even more than cowardice itself. . . .

Are these fears wrong? Are they stupid? Or are they healthy and right? I have been told to ignore my fear of censure and embarrassment and loss of reputations. But would it not be better to accept those fears? To yield to them? If inner peace is the true object, would I win it in exile?

Perhaps now you can see why I stress the importance of viewing obligations as a relationship between people, not between one person and some impersonal idea or principle. An idea, when violated, cannot make reprisals. A principle cannot refuse to shake my hand. Only people can do that. *And it is this social power, the threat of social consequences*, that stops me from making a full and complete break. (*GAC*, 320; my emphasis)

This scene of persuasion, from which I have deliberately quoted amply, is a classic instance of the discourse of hegemony, the analysis of which, in its differentiation between and yet identification of totalitarian and liberal democracy, constitutes, in my mind, the most important contribution of postmodern thought—from Antonio Gramsci and Louis Althusser, to Raymond Williams, Michel Foucault, and Edward Said—to the analysis of modern (i.e, post-Enlightenment, especially American) power relations. What is sadly obvious, however, is that neither this climactic scene from *Going After Cacciato* nor a multitude of analogous ones in the literature of the Vietnam War has been addressed from the critical—Said calls it "contrapuntal"[51]—perspective afforded by the analysis of the discourse of hegemony. As a result, this inviolable space of the American soul, I submit, has not simply remained intact in the sense, as I have noted, that its inviolability has enabled Americans, both liberal and conservative, to represent the horrors perpetrated by America against Vietnam—its land, its culture, and its people—as a "tragic mistake" or, at worst, a "betrayal" of the benign American exceptionalist ethos. As the first Gulf War and, especially, as we shall see in chapter 6, the global "war against terrorism" in the aftermath of 9/11 bears depressing and ominous witness, this failure of criticism has also enabled the dominant culture in America to "forget Vietnam," which is to say, to recuperate an even purer and more virulent form of the myth of American exceptionalism, now dedicated to the global mission of eradicating "terrorism," carrying out preemptive wars against and imposing American-style democracies on "rogue states" that harbor its perpetrators.

For these reasons, and despite what might appear to some as the obvious, I want to invoke at some length, here at the site of the peace table that brings Paul Berlin's imagined narrative—and *Going After Cacciato*—to its "close," the classic definition of hegemony that Raymond Williams derived from Gramsci's distinction between political and civil society and his interrogation of "the truth discourse" of the latter, the liberal discourse that is free from the violence of political society (the repressive states apparatuses) only so long as it gives its "spontaneous consent" to the values of the dominant capitalist culture.[52] This definition is crucial to an understanding of both Paul Berlin's speech and the power relations of the liberal capitalist society of which he is, in "Althusser's" term, an "interpellated" citizen:

> The concept of hegemony often, in practice, resembles these definitions of ["ideology"], but it is distinct in its refusal to equate consciousness with the articulate formal system which can be and ordinarily is abstracted as "ideology". It of course does not exclude the articulate meanings, values and beliefs which a dominant class develops and propagates. But it does not equate these with consciousness, or rather it does not reduce consciousness to

them. Instead it sees the relations of domination and subordination, in their forms as practical consciousness, as in effect a saturation of the whole process of living—not only of political and economic activity, nor only of manifest social activity, but of the whole substance of lived identities and relationships, to such a depth that the pressures and limits of what can ultimately be seen as a specific economic, political, and cultural system seem to most of us the pressures and limits of simple experience and common sense. Hegemony is then not only the articulate upper level of "ideology," nor are its forms of control only those ordinarily seen as "manipulation" or "indoctrination." It is the whole body of practices and expectations, over the whole of living: our senses and assignments of energy, our shaping perceptions of ourselves and our world. It is a lived system of meanings and values—constitutive and constituting—which as they are experienced as practices appear as reciprocally confirming. It thus constitutes a sense of reality for most people in the society, a sense of absolute because experienced reality beyond which it is very difficult for most members of the society to move, in most areas of their lives. It is, that is to say, in the strongest sense a "culture," but a culture which has also to be seen as the lived dominance and sub-ordination of particular classes.[53]

What Williams fails to convey by privileging the abstraction "domination" and its restriction of the interpellated victim to "particular classes" in this otherwise brilliant articulation of Gramsci's concept of hegemony is the violence, always at the service of the nation-state, that is *latent* in its appeal to liberal democracy (a failure, I think, that accounts for the tepidness, if not the impotence, of the so-called cultural criticism that his work inspired first in England and then in the United States). Nevertheless, it does convey with the force of illumination the insidious, but virtually irresistible distinction strategically intrinsic to the discourse of capitalist democracy (what Foucault called "the repressive hypothesis")[54] that always pits the latter's "benign," "ameliorative," and "humane"— truth-oriented—inquiry and ethos against the (vulnerable) violence of totalitarian power relations to obscure its complicity with totalitarianism. To put this in the terms of my reading of Berlin's commonsense argument at the peace table, it discloses with the force of authority that the discourse of hegemony has as its fundamental purpose not only the production of the (collective) soul—the "subjected subject"—which, in its assumed universality, is virtually invulnerable to the corrosiveness of history—"politics, principles or matters of justice"—but equally important the fear of alienation—of being exiled—from the collective national soul. As Berlin puts this ontological anxiety reiteratively—it is no accident that he does it in the language of war and peace—"If inner peace is the true object, would I win in exile?"

As I have shown by way of reconstellating Berlin's past into his imagined future, everything this young, "innocent" American has experienced in the military, politic, cultural, and ontological miasma of Vietnam would seem inexorably to point to his taking a different course from the one he does in this final scene of persuasion. He has, on the one hand, witnessed the disintegration of the plenary American war machine, the plenary politics of American political democracy, the plenary American representation of the Vietnamese earth, the plenary myth of American exceptionalism, and, on the other, the sudden irruption of another reality out of this self-destruction of the logical economy of America theory and practice (what I have been calling, after Heidegger, the unpresentable nothingness that the hegemonic discourse and practice of America "will have nothing to do with"). Despite his unhoming—his being precipitated into the realm of the uncanny (*die Unheimlichkeit*)—he has been so deeply *inscribed* by the discourse of hegemony and its binary logic that it utterly precludes the possibility of thinking the radically alternative reality of this "changed terrain" positively, which is to say, of perceiving the exilic condition—and its "nomadic" practical imperatives—as the essential lesson of his disillusioning experience in Vietnam.

What Paul Berlin sees symptomatically in the shatter of a Vietnam hitherto totally charted by the exceptionalist metaphysical/imperial gaze of America, but is incapable of registering consciously is proleptic of what Edward Said has articulated, especially in the eloquent conclusion of *Culture and Imperialism,* as the inevitable and fundamental project of the organic intellectual in the aftermath of the "end"—the fulfillment and demise—of the Western imperial narrative. I quote at some length to suggest not only why in O'Brien's "resolution" of the contradictions he exposes in *Going After Cacciato* is symptomatic of the disabling limitations of the oppositional literature of the Vietnam War and of the commentaries on this massive body of writing right up to the present moment, but also in what sense the novel is a "threshold text" that anticipates a yet to be realized future oppositional criticism of American imperialism. I mean a criticism that both understands the end, the disclosure of the closure, of imperialism as a continuum that includes the ontological and epistemological, as well as the economic, social, and the political sites, and as an imperative to think the pervasive condition of exile, however fraught with pain and suffering for the victims, as other than the deprivation of the self-identical community envisaged by the binarist logic of the Western discourse of hegemony, indeed, as its spectral Other.

Surely it is one of the unhappiest characteristics of the age to have produced more refugees, migrants, displaced persons, and exiles than ever before in history, most of them as an accompaniment to and, ironically enough, as afterthoughts of great post-colonial and imperial conflicts. As the struggle for independence produced new states and new boundaries, it also produced homeless wanderers, nomads, and vagrants, unassimilated to the emerging structures of institutional power, rejected by the established order for their intransigence and obdurate rebelliousness. And insofar as these people exist between the old and the new, between the old empire and the new state, their condition articulates the tensions, irresolutions, and contradictions in the overlapping territories shown on the cultural map of imperialism.

There is a great difference, however, between the optimistic mobility, the intellectual liveliness, and "the logic of daring" described by the various theoreticians [Deleuze and Guatarri, Virilio, Adorno] on whose work I have drawn, and the massive dislocations, waste, misery, and horrors endured in our century's migrations and mutilated lives. *Yet it is no exaggeration to say that liberation as an intellectual mission, born in the resistance and opposition to the confinements and ravages of imperialism, has now shifted from the settled, established, and domesticated dynamics of culture to its unhoused, decentered, and exilic energies, energies whose incarnation today is the migrant, and whose consciousness is that of the intellectual and artist in exile, the political figure between domains, between forms, between homes, and between languages.* From this perspective then all things are indeed counter, original, spare, strange. From this perspective also, one can see "the complete consort dancing together," contrapuntally. And while it would be the rankest Panglossian dishonesty to say that the bravura performances of the intellectual exile and the miseries of the displaced person or refugee are the same, it is possible, I think, to regard the intellectual as first distilling then articulating the predicaments that disfigure modernity—mass deportations, imprisonment, population transfer, collective dispossession, and forced immigrations.[55]

But Said does not end on this purely diagnostic note. Invoking another prominent modern intellectual exile, he goes on in a rhetoric that uncannily recalls Paul Berlin's intuition into the unaccountability of the spectral strategy of the Vietnamese insurgents that, like the many-headed hydra of antiquity, molecularized, stalled, and eventually defeated the American Ahabian juggernaut:

"The past life of emigrés is, as we know, annulled," says Adorno in *Minima Moralia* (subtitled *Reflections from a Damaged Life* . . . Why? "Because anything that is not reified, cannot be counted and measured, ceases to exist" or, as he says later, is consigned to mere "background." . . . Thus the emigré consciousness—a mind of winter, in Wallace Stevens's phrase—discovers in its marginality that "a gaze averted from the beaten track, a hatred of brutality, a search for fresh concepts not yet encompassed by the general pattern, is the last hope for thought." Adorno's general pattern is what in another place he calls the "administered world" or, insofar as the irresistible dominants in culture are concerned, "the consciousness industry." There is then not just the negative advantage of refuge in the emigré's eccentricity; there is also the positive benefit of challenging the system, describing it in language unavailable to those it has already subdued:

> *In an intellectual hierarchy which constantly makes everyone answerable, unanswerability alone can call the hierarchy directly by its name.*[56]

Haunted though he is by the inexorable presence of the nothing (in all its manifestations), Paul Berlin's metonymic American soul, in its programmed need to be answerable to the narrative of exceptionalist America, remains intact in the end. Although his corrosive experience in Vietnam has compelled him into awareness of the imperatives of the nothing—of being "in between," of a decentered condition that affirms questioning over the answer, exile over belonging to the homeland, unanswerability over answerability, the *polemos* of deviant or rhizomatic intellectual and practical struggle over the decisive dedifferentiating peace that has been the brutal end of the Western war machine since the Romans' invocation of the *Pax Romama*—he shrinks back from these difficult choices. He opts, instead, for the integrity of his "American" soul, hopelessly blinded by a national/imperial history that has had as its raison d'être the production of this type of interpellated and accountable citizen soldier to its constructedness—and, like virtually all of the liberal intellectuals and artists that protested and still protest the war, to the positive ontological, cultural, and political possibilities Said envisages in the multitudinous lives damaged by the binarist nationalist/imperial truth and practice of the Western nation-states. Sadly, this blindness, aided and abetted by the servile American media, has been and continues to be everywhere evident in America in the wake the inauguration of the symptomatically misnamed global "war on terror" on 9/11.

VI

What remains is the question of Tim O'Brien's attitude toward Paul Berlin's imagined "resolution" of his dilemma. I have said that the final ritual scene of persuasion comes all too obviously as a deus ex machina. By this I am not simply referring to the Western aesthetic convention established in antiquity and practiced throughout the history of Western literature, in which the writer defers to the gods—a Transcendental Signified—in the process of achieving a decisive resolution of the irresolvable crisis that is the inevitable condition of human being-in-the-world. I am also, and more precisely, referring to *either* the willful imposition by the writer of a resolution that the complex and erratic narrative action he or she has imagined has made otherwise impossible *or* the parodic imposition of such a decisive resolution for the purpose of exposing the ideological violence that narrative, like the metaphysics that informs it, always perpetrates on the radically differential disseminations of human temporality, that is, the alternative of the great postmodernists, Borges, Beckett, Pynchon, Rushdie, DeLillo, for example.[57]

The evidence of the fiction is, in my mind, inconclusive. But in the end it makes little difference which of these alternatives is attributable to O'Brien. In fact, the real liberatory force of *Going After Cacciato* resides precisely in the inexorability of this uncertainty. What matters is that, in the process of fulfilling its imaginative logic, the novel, both in its content and form, precipitates—bears decisive witness to—a reality about the Vietnam War, *this* war, that cannot finally be accommodated by the totalizing American exceptionalist narrative. I mean by this reality the spectral contradiction—the nothingness, in its ontological as well as military and political manifestations—that refuses to be answerable to and therefore haunts both Berlin's and O'Brien's reifying "stories." Ironically, this spectral reality manifests itself in the very literary criticism of this synecdochical modern American text about the Vietnam War, a criticism that, despite the manifest presence of this radical *Other* of the hegemonic discourse of America, has willfully shrunk back from "it," has, that is, evaded or rationalized—contradictorily "resolved—its menacing unpresentable presence by imposing a deus ex machina on the narrative "it" has shattered.

In referring to *Going After Cacciato* as a threshold synecdochical text, what I have wanted to emphasize is that the consequence of the long and systematic evasion or rationalization of the singularity of *this* war has not simply been the relegation of the Vietnam War—the difference between it and war-in-general as it has been represented in America (and beyond that, the West)—to the margins of history, or that it enabled, at least for the moment, especially after the attacks on the World Trade Center and the Pentagon on September 11, 2001, the recuperation of the lethal exceptionalist American national identity. I have also wanted to underscore the irresistible fact that these recuperative interpretive projects are haunted and therefore highly fragile initiatives. It may be that, in the wake of 9/11 and the American jeremiads proliferated by the media and the intellectual deputies of the dominant culture, the American public has temporarily forgotten the radical contradiction, disclosed by the Vietnam War, that haunts the hegemonic discourse and imperial practice of exceptionalist America— the Achilles' heel of American power—which, we recall, was one of the essential sources of the errant strategy of unanswerability that enabled the Vietnamese insurgents to defeat the infinitely more formidable American war machine. But the mutilated Others of the American empire have not forgotten. This is becoming manifest not only in the increasing isolation of the United States from its traditional Western allies. Far more tellingly, it is becoming increasingly evident in the recalcitrant and unaccommodating response of the unhomed victims of American imperialism in the Middle East to the culture- and life-destroying global mission of the American government, a government that, under the aegis of the revolutionary coalition of neoconservatives and evangelical Christians that constitutes the presidential administration of George W. Bush, would call them to account in the name of the recuperated narrative of American exceptionalism. The retrieval and reconstellation of the symptomatic witness of Tim O'Brien's *synecdochical* threshold novel—that is to say, of virtually the entire troubled discourse on the singular history of the Vietnam War—into this dangerous contemporary global occasion, is likely, as I have tried to suggest, to precipitate a metamorphosis—a "change of terrain"—of the contemporary globalized world recuperated and represented by the American government, its intellectual deputies, and the culture industry as an initiative toward world peace. Following the directives of this exilic witness, what, in this interregnum, is now only an invisible symptom could, as Said's shift of the focus of resistance from "the established, settled and domesticated dynamics of culture to its unhoused, decentered and exilic energies" suggests, become manifest in all its negative—and positive—possibilities: not simply a new perspective on resistance, but also one enabling us to perceive "'the complete consort dancing together' contrapuntally."

Chapter 6

AMERICAN EXCEPTIONALISM, THE JEREMIAD, AND THE FRONTIER, BEFORE AND AFTER 9/11

From the Puritans to the Neo-Con Men

In short, with all cavilers, it was best, both for them and everybody, that whoever had the true light should stick behind the secure Malakoff of confidence, nor be tempted forth to hazardous skirmishes on the open ground of reason. Therefore, he [the confidence-man] deemed it unadvisable in the good man [the confidence-man is duping] . . . to indulge in too much latitude of philosophizing, or, indeed, of compassionating, since this might beget an indiscreet habit of thinking and feeling which might unexpectedly betray him upon unsuitable occasions.

—Herman Melville, *The Confidence-Man*

The aide [a "senior advisor" in the George W. Bush administration] said that guys like me were "in what we call the reality-based community," which he defined as people who "believe that solutions emerge from your judicious study of discernible reality." I nodded and murmured something about enlightenment principles and empiricism. He cut me off. "That's not the way the world really works anymore," he continued. "We're an empire now, and when we act, we create our own reality. And while you're studying that reality—judiciously, as you will—we'll act again, creating other new realities, which you can study too, and that's how things will sort out. We're history's actors . . . and you, all of you, will be left to just study what we do."

—Ron Suskind, "Without a Doubt,"
New York Times, October 17, 2004

In the preceding chapters of this book, I have underscored what I take to be the determinative role that American exceptionalism played in the United States' devastation of Vietnam to thematize the contradictory violence latent in its "benign" logic and thus to suggest its illegitimacy as a justification of America's "war on terror" in the wake of September 11, 2001. By American exceptionalism, I have meant an *ontological* interpretation of the American national identity whose origins lay in the American Puritans' belief that their exodus from the Old World and their "errand in the wilderness" of the New was, on the prefigurative analogy of the Old Testament Israelites, divinely or transcendentally ordained and which became hegemonic in the course of American history with its secularization as Manifest Destiny in the middle of nineteenth century and as the end of history and the advent of the New World Order at the and of the twentieth century. But I have had another purpose, however implicit, in mind in thus pointing to the centrality of the myth of American exceptionalism in this history: to qualify, if not to entirely reject, the now pervasive thesis of postmodern globalization theory, identifiable, above all, with Fredric Jameson, Masao Miyoshi, Ajrian Appadurai, Antonio Negri and Michael Hardt, and Bill Readings. I mean the theory that asserts the demise of the sovereignty of the nation-state and the rise to hegemony of transnational capitalism (Negri and Hardt's "Empire") as a fait accompli, and, particularly, that differentiates the United States from the nations of Europe in that it is based on the social contract entered into by a diversity of immigrants, whereas the latter is grounded in a traditional homogeneous culture, and thus whose (peculiarly constitutive exceptional) logic produces the new sovereignty of transnational capitalism:

> Since the United States does not legitimate itself as a nation-state by appeal to any particular cultural content but only in terms of a contract among its subjects, there is no automatic political orientation to the excavation and inclusion of the popular. This was not the case in Great Britain, where the study of popular culture was automatically and systematically at the same time cultural critique, since it exposed the structural gap between the ideological state apparatuses and the people they regulated. In the United States, the system is described to itself so that it can work better; it is not overthrown. For example, in the United States it is possible to believe that capitalism's project is hindered by racism and sexism, which should be done away with so as to allow the process of expropriation to work more widely. In Great Britain, such a claim would have struck at the heart of the

ethnic cultural identity on which the nation-state was founded, while in the United States it represents no fundamental challenge to the state's promise to itself or the economic system it harbors.[1]

This distinction, which unquestioningly accepts the perennial thesis that America is, indeed, an exceptionalist nation (though it gives it a strange twist), fails to attend to the metaphysical basis of the American exceptionalist ethos and the centrality and mobilizing force of it *Logos* in American history: the inordinate degree to which it has served to render culturally diverse subjects into, in Negri and Hardt's term, "a people" no less nationalistic than the peoples of Western Europe. Furthermore, it fails, when applied to the present or "postmodern" historical global occasion, as Negri and Hardt do, to perceive that the nation-state as a system, is still, despite the pressures of late capitalism, very much intact. If this was not quite evident when this version of globalization theory began to emerge at the end of the twentieth century with the collapse of the Soviet Union and the end of the Cold War, it certainly became manifest in the wake of 9/11, when the United States, having recuperated its exceptionalist national identity—that is, cured itself of the "Vietnam syndrome"—drew on the mobilizing power of its ethos to launch its global "war on terror" in the overt name of the American empire and the *Pax Americana.*

Rather than pursuing the directives suggested by the United States' willful recuperation of the global exceptionalist discourse and practice that was decisively delegitimated by the Vietnam War, however, this globalization theory, since then, has opted instead to focus on accommodating this spectral contradiction to its thesis about the demise of the nation-state and the rise of transnational capital's "empire." Since the validity of my argument, both for the importance of the singularity of the Vietnam War in understanding the post-9/11 global occasion and against the global theory that has posited the waning of the nation-states as a completed project, finally depends on the force of my identification of American exceptionalism with the American national identity, it will be necessary to go beyond the generalizations about the history that I have relied in behalf of my argument thus far. My intention in this penultimate chapter is to retrieve the specific itinerary of this natural history by way of synecdochical citations ranging chronologically from its origins in the discourse of the Puritans to its fulfillment (and demise) in the post-9/11 discourse of the neoconservatives who now make American global policy, particularly that of Samuel P. Huntington, one of the most influential intellectual deputies of this dominant culture.

I

In his policy book entitled *Who Are We?: The Challenges to America's National Identity* published in 2004 in the aftermath of 9/11, Samuel P. Huntington lends his substantial authority as a prestigious scholar to the Bush administration's "argument" for "staying the course" in Iraq in the midst of a weakening of the American people's resolve to do so. Unlike his predecessor, Francis Fukuyama, however, and far more than Richard Haass, who modified the former's Hegelian end-of-history thesis to accommodate the global instability that followed the implosion of the Soviet Union, Huntington, in a surprisingly overt way, draws on the canonical cultural history of the United States to call for another "Great Awakening" as the means of sustaining the American national identity in the face of the challenges posed by the emergence of a discourse and practice of diversity to its unity—and power—and of enabling the "fulfillment" of America's History-ordained errand in the global wilderness. What Huntington means by a new Great Awakening cannot be entirely understood simply by attending to his invocation of earlier Great Awakenings that were defined by the original Great Awakening of the 1730s and 1740s identified with the great Puritan theologian Jonathan Edwards. His call, which should remind us, ironically, of the "Puritan/American calling" and, more specifically, the "American jeremiad," so enablingly analyzed by Sacvan Bercovitch, must be seen in the context of the origins of American exceptionalism in the Massachusetts Bay Puritans' exodus from the "Old World" into the "New," which is to say, the defining distinction they made between a *civilized* world that had become "old," "decadent," "sterile," "impotent," "tyrannical," "collective," "immobile," "effete," "profane" that is, *overcivilized*, and a civilized world that was "new," "creative," "manly," "productive," "free," "individualist," "kinetic," "progressive," "godly." More specifically, it must be seen in the context of the threat posed by the settled or sedentary life—the domesticating and familiarizing dynamics of civilization—to the youthful, virile, and creative energies that were precisely the characteristics the early settlers invoked to distinguished themselves from the Old World. Reconstellated into this inaugural American context, it will also be seen that Huntington's representative call for a new "great [Anglo-Protestant]Awakening" is a call for the reaffirmation or rejuvenation of the perennially American notion of the "frontier": that forward-moving boundary line between wilderness and settlement, the unfamiliar and the familiar, anxiety and complacency, distrust and confidence, violence and peace, "them" (an enemy) and "us," that became in the future the sine qua non of rejuvenating American civilization and the exceptionalist American national identity.

What I am suggesting, in other words, is that Huntington's blueprint for the maintenance of the vigorous nationalism on which America's global hegemony depends is not an anomaly, but the necessary adaptation of an ontopolitical perspective—American exceptionalism—that is chronologically simultaneous with the birth of the idea of America and the American national identity. This is not simply a scholarly matter; it is also and primarily a political one. Attending to these origins of Huntington's post-9/11 discourse will not only go far to explain the "revolutionary" domestic and foreign policies of the George W. Bush administration: the tacit annunciation of a state of exception that has increasingly enabled the abrogation of democracy by a sovereign neoconservative governing elite whose agenda is the imposition of American-style democracy on a global scale. It will also explain why the Democratic Party, far from being an opposition to the second Bush administration's preemptive wars against states that "harbor terrorists" and to its suppression of dissent in the United States, is, in fact, utterly complicitous with these neoconservative goals. It will also go far to explain why the American "Left," both intellectuals and political organizations, have been more or less impotent in their efforts to stall this neoconservative juggernaut.

In what follows, my intention is to offer a genealogy of this latest—and most totalizing and dangerous—discursive manifestation of the American exceptionalist errand in the wilderness. The demands for brevity will, unfortunately, make it necessary to overgeneralize about a long history, but the succinctness enabled by relying on synecdochical instances, will, I hope, provide directives that I believe are urgently needed in the context of the confusion that characterizes resistance to America's post-9/11 domestic and foreign policies.

II

Sacvan Bercovitch begins his magisterial book on the American jeremiad by invoking John Winthrop's sermon on board the *Arabella*, which "set forth the prospects of the infant theocracy in a provisional but sweeping prophecy of doom":

> The passengers were entering into a covenant with God, as into a marriage bond—and therefore, charged Winthrop, they might expect swift and harsh affliction. Invoking the ominous precedent of Israel, he explained that henceforth the Lord would survey them with a strict and jealous eye. They had pledged themselves to God, and He to them, to protect, assist, and favor them above

any other community on earth. But at their slightest shortcoming, for neglecting the "least" of their duties, He would turn in wrath against them and be revenged:

> If wee shall deale falsely with our god in this worke wee have undertaken and soe cause him to withdrawe his pres-ent help for us, wee shall be made a story and a by-word through the world, wee shall open the mouthes of enemies to speake evil of the wayes of god and all professours for Gods sake; wee shall shame the faces of many of Gods worthy servants, and cause theire prayers to be turned into Cursses upon us, till wee be consumed out of the good land whether wee are going.

Winthrop's grim forecast struck a familiar chord. Only several weeks before, as the passengers prepared to embark from South-ampton pier, John Cotton had similarly warned them about the perils of their high enterprise. Where much is given, he intoned, much is demanded. The same God who had sifted them as choice grain from the chaff of England, and who would soon plant them in the New World, might "also roote [them] out againe." Men generally succumbed to carnal lures, leaned towards profits and pleasures, permitted their children to degenerate. . . . Should the emigrants fall prey to such temptations, God would surely with-draw their "special appointment," weed them out, pluck them up, and cast them irrevocably out of His sight.[2]

In these resonant introductory sentences, Bercovitch gives us, in an epito-mized form, not only the historical origins of the American Puritans' "errand in the wilderness," but also the ideological raison d'etre of these origins *and* the necessary conditions that had to be met in order that this ideology become actualized and sustained over time. We are informed (1) of the Puritans' belief that they were, like the Jews of the Old Testament who prefigure them, God's chosen people, that is, of the certainty that their exodus from Europe was the "new" inaugural moment of a providential history—a history informed by the promise/fulfillment structure—the pur-pose of which was to replant the Word of God, betrayed by the Old World, in the New World wilderness and to redeem or renew mankind at large. We are also informed (2) of God's covenant with the Puritans, which both promised His commitment to their ultimate well-being and warned them of the immense difficulty of this global task. Finally, we are informed (3) of the Puritans' realization from the very beginning—and increasingly in the wake of what I will call temporarily the familiarization of the original event—of the fundamental threat to this divinely ordained "calling," the errand in the wilderness to build "the Citty on the Hill" as a beacon to the rest of the world.

At this point, Bercovitch goes on to distinguish his interpretation of the Puritan occasion's role in the history of the formation of America from that of the great Americanist Perry Miller by invoking the ubiquitous jeremiad. Though Miller acknowledges the ambiguity inhering in the Puritan jeremiad, he, according to Bercovitch, reads it primarily as castigation—the expression of the Puritan community's betrayal of the covenant and their drastic falling away from the original commitment to build the New Jerusalem into another Sodom—that resulted inevitably in the demise of the Puritan theocracy:

> What he [Miller] meant by ambiguity was opposition: the errand is either for oneself or for someone else; the jeremiads either discourage or encourage. Clearly, this stems from a "paradoxical realization" that somehow the errand functioned both ways, and that the jeremiads included both threat and hope. But for Miller the realization is an ironic one—it lies in the reader's capacity to see conflicting elements at work in the same act. The Puritans' sense of a failed errand [after the collapse of Cromwell's Protectorate], he claimed, led them to make the errand their own. Their "cry of repentance" furthered the community's "heinous conduct." And the reader's ironic awareness, in turn, builds upon a series of static oppositions: content versus form, social progress versus catalogues of denunciation, psychology versus theology, the march of settlements versus the ideal of theocracy, and summarily "the American experience" (manifest in land speculation, growing wealth, population dispersion) versus the Puritan lament, a "mounting wail of sinfulness" that issues in a self-defeating ritual of purgation. Methodologically, this implies the dichotomy of fact and rhetoric. Historically, it posits an end to Puritanism with the collapse of the church-state. (AJ, 10)

In opposition to Miller's reading, Bercovitch points persuasively to the paradoxical *optimism* that inheres in the ontology—the providential history—underlying the American jeremiad:

> But the Puritan clergy were not simply castigating. For all their catalogues of iniquities, the jeremiads attest to an unswerving faith in the errand; and if anything they grow more fervent, more absolute in their commitment from one generation to the next. The

most severe limitation of Miller's view is that it excludes (or deni-
grates) this pervasive theme of affirmation and exultation. . . . The
essence of the sermon that the first native-born American Puritans
inherited from their fathers, and then "developed, amplified, and
standardized," is its unshakable optimism. In explicit opposition
to the traditional mode, it inverts the doctrine of vengeance into a
promise of ultimate success, affirming to the world, and despite
the world, the inviolability of the colonial cause. (*AJ*, 6–7)

By thus attending to the paradoxical optimism endemic to the Puritans'
providential (teleological) view of history—to the confidence in the face of
the adversities of temporal/worldly life—Bercovitch was enabled to perceive the Puritan jeremiad not simply as an instrument that could turn any
threat to the community's charged unity in the pursuit of its errand—the
hostility of its Other or the familiarizing of the original existential event—
into a productive force in its behalf, but also as a means of renewing or rejuvenating the community at large, that is, though Bercovitch does not put
it this way, of always already escaping the fate of a civilization that had
become *overcivilized* "chaff," in Winthrop's metaphorics: old and decadent—an Old World:

The American Puritan jeremiad was the ritual of a culture on an errand—which is to say, a culture based on a faith in process. Substi-
tuting teleology for hierarchy, it discarded the Old World ideals of
stasis for a New World vision of the future. Its function was to create a climate of anxiety that helped release the restless "progressivist" energies required for the success of the venture. The
European jeremiad also thrived on anxiety, of course. Like all "tra-
ditionalist" forms of ritual, it used fear and trembling to teach ac-
ceptance of fixed social norms. But the American Puritan jeremiad
went much further. *It made anxiety its end as well as its means.
Crisis was the social norm it sought to inculcate.* The very concept
of errand, after all, implied a state of *un*fulfillment. The future,
though divinely assured, was never quite there, and New England's
Jeremiahs set out to provide the sense of insecurity that would ensure the outcome. Denouncing or affirming, their vision fed on the
distance between promise and fact. (*AJ*, 23; my emphasis)

It was, as Bercovitch persuasively demonstrates, the Puritan jeremiad, the
optimistic and always forwarding teleology of which enabled the exploitation of threat in behalf of renewal in the face of crisis, that, in its
secularized form, became the essential cultural instrument of the domi-

nant Anglo-Protestant core culture in maintaining its hegemony in the face of the astonishing cultural and political transformations America underwent in the long wake of the decline of the Puritan theocracy. It is also this profound insight into the formation of the American national identity that not simply revolutionized Puritan studies, but, despite reservations about the radicality of his commitment to dissensus,[3] provided the ground for the New Americanist revisions of American studies at the end of the twentieth century.

Having said this, however, one is entitled to ask: Is Bercovitch's formulation of the structure and, especially, the ideological effects of the American jeremiad on the American character and American historical practice adequate to the critical revisionary task? My contribution to the answer to this question will take its point of departure in a further, virtually parenthetical, remark Bercovitch makes about Perry Miller's (mis)representation of the Puritan jeremiad. After pointing to the latter's version as a tacit proclamation of the "end of Puritanism with the collapse of the church-state," that is, the demise of Puritanism's influence on the formation of the American national identity, he writes: "Miller's analysis lends support to the dominant anti-Puritan view of national development—that the 'American character' was shaped by what he called 'the fact of the frontier.'" He then goes on to posit his version of the Puritan jeremiad as the truer historical origin of the American national identity: "We need not discount the validity of this frontier thesis to see what it does *not* explain: the persistence of the Puritan jeremiad throughout the eighteenth and nineteenth centuries, in all forms of the literature, including the literature of westward expansion" (*AJ*, 10–11).

Bercovitch's tendency to distinguish between the American jeremiad and the frontier or, perhaps more accurately, to subordinate the frontier to the American jeremiad, signals a blindness to or, at any rate, a fatal deemphasis of, a crucial dimension of the Puritan jeremiad, one that renders his version, however heuristic it is, finally inadequate to the task of explaining the functioning of the American jeremiad in relation to historical "crises" of the national psyche throughout the eighteenth, nineteenth, and twentieth centuries, not least, as I will show, in the aftermath of 9/11. Though Bercovitch quite rightly says that the function of the jeremiad "was to create a climate of anxiety that helped release the restless 'progressivist' energies required for the success of the venture"—a locution that is intended to underscore the paradoxical optimism inherent in the Puritans' prefigural/providential view of history—it is not so much the actual sources of the anxiety that he emphasizes in his analysis as the familiarization of the difficult experience of adversity—the original existential conditions of Puritan life in the wilderness—that precipitated the anxiety and eroded the urgency of the community's sense of errand, that is, *that threatened a repetition in the New World of the entropic fate of the Old World.* What I want to suggest, in other words, is that it was (and continues to be) the frontier—the fluid boundary between "savagery" and "civilization," threatening forest and secure settlement, diabolic enemies and supportive friends, the uncertainty of the strange and confidence of the familiar—the not-at-home and the at-home, as it were—that was foremost in the mind of the Puritan Jeremiahs in their castigations of recidivism in the name of the founding moment. More precisely, I submit, the jeremiad and the frontier were indissolubly related. It is not quite adequate to say, as Bercovitch does, that in "inculcating" crisis as the "social norm," the jeremiad "set out to provide the sense of insecurity that would ensure the 'fulfillment' of the always *un*fulfilled errand" or that "the ritual import of the jeremiad" was "to sustain these two elements ['crisis' and 'direction and purpose'] by imposing control, and to justify control by presenting a certain form of process as the only road to the future kingdom" (*AJ*, 24). For these locutions imply a failure to see, or, perhaps more accurately, a minimizing of, the Puritan Jeremiahs' equally anxious concern that, in their desire to rationalize the wilderness in *majorem gloriam Dei*, to "clear," "settle," and "improve" the wilderness (these, not incidentally, are terms that saturate the frontier discourse of colonial novelists like James Fenimore Cooper, Robert Montgomery Bird, and antebellum and postbellum historians like Francis Parkman, George Bancroft, and Frederick Jackson Turner), their "New World" might "progress" full circle back into the Old. This Puritan fear—or, rather, this reliance on the terror of the frontier to sustain its optimistic dynamics—is, for example, at the heart of the "Preface" of Mary Rowlandson's captivity and restoration narrative written by one *Per Amicus* (probably Increase Mather) that turned the (remaining) ambiguities of her experience of "affliction" into a jeremiad that transforms suffering into an agency of optimism and celebrates earthly trial in the name of community renewal:

> This narrative was penned by the Gentlewoman her self. To be to her a memorandum of Gods dealing with her, that she might, never forget, but remember the same, and the several circumstances thereof, all the days of her life. A pious scope which deserves both commendation and imitation: Some friends having obtained a sight of it, could not but be so much affected with the many passages of working providence discovered therein as to judge it worthy of publick view, an altogether unmeet that such works of God should be hid for present and future Generations:

And therefore though this Gentlewomans modesty would not thrust it into the Press, yet her gratitude unto God made her not hardly perswadable to let it pass, that God might have his due glory and others benefit by it as well as herself. I hope by this time none will cast any reflections upon this Gentlewoman, on the score of this publication of her affliction and deliverance. If any should, doubtless they may be reckoned with the nine lepers, of whom it is said, *Were there not ten cleansed, where are the nine? but one returning to give God thanks.* Let such further know that this was a dispensation of publick note, and of universall concernment, and so much the more, by how much the nearer this Gentlewoman stood related to that faithful Servant of God, whose capacity and employment was publick in the house of God, and his name on that account of a very sweet savour in the churches of Christ [Her husband, the minister Joseph Rowlandson]. Who is there of a true Christian spirit, that did not look upon himself much concerned in this bereavement, this Captivity in the time thereof, and in this deliverance when it came, yea more than in many others; and how many are there, to whom so concerned, it will doubtless be a very acceptable thing to see the way of God with this Gentlewoman in the aforesaid dispensation, thus laid out and portrayed before their eyes.[4]

What I am suggesting in thus invoking this "Amicus's" transformation of Rowlandson's narrative into a jeremiad, in other words, is that, Bercovitch's emphasis on the threat to the progressive errand in his interpretation of the American jeremiad is incomplete. It does not clearly take into account the Puritans' equally urgent awareness of the need for a *perpetual frontier* between wilderness and civilization—the unending violent struggle it entails with a (usually defeatable) "enemy" who always threatens the "fulfillment" of the errand—that was the essential means by which their civilization would be, unlike an Old World that had run out of frontiers, always already rejuvenated, that is, would *always* remain an exceptional New World.

In pointing to Bercovitch's overdetermination of the unifying potentialities of the American jeremiad at the expense of its rejuvenating effects— the solidarity of the community in behalf of the errand at the expense of the renewal that would render its civil life immune to decay—I am not opting for the "frontier" thesis about the development of the American national identity. Rather, I am suggesting that Bercovitch's thesis about the role played by the American jeremiad needs to incorporate and emphasize the "fact of the frontier" instead of minimizing it. Bercovitch is right in singling out the jeremiad as that cultural ritual that more than any other explains the development of the American national character and the elect's domestic and foreign policies. But this cultural ritual—this communal agency for the renewal of the commonweal's covenant with God—must, I suggest, be understood not simply in domestic terms (the solidarity of civil society), but also and simultaneously in terms of its "foreign" relations (the threatening Other beyond the American frontier). In the wake of the demise of the Puritan theocracy and the constitutional separation of church and state, the "fact of the frontier" came to dominate the discourse of an ever-westward expanding America, but it is the jeremiad—and the concept of providential/ optimistic history on which it is founded—not in a purely secular form, as liberals have erroneously assumed, but in a religiosecular—"natural supernaturalist"—form, that has determined the meaning of its various and fluid historical manifestations. And, as in the case of the Puritans, though increasingly as America rationalized and banalized the "wilderness," its purpose has been not to close the frontier and terminate the errand, but to keep it perpetually open, even after the farthest western reaches of the continent had been settled and colonized. Its purpose has been to *always already produce crisis and the communal anxiety crisis instigates* not simply to mobilize the national consensus and a flagging patriotism, but also to inject by violence the American body politic with antibiotics against decay.

III   James Fenimore Cooper

It will not be my purpose in this chapter to undertake a comprehensive history of the indissoluble relation between the American jeremiad and the idea of the perpetual American frontier that has operated to render America perennially "exceptionalist," that is, always already a "New World," from the Puritan's errand in the New England wilderness, through the era of Manifest Destiny and westward expansion, to America's globalization of its errand in the aftermath of World War II and the onset of the Cold War, particularly its extension of the frontier into the Pacific and Southeast Asia and, after the event of 9/11, its transformation of the spatial (frontier) into a temporal metaphor (the unending "war on terror"). Such a history, at least up to the Civil War, can, I suggest, be inferred by reconstellating Bercovitch's *The American Jeremiad* into the countercultural history of American westward expansion encyclopedically documented by Richard Slotkin.[5] My intention is not to write history as such, but, by invoking a few exemplary moments in this cultural history, to shed urgent genealogical light on the post-Vietnam era, which, as we have seen, bore witness to a massive campaign to "forget" Vietnam and to the particular ominous turn that American exceptionalism has taken in the aftermath of the end of the Cold War, particularly in the wake of Al Qaeda's attacks on the World Trade Center and the Pentagon, when, in the eyes of the new America's elect, the limited geographical frontier metamorphosed into an illimitable temporal frontier.

Let me begin with the famous last paragraphs of James Fenimore Cooper's first Leatherstocking novel, *The Pioneers*, which have resonated like a *basso ostinato* throughout the previous chapters. In the novel, Cooper, it will be recalled, represents Natty Bumppo in old age and, at best, as an anachronism, fated, like his Indian friend, Chingachgook, the Mohegan, by his anticivilizational ways, to disappear from the face of the American earth. For Cooper, Templeton, New York, is the protagonist of the novel, the fledgling town on the frontier struggling, in the regulating discourse of the colonial period, to "clear," "settle," and "improve" the wilderness (Bumppo repeatedly animadverts against "betterment"), that is, to establish a civilization at its edge. At the end, however, Cooper rather suddenly, and famously, finds a new role for the backwoodsman to play in the civilizational process, one that will be overdetermined in the Leatherstocking novels that followed:

> Elizabeth raised her face, and saw the old hunter standing, look-ing back for a moment, on the verge of the wood. As he caught their glances, he drew his hard hand hastily across his eyes again, waved it on high for an adieu, and uttering a forced cry to his dogs, who were crouching at his feet, he entered the forest.
>
> This was the last that they ever saw of the Leather-stocking, whose rapid movements preceded the pursuit which Judge Tem-ple both ordered and conducted. He had gone far towards the set-ting sun,—the foremost in the band of Pioneers, who are opening the way for the march of the nation across the continent.[6]

In the process of writing the novel, Cooper becomes increasingly aware that the frontier settlement Templeton (i.e., the postrevolutionary American West), in its increasingly aristocratic reduction of cultural and ethnic diversity in the name of civilized justice (the squire-like Judge Tem-ple), could eventually degenerate into an Old World on the analogy not simply of the fate of Europe but also, as his reiterated references suggest, of the Atlantic seaboard states. It thus occurs to Cooper that the anxiety-producing frontier or, rather, the actions of the self-reliant, naturally sagacious, trail-blazing, and nature-oriented frontiersman—the antithesis of the British gentleman—both unifies and energizes its civil and political life. As the example of Mary Rowlandson's captivity narrative testifies, Cooper's Puritan predecessors rendered adversity and trial fundamental to the moral imperatives of their interpretation of the Fall as a *felix culpa* (fortunate fall) and their *divinely* ordained Adamic "errand in the wilderness." Similarly, though from a generally secular perspective, Cooper seems to have realized in the immediate aftermath of the American Revolution that the oppositions between wilderness and settlement, nomadic and sedentary, savagery and civility, manliness and bestiality are not, as it seemed, absolute, a matter of a narrative in which the first term exists to annihilate the second, but, rather, belong hierarchically together in a preordained ontological promise-fulfillment structure that anticipates an end (the City on the Hill), but, in fact, never arrives there, a relationship, that is, that renders America *always* exceptional.

This realization, I suggest, instigated Cooper's decision, again analogous to the Puritan Jeremiahs, in the next few years to resituate the American frontier experience depicted in *The Pioneers* (postrevolutionary 1793) to an earlier, clearly primal time and to present Natty Bumppo, who disappears into the wilderness at the end of the first Leatherstocking tale, in his youthful and vital prime. This was the original time, *in illo tempore*, of the prerevolutionary French and Indian Wars (1756–1763), when the struggle between the Old World and the New was as much a cultural as a political conflict. It was, that is, a time during which a certain aggressive subaltern constituency of "provincial America," acutely aware of the fatal flaws of imperial Britain—its aristocratic culture, its monarchical government, and its regimented army—was vociferously contrasting the Old World's clumsy and fruitless abstract efforts, epitomized by the blundering European arrogance of General Edward Braddock and then Sir Jeffrey Amherst, to defeat their European rival in the struggle for possession of the New World, to negotiate allegiances with the native Americans, and, not least, to attend to the knowledge of this foreign world—the alien wilderness and its nomadic denizens—gained by the "manly," "self-reliant," and "sagacious" American backwoodsmen by means of the interminable crisis incumbent on their frontier condition. Cooper began this temporal and ideological resituating process in his next novel, *The Last of the Mohicans* (1826), and he brought it to fulfillment in the novels that followed it, especially *The Deerslayer* (1841). His intention was not simply to mythologize the American backwoodsman, as it has traditionally been represented since John Filson's apotheosis of Daniel Boone, but also and, I think, primarily to *bear witness* for the *later*—that is, more civilizationally "mature"— America of the 1830s[7] to the *reversal* of the traditional relationship between civilizational and primitive knowledge symbolically epitomized by the historically burdened, collective, difference-reducing, and sluggish (i.e., anachronistic), Old World ethos, on the one hand, and the vigorous, immediate, and practical polyvalent Stoic and self-reliant ethos of the New

World. Not, however, to privilege this vital but errant New World ethos in an absolute binary opposition with the sterile and often effeminate but order-oriented ethos of the Old World, but, like his European conservative counterpart Alexis de Tocqueville, to assure the perpetual youthfulness ("manliness" in the discourse of the frontier) of an otherwise always aging/decaying and effeminate civilization. What matters in Cooper's representation of the Leatherstocking in *The Last of the Mohicans* is not the radical opposition between what he reiteratively calls the "sagacity" gained by the frontiersman by way of his self-reliance—his immediate relationship to nature—and the book-knowledge that distances the learned person from the grim realities one necessarily encounters in the forest, and thus either weakens his resolve to act decisively in contexts of crisis or, by generalizing them, blinds himself to the all important particularities.

It is not, in other words, the Leatherstocking figure's mythical rugged individuality that, as it has been reiteratively said by the custodians of the American memory, was the harbinger of entrepreneurial laissez-faire American democracy. That, Cooper, like de Tocqueville—and the founding Puritans—knew, would most likely end either in the anarchy of the multitude or the sterile tyranny of the sovereign people. What matters in Cooper's representation of the Leatherstocking, rather, is the *relationality* of the frontiersman's stoic "self-reliance" and the collective ethos of the British colonial world—the loyalist Effinghams in *The Pioneers*, Colonel Munro in *The Last of the Mohicans*, the garrison soldiers in *The Deerslayer*—that he both serves and shuns. This means, on the one hand, an attunement to "nature" that constitutes a willful break from the sterilizing bondage of a distancing "tradition," one enabling a different, more "immediate," practical and useful kind of knowledge, more amenable to surviving the murderous conditions of the wilderness than the book-knowledge privileged by Europe (an attunement that, in its most extreme form, is often symbolized in this frontier discourse by the abandonment of sword for the tomahawk).[8] When, for example Duncan, the haughty aristocratic young Virginian major in the British army, whom Hawkeye educates to the intricacies of the wilderness throughout the novel, unexpectedly volunteers to disguise himself as a painted madman in order to enter the Indian village where Cora is held captive by Magua, the backwoodman responds:

And now God bless you! You have shown a spirit that I like; for it is the gift of youth, more especially one of warm blood and a stout heart. But believe the warning of a man, who has reason to know all he says to be true. You will have occasion for your best manhood, and for a sharper wit than what is to be gathered in books, afore you outdo the cunning, or get the better of the courage of a Mingo! . . . I say, young gentleman, may Providence bless your undertaking, which is altogether for good; and remember, that to outwit the knaves, it is lawful to practice things, that may not be naturally the gift of a white skin.[9]

But this relationality between the backwoodsman's ethos and that of the British colonialist also and simultaneously means, on the other hand, that transcendentally justified authority (in Cooper's case, as in de Tocqueville's, a history-diluted Providence[10]) that, despite its tendency to wither, tethers the always erratic, differential singularities of nature to a stable center, compels them, in the last instance, to take their proper place in an ontologically prior larger whole. For Cooper, the Leatherstocking's manly individualism, including his uninhibited will to kill the threatening enemy, exists, like the decentralized and relatively errant local governments established by the Puritans in de Tocqueville's account of American democracy, to always already reinfuse force into a civilization the temporal course of which would otherwise, as in the case of the centralized polity of Europe, necessarily end in an unproductive and/or effeminate decadence.[11]

However remote from the Puritan jeremiad, Cooper's Leatherstocking novels, like so many of the novelistic romances written at that belated time, were, to reiterate, intended to bear witness to the antithetical limitations of the nomadic frontier ethos and the sedentary ethos of the settlement and thus to recall the Americans of the emergent Jacksonian era—an era of westward expansion and of civilizational consolidation—to the American exceptionalist calling, understood as an unexceptionalist exceptionalism.

IV   Francis Parkman

Like Cooper's Leatherstocking romances, which he admired,[12] Francis Parkman's celebrated histories of colonial America have their mise-en-scène in the French and Indian wars and thus their thematics in the frontier experience. It would seem an extravagant exaggeration to represent them as jeremiads reconstellated into the frontier context. And yet this is what I want to suggest by way of a brief reference to the first and most popular of these, *The Conspiracy of Pontiac* (originally published in 1851, but undergoing revisions until the sixth edition of 1870). Indeed, I will go as far as to say that *The Conspiracy* is more jeremiadic than Cooper's, more closely recalling its Puritan origins, precisely in the degree to which the antebellum America in which Parkman lives and writes has become more "civilized," which is to say, in the degree to which the ethos of settlement has come to overshadow that of the receding frontier. I am referring to Parkman's biography, to the fact that he was consciously a Boston Brahmin in the post-Jacksonian age, an inheritor of the Anglo-Protestant English, if not precisely the Puritan, tradition, and, as his memoir *The Oregon Trail* bears witness, that he also attempted to (re)live, as much as societal conditions made it possible, the stoic, self-reliant, and "manly" life of the earlier backwoodsman, who, like the Leatherstocking figure in Cooper's novels, plays a major symbolic role in his account of the development of the exceptionalist (and racist and patriarchal) American national identity in his histories.[13] But I am also referring to his "Preface" to the first edition of *The Conspiracy*, which, it is important to observe, speaks for the larger ideological intentions of the later histories:

> The Conquest of Canada was an event of momentous consequence in American history. It changed the political aspect of the continent, prepared a way for the independence of the British colonies, rescued the vast tracts of the interior from the rule of military despotism [the French, but implicitly also the English armies], and gave them, eventually, to the keeping of an ordered democracy. Yet to the red natives of the soil its results were wholly disastrous. Could the French have maintained their ground, the ruin of the Indian tribes might long have been postponed; but the victory of Quebec was the signal of their swift decline. Thenceforth they were destined to melt and vanish before the advancing waves of Anglo-American power, which now rolled westward unchecked and unopposed. They saw the danger, and, led by a great and daring champion, struggled fiercely to avert it. The history of the epoch, crowded as it is with scenes of tragic interest, with marvels of suffering and vicissitude, of heroism and endurance, has been, as yet unwritten, buried in the archives of governments, or among the obscurer records of private adventure. To rescue it from oblivion is the object of the following work. *It aims to portray the American forests and the American Indian at the period when both received their final doom.*[14] (my emphasis)

In these brief prefatorial remarks, so reminiscent of the preface, written by the *Amicus*, of Mary Rowlandson's captivity narrative, about the history that is to ensue, we encounter virtually the entire spectrum of the American exceptionalist ideology: the distinction that privileges the New World over the Old (democracy over despotism, Anglo-Protestantism over French Catholicism, "Popery," as Parkman puts it in his text), the racism that blames the victim for his extinction, the relentless momentum of Manifest Destiny, and so on. But, as the last, culminating, sentence of the quoted summary testifies, these, in the final analysis, are subordinate to the anxiety Parkman feels in the wake of the event that, so early on, rendered the "doom," not simply of the Indian, but also of the American "forests" inevitable. Like his Puritan ancestors in their jeremiads—and, in the contexts of severe covenantal crises, in their calls for "Great Awakenings"—what the Parkman of 1851 seems to be bearing witness to in behalf of his readers, in other words, is not the euphoric triumph of Anglophone civilization, but the demise of the negative conditions on which civilization depends for its renewal: the frontier and the morality of the trial, or, we might say, by way of anticipating the American exceptionlait discourse of the post-Cold War occasion, a threatening enemy.

Indeed, Parkman goes on to say that "to rescue" [the history of this epoch] from "oblivion" it "is evident that other study than that of the closet is indispensable to success in such an attempt." As a historian, he knew that "book-learning" was inadequate to this task, indeed, even detrimental insofar as it is compelled to rely on enervated and enervating abstractions. Like Americans in general, it was his obligation, he felt, not simply to get as close to the things themselves about which he intended to write, but in so doing to renew, to recharge, his learned sensibility:

> Habits of early reading had greatly aided to prepare me for the task; but necessary knowledge of a more practical kind has been supplied by the indulgence of a strong natural taste, which, at various intervals, led me to the wild regions of the north and west. Here, by the camp-fire, or in the canoe, I gained familiar acquaintance with the men and scenery of the wilderness. In 1846, I visited various primitive tribes of the Rocky Mountains, and was, for a time, domesticated in a village of the western Dahcotah, on the high plains between Mount Laramie and the range of the Medicine Bow. (*CP*, 347)

As a historian of the frontier era of American history, Parkman perceives his task on the analogy of the conditions of the wilderness and thus models his scholarly self, without irony, after the, by his time, long-textualized American frontiersman. Despite his claim to the objectivity that is enabled by "being there," his "new (world)" kind of historiography will be carried out according to the imperatives of what Edward Said has called "the textual

attitude": of the regulative *discourse* of the frontier: clearing, reclaiming, settling, and, if we see his project in terms of the belongingness of the New and
the Old World, always already renewing:

> The crude and promiscuous mass of [primary] materials presented
> an aspect by no means inviting. The field of the history was uncul-
> tured and unreclaimed, and the labor that awaited me was like that
> of the border settler, who, before he builds his rugged dwelling,
> must fell the forest-trees, burn the undergrowth, clear the ground,
> and hew the fallen trunks to due proportion. (CP, 348–349)[15]

The backwoodsman or borderer in Francis Parkman's histories
serves basically the same purpose as he does in Cooper. It is no accident
that the history he writes about the border wars between the British and
American and the Indians under Pontiac after the defeat of Montcalm at
Quebec in *The Conspiracy of Pontiac* is introduced and framed by the
American exceptionalist distinction he makes between, on the one hand,
the aggressively manly Protestant English, with whom he elides for this
inaugural purpose the American borderers and their attunement to the
particular exigencies of the New World wilderness ("Indian country"),
and, on the other, the passive Catholic French, whom he represents in the
stereotypical imagery of the Old World:

> The American colonies of France and England grew up to matu-
> rity under widely different auspices. Canada, the offspring of
> Church and State, nursed from infancy in the lap of power, its
> puny strength fed with artificial stimulants, its movements
> guided by rule and discipline, its limbs trained to martial exer-
> cise, languished, in spite of all, for the lack of vital sap and en-
> ergy. The colonies of England, outcast and neglected, but strong
> in native vigor and self-confiding courage, grew yet more strong
> with conflict and with striving, and developed the rugged pro-
> portions and unwieldy strength of a youthful giant.
>
> In the valley of the St. Lawrence, and along the coasts of the At-
> lantic, adverse principles contended for the mastery. Feudalism
> stood arrayed against Democracy; Popery against Protestantism;
> the sword against the ploughshare. The priest, the soldier, and the
> noble ruled in Canada. The ignorant, the light-hearted Canadian
> peasant knew nothing and cared nothing about popular rights and
> civil liberties. Born to obey, he lived in contented submission,
> without the wish or the capacity for self-rule. Power, centered in

the heart of the system, left the masses inert. . . . If we search the world for the sharpest contrast to the spiritual and temporal vassalage of Canada, we shall find it among her immediate neighbors, the Puritans of New England, where the spirit of non-conformity was sublimed to a fiery essence, and where the love of liberty and the hatred of power burned with sevenfold heat. The English colonist, with thoughtful brow and limbs hardened with toil; calling no man master, yet bowing reverently to the law which he himself had made; patient and laborious, and seeking for the solid comforts rather than the ornaments of life; no lover of war, yet, if need were, fighting with a stubborn, indomitable courage, and then bending once more with steadfast energy to his farm, or his merchandise,—such a man might well be deemed the very pith and marrow of a commonwealth. (*CP*, 390–391)

This crude American exceptionalist ideological differentiation between the French and British colonists, which, it should not be overlooked, reminds us of Alden Pyle's (and his real-life model's) disdain for the decadent French imperialists speaks for itself, but two particular points, pertinent to what will follow, are worth remarking: (1) Parkman's tendency, here and throughout his history, to identify and underscore the Anglo-Protestant New England culture not simply as the founding culture of America, but also as the *core culture* of America; (2) and closely related, his emphasis not simply on the American colonist's strength in "native vigor" and "self-confiding courage," attributes, no doubt, incumbent on their assumption of election, but also and primarily, his underscoring of the importance of "striving" and "conflict," however unwanted, as that condition that rendered the early British colonists' native vigor and self-confidence "yet more strong." This, as we have seen, was the condition that was the sine qua non of renewing the "commonwealth" the "bone and marrow" of the body politic.

Writing in the antebellum period, Parkman, the New England intellectual, was anxiously aware that the frontier that had nourished the "bone and marrow" of the highly civilized and vigorous New England body politic had by that time moved across the Mississippi into the West and that this movement was accompanied by a great migration that was multicultural and multiracial.For him, this meant two things: that New England, the *Logos* of the American national identity, was becoming an "Old" world and that the new West, with only gossamer threads binding its "errancy" to the East, a wilderness of a savage multitude. (Recall the Bush and the Hutter families in Cooper's *The Prairie* and *The Deerslayer*, respectively.) Reconstellated into this American exceptionalist context,

The Conspiracy of Pontiac thus comes to be seen as a call, in the manner of the Puritan jeremiad, for an awakening: not simply the recalling of a great paradigmatic moment of the founding of America that would reestablish the unity of the nation-state under the aegis of New England (the Anglo-Protestant core culture), but of the conditions of the frontier that were necessary for its perpetual renewal: the *proximity* of Civilization and the wilderness, Old World and New World, Us and them (an enemy), Optimism and anxiety, Order and errancy, Peace and violence, indeed, the indissoluble *belongingness* of these hierarchical opposites.

This American exceptionalist ideology of the renewing frontier is at the heart of *The Conspiracy*, and manifests itself everywhere in the text. I quote the following passage because it is synecdochical of both the content and rhetoric, but also because it clearly demonstrates the ontological and racist foundation on which Parkman's repugnant—and appallingly banal—American exceptionalism is grounded:

> When the European and savage are brought in contact, both are gainers, and both are losers. The former loses the refinements of civilization, but gains, in the rough schooling of the wilderness, a rugged independence, a self-sustaining energy, and powers of action and perception before unthought of. . . . Those rude and hardy men, hunters and traders, scouts and guides, who ranged the woods beyond the English borders, and formed a connecting link between barbarism and civilization, have been touched upon already. They were a distinct, peculiar class, marked with striking contrast of good and evil. Many, though by no means all, were coarse, audacious, and unscrupulous; yet, even in the worst, one might often have found a vigorous growth of warlike virtues, an iron endurance, an undespairing courage, a wondrous sagacity, and singular fertility of resource. In them was renewed, with all its ancient energy, that wild and daring spirit, that force and hardihood of mind, which marked our barbarous ancestors of Germany and Norway [the Anglo-Saxon race]. (*CP*, 465–466).

V   Daniel Webster

Daniel Webster's Bunker Hill orations are, of course, an entirely different genre from Parkman's histories, and their mise-en-scène—the Battle of Bunker Hill and the American Revolution in general—distant from the historian's.[16] But his historical perspective is the same, a sameness that testifies to this textual attitude's pervasiveness and its deeply backgrounded genealogy. Like Parkman's, it is an American exceptionalist problematic determined by his New England heritage and takes the rhetorical form of the jeremiad. If there is a difference, it lies in Webster's more immediate relationship to his Puritan roots and to the jeremiad than Parkman's. But to identify Webster's problematic with American exceptionalism and its form of articulation with the jeremiad as such is inadequate. No less than his Puritan predecessors (e.g., John Danforth and Increase and Cotton Mather) and, Cooper and Parkman, what is at stake for Webster at each of the occasions of his Bunker Hill orations is the perennial New World/ Old World opposition, the anxiety that the New World is becoming old (effete and/or dispersed) like Europe, and the need to identity a threat to the well-being of the covenanted nation that would both recuperate the failing consensus and renew the American peoples' productive energy. I quote from the representative last paragraph of the first of these commemorating orations, which Webster delivered at the laying of the cornerstone of the Bunker Hill Monument at the site of the battle on June 17, 1825, its fiftieth anniversary. After identifying himself and his audience as the belated filial offspring of those Puritan founders, whose "patience and fortitude" and "daring enterprise" had "set the world an example of founding civil institutions on the great and united principles of human freedom and human knowledge (the echo of Winthrop's sermon on board *The Arabella* is distinct),"[17] and, more immediately, of the great pioneers of the American Revolution who died at Bunker Hill in their behalf, and the ground on which they stand to commemorate them, the site of "the sepulchers of our fathers," Webster concludes:

> And let the sacred obligations which have devolved on this generation, and on us, sink deep into our hearts. Those who established our liberty and our government are daily dropping from among us. The great trust now descends to new hands. Let us apply ourselves to that which is presented to us, as our appropriate object. We can win no laurels in a war for independence. Earlier and worthier hands have gathered them all. Nor are there places for us by the side of Solon, and Alfred, and other founders of states. Our fathers have filled them. But there remains to us a great duty of defence and preservation, and there is opened to us, also, a noble pursuit, to which the spirit of the times strongly invites us. *Our proper business is improvement. Let our age be the age of improvement.* In a day of peace, let us advance the arts of peace and the works of peace. Let us develop the resources of our land, call forth its powers, build up its institutions, promote all its great interests, and see whether we also, in our day and generation, may not perform something worthy to be remembered. Let us cultivate

a true spirit of union and harmony. In pursuing the great objects which our condition points out to us, let us act under a settled conviction, and an habitual feeling, that these twenty-four States are one country. Let our conceptions be enlarged to the circle of our duties. Let us extend our ideas over the whole of the vast field in which we are called to act. Let our object be, OUR COUNTRY, OUR WHOLE COUNTRY, AND NOTHING BUT OUR COUNTRY. And, by the blessing of God, may that country itself become a vast and splendid monument, not of oppression and terror, but of Wisdom, of Peace, and of Liberty, upon which the world may gaze with admiration for ever! (*WS*, 253–254; my emphasis)

In this conclusion, Webster highlights by underscoring the ultimate raison d'être of the occasion. The great, manly American heroes who inaugurated the American Revolution at the Battle of Bunker Hill are gradually "dropping from among us," suggesting not simply this influential New England lawmaker's mourning over their demise, but also, and primarily, his anxiety over the belated present generation of Americans, who, living a half-century after the vital heroic and patriotic fathers in a time he represents as one of peace and prosperity, are thus susceptible to the enervating influences of the refinements of settled life. Webster underscores this anxiety by pointing to the absence (in the wake of the War of 1812) of an enemy that threatens the American way: "We can win no laurels in a war of independence. Earlier and worthier hands have gathered them all." This, as we have seen since Mary Rowlandson's captivity narrative, is the necessary enemy that is God's or History's means of trying and tempering the faith and confidence of Americans, the prerequisite of patriotism and rejuvenation of the covenantal people and their divinely ordained or destined errand. Thus he is compelled to turn precisely to that which threatens to enervate the will of his belated generation: the "defense," "preservation," and, above all, "improvement" of what the pioneers of the Battle of Bunker Hill accomplished.

But what is crucial to note in this paradoxical move is that, in invoking "improvement" as the task to which the "spirit of the age invites us," Webster is internalizing the wilderness, that is, reconstellating the spatial frontier into the ethos of the Anglo-Protestant American "core culture" in its advanced, democratic/capitalist allotrope, in which the "enemy" is identified as the laboring multitude, and, beyond that, the unimproved or, in the more current language of policy makers, underdeveloped, world at large. This transformation becomes clear when it is remembered that earlier in his oration, and in preparation for this duplicitous conclusion, Webster had said, in a way that echoes the Puritan calling—and Althusser's analysis of the *interpellated* subject[18]—and its work ethic:

A chief distinction of the present day is a community of opinions and knowledge among men in different nations, existing in a degree heretofore unknown. . . . Mind is the great lever of all things; human thought is the process by which human ends are ultimately answered; and the diffusion of knowledge, so astonishing in the last half-century, has rendered innumerable minds, variously gifted by nature, competent to be competitors or fellow-workers in the theatre of intellectual operation.

From these causes important improvements have taken place in the personal condition of individuals. Generally speaking, mankind are not only better fed and better clothed, but they are able also to enjoy more leisure; they possess more refinement and more self-respect. A superior tone of education, manners, and habits prevail. This remark, most true in its application to our own country, is also part true when applied elsewhere. It is proved by the vastly augmented consumption of those articles of manufacture and of commerce which contribute to the comforts and decencies of life; an augmentation which has far outrun the progress of population. And while the unexampled and almost incredible use of machinery would seem to supply the place of labor, labor still finds its occupation and its reward; so wisely has Providence adjusted men's wants and desires to their condition and their capacity. (*WS*, 248)[19]

"Our proper business is improvement. Let our age be the age of improvement." This is the moment in exceptionalist America's "destined" history when the Leatherstocking figure, under the aegis of "Jacksonianism," begins to metamorphose into the rugged and virile land speculator and, eventually, captain of industry. It is also the moment when the always rejuvenating frontier begins to transform itself into the problem of the gross national product, and the enemy into those "preterites," internal and global, who refuse in one way or another to be answerable to the democratic/capitalist calling.

VI   Frederick Jackson Turner

One could go on indefinitely citing important American cultural documents, such as the above, of nineteenth-century Westward expansionism and democratic capitalist development that, however rarified, take the form of the American jeremiad and are informed not simply by the optimistic American exceptionalist ethos, but an exceptionalist ethos that derives its always enabling domestic and global power from the belonging-ness together of the opposition between the New (frontier) World and the Old (frontierless) World. I will, however, restrict myself to one last example from the end of the century of this tacit national appeal to the violence endemic to the frontier in the name of renewing America's "benign" errand, that is, of escaping the laws of civilization that spelled the doomed fate of the Old World empires: that of the American historian Frederic Jackson Turner, the founder and still influential exponent of the theory that the frontier was the determining factor in the shaping of American history and the American national identity. In the "Preface" to the essays collected under the general title the *Frontier in American History* (1920), an encomium to the resiliency of the American frontier spirit he documents in his texts, Turner writes:

> The future alone can disclose how far these interpretations are correct for the age of colonization which came gradually to an end with the disappearance of the frontier and free land. It alone can reveal how much of the courageous, creative American spirit, and how large a part of the historic American ideals are to be carried over into the new age which has replaced the era of free lands and of measurable isolation by consolidated and complex industrial development and by increasing resemblances and connection between the New World and the Old.[20]

As in the case of predecessors such as the Puritan Jeremiahs, Cooper, Parkman, and Webster—and his imperialist contemporary Theodore Roosevelt—Turner frames these essays on the enabling operations of the frontier he had written in the previous twenty or thirty years (the first and most influential of these, "The Significance of the Frontier in American History," was given before the American Historical Association in Chicago, July 12, 1893) in the context not simply of the American errand in the western wilderness, but of the doomed frontier and the anxiety its inevitable passing precipitates. Specifically, this means the arrival of a "new age which has replaced the era of free lands and of measurable isolation," which is to say, the conditions of *movement* that fosters self-reliance, American style (decentralized) democracy, and communal renewal, "by [echoing Webster]consolidated and complex industrial development," that is, the *settlement* of the continent and the emergence to dominance of capitalism, the overdetermination of refinement as the measure of the good life, and the transformation of a dispersed and mobile frontier into a concentrated sedentary urban world that is coming increasingly and ominously to resemble the Old World.

Turner reiterates this belated jeremiadic theme throughout his essays. Indeed, it, and the anxiety that prompts its articulation, is enacted in the very structure of the book insofar as the various essays are organized to emphasize the paradoxical *advancing/waning* frontier, which, significantly, has its origin in the Anglo-Protestant Massachusetts Bay Colony, "the first official frontier," but moves inexorably to "new Wests"— the "Old West" ("the back country of New England, the Mohawk Valley, the Great Valley of Pennsylvania, the Shenandoah Valley, and the Piedmont"), the "Middle West," "the Ohio Valley," "the Mississippi Valley," and finally the "Far West"—as *settlement* comes to predominate each phase. But as in the case of the jeremiads of his predecessors, the anxiety that informs Turner's histories is also ideologically strategic, a productive agent of a philosophy of confidence. It is not by any means simply a manifestation of despair at the demise of the frontier. It is, as, according to Bercovitch, it was for the Puritan, John Danforth, over two hundred years before, also, and primarily, a reminder to his belated fin de siècle American readers of the essential resiliency at the heart of the exceptionalist American character that was formed by the frontier experience. Following his introduction of the theme of the ominous passing of the frontier in the preface, Turner adds:

> But the larger part of what has been distinctive and valuable in America's contribution to the history of the human spirit has been due to this nation's peculiar experience in extending its type of frontier into new regions; and in creating peaceful societies with new ideals in the successive vast and differing geographic provinces which together make up the United States. Directly or indirectly these experiences shaped the life of the Eastern as well as the Western States, and even reacted upon the Old World and influenced the direction of its thought and its progress. This experience has been fundamental in the economic, political and social characteristics of the American people and in their conceptions of their destiny. (*FAH*, preface)

Since America's "contribution to the history of the human spirit has been due to the nation's peculiar experience in extending its type of frontier into new regions," there is nothing intrinsic in the closing of the natural frontier that would warrant the demise of the optimistic American exceptionalist view of the world. The extended American experience of the literal moving frontier, Turner implies, has become over time a metaphor. Its character of "incessant expansion," that is, its imperialist élan, has been internalized as an attribute of "the American peoples' [democratic] destiny" and, therefore, has becomes applicable to any circumstance and time. Conscious of the "closed frontier," Turner concludes "The Significance of the Frontier in American History" by recapitulating the jeremiad prophetically:

> Since the days when the fleet of Columbus sailed into the waters of the New World, America has been another name for opportunity, and the people of the United States have taken their tone from the incessant expansion which has not only been open but has even been forced upon them. *He would be a rash prophet who would assert that the expansive character of American life has now entirely ceased.* Movement has been its dominant fact, and, unless this training has no effect upon a people, the American energy will continually demand a wider field for its exercise. But never again will such gifts of free land offer themselves. For a moment, at the frontier, the bonds of custom are broken and unrestraint is triumphant. There is not *tabula rasa*. The stubborn American environment is there with its imperious summons to accept its conditions; the inherited ways of doing things are also there; and yet, in spite of environment, and in spite of custom, each frontier did indeed furnish a new field of opportunity, a gate of escape from the bondage of the past; and freshness, and a confidence, and scorn of older society, impatience of its restraints and its ideas, and indifference to its lessons, have accompanied the frontier. What the Mediterranean Sea was to the Greeks, breaking the bond of custom, and offering new experiences, calling out new institutions and activities, that, and more, the ever retreating frontier has been to the United States directly, and to the nations of Europe more remotely. And now, four centuries from the discovery of America, at the end of a hundred years of life under the Constitution, the frontier is gone, and with its going has closed *the first period* of American history. (*FAH*, 37–39; my emphasis)

On the surface, this conclusion would seem to manifest Turner's pessimism concerning the future of America in the wake of the closing of the geographical frontier. Read in the light of the American jeremiad, however, the "pessimism" or, more accurately, the anxiety at the apparent demise of the literal frontier comes to be seen as an intensely nationalist ideological strategy that emphasizes the threat this demise poses to the dynamics of expansion and renewal in order to underscore the crucial significance of the frontier spirit to the American national identity and to mobilize the American people, in the wake of the closing of "the first period of American history," into a dynamic consensus committed to the inauguration, of a *second period* in which the frontier, and the self-renewing (democratic) expansion it enables, exists beyond the geographic borders of exceptionalist America, that is, also becomes a perpetual state of American mind.[21]

VII

It is no accident that Turner's tacit jeremiadic call at the end of the century for the extension of the American frontier beyond the Western boundary of the United States was (under the aegis of Theodore Roosevelt) enacted first by President McKinley, who extended the American errand into the "wilderness" of the Philippines, and, a half-century later, in the wake of World War II and the inauguration of the Cold War, by John F. Kennedy, into the "wilderness" of Vietnam, which, as we have seen, the American soldiers called "Indian country," a phrase they accommodated to the stereotypical narrative of the Hollywood western, the current American version of what Edward Said called "the textual attitude" that determines reality. At the time of the presidential election of 1960, the political and cultural exponents of the dominant culture were afflicted by a deep and widespread anxiety over the health of the American body politic, claiming that the American government's policies were becoming rigidified and the American people, "soft" as the threat of international communism began to rise. This anxiety, as we have seen in chapter 3, was epitomized by William Lederer and Eugene Burdick's novel *The Ugly American* (1959), which, as the title suggests, was, in part, intended as a counternarrative to that of Graham Greene. Like the American jeremiad, the purpose of their extraordinarily influential, if very bad, novel, whose mise-en-scène is an imaginary country, Sarkhan in Southeast Asia at the outset of the Cold War, was to remind America's effete leaders and its recidivist people of the enabling distinction between the Old World and the New—a reminder that, in the form of the difference between a decadent colonialist France and a vital and benign democratic United States, came to pervade the discourse of the latter in the early stages of its intervention in Vietnam[22]— and to recall them to the ideal of simple, vigorous, manly self-reliance that motivated the frontiersmen of America's glorious past.In a conscious response to this national anxiety, President Kennedy identified his campaign and later his administration as "the New Frontier," now, as in the case of Turner, envisioned as global, though the immediate errand was located in the wilderness of Southeast Asia, and he introduced domestic and foreign policies intended to capitalize on the persuasive power of the American exceptionalist myth of the frontier. As John Hellman puts the Kennedy administration's relocation and extension of the regenerative frontier (and its imperative of violence) in *American Myth and the Legacy of Vietnam*:

> The New Frontier proclaimed that the western frontier, officially closed in 1890 by the Superintendent of the Census to mark for Turner the ominous end of the first era of American history, could remain in its metaphorical dimensions an open landscape of challenge and possibility. In this symbolic frontier America could regenerate its traditional virtues while serving future progress. Here the individual American could flee the city yet spread the dominion of that city, take forth progress yet bring back natural virtue, and thus resolve in a middle landscape the conflict between contemporary American society and traditional American character and a purpose in the same way it had been resolved in American mythic experience since Cooper's Leatherstocking Tales. The Peace Corps, the Alliance for Progress, the domestic emphasis on physical fitness, the "get-the-country-moving-again" economic policies, the support for black civil rights, the space program, the "can-do" cabinet team—every aspect of the New Frontier evoked the ideal found in *The Ugly American*, the ideal central to the American mythic heritage: that America could preserve the rewards of grace only by a disregard for them in pursuit of its errand.[23]

There is, however, as I have shown, a crucial difference between this epochal contemporary occasion and the earlier history I have all too briefly invoked in this chapter. Whereas the benignity of the representation of the exceptionalist errand was rarely questioned in the past, no doubt because the logic of exceptionalism was in process (unfulfilled)—Turner's virtually absolute effacement at the end of the century of the history of the extermination of the native Americans in favor of his euphoric representation of "the frontier in American history" as the agent of the rise of (capitalist) democracy and the greatness of the American national identity is symptomatic—the errand in the Vietnam wilderness inadvertently produced a counterhistory. In the face of a determined resistance by the Vietnamese people, who succeeded at the site of the dissemination of information in demonstrating to the world that America's representation of its errand as "defense" was in fact aggression, and, as we have seen in chapters 4 and 5, a "postmodern" strategy of warfare that refused to be answerable to the exceptionalist narrative,

America, with the confidence of the righteousness of its divinely or History-ordained global errand, pursued the inexorable logical economy of its exceptionalism to its self-destructive fulfillment. In response to the invisibility of the enemy, it unleashed, as we have also seen, a ground and air war of attrition that indiscriminately killed and maimed an untold number of Vietnamese civilians, "cleared" their land with a vengeance, and transformed a rice culture into a society of urban refugees, all in the name of "saving it for the free world." In other words, this response not only exposed the relentless imperial will to power informing America's intervention in Vietnam; in undertaking this intervention in almost precisely the terms of the perennial exceptionalist discourse and practice of the frontier—like Parkman, as I have noted, the American military command and the soldiers invariably referred to the combat areas as "Indian country"—it also bore witness, as many of the "New Americanists' counterhistories reveal, to the historical continuity of the murderous violence informing the logic of America's benign exceptionalist mission from the Puritan errand in the New England wilderness to the American errand in the wilderness of Vietnam.

Indeed, in manifesting itself in an aggressive violence bordering on genocide, America's inexorable pursuit of the logic of exceptionalism to its virtual "end" in Vietnam bore resonant witness for the present, post-9/11 generation to the inevitable consequence of what Herman Melville, one of the few early writers of the so-called American Renaissance who, as I have argued, challenged the myth of the errand and the frontier to reveal its dark underbelly, called "the metaphysics of Indian-hating" in the process of thinking the logic of a particular—"diluted"—Indian-hater, "Colonel John Moredock, of Illinois," to its horrific end:

> The Indian-hater *par excellence* the judge [James Hall] defined to be one who, having with his mother's milk drank in small love for red men, in youth or early manhood, ere the sensibilities become osseous, received at their hand some signal outrage, or, which in effect is much the same, some of his kin have, or some friend. Now, nature all around him by her solitudes wooing or bidding him muse upon this matter, he accordingly does so, till the thought develops such attraction, that much as straggling vapors troop from all sides to a storm-cloud, so straggling thoughts of other outrages troop to the nucleus thought, assimilate with it, and swell it. At last, taking counsel with the elements, he comes to his resolution. An intenser Hannibal, he makes a vow, the hate of which is a vortex from whose suction scarce the remotest chip of the guilty race may reasonably feel secure. Next, he declares him-

self and settles his temporal affairs. With the solemnity of a Spaniard turned monk, he takes leave of his kin; or rather, these leave-takings have something of the still more impressive finality of death-bed adieus. Last, he commits himself to the forest primeval; there, so long as life shall be his, to act upon a calm, cloistered scheme of strategical, implacable, and lonesome vengeance. Ever on the noiseless trail; cool, collected, patient; less seen than felt; snuffing, smelling—a Leather-stocking Nemesis. In the settlements he will not be seen again; in eyes of old companions tears may start at some chance thing that speaks of him; but they never look for him, not call; they know he will not come. Suns and seasons fleet; the tiger-lily blows and falls; babes are born and leap in their mother's arms; but, the Indian-hater is good as gone to his long home, and "Terror" is his epitaph.[24]

What is remarkable about Melville's restrospective and proleptic coun-terhistorical metaphysical account of the metaphysics of Indian-hating is that the Indian is, as in Turner's end-of-the-frontier discourse, a polyva-lent metaphor for the enemy, whatever its specificity, who always lurks threateningly in the wilderness on the other side of the American "fron-tier." "For you must know," the narrator of the story tells his ironic lis-tener, "that Indian-hating was no monopoly of Colonel Moredock's, but a passion, in one form or other, and to a degree, greater or less, largely shared among the class to which he belonged [the frontier settlers]. *And Indian-hating still exists; and, no doubt will continue to exist, so long as Indians do*" (C-M, 142; my emphasis). What to Frederick Jackson Turner was a noble manifestation of the imaginative and practical resiliency of the self-reliant and enduring American national character, was for Melville, as it would become for his postmodern American heirs, not least Thomas Pynchon, another ignoble manifestation of an apparently incur-able national paranoia. When, Melville seems to be saying, America has finally exterminated this specific "Indian," its exceptionalist national logic will compel it to invent another to take his place.

VIII

In sum, America's brutal conduct of the Vietnam War precipitated the hypothetical self-destruction of the myth of American exceptionalism—and the metaphysics that is its source and justification—a self-destruction sym-bolically epitomized in the closing days of the war by the humiliating global spectacle of the American diplomatic core, in utter disarray, scrambling to be lifted to safety by helicopters off the roof of the American Embassy in Saigon as their South Vietnamese clients clamored for protection beyond the iron gates. And this symptomatic self-destruction was theorized in some degree by a new generation of Americanist scholars, who exposed the violence inhering in the logic of the exceptionalist errand in their scholarship. But a concatenation of historical events and (especially) the American government's and the culture industry's willful ideological representation of them have, as we have seen in the previous chapters, dimmed down, if they have not entirely erased this epochal disclosure. I am referring (1) to the systematic effort of the intellectual deputies of the dominant culture and the media to "forget Vietnam" inaugurated during the Reagan administration in 1982, at the time of the dedication of the Vietnam Veterans War Memorial, a recuperative process culminating in the representation of the healthy disillusionment of the American people by the sordid disclosures about their county's prevarications and its conduct of the war as a national neurosis, "the Vietnam syndrome"; (2) the implosion of the Soviet Union; and, fortified by these, (3) the United States' invasion of Iraq and its "surgical" defeat of Saddam Hussein's army in the first Gulf War, which the first President Bush represented as the event that enabled Americans to "kick the Vietnam syndrome at last." The consequences of this studied amnesiac reaction to the dispersion of the American national identity in the late 1960s and early 1970s were revolutionary. One was the decisive emergence at the end of the century of a nationalist neoconservative elite to political prominence, a culmination epitomized by a sequence of "triumphalist" representations of America's exceptionalist global mission (Fukuyama, Haass, and others) epitomized by the white paper entitled "Rebuilding America's Defenses," produced in September 2002 by neoconservative members of the Project for the New American Century (founded in 1997), that anticipated the later decision of the George W. Bush administration (many of whose members belonged to PNAC) to overthrow Saddam Hussein in the name of the *Pax Americana*, a "unipolar world" under the aegis of the United States. (The original membership of PNAC included William J. Bennett, Jeb Bush, Eliot Cohen, Dick Cheney, Francis Fukuyama, Donald Kagan, William Kristol, Norman Podhoretz, Donald Rumsfeld, Paul Wolfowitz, and John Bolton, many of whom became prominent members of the Bush administration.)[25] Another, equally important result of this amnesia was the precipitation of a virulently politically reactionary chauvinist strain of Evangelical Christianity remarkably reminiscent, in its racist and ethnic prejudices, of the theocratic perspective, that, despite the Constitutional separation of church and state and the rhetoric that obscures its fragility, has *always* been in some significant degree a powerful political force in America since the New England Puritans. A third was the election in 2000 of George W. Bush Jr., whose domestic and foreign policies have combined the neoconservatives' ("defensive") global imperialism with the religious right's Christian American exceptionalism.

In keeping with the paradoxical logic of the frontier myth, however, this post-Vietnam recuperation of American confidence in its global errand precipitated a new national anxiety in American officialdom: an anxiety, in the face of the demise of the "threat" of international communism with the annunciation of the *Pax Americana*, of no longer having a frontier/enemy to instigate the anxiety that, as we have seen, has been the sine qua non of the rejuvenating exceptionalist errand. Furthermore, this new anxiety over the threat of peace—i.e. the enervating indifference of the American body politic to the well-being of the nation-state it would foster—that, according to the American exceptionalist myth, ensues from the demise of the frontier, was exacerbated by the demographic transformation that had occurred in the United States since the decade of the Vietnam War and the civil rights movement. I mean the massive influx of immigrants, especially from Latin America, Mexico, and Asia, who, coupled with black Americans, are, unlike previous generations, resisting the seductions of assimilation to the Anglo-Protestant core culture.

This emergent double anxiety—over the demise of an anxiety-producing frontier or wilderness or enemy in the wake of peace, on the one hand, and over the disintegration of the national identity, on the other—was allayed by Al Qaeda's attacks on the two buildings of the World Trade Center and the Pentagon on September 11, 2001, which provided the dominant neoconservative elect with a new, unifying and rejuvenating frontier, now, however, no longer envisioned as a particular or local geopolitical space but as global in scope, as a polyvalent metaphor: "the war [without end] on terror." Since then, however, specifically, in the wake of the stalling of the preemptive American "missionary" initiative in Iraq and the disclosure of the Bush administration's flagrant deceptions concerning its justification for the invasion of Iraq, which has precipitated doubts in the American public's mind about "staying the course," this highly energized patriotic consensus has begun to wane. Responding to this "crisis," Samuel P. Huntington, one of the most influential intellectual deputies of the dominant neoconservative culture, published in 2004 a book appropriately entitled *Who Are We?: The Challenges to America's National Identity*, which, taking its point of departure in the events of 9/11, the United States' announcement of its "war on terror," and its preemptive armed interventions in the Middle East, lays out a systematic scenario for the accomplishment of America's errand, now in the global wilderness.

As the title and its historical context suggests, Huntington's *Who Are We?* modifies Francis Fukuyama's "triumphalist" thesis and gives greater "historical depth" than Richard Haass does in his version of America's role in the post-Cold War era by focusing its "argument" around two perennial ideological constants: (1) the concern for maintaining the integrity of the exceptionalist American national identity in the face of the internal historical forces that challenge its unity; and (2) the deeply backgrounded assumption that the maintenance of this vigorous national consensus is dependent on the equivalent of a frontier, that is, an enemy. These are not new in Huntington's policy writing. In 1975, he, with Michael Crozier and Joji Watanuki, published a study for the Trilateral Commission on the "crisis of democracy" precipitated by the civil rights and antiwar movement in the 1960s.[26] Anticipating the coming national amnesia, this "study," in effect, claimed that the extension of democracy in that decade had, in attending to the demands of women, blacks, and ethnic minorities, produced a volatile situation that now threatened "democracy," which is to say, the traditional unity of the nation and the national identity, thus jeopardizing America's global Cold War errand in the face of the threat of Soviet communism, and advised the American government to stem this disintegrative momentum by reaffirming the priority of the principle of a higher (national) authority. As Michael Hardt and Antonio Negri put this recuperative project,

> Huntington's diagnosis was that "democracy" in the United States has since the 1960s been put in danger by too much participation and too many demands from organized labor and newly activated social groups, such as women and Africans Americans. Too much democracy, he claimed paradoxically, had made U.S. democracy sick, resulting in a "democratic distemper". . . . In fact, Huntington's text is a resolutely antirepublican and antidemocratic gospel that preaches the defense of sovereignty against threats of all social forces and social movements. What Huntington fears most, of course, and this is the central thrust of his argument, is democracy in its proper sense, that is, as the rule of all by all. Democracy, he claimed must be tempered with authority, and various segments of the population must be kept from participating too actively in political life or demanding too much from the state. Huntington's gospel did, in fact serve as a guide in the subsequent years for the neoliberal destruction of the welfare state.[27]

A couple of decades later, in 1993, Huntington published the inordinately influential essay (fleshed out into a book in 1996), "The Clash of Civilizations," in *Foreign Affairs*, in which the anxiety he expresses over the threat of the disintegration of the American national identity in *The Crisis of Democracy* is tethered to the threat of the demise of the frontier, now, as we have seen, understood as a polyvalent metaphor. In typical American exceptionalist fashion, though unlike Fukuyama, he responds to the implosion of the Soviet Union by representing it to his clientele of government officials as the ominous demise of the perpetual enemy that has been historically the essential agent in the maintenance of consensus in America's violent pursuit of its errand and in the instigation of the cultural energy that has rendered America perennially a New World, and, then, in order to manage this new crisis, replaces the utterly reified Manichaean world of the Cold War by the equally Manichaean world envisaged by Orientalists such as Bernard Lewis, that represents its recalcitrant variety and complexity as a "clash of civilizations," specifically Western democratic/capitalist/Judeo-Christian against, primarily, an increasingly militant Islam. I will return to the virtually explicit reductiveness of Huntington's "scholarship" at the end of this chapter in order to call his history by its right name. It will suffice here to invoke Edward Said's decisive criticism of Huntington's "scholarly" method:

> Perhaps because he is more interested in policy prescription than in either history or the careful analysis of cultural formations, Huntington . . . is quite misleading in what he says and how he puts things. A great deal of his argument depends on second-and third-hand opinion that scants the enormous advances in our concrete and theoretical understanding of how cultures work, how they change, and how they can best be grasped or apprehended. A brief look at the people and opinions he quotes suggests that journalism and popular demagoguery rather than scholarship or theory are his main sources. For when you draw on tendentious publicists, scholars, and journalists like Charles Krauthammer, Sergie Stankevich, and Bernard Lewis you already prejudice the argument in favor of conflict and polemic rather than true understanding and the kind of cooperation between peoples that our planet needs. Huntington's authorities are not the cultures themselves but a small handful of authorities picked by him because they emphasize the latent bellicosity in one or another statement by one or another so-called spokesman for or about that culture. The giveaway for me is the title of his essay— "The Clash of Civilizations"—which is not his phrase but Bernard Lewis's.[28]

These earlier texts, so informed by the "textual attitude," by this influential deputy of the dominant neoconservative culture in the United States are, however, prolegomenal: though they are far from tentative, they address America's global role both before and in the wake of the demise of the Soviet Union according to the imperatives of the ideological policy abstractions of the Cold War era. On the other hand, *Who Are We?*, written in the aftermath of the attacks by Al Qaeda on 9/11 (which rendered American soil "ground zero" and reignited a patriotic concern for the nation, i.e., "homeland security"), the second, preemptive, invasion of Iraq, and the emergence of an insurgency that has increasingly taken on the disturbing character of another "quagmire," is Huntington's *Summum*. As its ideological form and historical content makes amply clear, this recent text, which, like his others, is primarily (strategically) addressed to and constitutes an ideological blueprint for the now ruling neoconservative/Evangelical Christian coalition, was not only intended to capitalize on the attacks in New York and Washington in behalf of justifying the Bush administration's invasion of Afghanistan and Iraq or, more broadly, its "war on terror," and the tacit normalization of the state of exception. It was also, and primarily, intended to endow "historical" weight to these policies by typically representing American aggression as acts of defense and then, more important, contextualizing this "crisis" of the "America's national identity" into the "history" that, according to him, produced it. Huntington's primary purpose, that is, was to justify and to proselytize in behalf of America's renewed and aggrandized exceptionalist global mission by way of recalling a glorious "history" that would show this latest example of American exceptionalist thought and practice to be, not a departure from, but the necessary fulfillment of the essential logic of the original Anglo-Protestant errand in the New World wilderness—which is to say, of America's benign global destiny as exceptionalist "redeemer" nation. In other words, Huntington's "history," as I will show, turns out to be a certain corrupted version of the American jeremiad, the unexceptional (imperial Old World) exceptionalist myth of divine election inaugurated by the Puritans and, *despite the constitutional separation of church and state, maintained in some significant degree after the American Revolution throughout the history of the westward and democratizing (rejuvenating) movement of the American frontier.*

Huntington's revealing overdetermination of the *crisis* of the American cultural or civilizational identity in the process of answering the framing question "Who Are We?" is signaled from the beginning by his dimming down of Fukuyama's euphoric Hegelian/Kojèvian representation of the end of the Cold War as the end of history and the advent of the New World Order under the aegis of American capitalist democracy. He does this in order to highlight, not the triumph of America, but the national anxiety precipitated by the *loss* of the necessary enemy (the frontier) on which, as we have seen, the dominant culture in America has relied throughout its history to sustain and to reinvigorate it's (version of) the American national identity and its exceptionalist errand. Unlike Fukuyama, Huntington rightly—and tellingly, in its subordination of democracy to religion—attributes the perennial strength and staying power of America, not so much to its democratic/capitalist "creed" as to the unity of its cultural or "civilizational" identity, a national identity (the incredibly reductive, prejudiced, and elitist "We" in his title). This presiding civilizational identity or "core culture" as Huntington euphemistically puts it, is the original "Anglo-Protestant culture" that "founded" America:

> The "American creed," as initially formulated by Thomas Jefferson and elaborated by many others, is widely viewed as the crucial defining element of American identity. The Creed, however, was the product of the distinct Anglo-Protestant culture of the founding settlers of America in the seventeenth and eighteenth centuries. Key elements of that culture include: the English language; Christianity; religious commitment; English concepts of the rule of law; the responsibility of rulers, and the rights of individuals; and dissenting Protestant values of individualism, the work ethic; and the belief that humans have the ability and the duty to try to create a heaven on earth, a "city on a hill." Historically, millions of immigrants were attracted to America because of this culture and the economic opportunities it helped to make possible. (*WAW*, xvi)

But this traditional Anglo-Protestant "core culture," according to Huntington, was thrown into crisis with the rise of what he contemptuously calls "subnational cultures" in the turbulent 1960s, cultures, in other words, that, encouraged by the "deconstructionist movement," ungratefully refused, unlike those of earlier "settlers" of America, to be assimilated to its "benign" Americanizing imperatives. It was this crisis of the Anglo-Protestant core culture (the American national identity)—and the means of resolving it—that the attacks by Al Qaeda and the resurgent patriotism they instigated retrospectively revealed. And it was to recuperate its dominant place and authority that Huntington undertook to "recall" the history of the development of the American national identity in the form and the content of his book. In so doing, he revealed more clearly than his neoconservative colleagues the specifics of the ideology that informs the Bush administration's unilateral global war on terror.

It is no accident, then, that the structure of Huntington's *Who Are We?* is, as the anxiety registered in the question suggests, modeled on the American jeremiad, or, rather, on a version of it that, in pursuing its difference-reducing logic to its systematic fulfillment, discloses the contradictions it cannot finally contain—the justified claims of America's Others (domestic and foreign)—and thus inadvertently self-destructs. Indeed,

Huntington, as we shall see momentarily, cites Sacvan Bercovitch's analysis of the American jeremiad in behalf of his ideological project at the precise moment he begins his "history" of the origins and development of the American national identity, though typically he fails to indicate that his source is fundamentally critical of the uses to which the jeremiad has been put in American history. Like the American jeremiad, Huntington's contemporary discourse seems to (strategically) assume the ontological validity of the Anglo-Protestant core culture (its "election"). And from this transcendental—and *essentially* optimistic—vantage point, it, like its predecessors, goes on to point dramatically to the eroding of the exceptionalist "national" errand and the vigor with which it was traditionally executed, and thus to the ominous signs of its disintegration and the loss of its covenantal authority: the emergence of recalcitrant and foreign constituencies within the American body politic that threaten to dilute, enervate, and disperse the Anglo-Protestant core culture. Thus, like the traditional jeremiad, as we have seen, Huntington attempts to reinstigate the unifying and invigorating communal anxiety that kept the covenant and the errand intact in the glorious American past by representing the contemporary, post-9/11 occasion in terms of the original conditions of the frontier: as a clash of civilizations, in which "militant Islam" has become, as Melville anticipated in his parody of the "metaphysics of Indian-hating," American Anglo-Protestant civilization's latest Indian.

Thus, after affirming the crisis of the exceptionalist American national identity as the fundamental condition of contemporary America, Huntington begins his "history" by recalling the inaugural and determinative importance of the Puritans' settlement of the Massachusetts Bay Colony, in the process of which he pointedly overdetermines its religious over its creedal significance. It is, significantly, a summary recollection that reiterates item by item the official representation and historical consequences of their figural interpretation of history (the belief that they were elected or "called" by God to fulfill the prefigurative history of the Old Testament Israelites in the New World): their divinely ordained exceptionalist "errand in the [American] wilderness":

> The settling of America was, of course, a result of economic and other motives, as well as religious ones. Yet religion still was central. . . . Religious intensity was undoubtedly greatest among the Puritans, especially in Massachusetts. They took the lead in defining their settlement based on "a Covenant with God" to create "a city on a hill" as a model for all the world, and people of the Protestant faiths soon also came to see themselves and America in a similar way. In the seventeenth and eighteenth

centuries, Americans defined their mission in the New World in biblical terms. They were a "chosen people," on an "errand in the wilderness," creating "the new Israel" or the "new Jerusalem" in what was clearly "the promised land." America was the site of a "new Heaven and a new earth, the home of justice," God's country. The settlement of America was vested, as Sacvan Bercovitch put it, "with all the emotional, spiritual, and intellectual appeal of a religious quest." This sense of holy mission was easily expanded into millenarian themes of America as "the redeemer nation" and "the visionary republic." (*WAW*, 64)

It is this original Anglo-Protestant "settler" culture, according to Huntington, not the later "immigrant cultures," that constitutes the origin, essence, and abiding character of the American national identity: "[Americans'] ancestors," he writes "were not immigrants but settlers, and in its origins America was not a nation of immigrants, it was a society, or societies, of settlers who came to the New World in the seventeenth and eighteenth centuries. Its origins as an Anglo-Protestant settler society have, more than anything else, profoundly and lastingly shaped American culture, institutions, historical development, and identity." To attribute the origins of the American national identity as some (liberal) historians have done to immigrants is to feed precisely those recent malignantly decadent forces in America that threaten to disintegrate the American national identity. Despite its rhetoric of objectivity, Huntington's discourse—the ideologically loaded positive resonance of the term "settler" is exemplary—is, in fact, pursuing the logic of the jeremiad (his encomium to the threatened origins of the covenant), and in the process, it manifests his strong—and offensive—prejudice against the latecomer and parasitical immigrant (not to say, his stereotypical indifference to its brutal colonialist implications):

Settlers and immigrants differ fundamentally. Settlers leave an existing society, usually in a group, in order to create a new community, a city on the hill, in a new and often distant territory. They are imbued with a sense of collective purpose. Implicitly or explicitly they subscribe to a compact or charter that defines the basis of the community they create and their collective relations to their mother country. Immigrants, in contrast, do not create a new society. They move from one society to a different society. Migration is usually a personal process, involving individuals and families. The seventeenth- and eighteenth-century settlers came to America because it was a *tabula rasa*. Apart from Indian

tribes, which could be killed off or pushed westward [the relegation of this genocidal history to subordinate clausal status epitomizes what can only be called the banality of the author's moral
sense] no society was there; and they came in order to create societies that embodied and would reinforce the culture and values
they brought with them from their origin country. Immigrants
came later because they wanted to become part of the society the
settlers had created. Unlike settlers, they experienced 'culture
shock' as they and their offspring attempted to absorb a culture
often much at odds with that which they brought with them. Before immigrants could come to America, settlers had to found
America. (*WAW*, 40)

After establishing this divinely ordained missionary errand as the
source and abiding center of the Anglo-Protestant core culture of America, Huntington, following the structural imperatives of the jeremiad—
and of the nationalistic purposes to which he is putting it in the post-9/11
occasion—then goes on to (selectively) recall and monumentalize the various crises this dominant Anglo-Protestant core culture has undergone
and, by way of its resiliency, survived in American history. That it is the
passing of the original and immediate threatening experience, the difficult
circumstances that enabled the individual members of the original community to identify themselves as an integral, coherent, and vital whole,
that is at stake is suggested by his subsequent invocation of the various
"Great Awakenings" that have historically revitalized and sustained the
Anglo-Protestant core culture and its missionary errand. In this jeremiadic memorialization, Huntington ostensibly identifies these Great Awakenings or "revivals" with evangelical moralism and its alleged correlate,
the political "reform ethic" of Anglo-Protestantism:

Historians identify four Great Awakenings in the history of American Protestantism, each of which was associated with and immediately followed by major efforts at political reform. Many
political, economic, and ideational factors came together to create
the American Revolution. Among the latter were Lockeian liberalism, Enlightenment rationalism, and Whig republicanism. Also of
central importance were the Revolution's religious sources, most
notably the Great Awakening of the1730s and 1740s. Led by
George Whitefield and other revivalist preachers and provided
with doctrine and justification by Jonathan Edwards, the Awakening swept across the colonies mobilizing thousands of Americans to commit themselves to a new birth in Christ. This religious

upheaval laid the basis for the political upheaval that immediately followed. . . . 'The evangelical impulse,' as Harvard scholar Alan Heimat said, 'was the avatar and instrument of a fervent American nationalism.'" (*WAW*, 76)

Huntington also overdetermines this identification of evangelical Protestant moralism with political reform in his analyses of the other three Great Awakenings: those of the 1820–1830s, which culminated in the abolitionist movement; of the 1890s, which was linked with the populist and Progressive drives that "attacked the concentrated power of corporate monopolies and by city machines and, in varying degrees, advocated antitrust measures, women's suffrage, and the initiative, referendum, and recall, prohibition, regulation of railroads, the direct primary"; and of the 1950s and 1960s, which challenged "the legal and institutional discrimination against and segregation of America's black minority" and, later, "the abuse of the institutions of established authority in the 1960s and 1970s," focused "on the conduct of the Vietnam War and the abuse of power in the Nixon administration" (*WAW*, 77–79).

But this emphasis on the "reformist" momentum of the national revivalist Great Awakenings Huntington invokes should not deflect attention, as it is intended to do, from their traditional jeremiadic function: the recuperation and rejuvenation of the national covenant (consensus). In attributing evangelical Protestant moralism as a primary source of the American Revolution, Huntington is *accommodating* the revolution—the multiple motives of the various revolutionaries—to the (imperial) ontology and politics of the Anglo-Protestant core culture. Similarly, in attributing the various political reform initiatives he enumerates—women's suffrage, black civil rights, the protestation of the Vietnam War, and the criticism of the abuse of power in the Nixon administration, for example—to this Anglo-Protestant core culture, he is by a sleight of hand willfully marginalizing the struggle of oppressed or radically disillusioned constituencies to gain their rights from or to challenge the perennial restricted cultural, racial, and political economy of the dominant culture in America. Huntington's identification of the various Protestant Great Awakenings with landmark "reform initiatives" in American history are intended both to claim benign openness to dissidence as a natural potential of the Anglo-Protestant "core culture" (as his inclusion of "dissent" as "a key element of [the Protestant] culture" testifies) and, to show, by way of always already accommodating this dissidence to its center, that crisis and the national anxiety it precipitates are a necessity for the rejuvenation of "America": a civilization threatened with erosion and disintegration by the temporal distancing from the original, mobilizing event, that is, by the waning of the enabling "frontier."

After establishing and memorializing Anglo-Protestantism as the core culture of the American national identity, Huntington, pursuing the logical imperatives of the jeremiad, goes on to identify the errant tendencies within American culture that currently, and in an unprecedented way, threaten its integrity and benign authority—and the safety of the American people in the face of the "rise" to global power of other "civilizations," namely, Chinese Confucianism and, above all, Islam. Rising in the turbulent 1960s and inadvertently abetted by the economic dynamics of a transnationalized capitalism, according to Huntington in a chapter tellingly entitled "Deconstructing America: The Rise of Subnational Identities," these ominous tendencies were embodied in the related denationalizing initiatives of what he contemptuously calls "subnational" cultures, most notably Hispanic and Asian, which, unlike their earlier immigrant counterparts, now increasingly refuse to accommodate (assimilate) themselves to the magnetic Anglo-Protestant core culture, and of the American "deconstructionist" intellectuals, who have appropriated the "destabilizing" thought of radical anti-Western European philosophers into this volatile American cultural context. Identifying himself (falsely), as his ideological forebears, the Puritans and the American Jeremiahs, invariably did, with a "heroic saving remnant"—the mythic bearers of the "Relic," or "Seed," or Word" of an eroding or disintegrating civilization[29]—Huntington demonizes these "deconstructionists" as subversives, who, by encouraging ethnic and racial groups to assert their subjectivities, threaten the traditional stabilizing authority of the Anglo-Protestant "core culture" and the "assimilative" process that previously molded immigrants into patriotic "Americans," a "multitude" in Negri and Hardt's terms, into a "people." Typical of the American Jeremiahs and their indifference to difference, Huntington (like Fukuyama) charges these "anti-American" deconstructionists (his use of the past tense should not be overlooked) with having undermined the vigorous confidence that has perennially distinguished America from the decaying Old World:

> The deconstructionists promoted programs to enhance the status and influence of subnational racial, ethnic, and cultural groups. They encouraged immigrants to maintain their birth country cultures, granted them legal privileges denied to native born Americans, and denounced the idea of Americanization. They pushed the rewriting of history syllabi and text book so as to refer to the "peoples" of the United States in place of the single people of the Constitution. They urged supplementing or substituting for national history the history of subnational groups. They down-

graded the centrality of English in American life and pushed bilingual education and linguistic diversity. They advocated legal recognition of group rights and racial preferences over the individual rights central to the American Creed. They justified their actions by theories of multiculturalism and the idea that diversity rather than unity or community should be America's overriding value. The combined effect of these efforts was to promote the deconstruction of the American identity that had been gradually created over three centuries and the ascendance of subnational identities. (WAW, 142)[30]

Indeed, at a certain point in Huntington's vulgar history of America, these subversive "deconstructionists" acquired governmental collaborators! Astonishingly indifferent to historical reality, to say nothing about what thinkers like Foucault and Said have to say about the duplicitous distinction he makes between colonialist violence and democratic nation-state benignity, Huntington's neoconservative policy preconceptions enables him to write:

Of central importance in this deconstruction coalition were governmental officials, particularly bureaucrats, judges, and educators. In the past, imperial and colonial governments provided resources to minority groups and encouraged people to identify with them, so as to enhance the government's ability to divide and rule. The governments of nation-states, in contrast, attempted to promote the unity of their people, the development of national consciousness, the suppression of subnational regional and ethnic loyalties, the universal use of the national language, and the allocation of benefits to those who conform to the national norm. Until the late twentieth century, American political and governmental leaders acted similarly. Then in the 1960s and 1970s, they began to promote measures consciously designed to weaken America's cultural and creedal identity and to strengthen racial, ethnic, cultural, and other subnational identities. These efforts by a nation's leaders to deconstruct the nation they governed were, quite possibly, without precedent in human history. (WAW, 143)

This grotesque representation of American history since the 1960s, not least the alleged complicity of deconstructive theory and national policy in "weakening America's cultural and creedal identity" in behalf of "strengthening" "subnational identities," is a telling measure of the antidemocratic politics of Huntington's version of American democracy—and of the success of the dominant neoconservative culture's amnesiac effort (aided by the attacks on American soil on 9/11) to rewrite (forget), once again, the actualities of the Vietnam decade.

It is at this point, after his instrumentalist discourse constructs a reality appropriate to the crisis-provoking purposes of his jeremiad, that Huntington brings into focus the matter of the "frontier," now, however, represented in the rhetoric adopted by the crisis-managing policy makers of his politically calculative generation to refer to this perennial condition: the new "fault line" between civilizations. Introduced at the beginning of the book, but held strategically in abeyance according to the dictates of the structure of the jeremiadic narrative, this motif reemerges climactically and decisively at the end of the chapter entitled "Deconstructing America." There, in a dramatically prophetic rhetoric, Huntington not only expresses his synecdochical "anxiety" over the "outcome of these battles ["over racial, bilingual, and multicultural challenges to the Creed, English, and America's core culture"] in the deconstructionist war." By way of invoking the threat to homeland security—the need for an enemy that he has inferred as a constant of America's exceptionalist history—he also points to the rejuvenating nationalist resolution of this anxiety-provoking dilemma that his book has strategically intended from the beginning to effect: "If external threats subside, deconstructionist movements could achieve renewed momentum. If America becomes continuously engaged with foreign enemies, their influence is likely to subside. If the external threats to America are modest, intermittent, and ambiguous, Americans may well remain divided over the appropriate roles of their Creed, language, and core culture in their national identity" (*WAW*, 177).

Unlike his neoconservative colleague, Francis Fukuyama, who greeted the demise of the Soviet Union euphorically, indeed, as biblically resonant "good news" (gospel),[31] Huntington, as we have seen, emphasizes its negative consequences for contemporary America: the loss of the decisive fault line—the anxiety-provoking enemy—that sustained America's unity and the vigor of its exceptionalist global missionary purpose from the end of World War II to the end of the Cold War in 1989. This difference, however, is not, as I have been suggesting, as contradictory a conclusion as it would seem to one who foresees a lasting peace as the end of conflict. On the contrary, in keeping with the always already renewing and reinvigorating function of the wilderness/frontier he has traced in the history of the development of the American national identity since the Puritan errand, Huntington's overdetermination of the "negative" consequences of the implosion of the Soviet Union is the necessary "positive" outcome of his

American exceptionalism. Following the paradoxical—one is tempted to call it paranoid—logic inhering in the belonging-togetherness of the New World and Old World intrinsic to the myth of American exceptionalism, Huntington assumes that civilizations decline as they advance, that is, necessarily lose their newness, erode, decay, become effeminate, and or incontinent with the fading of the fault lines that establish the conflictual logic of Us against them. Like that intrinsic to the discourse of the Puritan Jeremiahs, Cooper, Parkman, Webster, Turner, Burdick, and Lederer, and the many other American nationalists they represent, that is, Huntington's inexorable metalogic compels him to perceive the end of conflict as, in fact, a menace to the exceptionalism that has always distinguished "America" from the Old World, and thus the ontological necessity of a perpetual enemy to instigate collective anxiety over and identification with the national homeland. "At the end of the twentieth century," he writes,

> Democracy was left without a significant secular ideological rival, and the United States was left without a peer competitor. Among American foreign policy elites, the results were euphoria, pride, arrogance—and uncertainty. The absence of an ideological threat produced an absence of purpose. "Nations need enemies," Charles Krauthammer commented as the Cold War ends. "Take away one, and they find another." *The ideal enemy for America would be ideologically hostile, racially and culturally different, and militarily strong enough to pose a credible threat to American security.* The foreign policy debates of the1990s were already over who might be such an enemy. (*WAW*, 262; my emphasis)

In the mad rationality of these "foreign policy debates," which Huntington subsumes under the astonishingly frank title "The Search for an Enemy,"[32] it became clear to him that such a reinvigorating enemy of American exceptionalism could not be "creedal," since it was precisely the "triumph" of the Creed of Democracy that was contributing to the denationalization of exceptionalist America. "For over two centuries," Huntington writes, in keeping with his "civilizational" approach to the "problem" of the American national identity, "the liberal, democratic principles of the American Creed had been a core component of American identity. American and European observers had often referred to this creedal component as the essence of 'American exceptionalism.' Now, however, exceptionalism was becoming universalism, as democracy became more and more accepted around the world, at least in theory, as the only legitimate form of government. No other secular ideology existed to challenge democracy as fascism and communism had in the twentieth century" (*WAW*, 257).

In the face of this "dilemma," Huntington, like his jeremiadic predecessors in the face of the waning of the frontier, thus willfully *produces* this
anxiously sought-after reunifying and reanimating "civilizational" enemy
or fault line out of the complex, diverse, ambiguous—and thought-
demanding—postmodern or postnational global conditions largely produced by the depredations of British, French, and, more recently, American
imperialism in the nineteenth and twentieth centuries. Or, rather, he ratio-
nalizes this willful production by appropriating the attacks on the World
Trade Center and the Pentagon on September 11, 2001, to his jeremiadic
project. To underscore the crucial importance of the civilizational aspect of
this enemy, Huntington enumerates the various candidates proffered by the
policy experts in theses debates over America's post-Cold War enemy,
moving from the more or less unsatisfying creedal threats—a "revived nationalist, authoritarian Russia"; "small-time dictators like Slobodan Milosevic and Saddam Hussein"; China, "clearly a dictatorship with no respect
for political liberty, democracy, or human rights, with a dynamic economy,
an increasingly nationalist public, a strong sense of cultural superiority, and
among its military and some of her elite groups, a clear perception of the
United States as their enemy"—to the more satisfying cultural threat:

> Some Americans came to see Islamic fundamentalist groups, or
> more broadly political Islam, as the enemy, epitomized in Iraq,
> Iran, Sudan, Libya, Afghanistan under the Taliban, and to a
> lesser degree other Muslim states, as well as Islamic terrorist
> groups such as Hamas, Hezbollah, Islamic Jihad, and the Al
> Qaeda network. The attacks in the 1990s on the World Trade
> Center, the Khobar barracks, the U.S. embassies in Tanzania and
> Kenya, and the USS *Cole*, as well as other terrorist attempts that
> were successfully thwarted, certainly constituted an intermittent,
> low-level war against the United States. Five of the seven states
> the United States listed as supporting terrorism are Muslim.
> Muslim states and organizations threaten Israel, which many
> Americans see as a close ally. Iran and—until the 2003 war—
> Iraq pose potential threats to America's and the world's oils sup-
> plies. Pakistan acquired nuclear weapons in the 1990s and at
> various times Iran, Iraq, Libya, and Saudi Arabia have been re-
> ported to harbor nuclear weapons stockpiles, intentions, and/or
> programs. (*WAW*, 263)

And then, in a tone suggesting something akin to euphoric relief and a
rhetoric implying that History, not American policy makers, has deter-

mined America's new rejuvenating enemy, he concludes his narrative simply and decisively:

> The cultural gap between Islam and America's Christianity and Anglo-Protestantism reinforces Islam's enemy qualifications. And on September 11, 2001, Osama bin Laden ended America's search. The attacks on New York and Washington followed by the wars with Afghanistan and Iraq and the more diffuse "war on terrorism" make militant Islam America's first enemy of the twenty-first century. (*WAW*, 264–265)

But the attacks by Al Qaeda on the World Trade Center and the Pentagon did not only bring "America's search for an enemy" to a close; they produced, according to Huntington, a *civilizational*, particularly religious, enemy that served the purpose of the jeremiad. In establishing a permanent threat to "homeland security," this new religion-oriented civilizational enemy provided the inaugural impetus for the recuperation of a dispersing national solidarity under the aegis of the Anglo-Protestant core culture *and* the rejuvenation of an eroding American civilization, the symptomatic aspects of which were not simply a diversity indifferent to the ideal of the nation, but also a moral corruption that threatened its spiritual health. In Huntington's words, which echo those of all his predecessor Jeremiahs, the attacks of 9/11 brought to coalescence the growing concern, since the 1980s, of Americans over "issues that could be interpreted as evidence of moral decay: tolerance of sexual behavior previously considered unacceptable, teenage pregnancy, single-parent families, mounting divorce rates, high levels of crime, and the perception that large numbers of people were living the easy life on the welfare rolls funded by hardworking taxpayers. More broadly, there seemed to be feelings, first, that more meaningful forms of community and civil society had disappeared . . . and, second, that the prevailing intellectual mode, deriving from the 1960s, held there were no absolute values or moral principles and everything was relative" (*WAW*, 344). With this bizarrely paradoxical affirmation of the benignity of the threat posed by militant Islam, Huntington's post-9/11 American jeremiad come to its structural fulfillment. In affirming the threatening conditions that instigate a religiously oriented national anxiety over the fate of the chosen American nation, it announces the advent of a fifth Anglo-Protestant-inspired Great Awakening in American history, one that would be adequate to Huntington's Manichaean "clash of civilizations": "American identity began a new phase with the new century. Its salience and substance in this phase are being shaped by America's new vulnerability to external attack and by a turn to religion, a Great Awakening in America that parallels the resurgence of religion in most of the world" (*WAW*, 336).

At the end of his book, Huntington summarily—and rhetorically offers three "hypothetical" ways by which America could relate to the rapidly globalizing world in the wake the 9/11 Al Qaeda attacks: the cosmopolitan, the imperialist, and the nationalist. In keeping with the logic of his version of the American jeremiad, he goes on to reject both the cosmopolitan and the imperialist alternatives, the first because it would threaten America's national identity by compelling the subordination of its agency to the laws of international authorities, and the second because it would threaten America's national identity by affirming "the universality" of its creedal values. Both options, in other words, would result in the eventual demise of America's "civilizational" (Anglo-Protestant) identity: the annulment of that version of the American exceptionalist ethos that, as we have seen, has not only perennially defined American national identity, but also enabled America to remain, always already, a New World. For Huntington, like his American exceptionalist predecessors I have invoked, there is no alternative but that of a nationalism understood in "civilizational" terms, though this nationalism, as the general tenor of his book amply makes clear, does not preclude the imperial option as long as the latter remains subordinate to the imperatives of perpetual national renewal that are crucial to the former:

> Cosmopolitanism and imperialism attempt to reduce or to eliminate the social, political, and cultural differences between America and other societies. A national approach would recognize and accept what distinguishes America from those societies. America cannot become the world and still be America. America is different, and that difference is defined in large part by its Anglo-Protestant culture and its religiosity. The alternative to cosmopolitanism and imperialism is nationalism devoted to the preservation and enhancement of those qualities that have defined America since its founding. (*WAW*, 364–365)

As many dissenting American scholars, not least the so-called New Americanists (Richard Slotkin, Francis Jennings, Richard Drinnon, Sacvan Bercovitch, Donald Pease, Amy Kaplan, John Carlos Rowe, David Reynolds, and others), have persuasively demonstrated in recent years, this (naturalized) mythic exceptionalist national identity, which assumes that the American people are God's or History's "elect" and thus are obligated to fulfill His/Its missionary "errand in the [world's] wilderness," has by and large informed the discourse about the nation of public and academic American intellectuals from the colonial period through the so-called American Renaissance to the Cold War era and the founding of

American literary studies. Remarkably indifferent to the destabilizing disclosures of these New Americanist scholars, however, Huntington, like
his American exceptionalist predecessors, continues confidently to affirm
the absolute benignity of the idea of the "filiative" nation state and nationalism. In the process of privileging the "Anglo-Protestant culture"
over the "American Creed"—Huntington's contempt even for American-
style democracy is relentless—as the "core" of the American national
identity, he invokes Ernest Renan's famous essay "What Is a Nation?":

> People are not likely to find in political principles the deep emo-
> tional content and meaning provided by kith and kin, blood and
> belonging, culture and nationality. These attachments may have
> little or no basis in fact but they do satisfy a deep human long-
> ing for meaningful community. The idea that "We are all liberal
> democratic believers in the American Creed" seems unlikely
> to satisfy the need. A nation, Ernest Renan said, may be "a daily
> plebiscite," but it is a plebiscite on whether or not to maintain an
> existing inheritance. It is, as Renan also said, "the culmination of
> a long past of endeavors, sacrifice, and devotion." Without that
> inheritance, no nation exists, and if the plebiscite rejects that in-
> heritance, the nation ends. (WAW, 339)

What Huntington's American exceptionalist problematic compels him to
overlook—or, rather, enables him to repress—in thus citing Renan's famous definition of the nation is his ultranationalist—and Orientalist—
French authority's candid admission in the same essay that the nation (its
identity) is founded on an original and continuing violence committed by
one privileged cultural constituency against others and thus that the willed
forgetting of this violence is crucial to nation building and its survival:

> Forgetting, I would go so far as to say historical error, is a crucial
> factor in the creation of a nation, which is why progress in his-
> torical studies often constitutes a danger for [the principle of] na-
> tionality. Indeed, historical enquiry brings to light deeds of
> violence which took place at the origins of all political forma-
> tions, even of those whose consequences have been altogether
> beneficial. Unity is always effected by means of massacres and ter-
> ror lasting for the best part of a century. Though the king of
> France was, if I may make as bold as to say, almost the perfect in-
> stance of an agent that crystallized [a nation] over a long
> period; though he established the most perfect national unity that
> there has ever been, too searching a scrutiny has destroyed his
> prestige. The nation which he had formed has cursed him, and,

nowadays, it is only men of culture [the dominant culture] who know something of his former value and of his achievements.[33]

Like virtually all his exceptionalist predecessors, public and academic, who have written or spoken about the American national identity up to the postnational moment, Huntington, though far more explicitly and with far less nuance, overlooks or, at worst, suppresses, the dislocating fact that "forgetting" actual history or "historical error" is, as Renan (unwillingly) observes, "a crucial factor in the creation of a nation," that "deeds of violence" constitute the origins of "all political formations," that "massacres and terror" are the instruments that produce national unity, the "soul," as he puts it later in his essay, that *is* the nation.[34] And, as we have seen, despite the amnesiac monumentalist histories (I am using this term in Nietzsche's and Foucault's sense) that have celebrated its exceptionalism, America has been no exception.

Specifically, what Huntington (like Fukuyama, Haass, and other neo-conservative predecessors) "forgets" or willfully represses in his jeremiadic encomium to the exceptionalist Anglo-Protestant "core culture" of America and his call for another Great Awakening in the aftermath of 9/11 are all those act of "massacre and terror" that the monumentalist custodians of the American national memory—canonical historians, biographers, literary critics, and the culture industry in general—have relegated to oblivion in the process of building and renewing the American nation. These, as the New Americanists have gone far to bear historical witness in their destructive scholarship of retrieval, include the inhumane removal of and genocidal war against the native Americans (which began with the Puritans' extermination of the Pequods in the King Philip's War); the obscenities of slavery, and the ecological, cultural, and political ravages of Manifest Destiny, the depredations of the imperial Spanish-American War. Not least, as I have shown in the previous chapters, this repressed history of American violence includes the brutal devastation of Vietnam at the "new frontier"—the new West in the East.

IX

[The] political as an instance of community is a sharing that does not establish an autonomous collective subject who is authorized to say "we' and to terrorize those who do not, or cannot, speak in the "we."

—Bill Readings, *The University in Ruins*

In the process of identifying Huntington's post-9/11 recuperative nationalist project with the tradition of the American jeremiad, I have been compelled to overdetermine what it has in common with his predecessor Jeremiahs. There is, however, as I noted earlier, an easily discernible and, in my mind, crucial difference between them. The earlier American Jeremiahs I have invoked in this chapter by and large identified with what they professed in their jeremiads about the American national identity, particularly about its religious—that is, Protestant—foundation. Huntington (and most of the post-World War II generation of conservative intellectuals to which he belongs), on the other hand, is, as Edward Said has insistently shown, essentially a calculative "policy expert," not an ideological enthusiast; a "crisis manager" of the dominant political culture, not a "believer." Referring to Huntington's influential essay "The Clash of Civilizations," he writes:

> At the core of his essay, and this is what has made it strike so responsive a chord among post-Cold War policy-makers, is this sense of cutting through a lot of unnecessary detail, of masses of scholarship and huge amounts of experience, and boiling all of them down to a couple of catchy, easy-to-quote-and-remember ideas [such as Bernard Lewis's "the clash of civilizations"], which are then passed off as pragmatic, practical, sensible, and clear. But is this the best way to understand the world we live in? *Is it wise as an intellectual and scholarly expert to produce a simplified map of the world and then hand it to generals and civilian law makers as a prescription for first comprehending and then acting in the world?* Doesn't this *method* in effect prolong, exacerbate, and deepen conflict?[35]

As the "realist" tenor of Huntington's discourse everywhere suggests, what matters primarily to him, as it does to the neoconservative intellectual deputies of the Bush administration in general, is not the triumphant nationalization of Anglo-Protestant Christianity as such. There is no indication that Huntington is a practitioner of the Evangelical Christianity he identifies as the core of American civilization, which, he claims, is destined to clash with the civilization of Islam. It is, rather, a matter of the polyvalent political power that would accrue to the neoconservative political constituency he serves from a new Great Awakening. In other words, whereas Huntington's predecessors were, *mutatis mutandis,* American Jeremiahs only retrospectively (i.e., after Sacvan Bercovitch's analysis of the perennial type), Huntington, as his duplicitous reference to Bercovitch quoted earlier makes manifest, calculatively *uses* the genre—takes advantage of its deeply backgrounded, mobilizing cultural power—to harness this textualized nationalization of Anglo-Protestant Christianity to the neoconservative causes. We might say, invoking Herman Melville's proleptic disclosure of the pervasive abuse to which the optimism of American exceptionalism lent itself in *The Confidence-Man* (1857),[36] that Huntington masquerades as an American Jeremiah.

In the antebellum period, when the American frontier was receding beyond the Mississippi, Melville, unlike most writers of the so-called American Renaissance with which he has been misleadingly identified, perceived the contradictory violence endemic to the benign logic of American exceptionalism and, like his subversive creation, the spectral Bartleby, "preferred not to" be answerable to it imperatives of violence. In *The Confidence-Man; His Masquerades*, Melville's great Voltairian—and proto-Nietzschean—carnivalesque novel about the American national identity, he not only disclosed, through the ironic figure of the confidence-man, retrospectively and prophetically, the polyvalent—psychic, ecological, racial, cultural, and political—negative consequences of this deeply inscribed American exceptionalist perspective. Melville also perceived how the confidence inspired by this philosophy of Optimism—its lunatic Panglossian logic, according to him—that had its origins in the Puritans' exceptionalist providential/prefigural view of history, could be used by all manner of "confidence-men" to dupe a receptive American public. In this anti-jeremiadic novel, in other words, he not only retrospectively discloses the periodic fervent calls of the deputies of the dominant culture for national unity and renewal to be jeremiads; he also proleptically anticipates the calculated appropriation of the American jeremiad by post-Cold War confidence-men like Samuel P. Huntington.

In the novel, the confidence-man's indirect demythologization of the American exceptionalist ethos aboard the *Fidèle* (the steamboat on the Mississippi that is Melville's synecdoche for antebellum American society) is enabled by his awareness of the American's public's historically backgrounded ontological confidence in the ultimate benignity of an always threatening being, indeed, in its having been "elected" by God to fulfill His benign providential/destinarian design in the earth's pain- and anxiety-provoking wilderness. The demythologizing—anti-jeremiadic—strategy of Melville's ironic confidence-man has its origins in the early American Jeremiahs. These, as we have seen, were the spokespersons for a disintegrating dominant culture, who not only realized that settling, improving, and civilizing—that is, rationalizing—the New World wilderness and thus generating collective confidence in America's westward mission carried with it in the long run the potential for decay, corruption, and exhaustion, as in the case of their representation of the fate of the

Old World and its empires "*sine fine*." In so doing, these custodians of the American national memory—for Melville, they are, not incidentally, epitomized by Daniel Webster[37]—insistently, often hysterically, reaffirmed, by way of the ritual of the American jeremiad, the need for a perpetual "frontier" between the sedentary and the nomadic (i.e., civilization and savagery): a permanent threat to the unity of the American nation that would always renew the solidarity, the patriotism, and the youthful and optimistic vitality of its people. Despite the appeals to their "exceptionalist" New World origins, these American Jeremiahs, for Melville's ironic confidence-man, were not unlike those eighteenth-century Old World philosophers and poets—Leibnitz, Shaftesbury, Pope, and so on— whom Voltaire subsumes under the name of Pangloss and whose philosophies of Optimism derived their positive meaning and "progressive" practical force from their indissoluble relationality with adversity, hardship, and distrust or, rather, with the anxiety precipitated by natural or human-produced catastrophic events that threatened to undermine the legitimacy and authority of the optimistic view.

In the "confidence game" he is "playing," that is to say, Melville's confidence-man, attuned to the depth of his American victims' Panglossian optimism—knowing they, like Candide, are ensconced safely, with "the true light," in their "Malakoff of confidence" (*C-M*, 66)—actually, if indirectly, *exaggerates the threat* to their passive confidence posed by the apparent contradictions all the more to reactivate and rejuvenate its energy. The difference between Candide and most of the confidence-man's American victims is that the former eventually—by way of the reversal of the logical binary between confidence and distrust precipitated by the excess of violence he experiences—awakens to both the absurdity and cold-blooded inhumanity of Pangloss's "best of all possible worlds." In their gullibility—their deeply inscribed assurance that "whatever is [according to the American exceptionalist perspective], is right"—the confidence-man's American victims are incapable of perceiving the absolute incommensurability between their optimism and the disruptive and "blood-curdling" events that challenge its authority or of acting according to the responsible and humane imperatives of this disclosure. In thus carnivalizing American optimism—in thus "push[ing] the masquerade to its limit"—Melville, to appropriate Foucault's Nietszchean definition of parody in the genealogical mode, "prepare[s] the great carnival of time where masks are constantly reappearing. No longer the identification of our faint individualities with the solid identifies of the past [the pioneer, the backwoodman, the frontiersman, who turns out to be a "Leatherstocking Nemesis" or "Indian-hater par excellence"] but our 'unrealization' through the excessive choice of identities."[38]

This is Melville's anticipatory witness to the transformation the American jeremiad has undergone in the wake of the "closing of the frontier" and the end of the nineteenth century. The analogy between Melville's diagnosis of American national identity in the antebellum period and the disclosures of contemporary American history (theorized by the New Americanists), *especially since the national disaster of Vietnam War*, is uncannily revelatory not simply of the historical conditions that have produced the cultural discourse of the second Bush administration as it is synecdochically represented in Samuel P. Huntington's "jeremiad," but also of its new function as masquerade or confidence game. As Melville's anti-jeremiad, *The Confidence-Man*, testifies, American history has always been directed by confidence men. And this, as we have seen, is because the founding and abiding metanarrative of American exceptionalism, not least, in its jeremiadic mode, necessarily reproduces them. In the past, however, the inhuman (teleo)logic of their metanarrative of confidence remained obscured by its undeveloped status, its integral relationship with promise and process. It thus remained more or less "benign" in appearance to those Americans who paid the price for its practice. Since Melville's time, culminating in the period between the Vietnam War and the second Bush administration's response to the attacks on September 11, 2001, the potentiality of this "benign" logic has been fulfilled, that is, come to its end—and, in a theoretical way, to its demise. By this last I mean that its fulfillment in the "vision" of "the New American Century" has, like the carnivalesque strategy of Melville's confidence-man vis-à-vis the paradoxical logic of American optimism, precipitated into visibility not only the anachronism of this optimistic metanarrative (its willful indifference to the thrownness, contingency, and plurarity—and sufferings—of the contemporary human condition), but also, as in the self-parodic synecdochical example of Huntington's *Who Are We?*, its cynical spuriousness: its status as a cold-blooded masquerade, a neocon con game intended to obliterate the violence of America's past—not least the singularity of the Vietnam War—and to mobilize a differential American public by harnessing its deeply inscribed optimism to an aggressive and violent global Project for the New American Century and against an "erosive" and "debilitating" internal dissent by way of reinventing the American frontier in the guise of a permanent "war on [Islamic] terror" and the *normalization* of the anxiety-provoking state of exception.[39]

In the chapters of *The Confidence-Man* on the "metaphysics of Indian-hating," Herman Melville, attuned to the shadow that haunts the light of systemic interpretations of being like that of American exceptionalism, discloses the horrific violence latent in the benign trailblazing errand of the "backwoodsman—"the diluted Indian-hater, one whose heart proves not so steely as his brain" (*C-M*, 150)—by allowing the latter's contemporary exponent to pursue this unfulfilled logic to its limits, at which point the "Indian-hater par excellence" manifests himself as "Leatherstocking Nemesis," whose "hate . . .is a vortex from whose suction scarce the remotest chip of the guilty race may reasonably feel secure" and whose epitaph is "Terror" (*C-M*, 149–150).

As we have seen in the chapters analyzing Tim O'Brien's *Going After Cacciato*, Philip Caputo's *A Rumor of War*, and in a more indirect but nevertheless anticipatory way, Graham Greene's *The Quiet American*, Melville's reading of the metaphysical logic of American "Indian-hating"— his disclosure of the necessary continuity between the diluted Indian-hater and the Indian-hater par excellence—can teach us a great a deal about the deeply embedded exceptionalist (onto)logic that informed the United States' "benign" errand in the wilderness of Vietnam. Similarly, I suggest, we can learn much about the George W. Bush administration's policies vis-à-vis Islam, America's new Indian, in the wake of September 11, 2001, particularly about the continuity between the still-diluted logic of its exceptionalist errand in the Middle East and the prophetic discourse of Samuel P. Huntington, by attuning ourselves to Melville's carnivalization of the American optimism informing the "truth" of American exceptionalism and the American jeremiad that has sustained it over three centuries. For just as Melville's parodic geneaology exposes the implacable, unrelenting, and totalizing violence latent in the seemingly benign logic of the diluted Indian-hater, so, in pushing the logic of the Bush administration's diluted exceptionalism to its limits, America's latest Jeremiah, Samuel P. Huntington—the American Jeremiah par excellence—points to its horrific end—and the "unrealization of its 'truth.'"[40]

Chapter 7

CONCLUSION
The Vietnam War, 9/11, and Its Aftermath

Turning and turning in the widening gyre
The falcon cannot hear the falconer;
Things fall apart; the centre cannot hold;

—W. B. Yeats, "The Second Coming"

Well, if we can attrit the population base of the Viet Cong,
it'll accelerate the process of degrading the VC.

—Robert Komer, head of the pacification program
in Vietnam during the Vietnam War, quoted
in Frances Fitzgerald, *Fire in the Lake*[1]

The essence of American cultural history since the fall of Saigon in 1975 and the humiliating defeat the formidable U.S. army, both military and ideological, suffered at the hands of an infinitely weaker opponent has been, as I have insistently observed in this book, the systematic and increasingly nuanced forgetting of the Vietnam War, or, more precisely, the tellingly insistent remembering of the war that was intended to obliterate its singular history from the consciousness of the American cultural memory. This Herculean labor to lay the Hydra-headed specter of the Vietnam War to rest—which also meant the recuperation of the disintegrated American national identity—was undertaken not only by the state (and its intellectual deputies), but also by the media, Hollywood, the publishing houses, the educational institutions—what Adorno called the "consciousness industry"—that, however invisible, are its superstructural prosthetic instruments. As I have argued elsewhere,[2] the long but uneven amnesiac representational process underwent four continuous, if uneven, phases. The first, which actually preceded the end of what, after the Tet offensive of 1968, had come to be seen as a virtually unwinable war, was characterized by a belated effort, epitomized by John Wayne's state-sponsored "epic" film, *The Green Berets*, to rehabilitate the shattered image of the American military mission by attributing its failure to achieve victory to the alleged complicity of the media, which by then had in some degree turned against the war, with the mounting protest movement in the United States. The second phase, in the war's immediate aftermath, was characterized by a resonant national silence about it, a nonrepresentational representation that, in effect, rendered the returning soldiers who fought it the scapegoats for the dominant culture, which had inaugurated, planned, executed, and supported the disastrous war. The third and decisive phase of this amnesiac monumentalizing was inaugurated by the dedication of the Vietnam Veterans Memorial in 1982, a national commemoration that was in large part the consequence of the veterans' effort to rehabilitate their image, and culminated with the election of the conservative president Ronald Reagan. This was a turn in American politics that coincided with the massive representational and educational "reform" initiative (the reestablishment of the "core curriculum" in colleges and universities—and the modern affiliation of the idea of the university with the nation-state) sponsored by Harvard University and other "elite" institutions of higher learning and by public "intellectuals" such as William Bennett, Chair of the National Endowment for the Humanities and later Secretary of Education in the Reagan administration,[3] to recuperate and mobilize a cultural, political—and militaristic—national consensus that would enable America's imperial interventions in Granada, El Salvador, Nicaragua, and the Middle East, interventions, that is, that were intended to reestablish the Cold War against Soviet communism as the fundamental global reality. This third phase was subdivided into two moments. The first included the publication and promotion of numerous edited anthologies of personal reminiscences of the Vietnam War (*Everything We Had*, 1981; *To Bear Any Burden*, 1985; *Nam*, 1981; and *Bloods*, 1984, among others) and letters home written by American soldiers during the war (*Dear America*, 1985); several major Hollywood films (*The Deer Hunter*, 1978; *Coming Home*, 1978; *Go Tell the Spartans*, 1978; *Apocalypse Now*, 1979); and, more problematically, a number of veterans' memoirs and novels (Philip Caputo's *A Rumor of War*, 1977; Ron Kovic's *Born on the Fourth of July*, 1976; Tim O'Brien's *If I Die in a Combat Zone*, 1973, and *Going After Cacciato*, 1978; Gustav Hasford's, *Short Timers*, 1979; John Del Vecchio's *The Thirteenth Valley*, 1982; Larry Heineman's *Paco's Story*, 1987; and others). The ostensible raison d'etre of all of these was the rehabilitation of the veteran, but their ultimate cultural agenda was the "healing of the wound" suffered by the American collective psyche by way of transforming the corrosive uniqueness of the Vietnam War to war-in-general. In the second, culminating moment of this third representational phase, epitomized by the *Rambo* trilogy (1982, 1984, 1988) and the several *MIA* (missing in action films, 1984, 1985, 1988), this renarrativizing strategy, not incidentally, coincided with the emergence of a strident reactionary cultural discourse represented by the jeremiads of highly visible "public" intellectuals such as Allan Bloom, Roger Kimball, Hilton Kramer, David Lehman, and Dinesh D'Souza.[4] Emboldened by the momentum toward the "reconciliation" of the veteran with the American public and appealing to the traditional discourse of American exceptionalism—the very frontier mythology that had earlier justified America's intervention ("errand") in the Vietnamese wilderness—this combined political and cultural representational initiative foregrounded the decentering and randomization of the university, particularly the subversion of the "core curriculum" that had formerly inculcated the values of the dominant culture in students and reproduced the American nation-state, by those they called "tenured radicals"; vilified the protest movement for having unnerved the American public, that is, shaken, if not shattered, the American (perennially optimistic) national identity— what it called the "Vietnam syndrome"—and thus "prevented" America from winning the war. The fourth and "final" phase of the culture industry's renarrativization of the Vietnam War was inaugurated with the collapse of the Soviet Union, which was heralded by conservative policy makers like Frances Fukuyama as the end of history and the advent of the New World Order under the aegis of the United States.[5] This triumphalist discourse, the other (repressed) face of which was the forgetting of Vietnam, culminated in the recuperation of the American national identity and the invasion of Iraq in 1990. With the "surgically" executed "victory" over Saddam Hussein in the Gulf War, the long and laborious process of laying the ghost of Vietnam had ostensibly come to its end. As I put it before 9/11 and the United States' "preemptive wars" against Afghanistan and Iraq in the pursuit of its unending "war on terrorism":

> In this final phase . . . the earlier public need to "heal the wound"—
> a recuperative and conciliatory gesture of forgetting—became,
> in the words of President George Bush and official Washington,
> a matter of "kicking the Vietnam syndrome." Aided and abetted
> by the culture industry, this early gesture of forgetting metamorphosed at the time of the Gulf "crisis" into a virulently assured assumption that the resistance to America's intervention and conduct
> of the war in Vietnam in the 1960s was a symptom of a national
> neurosis. . . . Whatever its limitations, the protest movement in the
> Vietnam decade was, in fact, a symptomatic manifestation of a
> long-overdue and promising national self-doubt about the legitimacy of America's representation of its internal constituencies

(blacks, women, gays, ethnic minorities, the poor, the young, and so on) and about the alleged benignity of its historically ordained exceptionalist mission to transform the world (the barbarous Other) in its own image. In this last phase of the amnesiac process, this healthy and potentially productive self-examination of the American cultural identity came to be represented as a collective psychological sickness that, in its disintegrative momentum, threatened to undermine "America's" promised end. By this I mean the end providentially promised to the original Puritans and later, after the secularization of the body politic, by History: the building of "a city on the hill" in the "New World," which is to say, the advent of the New World Order and the end of history.[6]

With the fall of the Soviet Union, "the evil empire," as Reagan notoriously called it, and the end of the Cold War, however, the dominant culture in the United States lost the enemy that, given the binary "frontier" logic endemic to its perennial exceptionalist representation of the complexities of the world as a Manichaean struggle between the forces of good and evil, seems to have been an absolute necessity of American domestic and foreign policy. Coupled with the emergence to prominence of minority cultures within the United States, the residue of the civil rights movement, this evaporation of a mobilizing and rejuvenating enemy, was, as I have shown in chapter 6, represented by the policy experts as threatening, once again, to destabilize the American national identity. In a section of his post-9/11 book, *Who Are We?* tellingly entitled "In Search of an Enemy," Samuel P. Huntington, it will be recalled, bluntly put this anxiety in his jeremiad calling for the reconsolidation of the Anglo-Protestant "core culture" that had been at the heart of American civilization and the rise of the United States to global dominance in terms of the "civilizational"—as opposed to the secular "creedal" (i.e., political)—component of the exceptionalist American national identity. "The collapse of the Soviet Union," he wrote, "left America not only with no enemy, but also for the first time in its history without any clear 'other' against which to define itself." Echoing, yet modifying Francis Fukuyama's end-of-history thesis, he went on the say that, in the wake of the global triumph of democracy (against communism), this creedal component (American-style democracy) had become "universal"—the "only legitimate form of government." As a result "no other *secular* ideology existed to challenge democracy as fascism and communism had done in the twentieth century."[7] That is, the "American Creed" was no longer adequate to define the essence of the American national identity.

With the minimization of the role the "American Creed" formerly played in the identification of a world-substantial enemy and the inadequacy of "small-time dictators like Slobodan Milosevic and Saddam Hussein" to fill this role, the United States, according to Huntington, began tentatively to seek for this necessary enemy according to the imperatives of the religious (Anglo-Protestant) component of American culture, that is, by focusing more and more on "Islamic fundamentalist groups, or more broadly political Islam . . . epitomized in Iraq, Iran, Sudan, Libya, Afghanistan under the Taliban, and to a lesser degree other Muslim states, as well as in Islamic terrorist groups such as Hamas, Hezbollah, Islamic Jihad, and the Al Qaeda network." This anxious search for a defining enemy, Huntington declares, with what seems like exhilaration, came to its end on September 11, 2001, when Al Qaeda attacks on the World Trade Center and the Pentagon made "militant Islam American's first enemy of the twenty-first century" (*WAW*, 263–264).

As the all-too-representative rhetoric of dramatic closure of this influential American policy expert makes emphatically clear, the attacks on New York and Washington were received by American officialdom not as an outrage perpetrated on innocent civilians, but, echoing the public sponsor (the *Amicus*) of the anguish of Mary Rowlandson's captivity narrative, as something like an enabling gift. If there were any lingering doubts about America's civilizational "mission" in the world's "wilderness" in the minds of Americans, these remaining traces of the Vietnam syndrome, were now entirely effaced. Taking advantage of the patriotic fervor instigated by the attacks—and orchestrating its political potentialities—the Bush administration launched its "war on terrorism" and its "shock and awe" preemptive wars—preconceived, it turns out[8]—first on the Taliban regime in Afghanistan and then, by fabricating its claim that it possessed weapons of mass destruction, on the regime of Saddam Hussein in Iraq. Vietnam, it seemed, was, once again, "history."

I

What precisely was it, we are compelled to ask about the obsessive thirty-year effort of the American nation-state and its ideological apparatuses to obliterate Vietnam, that the collective American memory wanted desperately to forget? What, to invoke the irresistible rhetoric I have used in this book, was the demon that haunted, indeed, possessed the collective American soul for an entire generation following the shocking impingement on the national consciousness of the spectacle of the last Americans

boarding the helicopter that was to fly them out of Vietnam, while a multitude of America's South Vietnamese dependents, soldiers, and citizens,
who it had been its purpose to save for the free world, clamored outside
the gates of the American Embassy for sanctuary from the North Vietnamese army? What, in essence, was the Vietnam syndrome that, at the
time of the American army's decisive victory over Saddam Hussein in the
first Gulf War, President George Bush, with euphoric relief, thanked God
for enabling the American public to "kick"?

The purpose of this book, both the theoretical chapters and those
that interpret literary texts about the Vietnam War, has not only been to
"identify" and "name" this anxiety-provoking specter, but also to retrieve from the oblivion to which, in the aftermath of 9/11, the monumentalist dominant culture in America has attempted, finally in vain, to
bury "it." More precisely, its purpose has been to bring *this* war's irresistible spectrality to corporeal presence in behalf of soliciting (in the Der-
ridian sense of the word) the second Bush administration's representation
and justification of its "war on terror"—and its unrelenting will, as the
president insistently puts this narratological "structure of attitude," to
"stay the course" in the face of a situation that is increasingly coming to
resemble the Vietnam "quagmire." To achieve this "end," I have relied
heavily on certain fundamental aspects of the de*structuring* thought of a
number of "poststructuralist" theorists, above all Martin Heidegger,
Jacques Derrida, Jean-François Lyotard, Louis Althusser, Michel Foucault, Gilles Deleuze and Félix Guattari, Gayatri Spivak, and Edward
Said. But this reliance on poststructuralist theory, it needs to be emphasized, has been strategically heretical. Rather than attending meticulously
to the differences that distinguish one theory from another, as both the
theorists and their commentators have done more or less universally—
and disablingly—I have attended primarily to what they have in common
and to what I take to be the epochal historical circumstances—the more
or less simultaneous coming to the end (fulfillment and demise, in the
sense of decentering) of philosophy and imperialism—that contributed to
that commonality. And this is not only because the obsessive practice of
distinguishing has left the disciplinary (compartmentalizing) structure of
knowledge production of modernity—the alienating mechanism of divide
and conquer—intact and, in so doing, has minimized its political effectiv-
ity, if not, as Antonio Negri and Michael Hardt and, in a different way,
Timothy Brennan, have claimed, rendered these theories complicitous
with the very regime of truth they have wanted to oppose.[9] It is also, and
primarily, because such attention to the *relationality* of the various perspectives of poststructuralist theory, in collapsing the arbitrarily imposed
boundaries between the "sites" of knowledge production (the disci-

plines), reveals being—and its representations—to be an indissoluble *continuum*, that, *however unevenly at any particular historical conjuncture*, ranges from being as such (the ontological), the subject (the epistemological), and the ecos (the biological), through gender identities and relations, the family, race, and class, to economic, cultural, military, social, domestic political, and international or global formations. This multiple critical orientation, it has seemed to me, renders *visible*, in a way that no disciplinary perspective can, the kind of "realities" that the gaze of the empirical or instrumentalist problematic of the political leaders who decided to intervene in Vietnam, the bureaucrats in the Pentagon who planned the war, the military and cultural missions[10] that conducted it, were blind to and, despite the self-destruction of this gaze in that epochal decade, the American political leaders who decided to undertake pre-emptive wars in Afghanistan and Iraq after 9/11, the bureaucrats who have envisioned and planned them, and the military and cultural missions that are executing them continue to be blind to. In attempting to achieve my purpose in this book, I have relied on what Edward Said long ago called a "secular critical" approach to the representations of the Vietnam War during and after its non-ending end—if by "secular criticism" he means, as I think he does, a worldly criticism that not only rejects a religious but also an anthropological transcendental signified or natural supernaturalism, not only a *theo-logos*, but an *anthropo-logos*, if, that is, his well-known criticism of poststructuralist theory is intended, not as a rejection, but as a manifestation of the betrayal of its initial collaborative critical possibilities.[11]

Let me now return to the content of this book—my retrieval of the singular history of the Vietnam War from its representation in its aftermath and my reconstellation of this history into the post-9/11 global occasion. There, it will be recalled, I suggested that, however horrific, the attacks on the twin towers of the World Trade Center and the Pentagon were, as the symbolic significance of American power of these chosen sites clearly suggests, the consequence in large part of a very long history of what Said has called Western Orientalism, a history of representation/domination of the Orient culminating in the United States' ubiquitous indirect and overt economic, cultural, political, and military depredations over the last half-century in the oil-rich Middle East in the duplicitous name of stabilizing a recalcitrantly backward and unstable world: its clandestine orchestration of the overthrow of Muhammad Musaddiq in Iran, its support of unpopular despotic Middle Eastern regimes like Iraq, Saudi Arabia, Pakistan, and the Taliban, its massive financing of Israel's militaristic colonialist policies in the face of the obviously valid claims of the Palestinian people, to name only a few. I also suggested that the logic informing the United States' reductive binarist representation of and the swift and unequivocal response to the terrorists' attack on American soil was deeply backgrounded in American history, indeed, was simultaneous with its Puritan origins. This is the rejuvenating exceptionalist logic endemic to the American jeremiad, first theorized by the French intellectual Alexis de Tocqueville in *Democracy in America*,[12] that, in assuming Americans to be God's and, later, with the secularization of God's Word, History's chosen people, has perennially justified America's unilateral, "benign" "errand" in the world's "wilderness."[13] It is, therefore, as the nomadic English novelist Graham Greene, and the exilic American writers as distanced in time from one another as Herman Melville (in *Moby-Dick, Pierre, The Confidence-Man,* "Bartleby the Scrivener," and "Benito Cereno"),[14] Thomas Pynchon, Robert Coover, Don DeLillo, and, in the context of the Vietnam War, Philip Caputo, Tim O'Brien, and many others who fought in and later wrote about this first postmodern war, bear symptomatic witness, a "concentering" (Melville) metaphysical logic. Beginning inquiry from the *end*, it not only enables the demonization of anxiety-provoking multiplicity (thus precluding the opened-ended and productive strife of authentic dialogue), but also the *reduction* of this multiplicity (i.e., the differential dynamics of being) to a reified, comprehensible, and, in Melville's phrase, "practically assailable" One. As such a concentering monologic, this divine- or History-ordained American exceptionalism has predictably manifested itself over and over in history in a relentlessly deadly way—as a monomania (Melville) or paranoia (Pynchon)—whenever any differential constituency of the human community has refused its spontaneous consent to the "truth" of the American way of life: from the Puritans' annihilation of the Pequods in the name of their errand and the postrevolutionary Americans' removal and virtual extermination of the native American population in the name of Manifest Destiny, through the Spanish-American War and the imperial occupation of the Philippines to the Vietnam War, when, from a distant continent, the United States unleashed a technological fire power unprecedented in the history of warfare against a recalcitrant Southeast Asian people seeking its independence from colonial rule.

As my readings of Greene's *Quiet American*, Caputo's *A Rumor of War*, and O'Brien's *Going After Cacciato* have suggested, however, there are at least two significant and telling differences between the earlier historical manifestations of the violence inhering in this concentering exceptionalist American logic and that of the Vietnam War, both having to do with the globalization of geopolitical perspective. The former could be rationalized by appealing to a still intact nationalist understanding of international relations and/or to the Western "civilizational" ethos that easily justified "blaming the victim." America, on the other hand, undertook and conducted *this* war in a globalized—*postcolonial*—context. I mean a context that, as Edward Said observes in *Culture and Imperialism* by way of invoking the "contrapuntal" liberatory witness of postcolonial thinkers such as C. L. R. James, Frantz Fanon, George Antonius, Amilcar Cabral, and S. H. Alata, among others, who had made "the voyage in" to the metropolis, had gone far to delegitimize the authority of the nation-state and the identitarian binary logic of the Occidental imperial project.[15]

Reconstellated into the context of the *crisis* of the Truth discourse of the West precipitated by the postcolonial occasion, which is to say, the coming to its end—fulfillment/demise—of traditional Western imperialism, what was singular about the Vietnam War, in other words, was the *visible* incommensurability between America's justification of its intervention—to "save Vietnam" in the name of the "free world" ("civilization")—and its ruthlessly massive, brutal, and banal, though finally futile, execution of the war (of attrition), which killed and maimed possibly two million Vietnamese, mostly civilians, devastated a large portion of the Vietnamese earth, and in so doing destroyed its ancient rice culture, deracinated a deeply rooted people, and transformed them into a society of refugees. It is, as I have attempted to show, to this devastating paradox—this rendering visible of the violence hitherto hidden in the benign, accommodational logic of the American nation-state—that the literature of the Vietnam War I have written about bears symptomatic witness. At the beginning of *Dispatches*, where he meditates on an old map of Vietnam in his Saigon apartment, Michael Herr, in a gesture reminiscent of the parodic mode of Foucault's Nietzschian genealogy, pushes this devastating, but finally impotent territorializing logic (a logic that is reduced to its utterly dehumanized essence in the quotation from Robert Komer's press conference I have used as one of the epigraphs to this chapter) to its self-dissolving and carnivalesque end.[16] It thus may stand for the whole of the literature about *this* particular American war.

> *The Mission was always telling us about VC units being engaged and wiped out and then reappearing a month later in full strength, there was nothing very spooky about that, but when we went up against his terrain we usually took it definitively, and even if we didn't keep it you could always see that we'd been there. At the end of my first week in-country I met an information officer in the headquarters of the 25th Division at Cu Chi who showed me on his map and then from his chopper what they'd done to the Ho Bo Woods, the vanished Ho Bo Woods, taken off by giant Rome*

plows and chemicals and long, slow fire, wasting hundred of acres
of cultivated plantation and wild forest alike, "denying the enemy
valuable resources and cover."

It had been part of his job for nearly a year now to tell people
about that operation; correspondents, touring congressmen,
movie stars, corporate presidents, and staff officers from half the
armies in the world, and he still couldn't get over it. It seemed to
be keeping him young, his enthusiasm made you feel that even
the letters he wrote home to his wife were full of it, it really
showed what you could do if you had the know-how and the
hardware. And if in the months following that operation inci-
dences of enemy activity in the larger area of War Zone C had
increased "significantly," and American losses had doubled and
then doubled again, none of it was happening in any damn Ho
Bo Woods, you'd better believe it.[17]

The other difference, as we have seen, indissolubly related to the first, is that, despite its infinitely more powerful military might, the United States lost the war to the recalcitrant subaltern Other it would have subdued and accommodated to its *Logos*. And it lost it primarily because in this globalized postcolonial context—and by way of the disclosures released by the self-destruction of the end-oriented philosophical, epistemological, ecological, cultural, political, and military mechanisms of Western imperialism—America's Other, as Greene foresaw and Caputo, O'Brien, and many other veterans who have recalled their experience in writing have testified, *refused to be answerable* to the imperatives of the polyvalent American exceptionalist narrative. The Vietnamese's response rather was to be rhizomatically mobile, strategically indeterminate in its goals, erratic in its actions, indifferent to temporal and spatial boundaries, resistant (in its attunement to the slow motion of being) to the dictates of technological speed, and not least, invisible to America's techno-Ahabian gaze, all calculated to *decompose* the relay of American power extending back from its forward-oriented military machine through its progressivist capitalist cultural apparatus, to the instrumentalist (Franklinian "can-do") thinking that was envisioning, planning, and conducting the war from the remote distance of the Pentagon.

This double difference—an American war the ruthless, single-minded and banalized conduct of which disclosed the violence hidden in the benign American exceptionalist errand, on the one hand, and, by way of this banalized single-mindedness, enabled its Other to fracture its formidable war machine and reduce its power to impotence, on the other—constitutes the proleptic witness of Graham Greene's novel, written in the immediate aftermath of the Geneva Accords, about America's initial arrogant—and blind—intervention in Vietnam. Despite their efforts to personalize and then assimilate *this* war to war-in-general, this double difference, as I have shown, is also the symptomatic testimony of Philip Caputo's representative memoir, *A Rumor of War*, and Tim O'Brien's autobiographical novel, *Going After Cacciato*, whose mis-en-scènes span the period between 1965, when President Lyndon Johnson, justified by the fabricated Tonkin Bay incident, sent the first official combat troops to fight in the "Indian country" of Vietnam, and the Tet Offensive in 1968, which was the beginning of the end of the United States' bloody imperial involvement in that Southeast Asian country. This resonant witness to the visible contradiction between America's deeply backgrounded ontological justification of the Vietnam War and its single-minded, indeed, monomaniacal Ahabian practice has haunted the collective American consciousness since the fall of Saigon in 1975. This specter also explains the dominant culture's obsessive effort since then to forget Vietnam—an amnesiac monumentalizing process only apparently culminating in the first Gulf War and a triumphant "end-of-history" discourse—and its studied avoidance of reference to the Vietnam War in justifying to the American people and the world at large its ferocious retaliatory attack first on Afghanistan and then, using the language of "shock and awe," which resonates with the ferocity of Captain Ahab's "fiery pursuit" of the white whale, on Iraq.

This double difference is, I am suggesting, also why it is imperative that intellectuals, public and academic, who oppose the United States' representation and conduct of the "war on terror" retrieve the forgotten memory of the Vietnam War as Greene's, Caputo's, and O'Brien's representative texts articulate its singularity. For, as I have shown, their spectral witness to the terror of the "search-and-destroy" mentality inhering in the myth of American exceptionalism, despite the sustained effort to obliterate it from history, continues, in the aftermath of 9/11, to haunt the present American government's—and the American media's—reductive personification of the complex global conditions that Western imperialism and more recently America itself have largely produced in the name of its exceptionalist mission in the world's wilderness, in the demonized symbolic figures of Osama bin Laden and Saddam Hussein, its most recent Moby Dicks. The Vietnam War's spectral witness to a mighty America's humiliating defeat at the hands of an Other—*its* other that refused to answer to the accommodational imperatives of its exceptionalist story in Southeast Asia—has now, as the initial seemingly successful invasion of Iraq has turned unexpectedly into a destabilizing and volatile occupation, one resembling the Vietnam "quagmire," returned again to haunt America. As revenant, the singular history of the Vietnam War exposes America's metaphysical, epistemological, cultural, military, and political initiatives for what they are in a diverse and amorphous part of the world whose people have for centuries suffered the terrible consequences of being the second essentialized term in the Occident's binary logic. It is thus as likely as it was for the Vietnamese "enemy" that the decidedly undecidable "enemy" it is encountering there will turn the United States' inordinate power against itself.

To put all this in another way, the United States "succeeded" in its preemptive military mission to defeat the Taliban in Afghanistan and Saddam Hussein's army in Iraq. It has captured and hanged Saddam Hussein and may eventually capture and bring Osama bin Laden to trial (even, against the judicial tradition of democracy, to be tried by a military court). But granted these "accomplishments," President George W. Bush and his neoconservative intellectual deputies are no more likely to annul or even assuage the outrage that the United States has increasingly ignited both among its former European allies and the various Islamic peoples of the world at large by their concentering of the cultural, social, *and* political global morass their exceptionalist ethos has produced than Captain Ahab's "monomania"—was able to annul the self-defensive outrage of the ineffable "white" whale. This is becoming increasingly evident in the failure of this second Bush administration's monolithic effort to recreate the Afghanistani and Iraqi nation-states in its own (liberal capitalist) image (as the administrations of John F. Kennedy, Lyndon Baines Johnson, and Richard M. Nixon failed to recreate a Vietnamese nation-state in its own image in the 1960s and 1970s). It is also becoming increasingly evident in the diverse Iraqi peoples' spontaneous cultural and military resistance to the American occupation of their lands, a resistance that, ominously like that of the Vietnamese, refuses to be answerable to the United States' exceptionalist/Orientalist narrative and to the forwarding warfare that is endemic to it.

What I am suggesting by way of invoking the witness of the literature I have examined in this book about the ultimate consequences of America's predictably Ahabian response to the attacks on the World Trade Center and the Pentagon should become unequivocally manifest by reconstellating both these moments of American history into the "hidden history of the revolutionary Atlantic" (the period extending from the origins of the Atlantic slave trade to the revolutionary years) brilliantly retrieved by Peter Linebaugh and Marcus Rediker from the oblivion to which it has been relegated by the "Herculean" monumentalist historians of this earlier epochal moment of the march of Western civilization:

> The classically educated architects of the Atlantic economy
> found in Hercules . . . a symbol of power and order. For inspira-

tion they looked to the Greeks, for whom Hercules was a unifier of the centralized territorial state, and to the Romans, for whom he signified vast imperial ambition. The labors of Hercules symbolized economic development: clearing of land, the draining of swamps, and the development of agriculture, as well as the domestication of livestock, the establishment of commerce, and the introduction of technology. The rulers placed the image of Hercules on money and seals, in pictures, sculptures, and palaces, and on arches of triumph. . . . John Adams, for his part, proposed in 1776 that "The Judgment of Hercules" be the seal for the new United States of America. . . .

These same rulers found in the many-headed hydra an antithetical symbol of disorder and resistance, a powerful threat to the building of state, empire, and capitalism. The second labor of Hercules was the destruction of the venomous hydra of Lerna. . . .

From the beginning of English colonial expansion in the early seventeenth century through the metropolitan industrialization of the early nineteenth, rulers referred to the Hercules-hydra myth to describe the difficulty of imposing order on increasingly global systems of labor. They variously designated dispossessed commoners, transported felons, indentured servants, religious radicals, pirates, urban laborers, soldiers, sailors, and African slaves as the numerous ever-changing heads of the monster. But the heads, though originally brought into productive combination by their Herculean rulers, soon developed among themselves new forms of cooperation against those rulers, from mutinies and strikes to riots and insurrections and revolution.[18]

As Philip Caputo, Tim O'Brien, and virtually every American soldier who fought in Vietnam reiteratively testify, the insurgents of the National Liberation Front in Vietnam, like the many-headed hydra of European antiquity (and of the revolutionary Atlantic economy), were constantly defeated by the "Herculean" American military juggernaut, but they nevertheless kept rising up in unpredictable places and times to eventually bring their would-be monster-slayer to a dead end. Given the incommensurability of America's predictable invocation of the (mythical) logic of exceptionalism and the postcolonial globalized condition, there is little reason to believe that the hatred precipitated by the United States' perennial unilateral "defense" of its "interests" *in* the Islamic world—a defense expedited by its reduction of the diversity of this world to an abstract and predictable religioracist frontier stereotype, the "clash of civilizations"— will not also manifest itself as a "many-headed hydra" that will resurface

in unexpected places at unexpected times to constantly molecularize—
and neutralize the power of America—its narrative, its self-present will,
and its relentlessly forwarding military machine.

II

The consequence of the Vietnam War and the witness of those alienated
soldiers who fought it—they called themselves "grunts" in ironic awareness of their preterite status in the eyes of America's elect who sent them
to Vietnam—should have estranged the American national identity, unhomed it, changed its terrain, as it were. It should have shocked Americans into realizing that in this globalized postcolonial age—this age that
has borne massive witness to the paradoxical fulfillment and coming to
its end of Western imperialism—only a genealogically oriented rethinking
of America's perennial exceptionalist mission, a rethinking that understands America's arrogantly destructive modern (instrumentalist) global
policy in the light of the very formation of the American national identity,
will resolve the complex global conditions that are the dark legacy of
Western imperialism.

Despite the polyvalent witness of the Vietnam War—indeed, because of
it—the second Bush administration, in its arrogant, indeed, monomaniac
certainty of the History-ordained rightness of its crusade against "the axis of
evil" and the *Pax Americana*, has been studiedly impervious to the urgent
imperatives of such a rethinking. Indeed, like the Jeremiahs of the American past, its intellectual deputies, aware of the destabilizing demographic
transformations in the United States precipitated by the "deconstruction of
America" in the decade of the Vietnam War (the rise of recalcitrant "sub-
cultures" that threaten the hegemony of the "Anglo-Protestant core culture") have inaugurated an intellectual and cultural initiative intended to
re-"call" America to its founding exceptionalist ethos and mission. In his
highly orchestrated speech on September 11, 2006, commemorating the
fifth anniversary of the attacks on the World Trade Center and the Pentagon, President Bush, for example, echoing the long history of the American
jeremiad, said "the war against this enemy is more than a military conflict.
It is the ideological struggle of the 21st century, *and the calling of our generation.*"[19] Since the Vietnam War, a generation of New Americanists have
labored in their scholarship to bring to the surface the exceptionalist ideology that has been assimilated into the canonical literature and, through this,
inscribed in the cultural unconsciousness of the American people and to
point to the ravages that have been in large part its historical legacy. Their

purpose has not, as it has been crassly charged, been to instigate a rampant anti-Americanism,[20] but to stimulate a rethinking of American thinking that would be more sensitive to the complexities of the contemporary global occasion and commensurate to the threats these pose to all of humanity.[21] Now, in the post-Cold War period, when America has turned its geopolitical gaze to the Middle East, the policy makers of the Bush administration, when they do acknowledge dissent as legitimate rather than a form of collusion with terrorism, scoff at such proposals as symptomatic of Old World weakness (as Vice-President Dick Cheney did at the Republican National Convention in August 2004, in his sarcastic response to John Kerry's call for a more "sensitive" approach to foreign policy). And this arrogant reductiveness is, as I have shown, epitomized by the influential "policy expert," Samuel P. Huntington, who, willfully indifferent to this massively documented New Americanist scholarship (and to the testimony of the literature of the Vietnam War), reverts to the Orientalist Bernard Lewis's revisionist interpretation of the relationship of the West and Middle East during the Cold War era as "a clash of civilizations."[22] After September 11, 2001, calculatively attuned to the abiding centrality and enabling history of what Sacvan Bercovitch has identified as the "American jeremiad," Huntington openly and aggressively calls for a recuperation and reaffirmation of the "Anglo-Protestant core culture" and its exceptionalist ethos on which the fulfillment of America's divinely ordained errand in the wilderness depends—without, as we have seen, referring to the carnage and ravages, both on the continent and abroad, this providential errand has entailed.

The literature of the Vietnam War—and it is important to reiterate that it includes a great deal more than those "threshold texts" I have retrieved and reconstellated into the 9/11 aftermath—bears striking witness, like Greene's Fowler vis-à-vis Alden Pyle's blindness, to the innocent sea of blood spilled in the name of the unrelentingly banal American "vision" of those who inaugurated, planned, and executed the war. The "oversight" of what, after Althusser, I have called their American exceptionalist "problematic" precluded them from seeing this blood and, what is in the end the same thing, from realizing that this banalized way of seeing was a way of killing "at long range." As such, this witness is capable of estranging the world that the Bush administration, its intellectual deputies, and the American media "see" as a simple and inexorable "clash of civilizations," one good and the other evil. It enables us to retrieve and to *see* the world as infinitely various, differential, and complex—a "changed terrain," in Marx's resonant term—and thus to resist the territorialized world picture concocted by the neoconservative policy elite of the Bush administration to replace that of the Cold War. I mean a world picture that promises, not the *Pax Americana* they envision, but, as even they inadvertently acknowledge when they remind the American public that the "war on terror" does not have a foreseeable end, will be an ongoing undecidable war against an undecidable "terror"—not to say the establishment of a perpetual national state of emergency that, as the Patriot Act of 2002 and more recent presidentially enacted unconstitutional wiretapping promises, will play havoc with the civil rights of Americans who refuse their spontaneous consent to the truth discourse of the nation.

Let me invoke the theory of globalization that this book has tacitly questioned in overdetermining the (exceptionalist) nationalism that has relentlessly determined America's national identity and sociopolitical practice from its origins in the Puritan errand in the New World "wilderness" to its post-9/11 errand in the global "wilderness." What the spectral witness of this literature of the Vietnam War also enables us to see is that, however more complicated by the dynamics of a globalizing process propelled by the computerization of information transmission that is rendering time and space immediate, the rise of transnational capitalism and the globalization of the "free market," and the burgeoning of a proletariat of "immaterial labor," the contemporary global occasion remains tethered to the nation-state or to the metaphysics (and its panoptics) informing the idea of the nation-state as exemplified by the United States. It therefore directs us, not (yet) to the spectacle of a transnational capital that is automatically precipitating the sovereignty of "the multitude" as Negri and Hardt (and others) are alleging,[23] but to a global condition we might call an interregnum, to a resistance that, aware of the thinning out of the threads binding the periphery to the center endemic to the dynamics of the logic of accommodation of Enlightenment modernity, nevertheless remains tethered to the power relations of the center and periphery, or, rather, to the Achilles' heel of this nation-state model. I mean that contradiction in the logic of the nation-state which, at one extreme, manifests itself when the privileged center brutally "reduces" the peripheral corporeal Other to a specter that then comes back to haunt its authority—this is the way of nation-states that overdetermine totalitarian and overtly imperial ends. Or, antithetically, that contradiction which, at the other extreme, manifests itself when, in the process of increasingly accommodating its peripheral Other, the center self-destructs, when, to invoke my epigraph from Yeats, the widening gyre makes it no longer possible for the center to hold and "things fall apart." I have been arguing in this book that the United States has always identified itself with the latter, claiming to benignly accommodate the Other to democratic and anti-imperialist ends, while, in fact, its exceptionalist logic—and the perpetual frontier (or enemy) endemic to it—has perennially operated out of a barely concealed but virulent imperialism. Donald Pease and Amy Kaplan, among others, have led New Americanists in the exploration of American imperialism. Acutely aware of the reciprocality of the nation-state and imperialism, Kaplan, for example, argues that public under-standing of the American nation as a home became inextricable from the dynamics of empire: "Under the self-contained orderly home lies the anarchy of imperial conquest. Not a retreat from the masculine sphere of empire building, domesticity both reenacts and conceal its origin in the violent appropriation of foreign land. . . . 'Manifest Domesticity' turns an imperial nation into a home by producing and colonizing specters of the foreign that lurk inside and outside its ever-shifting borders."[24]

But the directives of the spectral witness (or witness of the spectral) of the threshold texts about the Vietnam War I have examined in this book suggest more than simply seeing the cultural variety that the American exceptionalist problematic has obscured from view. They also point to a way of *thinking* this singular cultural multiplicity positively. To rein-voke Edward Said's timely untimely meditation on the imperatives for perception and thought made urgent by the coming to its fulfillment and end of Western imperialism, they promise a new decentered, unhomed, or exilic thinking, a radically critical secularism, stripped of transcendental alibis, that would be commensurate to the task of transforming the dehumanizing discourse and practice of global clash into humanized global collaboration: a "'complete consort dancing together' contrapuntally."[25]

To return once more to Herman Melville's uncanny proleptic American witness, it will be recalled that Captain Ahab's "fiery pursuit" of the elusive white whale, like America's search and destroy mission in Vietnam, did not end in the decisive victory promised by its prophetic narrative; it ended, rather, in the destruction of the *Pequod*, Melville's symbol of the American ship of state. Only one survivor, who identifies himself as an or-phan—a defiliated, unfathered, and unhomed exile—remained to bear witness to America's devastating Adamic hubris. In this book about the literature of the Vietnam War, and by way of collaboratively invoking the post*structuralist* theory of non-American thinkers like Althusser, Heidegger, Foucault, Deleuze and Guattari, and Said and the corrosive "anti-American" fiction of Graham Greene, I have tried to show that Philip Caputo and Tim O'Brien—and the multitude of dead and mutilated veterans of the Vietnam War they resonantly represent—are all American Ish-maels who have *seen* America's shadow—and, in some degree or other, have become "it." It is finally this "Ishmaelite" witness that haunts the violence of America's Ahabian response to September 11, 2001.

III

Spy Story

The earth trembled,
a thread of fissure opened up,
and green fingers
reached out of the abyssal dark
grabbing at the asphalt street.
The people of the City
shuddered
and their good
their confident
their unerring
president
sent forth his tried team
of undercover agents
to get to the bottom
of this dreadful mystery.
With the help
of vernier calipers
they found the criminal
and called out
the army the navy the air force
to beat the old, many-headed
and irrepressible bitch
back in line.

NOTES

Preface

1. See Masao Miyoshi "'Globalization' and the University" in *The Cultures of Globalization*, ed. Fredric Jameson and Masao Miyoshi (Durham, N.C.: Duke University Press, 1998): "The opposition to the [Vietnam War] nearly split the country. Corporations such as GM, GE, and Dow chemical were often targets of fierce protest and denunciation, and labor demands for higher wages were also rising. It is thus no accident that huge corporations began to transfer their productions abroad in the 1960s and '70s, although there were other compelling reasons as well—such as increasing competition from Germany, and Japan, and other industrial nations. This is the time transnational corporations can be said to have commenced," p. 253.

2. Michael Hardt and Antonio Negri, *Empire* (Cambridge, Mass.: Harvard University Press, 2000), p. 142. See also Bill Readings, *The University in Ruins* (Cambridge, Mass.: Harvard University Press, 1996).

Chapter 1 History and Its Specter
Rethinking Thinking in the Post-Cold War Age

1. Francis Fukuyama, *The End of History and the Last Man* (New York: Free Press, 1992; originally published in essay form, "The End of History?," *The National Interest* (Summer 1989), 3–18. Further references will be abbreviated to *EH* and incorporated in the text in parentheses.

2. See, for example, Louis Montrose, "New Historicisms," in *Redrawing the Boundaries: The Transformation of English and American Literary Studies*, ed. Stephen Greenblatt and Giles Gunn (New York: Modern Language Association, 1992), 392–437. Some neo-Marxists took Fukuyama's annunciation seriously, but, paradoxically, not so much to challenge its claims about the end of history as to invoke certain

features of his argument to support their nostalgia for the metanarrative. See, for example, Fred Halliday, "An Encounter with Fukuyama," 89–95; Michael Rustin, "No Exit from Capitalism," 96–107, and Ralph Milliband, "Fukuyama and the Socialist Alternative," 108–113, all in *New Left Review*, No. 193 (May–June, 1992). The editors summarize these "encounters" with Fukuyama is the following way: "Though Fukuyama greatly overestimates the achievements and potential of liberal capitalism, and takes no account of the case for democratic socialism, his work, developing the tradition of Hegel's philosophy of history, has a scope and thoughtfulness that sets it apart from simple Western triumphalism." "Themes," p. 2.

3. Richard Haass, *The Reluctant Sheriff: The United States After the Cold War* (New York: Council on Foreign Relations, 1997). Further references will be abbreviated to *RS* and incorporated in the text in parentheses.

4. Alexis De Tocqueville, *Democracy in America*, vol. 1, trans. Henry Reeves, revised, Phillips Bradley (New York: Vintage, 1990), p. 6.

5. See, for example, Sacvan Bercovitch, *The American Jeremiad* (Madison: University of Wisconsin Press, 1978); Richard Drinnon, *Facing West: The Metaphysics of Indian Hating*, rev. ed. (New York: Schocken Books, 1990); and Richard Slotkin, *Regeneration Through Violence: The Mythology of the American Frontier, 1600–1860* (Hanover, N.H.: Wesleyan University Press, 1973), *The Fatal Environment: The Myth of the Frontier in the Age of Industrialization, 1800–1890* (Middletown, Conn.: Wesleyan University Press, 1985), and *Gunslinger Nation: The Myth of the Frontier in Twentieth-Century America* (New York: Athenaeam, 1992).

6. Francis Parkman, *France and England in North America*, 2 vols. (New York: Library of America, 1983) and *The Conspiracy of Pontiac* (New York: Library of America, 1991; originally published in 1851, followed by an expanded edition in1870); George Bancroft, *History of the United States*, 6 vols. (Port Washington, N.Y.: Kennikat Press, 1967); Frederick Jackson Turner, *The Frontier in American History* (New York: Henry Holt, 1953).

7. John Filson, *Life and Adventures of Colonel Daniel Boone* (1786); Joel Barlow, *The Columbiad* (1809); James Fenimore Cooper, *The Pioneers* (1823), *The Last of the Mohicans* (1826), *The Prairie* (1827), *The Pathfinder* (1840), and *The Deerslayer* (1841); Robert Montgomery Bird, *Nick of the Woods* (1837); William Gilmore Simms, *The Yemassee* (1835).

8. Tom Engelhardt, *The End of Victory Culture: Cold War America and the Disillusioning of a Generation* (New York: Basic Books, 1995).

9. Samuel P. Huntington, *Who Are We?: Challenges to America's National Identity* (New York: Simon and Schuster, 2004).

10. *Webster's Ninth New Collegiate Dictionary* (Springfield, Mass.: Merriam-Webster, 1984).

11. Jacques Derrida, *Specters of Marx: The State of the Debt, the Work of Mourning, and the New International,* trans. Peggy Kamuf (New York: Routledge, 1994), pp. 56–57. Further references will by abbreviated to *SM* and incorporated in the text in parentheses.

12. For a grotesque example of this rationalizing logic, see Robert McNamara, with Brian Van DeMark, *In Retrospect: The Tragedy and Lessons of Vietnam* (New York: Random House, 1995).

13. I am restricting my examples to nation-states that justified their exploitative imperial project in the name of some form of democracy or ameliorative higher cause, those, in fact, that always represent their intervention in the peripheral worlds by distinguishing it from that of such overtly rapacious nation states as Spain and Portugal (in Latin and South America), the Netherlands (in Indonesia), and Belgium (in the Congo), for example.

14. For a general interpretation of this history, see the chapter entitled "Vietnam and the *Pax Americana*: A Genealogy of the 'New World Order,'" in Spanos, *America's Shadow: An Anatomy of Empire* (Minneapolis: University of Minnesota Press, 2000), pp. 126–169.

15. See especially Fredric Jameson, *Postmodernism; Or the Logic of Late Capitalism* (Durham: Duke University Press, 1990); Michael Hardt and Antonio Negri, *Empire* (Cambridge, Mass.: Harvard University Press, 2000); Edward W. Said, *Humanism and Democratic Criticism* (New York: Columbia University Press, 2005); and Timothy Brennan, *Wars of Position* (New York: Columbia University Press, 2005).

16. See Richard Ohmann's still timely, though now more or less forgotten, analysis of the deadly banality of the memoranda that constitute the Pentagon Papers in *English in America: A Radical View of the Profession* (New York: Oxford University Press, 1976), pp. 190–206. See also pp. 202–203.

17. Michael Herr, *Dispatches* (New York: Vintage International, 1991), p. 71.

18. Antonio Gramsci, *Selections from the Prison Notebooks,* ed. and trans. Quintin Hoare and Geoffrey Nowell Smith (New York: International Publishers, 1971), p. 12.

19. General William C. Westmoreland, the commander of American forces in Vietnam, was even more precise in his representation of the American public's anxiety about America's conduct of the war: "I fear that one of the big losses, in fact, probably the most serious loss of the war, is what I refer to as the Vietnam pyschosis. Any time anybody brings up the thought that military forces might be needed, you hear the old hue

and cry 'another Vietnam, another Vietnam.' That can be a real liability to *us as we* look to the future." "Vietnam in Perspective," in *Vietnam: Four American Perspectives*, ed. Patrick J. Hearden (West Lafayette, Indiana: Purdue University Press, 1990), p. 45. My emphasis.

20. Niall Ferguson, *Colossus: The Rise and Fall of the American Empire* (New York: Penguin, 2004); Michael Mandelbawn, *The Case for Goliath: How America Acts as the World's Government in the Twenty-first Century* (New York: PublicAffairs, 2005).

21. See Foucault, *The History of Sexuality, Vol. I: An Introduction*, trans. Robert Hurley (New York: Pantheon Books, 1978), p. 10. See also Spanos, "Heidegger and Foucault: The Politics of the Commanding Gaze," in *Heidegger and Criticism*, pp. 168–171.

22. Joseph Conrad, *Heart of Darkness*, 3rd ed., ed. Robert Kimbrough (New York: Norton, 1988), p.11.

23. Edward W. Said, *Orientalism* (New York: Knopf, 1977), p. 92.

24. The massive effort of the Western (especially America) cultural memory to obliterate the actual history of the Vietnam War has not been restricted to the war as such. An important, indeed, fundamental, aspect of this will to forget has been—and continues to be—the project of delegitimizing the philosophical discourses that have theorized the ideological implications of this differential history. I am referring, of course, to destruction or deconstruction, which, more than any other "postmodern" discourse, has most decisively disclosed the contradictory violence informing the metaphysical principles—the anthropology—of Enlightenment liberal democracy. See Spanos, "Heidegger, Nazism and the 'Repressive Hypothesis,'" in *Heidegger and Criticism*, pp. 235–238. Related to this ideological initiative is that which identifies the oppositional (mainly "multicultural") educational practices enabled by these theoretical discourses as "political correctness," indeed, as a "new McCarthyism of the Left."

25. The significant exception to this state of affairs is that growing momentum called global studies, most forcefully represented by Fredric Jameson's *Postmodernism; Or the Cultural Logic of Late Capitalism*; Michael Hardt and Antonio Negri's *Empire* and *Multitude*; Bill Readings *The University in Ruins* (Cambridge, Mass.: Harvard University Press, 1996); Arjun Appudurai's *Modernity at Large: Cultural Dimensions of Globalization* (Minneapolis: University of Minnesota Press, 1996); the essays in *Cultures of Globalization*, ed. Fredric Jameson and Masao Miyoshi (Durham, N.C.: Duke University Press, 1998). All these have their point of departure in the thesis of the rise to global sovereignty of transnational capitalism and the waning of the nation-state. This is a welcomed turn in oppositional criticism, but insofar as this momentum assumes the rise to global sovereignty of transnational capitalism as a fait

accompli, as Negri and Hardt do, it is a representation of the contemporary occasion that is premature. This is borne witness to not only by the global imperialist role the United States—as a nation-state—has assumed since 9/11, but also, as I will show in chapter 6, by its philosophical (American exceptionalist) justification of this missionary role.

26. Martin Heidegger, "The Question Concerning Technology," pp. 17–19; "The Age of the World Picture," pp. 115–154, in *The Question Concerning Technology and Other Essays*, trans. William Lovitt (New York: Harper & Row, 1977).

27. I borrow this term from Antonio Gramsci by way of Paul Bové, "Introduction" to Marcia Landy, *Film, Politics, and Gramsci* (Minneapolis: University of Minnesota Press, 1994), p. xvii.

28. Heidegger, "Language in the Poem: A Discussion on Georg Trakl's Poetic Work," trans. Peter D. Hartz (New York: Harper & Row, 1971), pp. 178–179. Further references will be abbreviated to *LP* and cited in the text. My interpretation of the *Abgeschiedene* is indebted to Jacques Derrida's reading of Heidegger's essay on Trakl in *Of Spirit*, but it also contests it.

29. Martin Heidegger, "Hölderlin and the Essence of Poetry," trans. Douglas Scott, in *Existence and Being*, ed. with Introduction, Werner Brock (Chicago: Henry Regnery, 1949), p. 289.

30. Derrida, *Specters of Marx*, pp. 100–101. Though Derrida does not make the connection between this postmetaphysical reversal of the direction of this perennial Western gaze with the postcolonial project, it is not accidental that much colonialist literature self-destructs precisely at that point when it becomes conscious of this reversal, when the colonial protagonist realizes that he is being *looked at* by the indigene Other, when, that is, the imperial visitor becomes the visited. See, for example, Joseph Conrad's *Heart of Darkness* (New York: Norton, 1988): "And this stillness of life did not in the least resemble peace. It was the stillness of an implacable force brooding over an inscrutable intention. It looked at you with a vengeful aspect," p. 36; George Orwell's "Shooting an Elephant," in *A Collection of Essays* (New York: Anchor Books, 1957): "Here was I, the white man with his gun, standing in front of the unarmed native crowd—seeming the leading actor of the piece; but in reality I was only an absurd puppet pushed to and fro by the will of those yellow faces behind. I perceived in this moment that when the white man turns tyrant it is his own freedom that he destroys. He becomes a sort of hollow, posing dummy, the conventional figure of a sahib. For it is the condition of his rule that he shall spend his life in trying to impress the 'natives,' and as in every crisis he has got to do what the 'natives' expect of him. He wears a mask, and his face grows to fit it. I had got to shoot the elephant," p. 159; and Tim O'Brien's *The Things They Carried* (New

York: Penguin, 1990): "We called the enemy ghosts. 'Bad night,' we'd say, 'the ghosts are out.' . . . The countryside itself seemed spooky—shadows and tunnels and incense burning in the dark. The land was haunted. We were fighting forces that did not obey the laws of twentieth-century science," pp. 228–229.

Nor is it accidental that the rhetoric of much postcolonial theory and criticism finds its directive in this reversal of the panoptic imperial gaze. See, for example, Malek Alloula, *The Colonial Harem*, trans. Myrna Godzich and Wlad Godzich (Minneapolis: University of Minnesota Press, 1986); Mary Louise Pratt, *Imperial Eyes: Travel Writing and Transculturation* (New York: Routledge, 1992); Homi K. Bhabha, "Interrogating Identity: Frantz Fanon and the Postcolonial Prerogative," in *The Location of Culture* (New York: Routledge, 1994), pp. 40–65; and Ranajit Guha, "Not at Home in Empire," *Critical Inquiry*, vol. 23 (Spring 1997), 482–493. See, above all, Edward W. Said, "A Note on Modernism," in *Culture and Imperialism* (New York: Knopf, 1993). After noting that the Orient "impinges" on the anxious metropolitan artistic consciousness—Conrad, Malraux, T. E. Lawrence, Forster, Joyce, Mann—in a way it did not when Jane Austen wrote *Mansfield Park* in the 1820s, he adds, "only now instead of being *out there*, they are *here*, as troubling as the primitive rhythms of the *Sacre du printemps* or the African icons of Picasso's art," p. 188. I will return insistently in this book to this fundamental (optically articulated) *witness* of the American soldiers who fought in the Vietnam War.

31. Edward W. Said, *Culture and Imperialism*, pp. 331–333. (My emphasis.)

32. I am referring to the kind of institutional "postcolonial" criticism embodied in such texts as Bill Aschcroft, Gareth Griffiths, and Helen Tifflin, eds. *The Empire Writes Back: Theory and Practice in Post-Colonial Literatures*; Mary Louise Pratt, *Imperial Eyes: Travel Writing and Transculturation* (London: Routledge, 1989); Elleke Boehmer, *Colonial and Postcolonial Literature* (Oxford: Oxford University Press, 1995).

33. See Gayatri Spivak, "Explanation and Culture," in *In Other Worlds* (New York: Methuen, 1987), pp. 103–117, and "Marginality in the Teaching Machine," in *Outside in the Teaching Machine* (New York: Routledge, 1993), pp. 53–76. The critics of the Indian Subaltern Studies Group constitute exceptions to this disabling tendency to minimize the ontological question. See, for example, Ranajit Guha, *Elementary Aspects of Peasant Insurgency in Colonial India* (Delhi: Oxford University Press, 1983); Ashish Nandy, *The Intimate Enemy: Loss and the Recovery of Self under Colonial Rule* (Delhi: Oxford University Press, 1983); Partha Chatterjee, *Nationalist Thought and the Colonial World: A Derivative Discourse* (London: Zed Books, 1986) and *The Nation and Its Fragments: Colonial and Postcolonial Histories* (Princeton, N.J.: Princeton University

Press, 1993); Dipesh Chakrabarty, *Provincializing Europe: Postcolonial Thought and Historical Difference* (Princeton, N.J.: Princeton University Press, 2000) and *Habitations of Modernity: Essays in the Wake of Subaltern Studies* (Chicago: University of Chicago Press, 2002).

34. According to Heidegger, as I will show at length in later chapters, this epochal transformation began with the Romans' reduction of the Greeks' originative or errant thinking to a derivative and calculative thinking: a visualist mode that lends itself to imperial practice. In the process of thinking the Roman "*falsum*" (the opposite of *veritas*: truth), Heidegger observes: "The surmounting overseeing [that is intrinsic to the binary opposition between the true and the false] denotes the dominating 'sight' expressed in the often quoted phrase of Caesar: *veni, vidi, vici*—I came, I *oversaw*, and I conquered. The essence of the *imperium* resides in the *actus* of constant 'action.' The imperial *actio* of the constant surmounting of others includes the sense that the others, should they rise to the same or even to a neighboring level of command, will be brought down—in Latin *fallere* (participle: *falsum*)." Heidegger then goes on to distinguish between two kind of imperialism, the second of which, insofar as it overdetermines the indissoluble relation of truth and power that had hitherto been strategically represented as incommensurate and antagonistic categories (it is a version of what Foucault calls the "repressive hypothesis") constitutes the essence of the imperial project, of what has come to be called "neoimperialism." *Parmenides*, trans. André Schuwer and Richard Rojcewicz (Bloomington: University of Indiana Press, 1992), p. 41. See also the chapter entitled "Culture and Colonization: The Imperial Imperatives of the Centered Circle," in Spanos, *America's Shadow: An Anatomy of Empire* (Minneapolis: University of Minnesota Press, 2000).

35. By the "colonial project proper," I mean, in opposition to the connotations of "imperialism" (brutal conquest and exploitation), the process of ventriloquizing the voice of the Other by way of establishing *administerial* institutions—census-taking, administrative bureaucracies, schools, "self-governance," that is, those biopolitical instruments invented by the European Enlightenment to reduce the potential threat of the hitherto overtly oppressed to useful and docile bodies. See especially Frantz Fanon, *The Wretched of the Earth*, trans. Richard Wilcox (New York: Grove Press, 2004; originally published in 1961).

36. Since these by now sedimented key "concepts" of postmetaphysical thinking have been hitherto thought more or less independently of each other (i.e., disciplinarily), it might be useful, for the sake of suggesting their interrelatedness, to provide a selected bibliography that recalls their provenance: Martin Heidegger, "What Is Metaphysics?, *Basic Writings*, pp. 93–110; Jean-Paul Sartre, *Being and Nothingness: An Essay of Philosophical Ontology*, trans. Hazel Barnes (New York: Philosophical

Library, 1956); Jacques Derrida, *"Differance,"* in *Speech and Phenomena: and Other Essays*, trans. David B. Allison (Evanston, Ill.: Northwestern University Press, 1973); Emmanuel Levinas, *Totality and Infinity: An Essay on Exteriority*, trans. Alfonso Lingis (Pittsburgh: Duquesne University Press, 1969); Jean-François Lyotard, *The Differend: Phrases in Dispute*, trans. Georges Van Den Abbeele (Minneapolis: University of Minnesota Press, 1988); Louis Althusser, "From *Capital* to Marx's Philosophy," in Althusser and Étienne Balibar, *Reading* Capital (London: Verso, 1979).

37. Hannah Arendt, *The Origins of Totalitarianism* (San Diego: Harcourt Brace, 1979), pp. 61–62; Gilles Deleuze and Félix Guattari, *A Thousand Plateaus: Capitalism and Schizophrenia*, trans. Brian Massumi (Minneapolis: University of Minnesota Press, 1987); Homi Bhabha "DissemiNation: Time, Narrative, and the Margins of the Modern Nation," in *Nation and Narration*, ed. Bhabha (New York: Routledge, 1990), pp. 191–222, and "The Commitment to Theory," in *The Location of Culture*, pp. 19–39; Enrique Dusssel, *The Philosophy of Liberation*, trans. Aquilina Martinez and Christine Morkovsky (Maryknoll, N.Y.: Orbis Press, 1985), and *The Invention of America: Eclipse of the "Other" and the Myth of Modernity* (New York: Continuum Books, 1995); Gayatri Spivak, "Marginality in the Teaching Machine," in *Outside in the Teaching Machine* (New York: Routledge, 1993), pp. 53–76; Edward W. Said, *Culture and Imperialism*; Tomas Hammar, *Democracy and the Nation State: Aliens, Denizens, and Citizens in a World of International Migrations* (Brookfield, Vt.: Gower, 1990); Giorgio Agamben, "Beyond Human Rights," trans. Cesare Casarino, in *Radical Thought in Italy: A Potential Politics*, ed. Paolo Virno and Michael Hardt (Minneapolis: University of Minnesota Press, 1996) and *Homo Sacer: Sovereign Power and Bare Life*, trans. Daniel Heller-Roazen (Stanford: Stanford University Press, 1998); Teresa de Lauretis, *Alice Doesn't: Feminism, Semiotics, Cinema* (Bloomington: Indiana University Press, 1988); Eve Kosofsky Sedgwick, *Epistemology of the Closet* (Berkeley: University of California Press, 1990); Judith Butler, *Gender Trouble* (New York: Routledge, 1990); Michael Warner, *Public and Counterpublic* (Boston: Zone Books, 2002); Michael Hardt and Antonio Negri, *Empire* (Cambridge, Mass.: Harvard University Press, 2000), and *Multitude: War and Democracy in the Age of Empire* (New York: Penguin, 2004).

38. Toni Morrison, *Playing in the Dark: Whiteness and the Literary Imagination* (New York: Vintage Books, 1993), p. 33.

39. Martin Heidegger, "What Is Metaphysics?," pp. 95–96. I will amplify on this neglected yet fundamental Heideggerian thesis at greater length later in this book.

40. Jacques Derrida, "White Mythology: Metaphor in the Text of Philosophy," *Margins of Philosophy*, trans. Alan Bass (Chicago: University of Chicago Press, 1982), pp. 207–271. For notable exceptions to this forgetting, see Homi Bhabha, *The Location of Culture*; Gayatri Spivak, *Outside in the Teaching Machine*; Robert Young, *White Mythologies: Writing History and the West* (New York: Routledge, 1990); J. M. Coetzee, *White Writing: On the Culture of Letters in South Africa* (New Haven: Yale University Press, 1989); Syed Manzurui Islam, *The Ethics of Travel: From Marco Polo to Kafka* (Manchester: Manchester University Press, 1996); and the Subaltern Studies Group cited above in footnote 33.

41. G. W. F. Hegel, *The Philosophy of History*, trans. J. Sibree (New York: Dover, 1956), pp. 103–104. It is worth noting that Derrida quotes this passage in "White Mythology," *Margins*, p. 269, since it suggests that the exposure of the complicity of Western ontological representation with racist imperialism has been an abiding, if peripheral, intention of Derrida's deconstructive thinking from the beginning.

42. Michel Foucault, *Discipline and Punish: The Birth of the Prison*, trans. Alan Sheridan (New York: Pantheon, 1977), p. 205.

43. See especially Paul de Man, *Allegories of Reading* (New Haven: Yale University Press, 1979); Jonathan Culler, *On Deconstruction: Theory and Criticism after Structuralism* (Ithaca, N.Y.: Cornell University Press, 1982). Barbara Johnson, *The Critical Difference: Essays in the Contemporary Rhetoric of Reading* (Baltimore: Johns Hopkins University Press, 1980); Christopher Norris, *The Deconstructive Turn: Essays in the Rhetoric of Philosophy* (London: Methuen, 1983); J. Hillis Miller, *The Ethics of Reading: Kant, de Man, Eliot, Trollope, James, Benjamin* (New York: Columbia University Press, 1987).

44. See, for example, Benita Parry, "Problems in Current Theories of Colonial Discourses," in *Oxford Literary Review*, vol. 9 (1987); Rey Chow, *Writing Diaspora: Tactics of Intervention in Contemporary Cultural Studies* (Bloomington: Indiana University Press, 1993); Asha Varadharajan, *Exotic Parodies: Subjectivity in Adorno, Said, and Spivak* (Minneapolis: University of Minnesota Press, 1995).

45. As Foucault puts this kind of genealogical history, "I would like to write the history of the prison with all the political investments of the body that it gathers together in its closed architecture. Why? Simply because I am interested in the past? No, if one means by that writing a history of the past in terms of the present. Yes, if one means writing the history of the present." *Discipline and Punish*, p. 31.

46. Martin Heidegger, *Being and Time*, trans. John Macquarrie and Edward Robinson (New York: Harper & Row, 1962), p. 44. Heidegger's emphasis.

47. Fredric Jameson, *Postmodernism; or, The Logic of Late Capitalism*; Arjun Appadurai, *Modernity at Large: Cultural Dimensions of Globalization*; Bill Readings, *The University in Ruins*; Michael Hardt and Antonio Negri, *Empire*.

48. Michael Hardt and Antonio Negro, *Empire*, p. 138.

49. Edward Said, *Culture and Imperialism*, p. 233.

50. Said, *Culture and Imperialism*, p. 333. The quote within the quote is from T. S. Eliot's "Four Quartets."

Chapter 2   Althusser's "Problematic" Vision and the Vietnam War

1. This failure to think the meaning that Althusser attributes to his concept of the problematic is symptomatically disclosed in *The Althusserian Legacy*, ed. E. Ann Kaplan and Michael Sprinker (London: Verso, 1993), which purports to articulate that which in his Marxist thought remains fundamentally relevant to the contemporary occasion. What is noteworthy about this book, which contains essays on Althusser's legacy by a large number of prominent "Marxist" thinkers, is the paradox that none of the contributors sees fit to identify his concept of the problematic as one of his lasting legacies, while at the same time the word pervades their discourse. Ellen Rooney goes far to retrieve the original force of Althusser's concept in "Better Read than Dead: Althusser and the Fetish of Ideology," in *Yale French Studies* 88 (1995). Invoking Althusser's marginalized discussion of this concept in the introduction to *Reading* Capital, "From Capital to Marx's Philosophy," she asserts the importance the visual metaphorics of "blindness and insight" plays in its operations (p. 187). But insofar as she restricts the vision/blindness of the problematic to the question of reading in general at the expense of its ontological ground—the provenance of the problematic in Western metaphysics—she, unwittingly, overdetermines the resulting undecidability of meaning and thus comes precariously close to enacting what she would eschew (p. 192).

2. Gayatri Spivak, *Outside in the Teaching Machine* (New York: Routledge, 1993); and Edward W. Said, *Culture and Imperialism* (New York: Knopf, 1993), p. 332.

3. George Bush, to a group of legislators, reported in *Newsweek*, 117, March 11, 1991.

4. Francis Fukuyama, *The End of History and the Last Man* (New York, 1993), p. 45. The emphasis in the last sentence is mine. World events since the publication of Fukuyama's book have dampened the euphoria it first precipitated within the dominant (conservative and liberal) order. But

this should not suggest that they have delegitimized the end-of-history discourse. Rather, these events have precipitated a readjustment that has *accommodated* them to this discourse, one that, in admitting their reality, renders it more powerful. As I pointed out in chapter 1, an exemplary theorization of this accommodation can be found in Richard N. Haass, *The Reluctant Sheriff: The United States After the Cold War* (Washington, D.C.: Council on Foreign Relations, 1997).

5. See the chapter entitled "The Vietnam War and the *Pax Americana*: A Genealogy of the New World Order" in Spanos, *America's Shadow: An Anatomy of Empire* (Minneapolis: University of Minnesota Press, 2000), pp. 126–169. See also John Hellman, *American Myth and the Legacy of the Vietnam War* (New York: Columbia University Press, 1986); and Tom Englehardt, *The End of Victory Culture: Cold War America and the Disillusioning of a Generation* (New York: Basic Books, 1995); and Richard Berg and John Carlos Rowe, "Eyewitness: Documentary Styles in the American Representation of the Vietnam War," in *The Vietnam War and American Culture*, eds. Rowe and Rick Berg (New York: Columbia University Press, 1991), pp. 48–74.

6. Martin Heidegger, "The Age of the World Picture," in *The Question Concerning Technology and Other Essays*, trans. William Lovitt (New York: Harper and Row, 1977), 3–35.

7. Heidegger, *Introduction to Metaphysics*, trans. Ralph Manheim (New Haven: Yale University Press, 1959). Many years later, Enrique Dussels refers to this same global phenomenon as "the rational management of the world system" in "Beyond Eurocentrism: The World System and the Limits of Modernity," in *The Cultures of Globalization*, ed. Fredric Jameson and Masao Miyoshi (Durham, N.C.: Duke University Press, 1998), p. 19.

8. Martin Heidegger, "What Is Metaphysics?" in *Basic Writings*, ed. and trans. David Farrell Krell (New York: Harper and Row, 1993), p. 96.

9. Jacques Derrida, *Specters of Marx: The State, the Debt, the Work of Mourning, and the New International*, trans. Peggy Kamuf (New York: Routledge, 1994), pp. 6–7.

10. Louis Althusser, "Ideology and Ideological States Apparatuses: Notes towards an Investigation," in *Lenin and Philosophy and Other Essays*, trans. Ben Brewster (London: NLB 1971), p. 142.

11. Martin Heidegger, *Being and Time*, trans. John Macquarrie and Edward Robinson (New York: Harper and Row, 1962), p. 232.

12. Louis Althusser "From *Capital* to Marx's Philosophy," in *Reading* Capital, trans. Ben Brewster (London: Verso, 1979), p. 25; my emphasis. Further references will be abbreviated to CMP and incorporated in the text in parentheses.

13. Ben Brewster, "Glossary," in Althusser, *For Marx*, trans. Ben Brewster (London: NLB, 1977), p. 254.

14. Edward W. Said, *Orientalism* (New York: Vintage Books, 1979), p. 53.

15. Aijaz Ahmad, *In Theory: Classes, Nations, Literatures* (London: Verso, 1992); Christopher Norris, *Truth and the Ethics of Criticism* (Manchester: Manchester University Press 1994); Terry Eagleton, *The Illusions of Postmodernism* (Oxford: Oxford University Press, 1996); Timothy Bewes, *Cynicism and Postmodernity* (London: Verso, 1997); Perry Anderson, *The Origins of Postmodernity* (London: Verso, 1998).

16. Edward W. Said, *Humanism and Democratic Criticism* (New York: Columbia University Press, 2004). See Spanos, "Humanism and the *Studia Humanitatis* After 9/11: Rethinking the Anthropologos," *Symploké*, Nos. 1–2(2005), 218–262.

17. I am emphasizing the ontological dimension of Althusser's political theory—and its use value as an instrument of political critique in the post-Cold War occasion—simply because it is virtually systematically overlooked by the privileged forms of oppositional critique. What I am suggesting is that, for Althusser, ontology and politics, theory and practice, are indissolubly related, and that no critique of the dominant culture's representation of the post-Cold War occasion and its "war on terror" in the aftermath of 9/11 can be adequate that does not recognize this.

18. Edward W. Said, *Culture and Imperialism*, pp. 330–336.

19. Althusser, "Ideology and Ideological State Apparatuses": "Yes, the subjects 'work by themselves.' . . . In the ordinary use of the term, subject in fact means: (1) a free subjectivity, a centre of initiatives, author of and responsible for its actions; (2) a subjected being, who submits to a higher authority, and is therefore stripped of all freedom except that of freely accepting his submission. . . . [T]the individual *is interpellated as a (free) subject in order that he shall submit freely to the commandments of the Subject, i.e. in order that he shall (freely) accept his subjection*, i.e. in order that he shall make the gestures and actions of his subjection 'all by himself'. *There are no subjects except by and for their subjection. That is why they 'work all by themselves'*," pp. 181–182).

20. Paul A. Bové, *In the Wake of Theory* (Hanover, N.H.: Wesleyan University Press, 1992).

21. Jacques Lacan, *Écrit* (London: Tavistock, 1977).

22. Emmanuel Levinas, *Totality and Infinity: An Essay on Exteriority*, trans. Alphonus Lingis (Pittsburgh: Duquesne University Press, 1969), p. 45.

23. Jacques Derrida, *Specters of Marx*, p.100.

24. Jean-François Lyotard, *Differend: Phrases in Dispute*, trans: G. Van Den Abbele (Minneapolis: University of Minnesota Press, 1990).

25. Gilles Deleuze and Félix Guattari, *A Thousand Plateaus: Capitalism and Schizophrenia*, trans. Brian Massumi (Minneapolis, University of Minnesota Press, 1987), pp. 424 ff.

26. Derrida, "Structure Sign and Play in the Discourse of the Human Sciences," in *Writing and Difference*, trans. Alan Bass (Chicago: University of Chicago Press, 1977), p. 278.

27. Phillipe Lacoue-Labarthe, *La fiction du politique: Heidegger, l'art et la politique* (Paris: Christian Bourgeois Editeur, 1987), p. 59.

28. Enrique Dussel, *Philosophy of Liberation*, trans. A. Martinez and C. Morkovsky (Maryknoll, N.Y.: Orbis Press, 1985), p. 14. See also Dussel, *The Invention of America: Eclipse of 'the Other' and the Myth of Modernity* (New York: Continuum, 1992). See also Walter D. Mignolo, "Globalization, Civilizational Processes, and the Relocation of Languages and Cultures," in Jameson and Miyoshi, *The Cultures of Globalization*, pp. 32–53, particularly his discussion of "border [or "barbarian"] gnoseology," pp. 44–46.

29. Deleuze and Guattari, *A Thousand Plateaus*, pp. 21–22. See also the section entitled "Treatise on Nomadology," pp. 351–423.

30. See Herman Rapaport's brilliant Deleuzian reading of the NLF's "molecularizing" strategy in "Vietnam: The Thousand Plateaus" in *The Sixties without Apologies*, ed. Sonya Sayres et al. (Minneapolis: University of Minnesota Press, in cooperation with *Social Text*, 1984), p 139.

31. I am referring to the neoconservative think tank called Project for the New American Century (PNAC), which authorized "Rebuilding America's Defences," the policy paper that advocated total global domination by America and the unilateral invasion of Iraq long before George W. Bush was elected president in 2000.

32. Frantz Fanon, *The Wretched of the Earth*, trans. Richard Wilcox (New York: Grove Press, 2004).

Chapter 3   Who Killed Alden Pyle?
The Oversight of Oversight in Graham Greene's
The Quiet American

1. Graham Greene, *The Quiet American* (New York: Penguin, 1977; first published in 1955 by Heinemann), p. 140. Further references will be abbreviated as *QA* and incorporated in the text in parentheses.

2. The most succinct and accurate characterization of Gramsci's concept of hegemony is that of Raymond Williams in *Marxism and Literature* (Oxford: Oxford University Press, 1977), pp. 108–114.

3. See Jacques Derrida, "White Mythology: Metaphor in the Text of Philosophy," *Margins of Philosophy*, trans. Alan Bass (Chicago: University of Chicago Press, 1982), pp. 207–271.

4. See "Ideology and Ideological State Apparatuses," in *Lenin and Philosophy and Other Essays*, trans. Ben Brewster (New York: Monthly Review Press, 1971), p. 141.

5. Louis Althusser, "From *Capital* to Marx's Philosophy," in Althusser and Etienne Balibar, *Reading* Capital (London: Verso, 1979), p. 24. Further references will be abbreviated to CMP and incorporated in the text in parentheses.

6. Edward W. Said, *Orientalism* (New York: Vintage Books, 1979), pp. 91–92.

7. Martin Heidegger, "What Is Metaphysics?" in *Basic Writings*, rev. ed., ed. David Farrell Krell (San Francisco: HarperSanFrancisco, 1993), p. 96.

8. See Spanos, *The End of Education: Toward Posthumanism* (Minneapolis: University of Minnesota Press, 1993), pp. 71–78.

9. Paul de Man refers to this radical limitation of visualist perception as "the blindness of insight," but for obvious reasons, I prefer to call it the blindness of oversight. See de Man, *Blindness and Insight: Essays in the Rhetoric of Contemporary Criticism* (New York: Oxford University Press, 1971), pp. 106–107.

10. John Winthrop, "A Modell of Christian Charity," in *The American Puritans: Their Prose and Their Poetry*, ed. Perry Miller (New York: Doubleday, 1956), pp. 79–84. The phrase "errand in the wilderness" derives from the Puritan Samuel Danforth's election sermon, delivered on May 11, 1670: *A Brief Recognition of New England's Errand into the Wilderness*. See Sacvan Bercovitch, *The American Jeremiad* (Madison: University of Wisconsin Press, 1978), pp. 12–17.

11. In thus invoking the myth of American exceptionalism, indeed, its origins in the Puritans' divinely ordained "errand in the wilderness," Greene anticipates—perhaps is the source of—Michael Herr's brilliant genealogy of America's exceptionalist problematic, its intervention in Vietnam, and its conduct of the war: "You couldn't find two people who agreed about when it began, how could you say when it began going off? Mission intellectuals like 1954 as the reference date. . . . Anyway, you couldn't use standard methods to date the doom; might as well say that Vietnam was where the Trail of Tears [Indian Removal during, above all, the Andrew Jackson administration] was headed all along, the turnabout point where it would touch and come back to form a containing perimeter; might just as well lay it on the proto-Gringos who found the New England woods too raw and empty for their peace and filled them up with their imported devils. Maybe

it was already over for us in Indochina when Alden Pyle's body washed up under the bridge at Dakao, his lungs all full of mud; maybe it caved in with Dien Bien Phu. But the first happened in a novel, and while the second happened on the ground it happened to the French, and Washington gave it no more substance than if Graham Greene had made it up too. Straight history, auto-revised history, history without handles, for all the books and articles and white papers, all the talk and the miles of film, something wasn't answered, it wasn't asked. We were backgrounded, deep, but when the background started sliding forward not a single life was saved by the information." *Dispatches* (New York: 1991), pp. 49–50.

12. See Richard Slotkin, *Regeneration through Violence* (Hanover, N.H.: Wesleyan University Press, 1973).

13. See, for example, James Fenimore Cooper's Leatherstocking novels, particularly *The Pioneers* (1823) and *The Deerslayer* (1941), and Francis Parkman, *The Conspiracy of Pontiac* (1851).

14. Alexis de Tocqueville, *Democracy in America* (New York: Vintage Books, 1990): "The gradual development of the principle of equality [in America] is . . . a providential fact. It has all the characteristics of such a fact: it is universal, it is lasting, it constantly eludes all human interference, and all events as well as all men contribute to its progress," p. 6.

15. See John Hellman, *American Myth and the Legacy of Vietnam* (New York: Columbia University Press, 1986), p. 22. See also Sacvan Bercovitch, *The American Jeremiad*.

16. James Fenimore Cooper, *The Pioneers* (New York: Oxford University Press, 1991), p. 456. For a proleptic genealogy of the cultural apotheosis of the American backwoodsman that exposes the dark underside of the myth, see the chapter entitled "The Metaphysics of Indian Hating" in Herman Melville, *The Confidence-Man: His Masquerade* (Evanston, Ill.: Northwestern University Press, 1984), especially, pp. 149–150. See also Richard Drinnon, *Facing West: The Metaphysics of Indian-Hating and Empire-Building* (Minneapolis: University of Minnesota Press, 1980); and Anders Stephanson, *Manifest Destiny: American Expansion and the Empire of Right* (New York: Hill and Wang, 1996). I will amplify at length on this genealogy in chapter 6.

17. That Greene is conscious of Pyle's Puritan heritage is clearly suggested not simply by the fact that he is a Brahmin Bostonian, the offspring of a Harvard professor, but also, and not least, by his unusual first name Alden, which, we will recall, was the surname of one of the protagonists of the legendary Puritan triangular love story, "the courtship of Myles Standish," John Alden. See Samuel Adams Drake, *A Book of New England Folk Lore*, rev. ed. (Rutland, Vt.: Charles E. Tuttle, 1971), pp. 383–389.

18. Michael Herr, *Dispatches* (New York: Vintage Books, 1991), pp. 50–51.

19. Edward Geary Lansdale, *In the Midst of Wars: An American's Mission to Southeast Asia* (New York: Harper and Row, 1972), pp. ix–x. See also his reports in *The Pentagon Papers*. This same Colonel Lansdale, not incidentally, was Burdick's and Lederer's model for their self-reliant, acutely observant, and eminently practical "frontiersman" in Sarkhan (Indochina), Colonel Hillandale, "the Ragtime Kid," in their novel *The Ugly American* (New York: Norton, 1958).

20. Raymond Williams, *Marxism and Literature* (New York: Oxford University Press, 1977), p. 132.

21. Edward W. Said, *Culture and Imperialism* (New York: Knopf, 1993), p. 95.

22. See Edward Lansdale, *In the Midst of Wars*: "If there was any single act of mine in 1954 that made tongues wag more than usual among French gossips in Saigon, it was my becoming acquainted with the legendary rebel guerilla chief Trinh Minh Thé. It struck them as scandalous that an American would meet with someone whom the French had outlawed. As a farm boy turned soldier who had raised his own guerrilla army in the cause of Vietnamese independence, Thé had had the temerity to fight both the French colonialists and the Communist forces. Worst of all, in the eyes of his enemies, he had achieved considerable success. When I first met him, French Union troops still were trying to hunt him down, as were trigger squads of the Vietminh," p. 184. In this same vein, Lansdale goes on to refer to a bombing in Saigon to which Greene may be referring in *The Quiet American*. See pp. 187 and 191.

23. Edward W. Said, *Orientalism*, pp. 94–95.

24. Said, *Orientalism*, pp. 138–139. The phrase derives from M. H. Abrams, *Natural Supernaturalism: Tradition and Revolution in Romantic Literature* (New York: Norton, 1971).

25. Michel Foucault, *Discipline and Punish: The Birth of the Prison*, trans. Alan Sheridan (New York: Pantheon, 1977), p. 194.

26. Althusser, "From 'Capital' to Marx's Philosophy," p. 24.

27. I have emphasized the word "serious," which, along with "quiet," Fowler uses again and again to characterize Pyle, because it suggests that Greene is using it to underscore his (and America's) single-minded pursuit of its preconceived end (*QA*, 24). Very much like Nietzsche and the poststructuralists, vis-à-vis the "gravity" of the Western metaphysically oriented answerers, Greene is identifying this seriousness with the certain "implacable" single-mindedness of the teleological perspective of York Harding's books—and of the modern, Cold War, American national iden-

tity. Like the poststructuralists, Greene seems to be reversing the enabling principle of the Western philosophical tradition: that identity is the condition for the possibility of difference and not the other way around.

28. This blindness of what I have been calling Pyle's oversight and the banality of thought it entails are underscored in Fowler's last conversation with Pyle, when, in response to Fowler's references to the bloody carnage that occurred earlier that day, Pyle replies: "They were only war casualties. . . . It was a pity, but you can't always hit your target. Anyway they died in the right cause. . . . In a way you could say they died for democracy" (*QA*, 179).

29. Greene's striking metaphor recalls the famous figure one of the few American writers who have penetrated the benign American exceptionalist problematic inherited from the Puritan "elect" and disclosed its dark underside. I am referring to Herman Melville's devastatingly ironic portrayal of Father Mapple in *Moby-Dick*: "At my first glimpse of the pulpit, it had not escaped me that however convenient for a ship, these points in the present instance seemed unnecessary. For I was not prepared to see Father Mapple after gaining the height, slowly turn round, and stooping over the pulpit, deliberately drag up the ladder step by step, till the whole was deposited within, leaving him impregnable in his little Quebec. I pondered some time without fully comprehending the reason for this." *Moby-Dick*, eds. Harrison Hayford, Hershel Parker, G. Thomas Tanselle (Evanston, Ill.: Northwestern University Press, 1988), p. 39. For an amplification of this reading of Melville's portrayal of Father Mapple and his "little Quebec," see Spanos, *The Errant Art of* Moby-Dick: *The Canon, the Cold War, and the Struggle for American Studies* (Durham, N.C.: Duke University Press, 1995), pp. 87–114.

30. For a fuller account of this poststructuralist analysis of the detective story, see Spanos, "The Detective and the Boundary: Some Notes on the Postmodern Literary Imagination," *boundary 2*, vol. 1, 1 (Fall 1972), 147–168; reprinted in *Early Postmodernism: Foundational Essays*, ed. Paul A. Bové (Durham, NC: Duke University Press, 1995), 17–40.

31. Hannah Arendt, *Eichmann in Jerusalem: A Report on the Banality of Evil*, rev. and enl. ed. (New York: Penguin, 1994; first published in *The New Yorker* in February–March 1963). The parallel I am pointing to is uncanny: "[A] more specific and also more decisive flaw in Eichmann's character was his almost total inability to look at anything from the other fellow's view. . . . The longer one listened to him, the more obvious it became that his inability to speak was closely connected with his inability to *think*, namely, to think from the standpoint of. somebody else," pp. 48–49. See also pp. 276–279.

32. Greene's model for his characterization of Fowler is the Raskolnikov of Dostoievsky's *Crime and Punishment*. As Dostoievsky writes in *The Notebooks for Crime and Punishment*, ed. and trans. Edward Wasiolek (Chicago: University of Chicago Press, 1967): "His [Raskolnikov's] moral development begins from the crime itself; the possibility of such questions arise which would not have existed previously. [I]n the last chapter, in the prison, he says that without the crime he would not have reached the point of asking himself such questions and experiencing such desires, feelings, needs, and strivings, and development," p. 64). His ultimate source, however, is the Søren Kierkegaard of *The Sickness unto Death*, trans. Walter Lowrie (Princeton: Princeton University Press, 1954).

33. See R. W. B Lewis, *American Adam: Innocence, Tragedy, and Tradition in the Nineteenth Century* (Chicago: University of Chicago, 1955). For a critique of Lewis, see Spanos, *The Errant Art of* Moby-Dick: *The Canon, The Cold War, and the Struggle for American Studies*, pp. 144–147.

34. Edward W. Said, *Culture and Imperialism*, p. 332. See also Gilles Deleuze and Felix Guattari, "Treatise on Nomadology," in *The Thousand Plateaus*, trans. Brian Massumi (Minneapolis: University of Minnesota Press, 1987), pp. 351–424.

35. Hellman, *American Myth and the Legacy of Vietnam*, p. 15. The quotation is from a review of Greene's novel by A. J. Liebling in *The New Yorker*, April 7, 1956, p. 136. Alluding to his indictment of what I have called, after Edward Said, "the textual attitude" that mediates the actuality of *being there* in a commentary of a critical review of *The Quiet American* in *The New Yorker*, Greene writes, "When my novel was eventually noticed in the *New Yorker*, the reviewer condemned me for accusing my 'best friends'" (the Americans) of murder since I had attributed to them the responsibility for the great explosion—far worse than the trivial bicycle bombs—in the main square of Saigon when many people lost their lives. But what are the facts of which the reviewer needless to say was ignorant? The *Life* photographer at the moment of the explosion was so well placed that he was able to take an astonishing and horrifying photograph which showed the body of a trishaw driver still upright after his legs had been blown off. This photograph was reproduced in an American propaganda magazine published in Manila over the title 'the work of Ho Chi Minh' although General Thé had promptly and proudly claimed the bomb as his own. Who had supplied the material to a bandit who was fighting French Caodaist and Communists?" Greene, *Ways of Escape* (New York, Vintge, 1980), p. 139.

36. Joseph Mankiewicz, dir. *The Quiet American* (1958), starring Audie Murphy as Alden Pyle and Michael Redgrave as Thomas Fowler.

37. This effort to establish an American-style democracy in South Vietnam, that is, a puppet government that mouthed the American Cold War point of view, was a failed constant throughout the two decades of the Vietnam War. It began in 1955 with Ngo Dinh Diem, whose regime was represented by the U.S. government and the media as "The Miracle of Vietnam." The *New York Times*, for example, wrote on May 9, 1957: "In salvaging South Vietnam from the disorder that threatened its existence after partition in 1955 and by establishing democratic forms, President Diem has carved a deep niche in official esteem in Washington. This was evident in the character of the welcome. During the last four years, President Eisenhower had met only one other foreign leader, King Saud of Saudi Arabia, on arrival." Marvin E. Gettleman, Jane Franklin, Mar-ilyn Young, and H. Bruce Franklin, eds., *Vietnam and America: A Doc-umented History*, rev. ed. (New York: Grove Press, 1995), p. 136. Following the assassination, aided and abetted by the U.S. government, of Diem in 1963, the United States installed at least eight other South Vietnam governments, all of which failed to produce the "national democracy" their American sponsors ostensibly wished for.

38. This insane, but finally futile, logic of the American problematic is epitomized by Michael Herr in *Dispatches* (New York: Vintage Books, 1991): "We took space back quickly, expensively, with total panic and close to maximum brutality. Our machine was devastating. And versatile. It could do everything but stop. As one American major said, in a successful attempt at attaining history, 'We had to destroy Ben Tre [a province of Vietnam] in order to save it.' That's how most of the country came back under what we called control, and how it remained essentially occupied by the Viet Cong and the North until the day years later when there were none of us left there," p. 71.

39. See Spanos, "Vietnam and the *Pax Americana*: A Genealogy of the New World Order" in *America's Shadow*, pp. 126–169; and Richard Ohmann, *English in America: A Radical View of the Profession* (New York: Oxford University Press, 1976), pp. 190–206.

40. Spanos, *America's Shadow*, pp. 126–144.

41. Samuel P. Huntington, *The Clash of Civilizations and the Remaking of World Order* (New York: Simon and Schuster, 1996; originally published in essay form in *Foreign Affairs*, Summer 1993); *Who Are We?: The Challenges to America's National Identity* (New York: Simon and Schuster, 2004). Further citations will be abbreviated to *CC* and *WAW* incorporated in the text in parentheses.

42. Martin Heidegger, "The Age of the World Picture," in *The Question Concerning Technology and Other Essays*, trans. William Lovitt (New York: Harper & Row, 1977), pp. 129–130.

43. For a poststructuralist disclosure of the will to power informing the truth that derives from the reduction of the temporal dynamics of history to spatial image—being to "domain," "region," "field" or "province" of knowledge (all having their etymological roots in the idea of mastery)— see Michel Foucault, "Questions on Geography," in *Power/Knowledge: Selected Interviews and Other Writings, 1972–1977*," ed. Colin Gordon (New York: Pantheon Books, 1980), pp. 63–77.

44. See Richard Slotkin, *Regeneration through Violence: The Mythology of the American Frontier, 1600–1860* (Middletown, Conn.: Wesleyan University Press, 1973).

45. See Spanos, "Vietnam and the *Pax Americana*: A Genealogy of the 'New World Order'," in *America's Shadow*, pp. 144–169.

Chapter 4
Retrieving the *Thisness* of the Vietnam War
A *Symptomatic Reading of Philip Caputo's*
A Rumor of War

1. Gregory L. Vistica, *New York Times Magazine*, April 29, 2001. See also CBS, *60 Minutes II*, May 2, 2001.

2. See, for example, *Time Magazine*, May 7, 2001. The Kerrey story is the cover story of this issue, and, predictably, is entitled "The Fog of War."

3. See, for example, Daniel Lang, *Casualties of War* (New York: Pocket Books, 1989; originally published in *The New Yorker*, October 18, 1969); Tim O'Brien, *If I Die in a Combat Zone* (New York: Delacorte, 1973; revised, 1979); Ron Kovic, *Born on the Fourth of July* (New York: Pocket Books, 1976); Mark Baker, *Nam: The Vietnam War in the Words of the Soldiers Who Fought There* (New York: Morrow, 1981); Al Santoli, ed., *Everything We Had: An Oral History of the Vietnam War by Thirty-Three American Soldiers Who Fought It* (New York: Ballantine Books, 1981); Bernard Edleman, ed., *Dear America: Letters Home from Vietnam* (New York: Pocket Books, 1985); Lynda Van Devanter (with Christopher Morgan), *Home Before Morning: The Story of an Army Nurse in Vietnam* (New York: Warner Book, 1983); Wallace Terry, ed., *Bloods: An Oral History of the Vietnam War by Black Veterans* (New York: Ballantine Books, 1984); Kathryn Marshall, ed., *In the Combat Zone: Vivid Personal Recollections of the Vietnam War from the Women Who Served There* (New York: Penguin Books 1987).

4. Santoli, *Everything We Had*, p. xvi. Further references will be abbreviated to *EWH* and incorporated in the text in parentheses.

5. Philip Caputo, *A Rumor of War* (New York: Ballantine Books, 1977), p. 1. Further citations will be abbreviated to *ARW* and incorporated in the text in parentheses.

6. This reduction was not limited to the autobiographical literature of the Vietnam War; it also pervaded novelistic representations: John M, Del Vecchio's *The 13th Valley* (New York: Bantam Books, 1983) and Larry Heinemann's *Paco's Story* (New York: Farrar, Strauss, and Giroux, 1986), among many others; and filmic representations (Michael Cimino's *The Deer Hunter* [1978]; Oliver Stone's film *Platoon* [1986], among many others.

7. Caputo's personalized "eyewitness" approach to his representation of the Vietnam War is articulated even more clearly in the "Postscript" of the twentieth anniversary edition published in 1996: "I wanted *A Rumor of War* . . . to blow [Americans] out of their smug polemical bunkers into the confusing, disturbing emotional and moral no-man's-land where we warriors dwelled. I would do that . . . by writing about the war with such unflinching honesty and painstaking attention to detail as to put the reader there . . . I did not want to *tell* anyone about the war but to *show* it. . . . But I had greater ambitions. I strove to write a book that would reach beyond its time and place toward the universal, a story not only about Vietnam but about war itself, and the truth of war, and what poet Wilfred Owen called the pity of war." *A Rumor of War* (New York: Henry Holt, 1996), p. 350.

8. James Fenimore Cooper, *The Pioneers* (New York: Oxford University Press, 1991), p. 446. A number of books about the historical representation of the Vietnam War have shown the inordinate degree to which this founding myth of America, especially as it was mediated through the Hollywood western, was not only inscribed in the American discourse and practice of the Vietnam War (from the Pentagon in Washington to the military command in Saigon to the common soldier in the bush) but also in the representation of the war in its aftermath.. See, most notably, Michael Herr, *Dispatches* (New York: Vintage, 1991; originally published by Knopf, 1977); Richard Drinnon, *Facing West: The Metaphysics of Indian Hating and Empire-Building* (Minneapolis: University of Minnesota Press, 1980); John Hellman; *American Myth and the Legacy of Vietnam* (New York: Columbia University Press, 1986); Richard Slotkin, *Gunfighter Nation: The Myth of the Frontier in Twentieth-Century America* (New York: Harper, 1992); Loren Baritz, *Backfire: A History of How American Culture Led Us into Vietnam and Made Us Fight the Way We Did* (New York: Ballantine Books, 1985); James William Gibson, *Warrior Dreams: Paramilitary Culture in Post-Vietnam America* (New York: Hill and Wang, 1994); Tom Englehardt, *The End of Victory Culture: Cold War America*

and the Disillusioning of a Generation (New York: Basic Books, 1995); William V. Spanos, *America's Shadow: An Anatomy of Empire* (Minneapolis: University of Minnesota Press, 2000); Katherine Kinney, *Friendly Fire: American Images of the Vietnam War* (New York: Oxford University Press, 2000). What I want to stress, against a certain tendency in these studies to restrict analysis of this historical background to the site of cultural history, is the *metaphysical* ground of the founding American mythology, which is to say, its imperial European provenance.

9. This tension between settlement/improvement and the wilderness is especially visible in the early American literature devoted to nation-building from the perspective of American exceptionalism. It will be one of the main purposes of chapter 6 to undertake the genealogy of this resonant tension.

10. See Richard Slotkin, *Regeneration through Violence: The Mythology of the American Frontier, 1600–1860* (Middletown, Conn.: Wesleyan University Press, 1973), and, especially, the chapter in *Fatal Environment: The Myth of the Frontier in the Age of Industrialization* entitled "Regeneration through Violence: History of an Indian War, 1675–1820," pp. 51–80.

11. David Halberstam, *The Best and the Brightest* (New York: Random House, 1972): "[Bob McNamara] was a man of force, moving, pushing, getting things done, *Bob got things done*, the can-do man in the can-do society, in the can-do era," (p. 265). Caputo seems, at least retrospectively, to be aware of the inappropriateness of this strategy in the jungles of Vietnam when he refers pejoratively to "the modern army that Robert McNamara had molded into the corporate image of Ford Motor Company, an army full of 'team players' who spoke the glib jargon of public relations and practiced the art of covering their tracks" (*ARW*, p. 28).

12. For an early, but still powerful critique of the problem-solving logic of the Pentagon planners, see Richard Ohmann, *English in America: A Radical View of the Profession* (New York: Oxford University Press, 1976), pp. 190–206.

13. In speaking of this "can-do" instrumentalism, I am invoking Jean-François Lyotard's important discussion of the rise of "performativity" in the technological/capitalist era as the criterion of the legitimacy of knowledge. See *The Postmodern Condition: A Report on Knowledge*, trans. Geoff Bennington and Brian Massumi (Minneapolis: University of Minnesota Press, 1984), pp. 41–67. See also Bill Readings, *The University in Ruins* (Cambridge, Mass.: Harvard University Press, 1996). What I ultimately have in mind, as will become clear, is Hannah Arendt's controversial, but still to be understood, identification of the thought and practice of the Nazi functionary, Adolph Eichmann as "the banality of

evil." For an extended analysis of this constellation, see Spanos, "American Studies in the Age of the World Picture," in *The Futures of American Studies*, ed. Donald E. Pease and Robyn Wiegman (Durham, N.C.: Duke University Press, 2002), pp. 387–415.

14. Michel Foucault, "Space, Knowledge, and Power" (an interview with Paul Rabinow and Christian Hubert) in *The Foucault Reader*, ed. Paul Rabinow (New York: Pantheon, 1984), pp. 239–256. All these terms are what Derrida would call "white metaphors," the telling ideological import of which has been effaced by usage: "region," from the Latin *regerer* (to rule over), "domain," from *dominus* (ruler), "province" from *vincerer* (to conquer), and so on: See also Gilles Deleuze and Félix Guattari, *A Thousand Plateaus*, trans. Brian Massumi (Minneapolis: University of Minnesota Press, 1987), particularly sections 13, "Apparatus of Capture," and 14, "The Smooth and the Striated," pp. 424–500.

15. Tom Engelhardt, *The End of Victory Culture*: "Between 1945 and 1975, the U.S. military reduced first Japan, then Korea, and finally Indochina to ruin. In each case, however, the end result proved disconcertingly unlike the one that the war story assured Americans would come. In each, that narrative began to suffer statistical breakdown as the link between the spectacle of slaughter and its predictable results, between dead bodies recorded and mastery over the Other, was called into question," p. 55.

16. See Mary Louise Pratt, *Imperial Eyes: Travel Writing and Transculturation* (New York: Routledge, 1992).

17. Jacques Derrida, *Specters of Marx: The State of the Debt, the Work of Mourning, and the New International*, trans. Peggy Kamuf (New York: Routledge, 1994), pp. 6–9.

18. Richard Slotkin points to, without naming, this paradoxical juxtaposition in the Kennedy administration of the Arthurian myth and the American exceptionalist myth of the frontier (European aristocracy and American democracy) in *Gunfighter Nation*: "By identifying with the complex of chivalric and gunfighter/Indian-fighter imagery that invested the New Frontier Americans as a people gave their consent to the project of 'caring for' the poor of the Third World. But with their consent given, the deeds of charity would be vicarious. The actual work would be entrusted to small, elite cadres of volunteers who would live among the natives and learn their ways but who would resist the temptation to 'go native.' Instead, they would begin the process of modernizing—which is to say, Americanizing—the indigenous cultures. The Peace Corps and the Green Berets were the political instruments most closely identified with Kennedy-style heroism. . . . Both would begin by achieving mastery of the local rules, mirroring the wiles of the native enemy to defeat that enemy on his own ground," p. 503.

19. Joseph Conrad, *Heart of Darkness*, 3rd ed., ed. Robert Kimbrough (New York: Norton Critical Editions, 1988). The fundamental presence of Conrad's novel in Caputo's memoir is further verified by his plagiarizing of Marlowe's first words—"'And this also,' said Marlow suddenly, 'has been one of the dark places of the earth.'"—to describe the unfriendly and frightening Vietnamese bush: "its was one of the last of the dark regions on earth," p. 105.

20. Martin Heidegger, "What Is Metaphysics?," trans. David Farrell Krell in *Basic Writings*, rev. and exp. ed. (New York: Harper SanFrancisco, 1993), p. 101.

21. Ibid., p. 96.

22. As I will show in the next chapter, the protagonist of Tim O'Brien's *Going After Cacciato* (New York: Delacorte Press, 1978) is haunted by this same eerie sense of "visitation," p. 252.

23. As Enrique Dussel puts this imperial ontological binary: "The center *is*; the periphery *is not*. Where Being reigns, there reign and control the armies of Caesar, the emperor. Being *is*; beings are what are seen and controlled," pp. 5–6. My emphasis.

24. This relay of racist binaries that pervades Caputo's text (and virtually all the memoirs or reminiscences of American veterans) can be traced back to the representation of the native American as cunning, duplicitous, wily, deceitful, perfidious, and so forth—that is, as sharing the instinctive characteristics of brutes (above all, the reptile) in the nation-building literature of early colonial and postrevolutionary America. Francis Parkman's "unsentimental" (racist) characterization of the Indian in *The Conspiracy of Pontiac* (pp. 387–388) is exemplary, as I will show in chapter 6. In *Dispatches*, Michael Herr captures the ironic racial essence of the American soldiers' uncomprehending disdain of the Vietnamese insurgents' refusal to fight in a "manly" way. Recalling the American military command's euphoric anticipation of a "set-piece battle" at Khe Sanh, he writes, "Victory! A vision of as many of 40,000 of them out in the open, fighting it out on our terms, fighting for once like men, fighting to no avail," p. 107.

25. Hannah Arendt, *The Human Condition* (Chicago: University of Chicago Press): "Man, in so far as he is *homo faber*, instrumentalizes, and his instrumentalization implies degradation of all things into means, their loss of intrinsic and independent value, so that eventually not only the objects of fabrication but also 'the earth in general and all forces of nature,' which clearly came into being without the help of man and have an existence independent of the human world, lose their value," pp. 156–157.

26. Tim O'Brien underscores this same point in *Going After Cacciato*, p. 270. See chapter 5.

27. William J. Duiker, *Ho Chi Minh: A Life* (New York: Hyperion, 2000), p. 27. See also p. 45.

28. Herman Rapaport, "Vietnam: The Thousand Plateaus," in *The Sixties without Apologies*, ed. Sohnya Sayres et al. (Minneapolis: University of Minnesota Press, 1984), p. 139.

29. Caputo uses this same evasive subordinate grammatical structure in justifying his request in November to be transferred from the Headquarters Company, where he served as "death's bookkeeper": "My convictions about the war had eroded almost to nothing; I had no illusions, but I volunteered for a line company anyway. There were a number of reasons, of which the paramount was boredom. . . . I cannot deny that the front still held a fascination for me. *The rights and wrongs of the war apart*, there was a magnetism about combat" (*ARW*, 218; my emphasis).

30. See, for example Thomas Myers, *Walking Point: American Narratives of Vietnam* (New York: Oxford University Press, 1988), p. 98.

31. For an extended discussion of this dehistoricizing consequence of tragedy, see Spanos, *The Errant Art of* Moby-Dick: *The Canon, the Cold War, and the Struggle for American Studies* (Durham, N.C.: Duke University Press, 1995), pp. 36–42, 47–60.

32. Andrew F. Krepinevich, Jr., *The Army and Vietnam* (Baltimore: Johns Hopkins University Press, 1986), p. 5.

33. Herman Melville, *Moby-Dick or The Whale*, ed. Harrison Hayford, Hershel Parker, G. Thomas Tanselle (Evanston and Chicago: Northwestern University Press, 1988), p. 184; my emphasis. Melville underscores the violent practical consequence of this metaphysical concentering of the many into the one by repeating the metaphor a page later: "That before living agent, now became the living instrument. If such a furious trope may stand, his special lunacy stormed his general sanity, and carried it, and turned all its concentred cannon upon its own mad mark," p. 185. See Spanos, *The Errant Art of* Moby-Dick, pp.114–131.

34. I have invoked Melville's characterization of Captain Ahab's monomaniacal obsession for revenge against the white whale to suggest that Caputo is here, at this limit experience, personifying a fundamental trait of the American national character. It would be equally, if not more appropriate to invoke Melville's characterization, analogous to his portrayal of Ahab, of the "Indian-hater *par excellence*"—who fulfills the logical economy of the American backwoodsman—"captain in the vanguard of conquering civilization"—in becoming "a Leatherstocking Nemesis" in the chapters on "the metaphysics of Indian-hating" in *The Confidence-Man*, eds. Harrison Hayford, Hershel Parker, G. Thomas Tanselle (Evanston and Chicago: Northwestern University Press, 1984), pp. 149–150. I will develop this recurrent "furious trope" at length in chapter 6. Suffice it here

to note that, as Jeanette McVicker suggested to me, it has had its supreme parodic manifestation (in the Nietzchean/Foucauldian sense of the word) in Stanley Kubrik's *Dr. Strangelove: Or How I Learned to Stop Worrying and Love the Bomb*, particularly in the denouement of this great film, in which we see Slim Pickens, captain of the strategic B-52 bomber, straddling the phallic atomic bomb, released and directed at the heart of the "evil empire," as if he were riding a stallion into Indian country. The film, not incidentally, was made in 1966, thus overlapping the period of Caputo's tour of duty.

35. In his "Postscript" to the 1996 edition of *A Rumor of War*, Caputo acknowledges that "Vietnam was the epicenter of a cultural, social, and political quake that sundered us like no other event since the Civil War," p. 353. Nevertheless he remains faithful to his original understanding of the purpose of his memoir, which, along with Santoli and many other veterans—indeed, the culture industry at large—was intent on "healing the wound" suffered by the collective American national identity during the Vietnam War: "Though I didn't write *A Rumor of War* as personal therapy, I think that it and the best of the other books about the war have been therapeutic for a wounded nation. . . . It would be inaccurate, dangerously so, to say that that disruption has ended. . . . But for all our present troubles, the nation has pulled far back from the brink it was edging toward twenty-five years ago," p. 354. Despite his symptomatic insights about the dark underside of the American national identity and the alienation from his homeland that entailed, Caputo's avowed purpose remains complicitous, however inadvertently, with the ideology of that early moment in the aftermath of the war that would recuperate the national consensus that had been shattered by the self-destruction of the myth of American exceptionalism—and had released alternative possibilities of democratic thought and practice.

36. See Spanos, "American Studies in the 'Age of the World Picture': Thinking the Question of Language," in *The Futures of American Studies*, pp. 387–415.

37. I am referring to that liberal nationalist concept of power relations in which the individual subject is guaranteed human rights only when he or she cedes ultimate sovereignty to the nation-state and thus, in seeking redress for acts of violence, is restricted to the terms of negotiation.

38. Noam Chomsky, *Deterring Democracy* (New York: Hill and Wang, 1992).

39. See Fredric Jameson, *Postmodernism; Or, the Logic of Late Capitalism* (Durham, N.C.: Duke Universssity Press, 1991); Arjun Appadurai, *Modernity at Large: Cultural Dimensions of Globalization* (Minneapolis: University of Minnesota Press, 1996); Bill Readings, *The University in Ruins* (Cambridge, Mass.: Harvard University Press, 1996);

and Michael Hardt and Antonio Negri, *Empire* (Cambridge, Mass.: Harvard University Press, 2000).

40. An example of this kind of failure is Christopher Hitchens's argument for bringing Henry Kissinger to trial for war crimes in "The Case Against Henry Kissinger: The Making of a War Criminal, Part One," in *Harper's Magazine* (February 2000), 33–58. Like Caputo in the context of the Johnson administration, Hitchens forcefully demonstrates the complicity of American foreign policy and its conduct of the war during the Nixon administration with the mass murder of innocent civilians. Unlike Caputo, Hitchens indicts a single figure in the government of Richard Nixon, Henry Kissinger, who, he claims, played a primary and often unilateral role in the decisions that led to "war crimes, crimes against humanity, and offenses against common or customary or international law, including conspiracy to commit murder, kidnapping and torture," p. 33. On the basis of the evidence he bring to bear on this "case against Henry Kissinger," Hitchens has every justification to call for bringing him to trial as a war criminal. But this indictment should not at the same time deflect attention, *as it does by its narrowly personal focus*, from the complicity of the American national identity at large in these crimes against humanity in Vietnam (and elsewhere). In singling out and separating Kissinger from the issue of the American national identity, Hitchens, like Caputo vis-à-vis the military command in Saigon, not only implies that Kissinger, the criminal, betrayed the ideals of America; he also transforms him into a scapegoat, an identity that not only liberals but even conservatives who want to forget Vietnam have little problem entertaining at this post-Cold War moment in American history. This, not incidentally, is one of the essential problems of political criticism, whether journalistic or academic, that is either not conversant with the genealogy of American cultural history (including its ontological foundations) or thinks it is essentially irrelevant to political critique. After all, it is not expiation for the crimes of the Vietnam War that should be the primary concern of criticism (as it seems to be implicitly for Caputo and explicitly for Hitchens). That demand has all the connotations of retribution. What should be the primary concern of criticism is an understanding of the American national character, which will enable the transformation of a democracy that is essentially imperial and latently violent into a true social democracy.

Chapter 5   "The Land Is Your Enemy"
Tim O'Brien's *Going After Cacciato*

1. Francis Fukuyama, *The End of History and the Last Man* (New York: Free Press, 1992).

2. Richard Haass, *The Reluctant Sheriff: The United States After the Cold War* (New York: Council on Foreign Relations Books, 1997).

3. "Rebuilding America's Defences: Strategy, Force, and Resources for a New Century," a "white paper" prepared by PNAC, September 2000.

4. Niall Ferguson, *Colosssus: The Rise and the Fall of American Empire* (New York: Penguin, 2005).

5. Samuel P. Huntington, *Who Are We?: Challenges to America's National Identity* (New York: Simon and Schuster, 2004).

6. Michael Mandelbaum, *The Case for Goliath: How America Acts as the World's Government in the Twenty-first Century* (New York: Pubic Affairs, 2005).

7. For other prominent texts of this autobiographical genre that in a virtually systematic way reduce the singularity of the Vietnam War to war-in-general, see note 3 of chapter 4. Even *Bloods: An Oral History of the Vietnam War by Black Veterans*, ed. Wallace Terry (New York: Ballantine Books, 1984), which ostensibly was intended, in part, to counter the blindness of Santoli's and others' anthologies of reminiscences to the race question does not escape this reductive representation of the Vietnam War.

8. See Jean-Paul Sartre's inaugural postmodern distinction between *la vie* and *l'aventure* (life and adventure) in *Nausea*, trans. Lloyd Alexander (New York: New Directions, 1964): "That's living. But everything changes when you tell about life; it's a change no one notices: the proof is that people talk about true stories. As if there could possibly be true stories; things happen one way and we tell about them in an opposite sense. You seem to start at the beginning. . . . And in reality you have started at the end. It was there, invisible and present, it is the one which gives to words the pomp and value of a beginning. . . . And the story goes on in reverse. . . . 'It was night, the street was deserted.' This phrase is cast out negligently, it seems superfluous; but we do not let ourselves be caught and we put it aside: this is a piece of information whose value we will subsequently appreciate. And we feel that the hero has lived all the details of this night like annunciations, promises, or even that he lived only those that were promises, blind and deaf to all that did not herald adventure," pp. 39–40.

9. Tim O'Brien, *Going After Cacciato* (New York: Broadway Books, 1999), p. 1 Further references will be incorporated in the text and cited as *GAC*.

10. See John Hellman, *American Myth and the Legacy of Vietnam* (New York: Columbia University Press, 1986), pp. 160–167.

11. In *The Green Berets* it is a huge sign bearing the name "Fort Dodge" that the camera quite pointedly pans in on when the A-team commanded by Colonel Kirby (John Wayne) arrives at the outpost fire base in Vietnam, which it is their mission to defend against the Vietnam hordes.

12. For a brilliant critique of the imperial uses to which the custodian of American culture of the eighteenth and nineteeenth centuries put this "American sublime," see Rob Wilson, *American Sublime: The Genealogy of a Poetic Genre* (Madison: University of Wisconsin Press, 1991).

13. Richard Slotkin, *Regeneration Through Violence* (Hanover, N.H.: Wesleyan University Press, 1973). This dark underside of the myth of American exceptionalism is also symptomatically present in much of the literature of the Vietnam War. As I have shown in chapter 4, it is especially prominent in Philip Caputo's memoir, *A Rumor of War*, in which, like Paul Berlin, Caputo invokes nostalgically the sublime, pristine—and rejuvenating purity—"that savage, heroic time"—of the midwestern frontier space where he was born. See also chapter 4.

14. Jame Fenimore Cooper, *The Pioneers*, ed. James D. Wallace (Oxford: Oxford University Press, 1991), p. 456.

15. Edward W. Said, *Orientalism* (New York: Vintage Press, 1979), pp. 92–93.

16. For a technical account (and critique) of "the Army Concept" that determined America military strategy in Vietnam, see Andrew F. Krepinevich, Jr., *The Army and Vietnam* (Baltimore: Johns Hopkins University Press, 1986). p. 5. What Krepinevich's rhetoric insistently obscures in his identification of the "Army Concept" with European warfare is precisely what the National Liberation Front and the North Vietnamese Army exploited: the American army's Eurocentric commitment to a narrative of closure (the promise/fulfillment structure that terminates in unconditional victory). This, as we have seen, is what Philip Caputo's memoir intuits. It is also, to anticipate, what O'Brien will symptomatically disclose by way of his portrayal of Paul Berlin.

17. It is this kind of unspeakable "narrative," in which what comes resonantly through is a baffling and frightening silence that constitutes the essential Vietnam "war story." Michael Herr, for example, implies this in inaugurating *Dispatches* with the "story" he hears from the 4th Division Lurp (long-range reconnaissance patroller) he meets early in his tour as a reporter for *Esquire* in Vietnam:

> But what a story he told me, as one-pointed and resonant as any war story I even heard, it took me a year to understand it:
> "Patrol went up the mountain. One man came back. He died before he could tell us what happened.
> I waited for the rest, but it seemed not to be that kind of story; when I asked him what had happened he just looked like he felt sorry for me, fucked if he'd waste time telling stories to anyone dumb as I was. *Dispatches* (New York: Vintage Books, 1991), p. 6.

18. Heidegger, "What Is Metaphysics?" in *Basic Writings*, rev. and exp. Ed., ed. David Farrell Krell (New York: Harper, 1993), p. 101. See also *Being and Time*, trans. John Macquarrie and Edward Robinson (New York: Harper and Row, 1962), pp. 231–232. This central and enabling ontological concept of Heidegger's "existential analytic" of *Dasein* derives ultimately from Søren Kierekegaard, *The Concept of Dread*, trans. Walter Lowrie (Princeton: Princeton University Press, 1957), p. 38.

19. Martin Heidegger, "What Is Metaphysics?," p. 96.

20. Heidegger, "What Is Metaphysics?," p. 101. Here, one should recall the grim jokes the remaining members of Berlin's platoon tell about the deaths of their comrades in the opening pages of the novel.

21. Heidegger, "Letter on Humanism," in *Basic Writings*, p. 221. My emphasis.

22. Fredric Jameson, *Postmodernism; Or, the Cultural Logic of Late Capitalisms* (Durham, N.C.: Duke University Press, 1991), p. 44. For a critique of Jameson's identification of the postmodernity of the Vietnam War with the "blank parody" intrinsic in the "logic of late capitalism," see Spanos, "*Moby-Dick* and the Contemporary American Occasion," in *The Errant Art of* Moby-Dick: *The Canon, the Cold War, and the Struggle for American Studies*, pp. 252–257.

23. See Tom Engelhardt, *The End of Victory Culture* (New York: Basic Books, 1995).

24. For an encyclopedic cultural history of this system of binaries, whose origins lay in imperial Rome, see Richard Waswo, *The Founding Legend of Western Civilization: From Virgil to Vietnam* (Hanover, N.H.: Wesleyan University Press, 1997), p. 6.

25. I am indebted for this and the following analysis of the distinction between the nomadic "guerilla" strategy of the National Liberation Front (the Viet Cong) and the "European" strategy of the American military command to three indispensable books that treat the sedentary/nomadic binary in terms of the ontology of the land: Gilles Deleuze and Félix Guattari, *A Thousand Plateaus: Capitalism and Schizophrenia*, trans. Brian Massumi (Minneapolis: University of Minnesota Press, 1980), especially the section entitled "Treatise on Nomadology"; Manuel De Landa, *Warfare in the Age of Artificial Intelligence* (Cambridge: MIT Press, 1991); and Robert Marzec, *An Ecological and Postcolonial Study of Literature: From Daniel Defoe to Salman Rushdie* (New York: PalgraveMacmillan, 2007).

26. As I have shown in the previous chapter on Caputo's *A Rumor of War*, this yearning for the "decisive" battle precipitated by the indeterminacy of military actions pervades the written and oral testimony of the American veterans of the Vietnam War, thus bearing witness to the

depth to which the "victory culture" narrative has been inscribed in the American national identity.

27. See especially Heidegger, "What Is Metaphysics?," p. 95.

28. See Herman Rapaport, "Vietnam: The Thousand Plateaus," in *The Sixties without Apologies*, ed. Sohnya Sayres et al. (Minneapolis: University of Minnesota Pres, 1984), pp. 137–147. See also the chapter entitled "Vietnam and the *Pax Americana*," in Spanos, *America's Shadow*, pp. 126–169; and Peter Linebaugh and Marcus Rediker, *The Many-Headed Hydra: Sailors, Slaves, Commoners, and the Hidden History of the Revolutionary Atlantic* (Boston: Beacon Press, 2000).

29. Jacques Derrida, *Specters of Mars: The State of the Debt, the Work of Mourning, and the New International*, trans. Peggy Kamuf (New York: Routledge, 1994): "The [metaphysical] perspective has to be revered . . . ghost or *revenant*, sensuous-non-sensuous, visible-invisible, the specter first of all sees *us*. From the other side of the eye, *visor effect* [the reference is to the visitation of Hamlet's murdered father], it looks at us even before we see *it* or even before we *see* period. We feel ourselves observed, sometimes under surveillance by it even before any apparition. Especially—and this is the event, for the specter is of the event—it sees us during a *visit*. It (re)pays us a visit [*Il nous rend visite*]. Visit upon visit, since it returns to see us and since *visitare*, frequentative of *visere* (to see, to examine, contemplate), translates well the recurrence or returning, the frequency of a visitation," p. 101. See also Mary Louise Pratt, *Imperial Eyes: Travel Writing and Transculturation* (New York: Routledge, 1992).

30. Philip Caputo, *A Rumor of War* (New York: Owl Books, 1996), p. 85. As in the case of O'Brien, it is not the land itself that instigates this anxiety; it is, rather, the invisible Vietnamese insurgents who know, live, and fight according to the land's spectral imperatives.

31. The name O'Brien gives to the Viet Cong officer is an ironic allusion to Vincent Van Gogh, the modern Western artist whose paintings depict the earth and those who dwell on it in a way that resonates with a meaning that is similar to the meaning implied in the Vietnamese word, *Xa*.

32. See Philip Jones Griffiths, *Vietnam, Inc.* (New York: Macmillan, 1971). Several photographs of this great photographic history of the American destruction of the (rice) culture of Vietnam, depict peasants planting or harvesting rice in the paddies alongside gravestones. In his commentary Griffiths writes:

> The Vietnamese are rice-growing people. For two thousand years their adeptness at pursuing this perennial task has been sustained by their belief in a harmony between man and nature. This belief, born of Buddhism,

> structured by Confucianism, and mystified by Taoism, sees every man, every thought, every action as significant and interrelated within a universal order. . . .
>
> The environment, their world, is the paddy field, and their horizons are delineated by the borders of these flat rice lands. . . .
>
> The secret of their strength lies in the nature of their society. The foundation of their society is the village. Set amid the sea of rice fields, villages rise like identical islands, surrounded by sheer cliffs of bamboo. Inside live those who tend the rice, in great proximity to one another (every precious bit of land is needed for rice-growing), but within a well-organized whole. . . . Harmony is the supreme virtue—and becoming part of that harmony— was the motivating force, enabling the villages to accept toil in the fields. Rites and rituals gave meaning to the work far beyond simply providing food to eat. In the field were buried one's ancestors whose spirit passed through the soil into the rice so that eating it became the ritual by which one inherited one's ancestor's soul. (p. 12)

After the publication of this powerful visual indictment of American thinking and practice, the British photojournalist was refused reentry to Vietnam by the American authorities. See Spanos, *Heidegger and Criticism* (Minneapolis: University of Minnesota Press, 1993), pp. 205–216.

33. Robert Marzec, *An Ecological and Postcolonial Study of Literature*, pp. 27–75. Ultimately, I suggest, this enclosure, classification, and "tablizing" of the land that came to define the relation of the Western subject with the earth on which he or she dwells had its origin in the Roman introduction of census taking and *administration* as essential instruments of the imperial project.

34. Heidegger, *Parmenides*, trans. André Schuwer and Richard Rojcewicz (Bloomington: Indiana University Press, 1982), p. 60. There is, as far as I know, no etymology for the Latin *terra*, but given the distinction Heidegger makes between it and the Greek word signifying earth (*Gea*), one wonders if it might lie in the Greek word *teras*, which means "monster." See also Gilles Deleuze and Félix Guattari, "Treatise on Nomadology," in *A Thousand Plateaus*; Michel Foucault, "Questions on Geography" (interview with the editors of *Hérodote*), in *Power/Knowledge: Selected Interviews and Other Writings, 1972–1977*, ed. Colin Gordon (New York: Pantheon Books, 1980), pp. 63–77; and Rober Marzec, *An Ecological and Postcolonial Study of Literature*.

35. Michael Herr articulates the violent—but finally futile—Eurocentric imperial essence of this Western cartographic obsession on the first page of *Dispatches*: "There was a map of Vietnam on the wall of my apartment in Saigon and some nights, coming back late to the city, I'd lie out on my bed and look at it. . . . Vietnam was divided into its older territories of Tonkin, Annam, Cochin China, and to the west past Laos and Cambodge sat Siam, a kingdom. That's old, I'd tell visitors, that's a really old map. If the dead ground could come back and haunt you the way dead people do, they'd have been able to mark my map CURRENT and burn the ones they'd been using since '64. But count on it, nothing like that was going to happen. It was late '67 now, even the most detailed maps didn't reveal much anymore; reading them was like trying to read the faces of the Vietnamese, and that was like trying to read the wind. We knew that the uses of most information were flexible, different pieces of ground told different stories to different people. We also knew that for years now there had been no country here but the war," p. 3. Later, in his book, Herr applies this imperial cartographic obsession to the American military command's more detailed division of South Vietnam into four tactical corps: "The terrain above II Corps, where it ran along the Laotian border and into the DMZ, was seldom referred to as the Highlands by Americans. It had been a matter of military expedience to impose new sets of references over Vietnam's older, truer being, an imposition that began most simply with the division of one country into two and continued its logic—with the further division of South Vietnam into four tactical corps. It had been one of the exigencies of the war, and if it effectively obliterated even some of the most obvious geographical distinctions, it made for clear communications, at least among the members of the Mission and the many components of the Military Assistance Command Vietnam, the fabulous MACV," p. 92. As we have seen, Philip Caputo, like O'Brien and Herr, also bears symptomatic witness early on and throughout *A Rumor of War* to the disabling consequences of this reductive American spatializing, cartographic gaze (*ARW*, 21). John M. Del Vecchio makes much of this deconstructive tension between the intransigent flow of Vietnam reality and American mapping in *The 13th Valley* (New York: Bantam Books, 1982).

36. Edward W. Said, *Orientalism* (New York: Vintage Books, 1979). "In any instance of at least written language, there is no such thing as a delivered presence, but a *re-presence*, or representation. The value, efficacy, strength, apparent veracity of a written statement about the Orient therefore relies very little, and cannot instrumentally depend on the Orient as such. On the contrary, the written statement is a presence to the

reader by virtue of its having excluded, displaced, made supererogatory any such *real thing* as 'the Orient.' . . . [T]hat Orientalism makes sense at all depends more on the West than on the Orient, and this sense is directly indebted to various Western techniques of representation that make the Orient visible, clear, 'there' in discourse about it," pp. 21–22.

37. Herman Melville, *Moby-Dick*, ed. Harrison Hayford, Hershel Parker, and Thomas Tanselle (Evanston, Ill.: Northwestern University Press, 1988), p. 184; my emphasis.

38. Tim O'Brien, *The Lake of the Woods* (New York: Penguin Books, 1995), p. 103.

39. Martin Heidegger, *Being and Time*, pp. 105–106. It is, not incidentally, this disintegration of and estrangement from the charted "world" occasioned by the American soldiers' encounter with a radically different culture—and a kind of warfare that was endemic to it—that explains their reiterated yearning to return "to the world."

40. Edward W. Said, *Culture and Imperialism*, pp. 69–70. To thematize the *ontologic* that informs Said's identification of the Western novel with Western imperialism, I would add to Said's parabolic enabling conclusion that, without empire, there is not simply "no European novel as we know it"; there is no "Europe." See Spanos, *America's Shadow*, pp. 95–96.

41. Herman Melville, *Moby-Dick*, p. 168.

42. Katherine Kinney, *Friendly Fire:American Images of the Vietnam War* (New York: Oxford University Press, 2000), p. 53. The quotation in her text is from *GAC*, 206.

43. Actually, Sarkin Aung Wan is from Cholon, the Chinese section of Saigon.

44. Kinney, *Friendly Fire*, p. 58.

45. Michel Foucault, "Truth and Power," in *The Foucault Reader*, ed. Paul Rabinow (New York: Pantheon Books, 1984), p. 74.

46. I am alluding to that disposition of the American mind, from the Pentagon planners down to the soldiers in the killing fields of Vietnam, that, in perceiving the death of human life in the terribly banal terms of the "body count," warrants the analogy with Hannah Arendt's representation of the Nazi functionary Adolf Eichmann in *Eichmann in Jerusalem: Report on the Banality of Evil* (New York: Penguin Books, 1977), p. 278. See also Arendt, *The Life of the Mind* (New York: Harcourt Brace Jovanovich, 1977), pp. 3–4.

47. In putting Paul Berlin's present frame of mind in terms of Graham Greene's prophetical novel, *The Quiet American*, I want to point to the radical difference between the early "prewar" American exceptionalist perspective on Vietnam—that of Alden Pyle (and the American on whom he was modeled, Colonel Edward Lansdale), whose deadly reductive reading of York Harding's Orientalist Cold War narrative is utterly

unshakable, despite the innocent blood he has indirectly shed—and the later American exceptionalist perspective that *this* war has weakened, if not entirely shattered. See chapter 3.

48. I am invoking Michel Foucault's compelling Nietzschean definition of this much abused word: "The history of this micro-physics of punitive power would then be a genealogy or an element in a genealogy of the modern 'soul.' . . . It would be wrong to say that the soul is an illusion, or an ideological effect. On the contrary, it exists. It has reality. It is produced permanently around, on, within the body by the functioning of a power that is exercised . . . on those one supervises, trains, corrects, over madmen, children at home and at school, the colonized, over those who are stuck at a machine and supervised for the rest of their lives. This is the historical reality of the soul, which, unlike the soul represented by Christian theology, is not born in sin and subject to punishment, but is born rather out of methods of punishment, supervision and constraint." *Discipline and Punish: The Birth of the Prison*, trans. Alan Sheridan (New York: Pantheon Books, 1977), pp. 29–30.

49. See Raymond Williams's analysis of the "structures of feeling" that are produced by the discourse of hegemony in *Marxism and Literature* (Oxford: Oxford University Press, 1977), pp. 128–135. Clearly drawing from Williams, Edward Said refers to this aspect of hegemony in *Culture and Imperialism*, particularly in his brilliant contrapuntal reading of Jane Austen's *Mansfield Park* as "structures of attitude and reference," pp. 74–75.

50. This blinded, essentially duplicitous, representation of the singularity of the Vietnam War has pervaded (and continues to pervade) the retrospective discourse of the liberal establishment, but its most telling example is Robert McNamara's *In Retrospect: The Tragedy and Lessons of Vietnam* (New York: Times Books, 1995), where he attributes his share of the blame for the "tragedy" of the Vietnam War to his failure to rigorously follow the dictates of the managerial instrumentalist thinking he brought to the Pentagon from Ford Motors, the very exceptionalist mindset that reduced Vietnam to a "problem to be solved"—and the indiscriminate destruction of that Third World land and the killing of untold numbers of its people, p. 203.

51. By "contrapuntal reading," Said means (among other things) one that, in attending to the "structures of attitude and reference" of a cultural text, exposes that which is unsaid, that which contradicts the truth of what is said in the text. See *Culture and Imperialism*, pp. 66–67.

52. Antonio Gramsci, *Selections from the Prison Notebooks*, ed. and trans. Quintin Hoare and Geoffrey Nowell Smith (New York: International Publishers, 1971), p. 12.

53. Williams, *Marxism and Literature*, p. 110.

54. Michel Foucault, *The History of Sexuality, Vol. I, An Introduction*, trans Robert Hurley (New York: Pantheon Books, 1978), pp. 17–49.

55. Said, *Culture and Imperialism*, pp. 332–333. My emphasis.

56. Said, *Culture and Imperialism*, p. 333. My emphasis.

57. See also Michel Foucault's parodic Nietzschean version of critical genealogy in "Nietzsche, Genealogy, History," in *Language, Counter-Memory, Practice: Selected Essays and Interviews* (Ithaca, N.Y.: Cornell University Press, 1977): "The new historian, the genealogist . . . will not be too serious to enjoy it [the monumentalist historian's imposition of an abstract heroic identity on the differential dynamics of history]; on the contrary, he will push the masquerade to its limits and prepare the great carnival of time where masks are constantly reappearing. No longer the identification of our faint individuality with the solid identities of the past, but our 'unrealization' through the excessive choice of identities," p. 161.

Chapter 6   American Exceptionalism, the Jeremiad, and the Frontier, before and after 9/11
From the Puritans to the Neo-Con Men

1. Bill Readings, *The University in Ruins* (Cambridge, Mass.: Harvard University Press, 1996), p. 102. See also Michael Hardt and Antonio Negri, *Empire* (Cambridge, Mass.: Harvard University Press, 2000), particularly the section "Network Power: U.S. Sovereignty and the New Empire," pp. 160–204. This version of globalization theory has its origins in Fredric Jameson's influential essay, "Postmodernism; or, The Cultural Logic of Late Capitalism," *New Left Review*, no. 146 (July–August 1984), 59–92; republished in *Postmodernism; or, The Cultural Logic of Late Capitalism* (Durham, N.C.: Duke University Press, 1991).

2. Sacvan Bercovitch, *The American Jeremiad* (Madison: University of Wisconsin Press, 1978), pp. 2–4. Further references will by abbreviated *AJ* and incorporated in the text.

3. See Donald Pease, "New Americanists: Revisionist Interventions into the Canon," in *New Americanists*, a special issue of *boundary 2*, vol. 17, 1 (Spring 1990), pp. 28–29.

4. Mary Rowlandson, *The Sovereignty and Goodness of God*, ed. Neal Salisbury (Boston: Bedford Books, 1997), pp. 65–66.

5. See *Regeneration through Violence: The Mythology of the American Frontier, 1600–1860* (Middletown, Conn.: Wesleyan University Press, 1973); and, above all, *Fatal Environment: The Myth of the Frontier in the Age of Industrialization, 1800–1890* (Middletown, Conn.:

Wesleyan University Press, 1985). Despite the resonant title of the first of these, it is the second to which I am most indebted. The problem with the first volume is that it addresses the question of the American national identity primarily in terms of the archetypes of myth criticism rather than culture and sociopolitics. The result is a tendency to universalize the American frontier experience that runs counter to the imperatives of historicity. The second volume, which tellingly recapitulates the first in a chapter entitled "Regeneration through Violence" but minimizes the mythic, is more satisfactory in this respect, drawing as it does on Bercovitch's work. But even in this volume Slotkin, in my mind, does not render the object of the regeneration through violence clear.

     6. James Fenimore Cooper, *The Pioneers*, ed. James D. Wallace (New York: Oxford University Press, 1991), p. 456.

     7. This "jeremiadic" intent, which represents an earlier, more vital, time for a later, more mature, but less energetic and active—"degenerating"— America, is a constant of colonial and postrevolutionary American cultural production pertaining to nation building. For example, despite Robert Montgomery Bird's quarrel with Cooper (and his European allies, Rousseau, Chateaubriand, Robert Southey, Coleridge, and other Romantics) over his subscription to the notion of the noble savage, his novel *Nick of the Woods, or The Jibbenainsonay: A Tale of Kentucky*, rev. ed. (Redfield: New York, 1854), is at one with him in this:

> The exiles of America, who first forsook their homes on the borders of the Atlantic, to build their hearths among the deserts of the West, had a similar consolation [as Adam and Eve's in their encounter with "an earthly and unsanctified" Paradise]; they were bending their steps towards a land, to which rumor at first, and afterwards the reports of a thousand adventurous visitants, had affixed the character of a second Elysium. . . .
>
> It might be difficult, *in these degenerate days*, to find fruits and flowers adorning any forest in Kentucky at Christmas; yet there was enough, and more than enough, in the wild beauty and unexampled fertility of the country, to excuse the rapture of the hunter [like Danial Boone] and to warrant high expectations on the part of the eastern emigrant, to whom he had opened a path through the wilderness, which they were not slow to follow. A strong proof of the real attractions of the land was to be seen in the crowds rushing towards it, year after year, regardless of all adverse circumstances. (pp. 13–14; my emphasis)

8. This motif in colonial American fiction had its origins in Benjamin Church (*Entertaining Passages, Relating to PHILIP'S . . . with Some Account of the Divine Providence towards Benj. Church , Esqr*) and, above all, John Filson's legend of Daniel Boone (*The Discovery, Settlement, and Present State of Kentucke*), and its historical "verification" in historians like Francis Parkman. It is central to the ideological purpose of Robert Montgomery Bird's, *Nick of the Woods*, which is the story of the education into manliness of the aristocratic Virginian, Roland Forrester, who has been exiled into the Kentucky wilderness from a settled Virginia characterized by greed, deception, and immorality, that is, as a state in the new nation that threatens to revert to the conditions of the Old World, by the backwoodsman Nathan Slaughter.

9. James Fenimore Cooper, *The Last of the Mohicans*, ed. John McWilliams (Oxford: Oxford University Press, 1990), p. 229.

10. Alexis de Tocqueville, *Democracy in America*, Vol. 1, rev. ed., ed. Phillips Bradley (New York: Vintage Books, 1990), p. 6.

11. See especially the chapter entitled "Political Effects of Decentralization in the United States" in de Tocqueville, *Democracy in America*, Vol. 1, pp. 85–97.

12. See Parkman's review of Cooper's works in *North American Review* (1852)

13. *The Oregon Trail*, significantly subtitled *Or a Summer's Journey Out of Bounds: By a Bostonian*, was published in twenty-one installments in *Knickerbocker Magazine* beginning in February 1847. Parkman's commitment to the virtues of American manliness and his anxiety over the feminizing of the American exceptionalist ethos incumbent on the civilizing process was not simply a cultural characteristic; he was, as his tracts against women's suffrage in the 1870s testify, a consciously political antifeminist.

14. Francis Parkman, *The Oregon Trail* and *The Conspiracy of Pontiac* (New York: Library of America, 1991), p. 347. Further references will be abbreviated to *CP*, and incorporated in the text in parentheses.

15. In referring to Parkman's image of the frontiersman experience as "long-textualized," I am invoking Edward Said's critically enabling notion of "the textual attitude" that invisibly mediates and distorts Western representations of the Orient. The irony, in the case of Parkman, is that he represents his "textualized" (i.e., ideologized) frontiersman as the consequence of immediate experience. In this, he prefigures not only Alden Pyle's reliance on the books of the area expert York Harding in Graham Greene's *The Quiet American* (London: Penguin Books, 1962), but also all those Americans, like Al Santoli, who claimed, against the distanced accounts of "ideologues," that their representations of the Vietnam War were true because they were eyewitness accounts. See especially chapter 4.

16. I have reversed the chronology between Parkman and Webster to maintain thematic continuity between the former and Cooper.

17. Daniel Webster, "The Bunker Hill Monument," in *The Writings and Speeches*, Vol. 1 (Boston: Little, Brown, 1903), p. 236. Further references will be abbreviated to *WS*, and incorporated in the text in parentheses.

18. Louis Althusser, "Ideology and Ideological State Apparatuses," in *Lenin and Philosophy and Other Essays*, trans. Ben Brewster (New York: Monthly Review Press, 1971). As Althusser puts this "calling" or "hailing" by a transcendental Subject (the dominant capitalist culture) that transforms the singular individual into a subjected subject, "the individual *is interpellated as a (free) subject in order that he shall submit freely to the commandments of the Subject, i.e. in order that he shall (freely) accept his subjection. . . . There are no subjects except by and for their subjection.* That is why they 'work all by themselves'," p. 182.

19. In *Emerson and the Climates of History* (Stanford: Stanford University Press, 1997), Eduado Cadava invokes Emerson's essay "Nature" to mount a forceful critique of Webster's first Bunker Hill oration, especially his identification of the emergent capitalist culture with the American Revolution and the founding fathers at the expense of the emergent working class, pp. 106–114. Ironically, however, it is Emerson's essay, not Webster's orations, that Cadava identifies as a jeremiad (without attending to the teleological view of history it entails). In so doing, he not only undermines his representation of Emerson as a radical American thinker; more important, he fails to perceive the (strained) reactionary jeremiadic function of Webster's oration.

20. Frederick Jackson Turner, "Preface," *The Frontier in American History* (New York: Dover Publications, 1996), nonpaginated. Further citations will be abbreviated to *FAH* and incorporated in the text in parentheses. Henry Nash Smith's *Virgin Land: The American West as Symbol and Myth* (Cambridge, Mass.: Harvard University Press, 1950) constitutes, in some fundamental way, a literary/cultural history of Turner's frontier thesis. But as the omission of any reference to the Puritans' "errand in the wilderness" testifies, his history idealizes the westering movement, while pointing, against itself, to the ideological motives subsuming it: the relentless consistency of the American exceptionalist theme as defined by the mobilizing and rejuvenating energies of the frontier—including, as the very title of the book suggests, its indifference to the genocidal violence this westward movement inflicted on the native inhabitants. See Donald E. Pease, "New Americanists: Revisionary Interventions into the Canon," in *boundary* 2, vol. 17, 1 (Spring 1990), 13–15. In romanticizing the westward movement, which is to say, in

overlooking the jeremiadic discourse accompanying it, Smith's history also overlooks the optimism that, in fact, informs Turner's apparent pessimism at the "closing of the American frontier." In so doing, this oversight precludes the possibility of his perceiving America's globalization of the frontier in the ensuing half-century. See the chapter of *The Virgin Land* entitled "The Myth of the Garden and Turner's Frontier Hypothesis," pp. 250–260.

21. One of the great ironies of Hardt and Negri's *Empire* is its remarkable similarity with Turner's frontier thesis. In interpreting the period of Westward expansion from Thomas Jefferson to Andrew Jackson as a momentum symptomatic of the production not only of the new sovereignty of "Empire" but of the republican "multitude," they, like Turner, accept the myth of American exceptionalism in the terms it was understood and practiced since the Puritans and thus virtually obliterate the history of the genocidal violence perpetrated by the white pioneering "multitude" on the native Americans in the name of the production of the nation-state. See the section in *Empire* on "Open Frontiers," pp. 167–172 and Negri, *Insurgencies: Constituent Power and the Modern State*, trans. Maurizia Boscagli (Minneapolis: University of Minnesota pres 1999), pp. 141–155. For a powerful critique of Hardt and Negri's interpretation of the American frontier experience in the light of its continuity with Turner's frontier thesis, see Peter Fitzpatrick, "The Immanence of *Empire*," in Paul A. Passavant and Jodi Dean, eds., *Empire's New Clothes: Reading Hardt and Negri* (New York: Routledge , 2004), pp. 49–50.

22. Lederer and Burdick's emphasis on this ideological distinction was no doubt intended to recall and counter its decisive demythologization by Graham Greene in *The Quiet American*. Like Greene vis-à-vis Alden Pyle, Burdick and Lederer, not incidentally, model one of their self-reliant American frontiersmen, Colonel Edward B. Hillandale, on Colonel Edward Lansdale, though their evaluation, needless to say, of this figure is absolutely antithetic to Greene's. See chapter 3.

23. John Hellman, *American Myth and the Legacy of Vietnam* (New York: Columbia University Press, 1986), pp 35–36.

24. Herman Melville, *The Confidence-Man; His Masquerade*, ed. Harrison Hayford, Hershel Parker, G. Thomas Tanselle (Evanston and Chicago: Northwestern University Press, 1984), pp. 149–150. Further references will be abbreviated to *C-M,* and incorporated in the text.

25. See http://.dkosopedia.com/index.php/Project_for_the_New_American_Century.

26. Samuel P. Huntington, H. Michael Crozier, and Joji Watanuki, *The Crisis of Democracy* (New York: New York University Press 1975).

27. Michael Hardt and Antonio Negri, *Multitude: War and Democracy in the Age of Empire* (New York: Penguin, 2004), p. 33.

28. Edward W. Said, "The Clash of Definitions," in *Reflections on Exile and Other Essays* (Cambridge, Mass.: Harvard University Press, 2000), pp. 571–572.

29. For an amplification of this motif, which, in America originated with the Puritans' typological identification of their exilic/seed-bearing status with the Old Testament Israelites and, not incidentally, with Virgil's Aeneas, see Spanos, *America's Shadow: An Anatomy of Empire* (Minneapolis: University of Minnesota Press, 2000), pp. 99 and 240–241.

30. Huntington devotes an entire chapter to this effort to demonize "deconstructionism." Typical of the policy experts to which he belongs, however, nowhere in it does he indicate that he has read any of the major articulations of this discourse or understood its essential tenets.

31. Francis Fukuyama, *The End of History and the Last Man* (New York: Free Press, 1992), p. xiii. As we have seen in chapter 1, Jacques Derrida identifies Fukuyama's apocalyptic history with the Christian evangelical rhetoric in *Specters of Marx: The State of the Debt, the of Work of Mourning, and the New International*, trans. Peggy Kamuf (New York: Routledge, 1994), pp. 56 ff. In the end, however, even Fukuyama manifests anxiety over the loss of an enemy, though he calls this last, after Hegel, "*thymos.*" This is why, as I have argued, one must read *Who Are We?* as a continuation rather than as a rejection of Fukuyama's "end-of-history" thesis.

32. Typical of his ideological distortions of cultural evidence, Huntington invokes the last lines of Constantine Cavafy's great anti-imperialist poem "Waiting for the Barbarians" in behalf of his affirmation of America's need for an enemy: "And now [that the barbarians awaited by the effete metropolitan leaders "have not come"] what will become of us without barbarians?/ Those people were a kind of solution." In doing so, Huntington turns a poem that in reality constitutes a devastating carnivalesque parody of an exhausted purist imperial civilization (epitomized by the bewildered effete speaker)—and a celebration of "barbaric" multiplicity—into its antithesis.

33. Ernest Renan, "What Is a Nation?," trans. Martin Thom, in Homi Bhabha, ed., *Nation and Narration* (London: Routledge, 1999), p. 110. For a forceful critique of the foundations of nationalism, one quite relevant to this context, see, William Connolly, *Why I Am Not a Secularist* (Minneapolis: University of Minnesota Press, 1999), p. 81. See also Partha Chatterjee, *Nationalist Thought and the Colonial World: A Derivative Discourse?* (London: Zed Books, 1986); Benedict Anderson,

Imagined Communities: Reflections on the Origins and Spread of Nationalism (London: Verso, 1991); Bill Readings, *The University in Ruins* (Cambridge, Mass.: Harvard University Press, 1996) ; Arjun Appadurai, "Life After Primordialism," in *Modernity at Large: Cultural Dimensions of Globalization* (Minneapolis: University of Minnesota Press, 1996), pp. 139–157; and Negri and Hardt, *Empire*.

34. Renan, p. 19.

35. Edward W. Said, "The Clash of Definitions," pp. 571–572.

36. Herman Melville, *The Confidence-Man: His Masquerade*, ed. Harrison Hayford, Hershel Parker, and G. Thomas Tanselle (Evanston and Chicago: Northwestern University Press, 1984). Further references will be abbreviated to C-C and incorporated in the text in parentheses.

37. Melville's novel *Israel Potter: Fifty Years of Exile* (1854–1855), which begins with an ironic dedication "To His Highness the Bunker-Hill Monument," constitutes a satire of the nationalist monumentalism of Daniel Webster as this is expressed in his jeremiadic Bunker Hill orations.

38. Michel Foucault, "Nietzsche, Genealogy, History," in *Language, Counter-Memory, and Practice: Selected Essays and Interviews*, ed. and trans. Donald F. Bouchard (Ithaca, N.Y.: Cornell University Press, 1977), pp. 160–161.

39. Giorgio Agamben's theorization of the state of exception in *State of Exception*, trans. Kevin Attell (Chicago: University of Chicago Press, 2005) goes far to explain the Bush administration's foreign and domestic policies after 9/11. But insofar as his analysis focuses on its European origins (the Napoleonic era), it cannot, necessarily, perceive the unique twist this doctrine of the state of exception undergoes in the context of the exceptionalist history of the United States. But this is the matter of another project.

40. For an amplification of Melville's proleptic critique of the uses to which the dominant culture of post-9/11 America has put the myth of American exceptionalism, see Spanos, *Herman Melville and the American Calling: The Fiction After* Moby-Dick, *1851–1857* (Albany, N.Y.: State University of New York Press, forthcoming).

Chapter 7　Conclusion
The Vietnam War, 9/11, and Its Aftermath

1. This is the influential CIA agent, Robert Komer, to whom Michael Herr refers in *Dispatches* as "Robert 'Blowtorch' Komer, chief of COORDS, spook anagram for Other War, pacification, another word for war": "If William Blake had 'reported' to him that he'd seen angels in

the trees, Komer would have tried to talk him out of it. Failing there, he'd have ordered defoliation," p. 44.

2. Spanos, *America's Shadow: An Anatomy of Empire* (Minneapolis: University of Minnesota Press, 2000), pp. 128–144.

3. Henry Rosovsky, "Report on the Core Curriculum" (Cambridge, Mass.: Faculty of Arts and Sciences of Harvard University, February 15, 1978); republished by the Rockefeller Foundation with modifications in *Toward the Restorations of the Core Curriculum*. See also William Bennett, "To Reclaim a Legacy: Report on the Humanities in Education," *Chronicle of Higher Education* (November 28, 1984).

4. Allan Bloom, *The Closing of the American Mind: How Higher Education Has Failed Democracy and Impoverished the Souls of Today's Students* (New York: Simon and Schuster, 1987); Roger Kimball, *Tenured Radicals: How Politics Has Corrupted Our Higher Education* (New York: Harper and Row, 1990); David Lehman, *Signs of the Times: Deconstruction and the Fall of de Man* (New York: Poseidon Books, 1991); Dinesh D'Souza, *Illiberal Education: The Politics of Race and Sex on Campus* (New York: Free Press, 1991).

5. Frances Fukuyama, *The End of History and the Last Man* (New York: Free Press: 1992).

6. William V. Spanos, *America's Shadow: An Anatomy of Empire*, p. 142.

7. Samuel P. Huntington, *Who Are We?: The Challenges to America's National Identity* (New York: Simon and Schuster, 2004), p. 257; my emphasis. Further references will be abbreviated to *WAW* and incorporated in the text in parentheses.

8. I am referring to the white paper of the neoconservative think tank Project for the New American Century (PNAC), "Rebuilding America's Defenses" (September 2000, circulated in Washington long before 9/11), whose vulgar shorthand rhetoric, as I have shown in chapter 6, is reminiscent of the memoranda of the Pentagon Papers that exposed the utterly dehumanized thought of the Washington bureaucrats who planned the Vietnam War.

9. See Antonio Negri and Michael Hardt, "Symptoms of Passages," in *Empire* (Cambridge, Mass.: Harvard University Press, 2000), pp. 137–158. See also Timothy Brennan, "Humanism, Philology, and Imperialism," in *War of Position: The Cultural Poltics of Left and Right* (New York: Columbia University Press, 2006), pp. 93–125.

10. It should not be forgotten that the United States' intervention in Vietnam was not simply a military/political action, but also, especially after 1966, a massive "cultural" operation that had as its purpose the

"winning of the hearts and minds" of the Vietnamese people, as Francis Fitzgerald observed (in a way reminiscent of Foucault's Nietzschean understanding of genealogy in it parodic or carnivalesque mode) long ago in *Fire in the Lake: The Vietnamese and the Americans in Vietnam* (New York: Vintage Books, 1988; first published in 1972), pp. 433–434.

11. Edward W. Said, "Secular Criticism" in *The World, the Text, and the Critic* (Cambridge, Mass.: Harvard University Press, 1983), pp. 1–30. I am aware, of course, that Said increasingly distanced himself from poststructuralist theory not simply for its tendency to systematize thinking (and to deny agency), but also, as his last posthumously published book *Humanism and Democratic Criticism* (New York: Columbia University Press, 2004) testifies, for its "antihumanism." It is my contention, however, that it was not so much poststructuralist theory *as such* that he was criticizing as its practitioners who abused its revolutionary potential by disciplining and systematizing the decentering of the polyvalent *Logos*. Indeed, I would go so far as to say, Said's "secular criticism" fulfills that revolutionary potential, above all, by thinking the decentering of the Western *Logos* in an anti- or transdisciplinary way, as a continuum that ranges from the ontological site, through the cultural, all the way across to the site of global politics. See Spanos, "Humanism and the *Studia Humanitatis* After 9/11/01: Rethinking the Anthropologos," *Symploke*, vol. 13, 1–2 (2005), 219–262, and *The Legacy of Edward W. Said* (forthcoming from University of Illinois Press).

12. Alexis de Tocqueville, *Democracy in America* (New York: Vintage Books, 1990), p. 6.

13. For an amplified account of this argument, see the chapter entitled "Vietnam and the *Pax Americana: A Genealogy of the 'New World Order'*," pp. 126–169.

14. See Spanos, *The Errant Art of* Moby-Dick: *The Canon, the Cold War and the Struggle of American Studies* (Durham, N.C.: Duke University Press, 1995).

15. Edward W. Said, *Culture and Imperialism* (New York: Knopf, 1993), p. 312.

16. See Michel Foucault "Nietzsche, Genealogy, History," in *Language, Counter-Memory, Practice: Selected Essays and Interviews*, ed. Donald F. Bouchard, trans. Bouchard and Sherry Simpson (Ithaca, N.Y.: Cornell University Press, 1977), pp. 160–161.

17. Michael Herr, *Dispatches* (New York: Vintage Books, 1991), pp. 4–5. The echo of the John Wayne voice at the end should not be overlooked.

18. Peter Linebaugh and Marcus Rediker, *The Many-Headed Hydra: Sailors, Slaves, Commoners, and the Hidden History of the Rev-*

olutionary Atlantic (Boston: Beacon Press, 2000), pp. 3–4. See also Paul Gilroy, *The Black Atlantic: Modernity and Double Consciousness* (Cambridge, Mass.: Harvard University Press, 1993), especially chapter 1, "The Black Atlantic as a Counterculture of Modernity," pp. 1–40.

19. President's "Address to the Nation. " My emphasis. http://www. whitehouse.giov/news/reqlses/2006/09/20060911-3.html.

20. See Alan Wolf, "The Difference Between Criticism and Hatred (Anti-American Studies)," a review of Donald E. Pease and Robyn Wiegman, *The Futures of American Studies* (Durham, N.C.: Duke University Press, 2002), in *The New Republic*, 1/30/2003.

21. See, above all, the exemplary and far-reaching New Americanist work of Donald E. Pease, the most pertinent of which are: *Visionary Compacts: American Renaissance Writings in Cultural Context* (Madison: University of Wisconsin Press, 1987); "New Americanists: Revisionist Interventions into the Canon," in *New Americanists*, a special issue of *boundary* 2, vol. 17, 1 (Spring 1990); *The Futures of American Studies*, eds. Pease and Robyn Wiegman (Durham, N.C.: Duke University Press, 2002); "C. L. R. James's *Mariners, Renegades and Castaways* and the World We Live In," in *Mariners, Renegades and Castaways: The Story of Herman Melville and the World We Live In*, ed. Pease (Hanover, N.H.: University Press of New England, 2001). See also Amy Kaplan, *The Anarchy of Empire in the Making of U.S. Culture* (Cambridge, Mass.: Harvard University Press, 2002); and John Carlos Rowe, *At Emerson's Tomb: The Politics of Classic American Literature* (New York: Columbia University Press, 1997) and *Literary Culture and U.S. Imperialism: From the Revolution to World War II* (New York: Oxford University Press, 2000).

22. Bernard Lewis, *The Middle East and the West* (New York: Harper Torchbooks, 1968), p. 135.

23. See Hardt and Negri's discussion of the American Constitution, which, they claim, represents an epochal "rupture in the genealogy of modern sovereignty": "Against the tired transcendentalism of modern sovereignty, presented either in Hobbesian or in Rousseauian form, the American constituents thought that only the republic can give order to democracy, or really that the order of the multitude must be born not from a transfer of the title of power and right, but from an arrangement internal to the multitude, from a democratic interaction of powers linked together in networks. The new sovereignty can arise, in other words, only from the constitutional formation of limits and equilibria, check and balances, which both constitutes a central power and maintains power in the hands of the multitude. There is no longer any necessity or room here for the transcendence of power." *Empire* (Cambridge, Mass.: Harvard University Press, 2000), p. 161. This, according to Hardt and Negri, made it

inevitable that the United States would take the lead in the transference of sovereignty from the national state to transnational capital (and eventually) to the multitude. See also Bill Readings, *The University in Ruins* (Cambridge. Mass.: Harvard University Press, 1996).

24. Amy Kaplan, *The Anarchy of Empire in the Making of U.S. Culture* (Cambridge, Mass.: Harvard University Press, 2002), p. 50.

25. Edward W. Said, *Culture and Imperialism* (New York: Knopf, 1993), p. 332; my emphasis. The quoted passage is from T. S. Eliot's "Little Gidding," *Four Quartets*.

INDEX

Abrams, M. H., *Natural Supernaturalism: Tradition and Revolution in* Romantic literature, 276n; natural supernaturalism, 77

Adams, John, 6, 255

Adorno, Theodor, 24–25; on the consciousness industry, 59, 148, 243; *Minima Moralia: Reflection on a Damaged Life*, 24; on non-answerability, 24–25, 182–183

Ahmad, Aijaz, 46, 272

Agamben, Giorgio, "Beyond Humana Rights," 268n; *Home Sacer: Sovereign Power and Bare Life*, 268n; *State of Exception*, 302

Alata, S. H., 251

Alloula, Malek, 26; *The Colonial Harem*, 266n

Al Qaeda, xvi, xvii, 3, 6, 40, 46, 56, 67, 95, 140, 199, 219, 222, 233–234, 247

Althusser, Louis, xi, 24, 165, 179, 259; and the absent cause, 28; and agency, 50–53; and changed terrain, 53, 56, 78, 85, 172, 181, 185; " From *Capital* to Marx's Philosophy," 43–53, 61, 268n; "Ideology and Ideological State Apparatuses: Notes towards an Investigation," v, 41, 64, 274n, 299n; and the jeremiad, 209–210; and symptomatic reading (*lecteur symptomale*), 61, 64–65, 122; and the problematic, 7, 35, 41–53, 60–64, 78, 89, 118–119, 257, 270n ; and interpellated s ubject, 25, 48–49, 179–180, 209, 272n, 299n; and ontological emphasis, 39–46; an spectrality, 45, 49–51; and vision, 44–51, 6–65, 257–258; and the invisible, 49–51 and the Vietnam War, 39, 46–47; 53–56. *See also, Quiet American, The; Rumor of War, A;* problematic,

America, xiii; and Adamic mission, 19, 87, 134–135, 200, 252–253, 259; and Ahabian monomania, xiv, xv, 96, 133–135, 141–43, 173–174, 182, 250, 253–254, 259, 285n; and amnesia , 15, 38–41, 47, 54–55, 101, 140, 145–150, 179, 218, 234–236, 243–247, 264n; and Anglo-Protestant core culture, 203–206, 223–230, 233–236 ; and banality of thought, 24; and blaming the victim, 250–251; and the "calling," 190, 299n; and "can do" thinking, 118–119, 252, 282n; and the Cold War, 18–19, 57, 65–66, 70–77, 84–85, 92–97, 276–277; and cultural memory of,19–20 ; and "errand in the wilderness", xi; 12, 140, 147, 173, 250; and the frontier, 190, 195–198, 210–214, 215–217, 219, 232, 300n; and hegemonic

307